St. Jerome's Commentaries

on Galatians, Titus,

and Philemon

St. Jerome's

Commentaries

on Galatians, Titus,

and Philemon

University of Notre Dame Press

Notre Dame, Indiana

Translated by

THOMAS P. SCHECK

Manufactured in the United States of America

Library of Congress Cataloging-in-Publication Data

Jerome, Saint, d. 419 or 20.
[Commentaries. English. Selections]
St. Jerome's commentaries on Galatians, Titus, and Philemon /
translated by Thomas P. Scheck.
    p.   cm.
Includes bibliographical references and indexes.
ISBN-13: 978-0-268-04133-5 (pbk. : alk. paper)
ISBN-10: 0-268-04133-4 (pbk. : alk. paper)
1. Bible. N.T. Galatians—Commentaries. 2. Bible. N.T. Titus—Commentaries.
3. Bible. N.T. Philemon—Commentaries.   I. Scheck, Thomas P., 1964–
II. Title.   III. Title: Saint Jerome's commentaries on Galations, Titus, and Philemon.
BR65.J472E64   2010
227'.077—dc22

                                                                2010024339

Dedicated in friendship and affection to my mentor
and colleague, Father Joseph T. Lienhard, S.J.,
of Fordham University

Contents

Abbreviations

ACC	Ancient Christian Commentary on Scripture
Adv Haer	Irenaeus's *Adversus haereses*
ANF	Ante-Nicene Fathers
CCSL	Corpus christianorum, series latina
CRm	Origen's *Commentary on the Epistle to the Romans*
CSEL	Corpus scriptorum ecclesiasticorum latinorum
CWE	Collected Works of Erasmus
DCB	*A Dictionary of Christian Biography.* Ed. W. Smith and H. Wace. 4 vols. London, 1877–87.
DSA	Luther's *De servo arbitrio*
DTC	*Dictionaire de théologie catholique.* Ed. A. Vacant et al. 15 vols. Paris, 1903–50.
EEC	*Encyclopedia of the Early Church.* Ed. A. Di Berardino. 2 vols. New York, 1992.
Ep.	Epistle
FOTC	Fathers of the Church
HE	Eusebius's *Historia ecclesiastica*
ICC	International Critical Commentary
JBC	*Jerome Biblical Commentary.* Ed. R. E. Brown et al. Englewood Cliffs, 1968.

LW   Luther's Works, American edition

NICNT   New International Commentary on the New Testament

NJBC   New Jerome Biblical Commentary. Ed. R. E. Brown et al. Englewood Cliffs, 1990.

NPNF1   Nicene and Post Nicene Fathers, first series

NPNF2   Nicene and Post Nicene Fathers, second series

OCD   *The Oxford Classical Dictionary*, 3rd edition. Ed. S. Hornblower and A. Spawforth. Oxford, 1996.

PL   Patrologia Latina. Ed. J. P. Migne. 217 vols. Paris, 1844–64.

RSV   Revised Standard Version

TNTC   Tyndale New Testament Commentaries

Vir Ill   Jerome's *De viris illustribus*

WBC   Word Biblical Commentary

WHTO   *The Westminster Handbook to Origen.* Ed. McGuckin. Louisville, 2004.

Acknowledgments

I am grateful to Bradley Ritter, my colleague in the classics department at Ave Maria University, for assisting in the translation of a number of difficult passages in the *Commentary on Galatians*. Also the diligence of librarians Christina Kennedy and Henry Stachyra was much appreciated.

Introduction

Saint Jerome (347–420) was undoubtedly one of the most learned of the Latin Church Fathers. The staggering range and depth of his reading can be glimpsed from his work *De viris illustribus* (*On Famous Men*), a pioneering work of patrology, written around 385 and modeled on Suetonius's *Lives of the Caesars*. To this day his survey is considered indispensable for much of our knowledge of the literature of the Church's early centuries.[1] *De viris illustribus* offers proof that Jerome had mastered nearly the entirety of the antecedent exegetical and theological tradition, both Greek and Latin. It is also well known that Jerome learned the biblical languages: Greek, Hebrew, and Aramaic. He put this knowledge to work in his most famous editorial achievement, the Latin Vulgate translation of the Bible. Such linguistic learning makes Jerome stand out in dramatic contrast with his contemporary Augustine, who knew well the Latin language but was almost completely unacquainted with the Greek exegetical tradition. While Augustine was a far more influential *theologian* in the Church of the West, because of his ranking as a bishop and for his more systematic and dogmatic approach to theological topics, Jerome's philological learning was deeper and his legacy as an *exegete* was greater.

---

1. For English translations see NPNF2 3.359–84 and FOTC 100.

It is therefore regrettable that the majority of Jerome's commentaries on Scripture have never been translated into English.[2] As late as
the mid-twentieth century, Popes Benedict XV and Pius XII were
warmly commending Jerome's Scripture scholarship to Catholic scholars.[3] In *Dei Verbum 23,* the bishops of the Second Vatican Council encouraged exegetes to study the Holy Fathers of both East and West.
Unfortunately, such exhortations fell and continue to fall on deaf ears.
Indeed, in modern Scripture scholarship, St. Jerome's commentaries
are almost completely neglected, even in Catholic circles.

It is true that the modern Catholic Scripture commentary edited
by R. E. Brown, J. Fitzmyer, and R. Murphy was entitled *The Jerome
Biblical Commentary,* and that this title has probably made Jerome's
name more familiar to American readers. But neither the principles
nor the substance of Jerome's exegesis are taken into consideration in
this work. Even the Protestant D. L. Dungan criticized the JBC and the
NJBC for its uncritical surrender to liberal German Protestant historical criticism and observed that none of the commentaries in this
work are informed by Catholic principles of exegesis.[4] The neglect of
such principles seems to have been deliberate, since the chief editor,
R. E. Brown, has published his own opinion: "I think we must recognize that the exegetical method of the Fathers is irrelevant to the study
of the Bible today."[5] Likewise, Brown's colleague and fellow contribu-

---

2. To my knowledge, the only commentaries of Jerome available in English
thus far are Gleason Archer's translation of *Jerome's Commentary on Daniel* (Grand
Rapids, Mich.: Baker, 1958), Ronald Heine, *The Commentaries of Origen and Jerome
on St Paul's Epistle to the Ephesians* (Oxford: Oxford University Press, 2002), and my
translation of St. Jerome's *Commentary on Matthew,* FOTC 117. Intervarsity Press
has announced their intention to publish a translation of Jerome's *Commentary on
Jeremiah* in the series Ancient Christian Texts. I have in preparation a new translation of Jerome's *Commentary on Isaiah.*

3. Cf. *Spiritus Paraclitus,* encyclical of Pope Benedict XV on St. Jerome, September 15, 1920 (*Acta Apostolicae Sedis* 12:385–420); *Divino afflante Spiritu,* encyclical of Pope Pius XII, September 30, 1943.

4. *A History of the Synoptic Problem: The Canon, the Text, the Composition,
and the Interpretation of the Gospels* (New York: Doubleday, 1999), pp. 365–67.

5. "The Problems of the Sensus Plenior," *Ephemerides Theologica Lovanienses*
43 (1967), p. 463.

tor to the JBC, J. L. McKenzie, SJ, wrote: "The Old Testament in no way predicts or leads one to expect the historical reality of Jesus of Nazareth nor the saving act which the disciples of Jesus proclaimed as accomplished in him."[6] Such an opinion is rationalist and more closely resembles Marcionism than St. Jerome's theology of the Old Testament. It would not be difficult to demonstrate that Brown's and McKenzie's prejudices prevailed in the JBC's essays and commentaries, which either minimize Jerome as a significant figure for Catholic exegesis or betray ignorance of his writings.[7] It appears that the editors of this volume wanted their work to be associated with the *name* of St. Jerome rather than with the *substance* of his exegesis.

In spite of this neglect and indeed repudiation of St. Jerome's principles of exegesis by modern Catholic interpreters, F. X. Murphy has correctly observed that Jerome is nevertheless "an indispensable witness to the mind of the Church in dealing with the Word of God."[8] Therefore, it is to be hoped that this first English translation of St. Jerome's commentaries on Galatians, Titus, and Philemon will be received with interest and attention.

A Brief Biography of Jerome

Jerome was born in Stridon, a village in the western Balkans under northern Italian influence. His wealthy parents seem to have been devout Christians, the evidence being that three of their children later entered religious life. Jerome was not baptized as an infant, in keeping

---

6. *A Theology of the Old Testament* (Garden City: Doubleday, 1976), p. 279. For a critique of McKenzie's own scholarship, see Guillermo V. Villegas, *The Old Testament as a Christian Book: A Study of Three Catholic Biblical Scholars: Pierre Grelot, John L. McKenzie, Luis Alonso Schökel* (Manilla: Divine Word Publications, 1988).

7. For instance, in his essay on "Hermeneutics," JBC, p. 612, Brown writes: "In his early days Jerome (d. 419) followed Origen's principles, but the commentaries written at the end of Jerome's life betray greater interest in the literal sense." This summary statement could only have been written by someone who is completely ignorant of both Jerome's and Origen's commentaries.

8. "Saint Jerome," *New Catholic Encyclopedia,* 2d ed., 7.759.

with a common custom of the time. At the age of twelve he was sent to Rome to complete his literary studies. For the next eight years he acquired a thorough education in grammar, the humanities, rhetoric, and dialectics. In Rome Jerome studied under Aelius Donatus, who was the most famous teacher of literature of the period. He honed his skills as a young scholar by transcribing a great number of Latin authors for his personal library. His own competence in Latin prose was such that to this day Jerome's letters rank alongside the epistolary collections of Cicero, Seneca, and Pliny the Younger as the most celebrated in Latin literature. Jerome also learned the rudiments of Greek in Rome, though his eventual mastery of the Greek language would only be attained later, after living in the East for many years.

Jerome may have allowed himself some experience of the *dolce vita,* "since he was not yet baptized."[9] His comment under the lemma to Gal 6.1 may even be autobiographical in this respect.[10] Yet he did not break off his ties with his Christian friends with whom he was accustomed on Sundays to visit the tombs of the apostles and martyrs.[11] At the age of eighteen or nineteen, Jerome asked for baptism, which he received in Lent 367, possibly from Pope Liberius. Later that year he traveled to Gaul, where, in Trier, he made a decision to pursue the monastic life. Here he made copies of some works by Hilary of Poitiers (d. 368). In *Vir Ill* 100, Jerome reports that Hilary, in his commentaries on the Psalms, had imitated Origen, but also added some original material. Jerome further mentions that Hilary, in his *Commentary on Job,* had translated freely from the Greek of Origen. Observing orthodox Latin and Greek interpreters assimilate the writings of the Greek exegete Origen of Alexandria (185–254) into their own works will estab-

---

9. J. Gribomont, "Jerome," in J. Quasten, *Patrology,* 4 vols. (Utrecht-Antwerp: Spectrum, 1975–), 4.213. Though some of his medieval hagiographers assigned virginity to him, Jerome denied that he himself possessed virginity; Ep. 48.20 to Pammachius (NPNF2 6.87); Ep. 7.4 to Chromatius, Jovinus, and Eusebius (NPNF2 6.9).

10. "If someone remains a virgin until old age, he should pardon one who was once deceived by the burning passion of youth. For he knows how difficult it was for him to pass through that period of life."

11. *Commentary on Ezekiel,* 12.244–53.

lish a paradigm for Jerome. Repeatedly, he will encounter theologians of untainted orthodoxy who recognized Origen as an exegete *par excellence*. One point of attraction to Origen, of course, was his famous knowledge of the Bible. Jerome later remarked that he would gladly trade his knowledge of Scripture with Origen, who "knew the Scriptures by heart."[12]

Jerome moved to Aquileia in northeastern Italy, where he continued to study theology and lived as an ascetic for seven years. In 374 he began living as a hermit in the desert of Chalcis, a region located slightly east of Syrian Antioch.[13] During this period Jerome was introduced to the Hebrew language by a converted Jew named Baranina. Jerome was the first Latin Christian to attempt to learn the original languages of the Old Testament in this manner and to use this knowledge in his scholarship. He would eventually master both Hebrew and Aramaic. A famous incident in his life occurred at Chalcis: Jerome dreamed that he stood before the judgment seat of Christ. In the vision he was accused of being a Ciceronian rather than a Christian and was ordered to be flogged. In the midst of the scourging, he begged Christ for mercy and vowed never to touch pagan literature again. Jerome recounts the experience in Ep. 22.30 to Eustochium. He seems also to allude to it in the preface to book 3 of the commentary on Galatians.

Jerome went to Antioch in 379, where he was ordained by Bishop Paulinus. He heard lectures there from Apollinaris of Laodicea, an Alexandrian grammarian, who had mastered Greek literature and philosophy and had written an important apologetic work in thirty books, *Against Porphyry*. Apollinaris's work, which does not survive, had a formative influence on Jerome. In Ep. 84.3, Jerome said that he had learned biblical interpretation from Apollinaris, though he distanced himself from Apollinaris's heterodox understanding of the Incarnation. Certainly the influence of "Alexandrian," that is, Origenian methods of exegesis would influence Jerome in a decisive way.

---

12. Ep. 84.8.
13. For a study of the letters Jerome wrote during this period, see Cain, "*Vox Clamantis.*"

From Antioch Jerome went to Constantinople, where he became a pupil of St. Gregory Nazianzus (d. 389). This famous Cappadocian Father likewise encouraged Jerome to study and assimilate Origen's scriptural exegesis. Jerome continued to do so in emulation of his orthodox predecessors. More than that, Jerome would adopt Origen's comprehensive pattern of life, scholarship, and asceticism as a model for his own. Jerome's fluency in Greek at this point is demonstrated by the fact that he undertook translations of Origen's homilies on Jeremiah, Ezekiel, and Isaiah. He also translated Eusebius of Caesarea's *Chronicle of World History*. These projects were completed around 381. Jerome also translated Origen's homilies on the Song of Songs, which he dedicated to Pope Damasus (d. 384), and Origen's homilies on Luke around 389. At about this time he also wrote his *Commentary on Ecclesiastes*.

Jerome spent the early 380s in Rome where he had become embroiled in controversy with his brother monks and priests as a result of the insulting and defamatory style of his satirical writings. The situation became so serious that, after Pope Damasus's death in December 384, an official ecclesiastical inquiry was conducted and Jerome was condemned in a formal judgment that was delivered orally.[14] Thus around 385 the atmosphere in Rome had become so hostile toward Jerome that he was asked to leave the city altogether.[15] After traveling to Palestine and visiting the holy sites, Jerome made a brief visit to Egypt, where he stayed for thirty days with Didymus the Blind (d. 398). Soon he would publish his own translation of Didymus's *Treatise on the Holy Spirit*. Jerome was well aware that Didymus too had been immersed in the writings of Origen, and Jerome wanted to make this material available to Latin readers.[16] Unfortunately he was inspired to translate Didymus partly by a rather base motive: he aimed to show Latin readers that St. Ambrose, whom he intensely disliked, had pla-

14. For a very recent and fine study of this controversy, see Cain, *The Letters of Jerome*, 99–128.

15. Cf. Kelly, *Jerome*, p. 113.

16. See R. A. Layton, *Didymus the Blind and his Circle in Late-Antique Alexandria* (Urbana: University of Illinois Press, 2004).

giarized much of his own book on the Holy Spirit from Didymus. Rufinus of Aquileia will later expose Jerome's ill will and come to Ambrose's defense in his *Apology against Jerome* 2.22–25.[17]

In 385 Jerome settled in Bethlehem, where he set up a monastery. Being within range of Caesarea, he traveled there frequently to consult its magnificent library,[18] which included a copy of Origen's *Hexapla*, or "six-fold Bible." In this work, which does not survive, on which he dedicated twenty-eight years of research, Origen displayed the text of Scripture in six or more parallel columns: (1) Hebrew text; (2) Hebrew transliterated into Greek; and the Greek versions of (3) Aquila, (4) Symmachus, (5) the Septuagint, and (6) Theodotion. For the Psalms Origen displayed two or three other Greek translations. The *Hexapla* would assist Jerome immensely in his own biblical translations and commentaries. He mentions Origen's *Hexapla* in the *Commentary on Titus* 3.9. Jerome copied and otherwise obtained important manuscripts of the Scriptures and the writings of Origen. It was precisely at this time, in the early Bethlehem period, when Jerome completed the three commentaries contained in the present volume, those on Philemon, Galatians, and Titus, in that order. Jerome informs his readers that he originally intended to treat all the Pauline letters.[19] Just as he did not fulfill his original intention of translating Origen's writings, so his planned commentaries on Paul remained an incomplete work.

The remaining period during which Jerome lived in Bethlehem until his death in 419/20 was also very productive. He produced his Old Testament translations and massive commentaries on the prophets. Jerome also continued his famous epistolary exchanges and later combated the Pelagian heresy.

---

17. Cf. NPNF 3.470–71. For an assembly of passages in Jerome that attack Ambrose, see D. Hunter, *Marriage, Celibacy, and Heresy in Ancient Christianity: The Jovinianist Controversy* (Oxford: Oxford University Press, 2007), pp. 234–36.

18. For a description of the library see the article on "Disciples of Origen" in *WHTO*.

19. In *Commentary on Ephesians,* preface to book 2. Jerome's *Commentary on Ephesians* has been translated by Heine, *The Commentaries of Origen and Jerome.*

Exegetical Predecessors: Origen

The commentaries presented in this volume were written shortly after Jerome's arrival in Bethlehem in ca. 386–388.[20] They were composed in the following order: Philemon, Galatians, [Ephesians], Titus.[21] They are presented in this volume not in their chronological order, but in the order in which I have translated them: Galatians, Titus, Philemon. This rearrangement has been done to make the footnoted material more coherent for the reader. Jerome began his treatment of the Pauline letters with the briefest one, that to Philemon. In spite of his not mentioning his exegetical predecessors and sources in the preface to the *Commentary on Philemon*, it is clear that he depended on Origen. Excerpts from Pamphilus's *Apology for Origen* and Rufinus's *Apology against Jerome* confirm this. The discussion of the symbolic meaning of names under verse 25 plainly derives from Origen.[22] Generally, however, it is noticeable that Jerome completely avoids allegory in this work and in the other Pauline commentaries. The subject matter does not lend itself to allegory. This method applies chiefly to the interpretation of the Old Testament, not the epistles of St. Paul. In the *Commentary on Philemon* an important theological defense of the free will is found under verse 22, and his treatment of the exegetical difficulty contained in verse 4 is worth reading, where Paul speaks of faith in God and in the saints. On the whole Jerome offers a practical and quite literal exposition of the brief Pauline letter to Philemon, an exposition that draws heavily on Origen, who is not credited.

A few days after completing the *Commentary on Philemon*, Jerome began working on the *Commentary on Galatians*. In the preface to Galatians Jerome admits that Origen is the principal exegetical authority he is following in his interpretation of Galatians. Origen had written five books on Galatians and had devoted the tenth book of his *Stro-*

---

20. Kelly, *Jerome*, p. 145 dates them at 387/88.
21. See below in the prefaces and *Commentary on Titus* 1.10–11.
22. Cf. Grützmacher, *Hieronymus*, 2.24.

mateis to it. Jerome's work in fact contains lengthy verbatim translations from Origen's *Stromateis,* a work that is no longer extant.[23] Fragments from Origen's now lost exegesis of Galatians and Titus that are preserved in Pamphilus's *Apology for Origen* confirm the extent of Jerome's dependence on Origen.[24] Giacomo Raspanti suggests that one of the reasons Jerome tackled Galatians was that the exegesis of this letter provided him an opportunity to illustrate and defend his translation agenda for the Old Testament, in which he would rely at least to some extent on the Hebrew text, compare it with the Greek text in the context of the Greek exegetical tradition, and take some liberties occasionally to suggest exegetical and translational changes on the basis of the Hebrew original.[25] There are many instances in the *Commentary on Galatians* when Jerome does do precisely this, as Raspanti shows.

After completing the Galatians commentary, Jerome wrote his commentary on Ephesians.[26] This was followed by his *Commentary on Titus.* The *Commentary on Titus* 1.5 contains a significant theological discussion in which Jerome argues that in the apostolic age the terms "bishop" and "priest" were synonymous, each church being governed by a council of coequal priests. The emergence of the episcopate proper, Jerome argues, was due not to any ordinance of the Lord Jesus but to ecclesiastical custom, with the object of excluding schisms. Jerome is thus an important ancient source for subsequent controversies in the Church over the divine institution of monarchical episcopacy.[27]

I will provide one historical example of such a controversy spawned by Jerome's views. In the early sixteenth century, the Catholic priest-scholar Erasmus of Rotterdam (1466–1536) had obtained a very exact knowledge of St. Jerome's writings and even published the first printed

---

23. See *Commentary on Galatians* 5.13; 5.24.

24. Cf. *Commentary on Galatians* 1.1; 1.11–12; *Commentary on Titus* 3.10–11. See my forthcoming translation of Pamphilus's *Apology for Origen,* FOTC 120.

25. "The Significance of Jerome's Commentary on Galatians in his Exegetical Production," in Cain and Lössl, eds., *Jerome of Stridon,* pp. 163–71, at 171.

26. See Heine, *The Commentaries of Origen and Jerome.*

27. Cf. J. Forget, "Jerome" DTC 8.965–76; Y. Bodin, *Saint Jerome et l'eglise* (Paris: Beauchesne et ses fils, 1966).

edition of them in 1516. As a result he questioned whether papal monarchy was recognized or exercised at the time of Jerome. Erasmus did not call into question whether papal sovereignty existed, but whether it was universally acknowledged. In a letter to Lorenzo Campeggi, Erasmus defends observations he had made in his scholarly notes to his *Edition of St. Jerome* (1516) against an attack upon his orthodoxy by a rabid critic named Zuniga (who was later officially silenced by consecutive popes). Erasmus writes:

> As to the sovereignty of the pope I have never doubted; but whether that sovereignty was recognized in Jerome's day or exercised is a doubt I do raise somewhere when prompted by the context, I think in my published notes on Jerome. But this has two sides: in one passage I set down what happens to support this view, and again in others I record in the same notes what leads to a different opinion. And there are so many other places where I call Peter first in rank among the apostles, Roman pontiff, Vicar of Christ, and head of the church, assigning him the chief power after Christ himself. All this is concealed by Zuniga, who picks out only what can be distorted to my discredit.[28]

In other words, Erasmus does not call into doubt that Christ intends the bishop of Rome to hold the primacy over the universal Church, but he questions whether, historically, this primacy was universally acknowledged or practiced in Jerome's day. It seems that evidence from St. Jerome's commentaries provided Erasmus with the historical grounds for raising these questions.

Use of the Septuagint

It is evident that the text of the Old Testament that Jerome cites as Scripture in these commentaries is that of the Septuagint, that is, the

---

28. See Desiderius Erasmus, CWE Ep. 1410, 19 January 1524.

Alexandrian Greek translation of the Old Testament, which was Origen's Bible.[29] Jerome has no hesitation in quoting from the Greek books that were added to the Alexandrian canon of Scripture, such as Sirach, Wisdom, Tobit, and the additions to Daniel. He treats these books as inspired Scripture and ecclesiastically authoritative, as did Origen. Later they were called the deuterocanonical writings by the Council of Trent. Jerome's free use of them confirms the insight that Jerome's subsequent theory about the authority of the Hebrew canon over against the Alexandrian canon was not consistent with his actual practice. In his early commentaries and in his correspondence, he continued to cite as Scripture texts from the Septuagint canon.[30] To my knowledge Jerome never challenged the divine inspiration of the Septuagint translation, but he accepted its ecclesiastical authority.

Jerome's *Commentary on Galatians*

The remainder of this introduction will focus on the content of Jerome's *Commentary on Galatians,* which was largely a compilation drawn from Origen's writings. Although Origen's original exegesis of Galatians does not survive, in 406 Rufinus of Aquileia translated into Latin Origen's *Commentary on the Epistle to the Romans.* This was a felicitous enterprise for Christians of the West, since otherwise we would not possess Origen's Pauline exegesis. The Greek text of Origen's *CRm*

---

29. I have always cited Scripture references according to the RSV chapter and verse. However, the reader needs to be aware that Jerome's citations of the Old Testament are based on the Septuagint, which does not always have an identical versification.

30. For discussions of Jerome's view of the canon, see D. Brown, *Vir Trilinguis: A Study in the Biblical Exegesis of Saint Jerome* (Kampen: Kok Pharos Publishing House, 1992), 62–86; P. Skehan, "St. Jerome and the Canon of the Holy Scriptures," in *A Monument to Saint Jerome,* ed. F. X. Murphy, 257–87 (New York: Sheed & Ward, 1952); E. F. Sutcliffe, "Jerome," in *The Cambridge History of the Bible,* vol. 2, *The West from the Fathers to the Reformation,* 80–101 (Cambridge: Cambridge University Press, 1969).

is preserved only in fragments.[31] The preservation of Rufinus's Latin translation of the *CRm* offers scholars a golden opportunity to compare Origen's Pauline exegesis with Jerome's. A comparison shows substantial agreement in the substance of the exegesis.[32] As an interpreter of St. Paul, Origen's exegesis was embraced by Catholic theologians.[33] In the footnotes of the present translations I have attempted to identify parallel passages.

It is noteworthy that in the epilogue of Rufinus's translation of Origen's *CRm*, Rufinus describes some malicious contemporaries who are encouraging him to steal the title from Origen and to put his own name on the title page of the translation. Rufinus refuses to do this, he says, since Origen is responsible for the exegetical material that he has rendered into Latin. Hammond underscores Rufinus's intention in this passage and notes that his words are really aimed at Jerome. She writes:

> Rufinus' stand against such plagiarism . . . was an implied criticism of Jerome's methods in his biblical commentaries. The procedure that he [Rufinus] refuses here . . . is similar to that for which he had attacked Jerome and those like him earlier. By directly translating Origen, he himself will reveal to Latin readers the source of Jerome's vaunted learning as a biblical commentator.[34]

This analysis seems quite accurate, and it answers the question of why Jerome himself never wrote a commentary on Romans: Rufinus's Latin translation of Origen left him with nothing to say of his own on Paul's epistle. Harnack confirms my conjecture in this regard when he raises

---

31. See the introduction to my translation (FOTC 103) and my study, *Origen and the History of Justification.*

32. For proof that Jerome had direct access to Origen's Greek commentary on Romans, see Hammond Bammel, "Philocalia IX," and Bammel, "Patristic Exegesis."

33. This is essentially the thesis of my book, *Origen and the History of Justification.* Cf. C. Verfaillie, *La doctrine de la justification.*

34. "The Last Ten Years," p. 404.

the question of why Jerome commented only on the letter to Titus among the Pastoral Epistles and answers: "Because a commentary of Origen was available only for this letter. Enough said!"[35]

I have not called attention to this in order to reproach Jerome or to single him out. He was doing precisely what his predecessors Ambrose and Hilary had done and what Didymus and Gregory Nazianzen had encouraged him to do. In fact Jerome himself was never embarrassed by the fact that he relied on Origen's exegesis in his own. He recommended Origen's works for study throughout all periods of his life. In 392 Jerome responded to critics who accused him of dependence on Origen in his own exegetical writings with these words:

> They say that I made excerpts from Origen's works, and that it is illegitimate to touch the writings of the old masters in such a way. People think that they gravely insult me by this. For myself, however, I see in this the highest praise. It is my express desire to follow an example of which I am convinced that it will please all men of discernment and you too.[36]

In 400, at the height of the Origenist controversies,[37] Jerome wrote in Ep. 85 to Paulinus of Nola an endorsement of Origen's defense of the free choice of the will found in *Peri Archon* (which was supposedly the most dangerous of Origen's works). To explain the meaning of the hardening of Pharaoh's heart, Jerome recommended Origen's explanation. Jerome's later Old Testament commentaries also display massive assimilation of Origen's exegesis. All of this confirms that Jerome did not substantially differ from his ecclesiastical contemporaries such as Rufinus and Ambrose in his method of appropriating Origen. Origen's best exegetical and spiritual insights were adopted, while his errors and controversial speculations were set aside. Jerome is not to be

---

35. *Der kirchengeschichtliche Ertrag*, p. 165, n. 1.

36. *Commentariorum in Michaeum, libri 2*, PL 25: 1189.

37. I have not discussed these controversies in detail here. See the introduction to my translation of St. Jerome's *Commentary on Matthew*, FOTC 117. See also F. X. Murphy, *Rufinus of Aquileia*, and Kelly, *Jerome*.

faulted for assimilating Origen, but for the way he attacked others, such as Rufinus, for refusing to publicly denounce Origen, and Ambrose, for allegedly stealing his exegesis from Origen. Both accusations are hypocritical, because Jerome himself had once praised Origen to the skies, and because his own exegesis relies heavily on Origen's insights.

Neglect of Ambrosiaster

In the preface to the *Commentary on Galatians,* Jerome discusses his exegetical predecessors, but he is completely silent about the Roman Churchman and scholar, Ambrosiaster, who had preceded him as a Latin commentator on Galatians.[38] Kelly suggests that something deeply personal to Jerome accounts for this deliberate neglect.[39] The unedifying story goes like this. Under the patronage and commission of Pope Damasus, Jerome had been asked by the pope to systematically revise existing Latin versions of the four Gospels and the Psalter. This was the beginning of Jerome's editorial work that became the Latin Vulgate Bible, though he did not touch the New Testament Epistles. Ambrosiaster, a Greek-less churchman from Rome, had criticized Jerome's revision and given outspoken preference for the Old Latin version of the New Testament over the Greek original. Jerome expressed his anger at the "two-legged asses" who had attacked his attempts to improve the Old Latin of the Gospels. Kelly argues that since he had clashed with Ambrosiaster on this earlier issue, Jerome avenged himself on his opponent by relegating Ambrosiaster's *Commentary on Galatians* to oblivion.[40]

---

38. Ambrosiaster's commentaries on St. Paul have been recently translated into English by G. Bray, *Ambrosiaster: Commentaries on Romans and 1–2 Corinthians,* Ancient Christian Texts (Downers Grove: Intervarsity, 2009), and *Ambrosiaster: Commentaries on Galatians-Philemon* (Downers Grove: Intervarsity, 2010).

39. Kelly, *Jerome,* p. 149.

40. Ibid.

Disparagement of Marius Victorinus?

On the other hand, in the preface to the *Commentary on Galatians* Jerome does not fail to report that Gaius Marius Victorinus, his former teacher of rhetoric in Rome, had published a commentary on the apostle. But he did so, Jerome goes on to say, "while he was occupied by the task of instructing in secular literature, and he was completely ignorant of the Scriptures. And no matter how eloquent someone is, he cannot discuss a subject well that he does not know." Few today would deny that Victorinus knew Platonism much better than he knew Christian theology and Scripture. Nevertheless, Jerome's disparaging assessment of Victorinus's *Commentary on Galatians* has been received as a haughty dismissal.[41] This too requires an explanation.

Marius Victorinus (280?–380?), known also as Afer (from Africa, the country of his birth), taught rhetoric in Rome, where his success earned him a statue in the forum. He abandoned his chair in 362 following Julian's edict forbidding Christians to teach. In old age he converted to Christianity.[42] Victorinus was the first to comment on Paul in Latin.[43] He did not use Greek sources but applied his experience in commenting on pagan texts to Paul's letters. At first glance Jerome's negative assessment of Victorinus's work seems excessive and arrogant. However, closer analysis of the respective commentaries suggests that Jerome is probably referring to Victorinus's complete neglect of the early Greek exegetes and to his total ignorance of the Old Testament, and even of the Gospels.

For Jerome a basic principle of Christian scriptural exegesis is to consult the mind of the Church as it is embodied in the antecedent exegetical tradition. This applies to Origen above all, its premiere

---

41. Cf. Quasten, *Patrology*, 4.232. Good discussions are found in Cooper, *Marius Victorinus' Commentary on Galatians,* pp. 107–10; E. Plumer, *Augustine's Commentary on Galatians,* pp. 41–47.

42. His conversion is the subject of Augustine's *Confessions* 8.2–5.

43. See Cooper, *Marius Victorinus' Commentary on Galatians.*

exegete, and especially to Origen's exegesis when that exegesis had been consensually approved by subsequent orthodox exegetes. Origen's great gift was identifying the Old Testament sources for the thoughts of the New Testament. In Jerome's estimation, an ecclesiastical commentator should report what the interpretive tradition has said about the Scriptures under examination. Victorinus fails to do this.

Moreover, even a cursory reading of Victorinus's exegesis of St. Paul shows that he simply does not consult the Old Testament or even the Gospels for clarification of Paul's meaning. He interprets Paul solely from Paul in the manner in which the Greeks explained Homer solely from Homer. A comparison of the Scripture indexes of Victorinus's and Jerome's commentaries reveals the real distinction between these two approaches. Victorinus's commentary does not contain a single explanatory reference to the Old Testament; moreover it offers very minimal consultation of the Gospel traditions to shed light on Paul's teaching and intentions. The contrast with St. Jerome's exegesis could not be greater. Stephen Cooper nicely summarizes their different exegetical approaches as follows:

> While Victorinus' method of interpreting authors with respect to their corpus of writing conformed to the academic procedures developed by the schools of his day, it was a notable departure from the tradition of Christian commentary. Origen's work exemplifies a standard feature of this tradition: an individual scripture must be explained by recourse to relevant, usually lexical parallels from the entirety of Scripture, whereby potential conflicts could be resolved. This manner of proceeding, reminiscent of rabbinic discussion, had its rationale not only in the theological desideratum to assert the unity of scriptural truth. It was also necessary to combat heretical rejections of the Old Testament (e.g. Marcion's *Antitheses*) or pagan attacks upon Christianity which often exploited discrepancies between the Gospels or between the Old Testament and the New. The tradition of Christian commentary . . . involved not only philological clarifications of the text (a technique of Latin grammarians and rhetors as well) but also discussion of the interpretive options explored by earlier exegetes. Victorinus' almost complete neglect of

this latter task may have been the thing that earned his commentaries the disdain of Jerome, who considered a comparison of opinions to be the essence of commentary both sacred and secular.[44]

Excursus: Did Paul Know the Gospel Traditions?

Ironically, the features that seem to have offended Jerome in Victorinus's approach to Pauline interpretation have made Victorinus a more interesting and attractive exegete to some streams of modern scholarship. Whereas Jerome's way of reading Paul is to see the apostle as completely rooted in the Old Testament, and as a faithful follower of the teaching of Jesus in the Gospels, many modern scholars wish to disassociate Paul both from the Old Testament and from the broader Christian tradition. In fact, much modern New Testament scholarship has been heavily influenced by the assertions of the radical New Testament critic Rudolph Bultmann, who claimed said that "Jesus' teaching is—to all intents and purposes—irrelevant for Paul."[45] Bultmann's school of thought pits Paul *against* the Jesus tradition. With two exceptions, 1 Cor 7.10 and 1 Cor 9.14, Paul purportedly never cites or alludes to sayings of Jesus. In Bultmann's case, this manner of reading Paul dovetailed with his existential philosophy according to which the historical existence and crucifixion of Jesus are indispensable, but otherwise the historical Jesus and traditions about him are irrelevant for faith.

The Bultmannian approach to Paul entered Catholic Scripture scholarship with a vengeance after 1968. For example, notice how Joseph Fitzmyer minimizes Paul's knowledge of the Gospel traditions:

It is remarkable how little he [Paul] knew of Jesus the Galilean rabbi or even of what is recorded in the Gospels about him. One reason

---

44. Cooper, *Marius Victorinus' Commentary on Galatians,* p. 109.

45. "The Significance of the Historical Jesus for the Theology of Paul," in *Faith and Understanding: Collected Essays,* 220–46 (London: SCM, 1969), p. 223.

for this is the early date of Paul's letters—almost all of them were written before the Gospels took the form we know. . . . He is not interested in the historical Jesus as a teacher, a prophet, or as the chronological source and the first link in the chain of such transmission. Rather, Paul is interested in the exalted Lord who is the real agent of all the tradition developing in the bosom of the apostolic Church.[46]

The presupposition here is that knowledge about Jesus was severely restricted until the Gospels took written form, and that the alleged silence of Paul's letters proves that Paul was not interested in Jesus as a teacher and prophet. Elsewhere, Fitzmyer claims that precisely because of his lack of interest in Jesus of Nazareth, Paul's writings "create an anomaly for Christians of later generations."[47] It is not clear which Christians Fitzmyer may be referring to here who found Paul to be an anomaly, but it is clear that Fitzmyer stands firmly in the Bultmannian tradition of interpretation. Fitzmyer claims that Paul's Damascus road insight did not give him a "cinematic reproduction of the ministry of Jesus of Nazareth, but the understanding of Jesus for humanity."[48]

Along similar lines Paula Fredriksen mimics Bultmann and says: "About Jesus of Nazareth Paul evinces little interest."[49] Such a minimalist approach to Paul's writings, which severs Paul from the Gospel traditions, differs radically from the presuppositions of Origen and Jerome respecting St. Paul's theology. Consider, for example, all the references to the Gospels in the Scripture index of the present commentary or in Origen's *CRm* and contrast that with the claims of the Bultmann school of interpretation.

Although at first glance it seems that Origen and Jerome offend against the "best and most assured results" of modern historical criti-

---

46. JBC, 79:17.

47. "Abba and Jesus' Relation to God," in *According to Paul: Studies in the Theology of the Apostle* (New York: Paulist Press, 1993), p. 108.

48. Ibid.

49. *From Jesus to Christ: The Origins of the New Testament Images of Christ* (New Haven: Yale University Press, 2000), p. 174.

cism, a radical paradigm shift is now occurring in the modern scholarly treatment of this problem. Bultmann's influence is lessening. Recently, the Protestant New Testament scholar, David Wenham has demonstrated in two important books that Paul was a devoted follower of the teaching of Jesus.[50] Wenham challenges the Bultmannian approach to interpreting Paul's writings and shows that Paul's epistles manifest a deep rootedness in the Gospel traditions. Wenham's point is not that the Gospels had already taken written form during Paul's ministry period; rather, he argues that the oral tradition that was later recorded in the Gospels was very much alive to Paul and that Paul had direct access to it.

Far from "evincing little interest" in Jesus's life and teaching, far from creating "an anomaly for Christians of later generations" by his insight into Jesus's existential significance for humanity, Paul's letters allude to the Gospel traditions on a massive scale. Some of Paul's knowledge was directly revealed to him by the appearance of the risen Christ. But he also learned a great deal from other Christians. According to Gal 1.18 he stayed with Peter for two weeks in Jerusalem. The book of Acts and the evidence from Paul's letters document massive contact between Paul and the early Hebrew-Christian disciples. Of great interest is the way Wenham shows that Paul's allusions to the Gospel tradition in his letters are *accidental,* that is to say, Paul uses the sayings and teachings of Jesus in his letters only as a reflection of the particular issues that he is dealing with in his relation to particular churches.

For instance, the echoes of Jesus's teaching in 1 Corinthians overlap a little with the echoes found in Galatians and 1 and 2 Thessalonians, but to a large extent they are different. This shows that the selection of echoes in each letter is determined by the problems in the particular church. Thus in 1 Cor 11 there is a specific focus on the Last Supper, because the Corinthians' Eucharistic meals were filled with liturgical abuses. Likewise, in 1 Cor 15 there is a specific reference to the

---

50. *Paul* and *Paul and Jesus.*

resurrection appearances, but only because resurrection was a debated issue in Corinth. The fact that Paul does not describe the crucifixion is not because he had not taught the Corinthians about it, obviously, but because it was unnecessary to retell the story in the letter. It would have been wasted ink. Wenham summarizes:

> It is salutary to reflect that, if the Corinthians had not had problems in their eucharists, we would have no evidence at all that Paul knew or taught about the Last Supper in any of his churches. He does not need to mention it in his other letters. We conclude that silence does not prove ignorance—not at all. The references that we do have to the stories and sayings of Jesus are the tip of an iceberg that is mostly concealed from us.[51]

Wenham draws the far-reaching conclusion that the Jesus tradition was central to Paul's theology. Therefore it is ludicrous to suggest that Paul was the real founder of Christianity or that Paul's writings are inconsistent with the rest of the New Testament. On the contrary, the anomaly comes about when we assume that Paul would have spoken about Christ without providing for his congregations information about Jesus's teaching and deeds.[52]

For Paul the fountain of theology was the Jesus whom he met on the Damascus road, who was identical with the one about whom he learned from the Christian tradition. He considered himself Jesus's slave; he did not view himself as the founder of Christianity. Wenham writes:

> If the primary text that Paul is expounding in his writings is the text of Jesus, then instead of reading Paul's letters in isolation from the Gospels, it will be important to read them in the light of the

---

51. *Paul,* p. 409.

52. This is Denis Farkasfalvy's criticism of Fitzmyer in "Jesus Reveals the Father: The Center of New Testament Theology," *Communio* 26 (1999), pp. 235–57, at p. 247, n. 25.

Gospels—not falling into naïve harmonization, but recognizing that Paul was above all motivated by a desire to follow Jesus.[53]

Wenham's way of reading Paul, as a theologian who knew the Gospel traditions intimately, is the way Origen and St. Jerome read Saint Paul. In spite of what may be naïve assumptions on Origen and Jerome's part about the extremely early dating of the written form of the Gospels,[54] Origen and Jerome seem to have rightly understood that Paul was thoroughly acquainted with Jesus's teaching and based his own upon it. Wenham's analyses suggest that Origen and Jerome's way of reading Paul is the right way to read him, while Bultmann's (and to some extent Marius Victorinus's) approach is the wrong way.

End of Excursus

Surely from Jerome's point of view another negative result of Marius Victorinus's "complete ignorance of the Scriptures" was the way his interpretation of St. Paul pits the apostles against each other. Under the lemma to Gal 1.19, for example, Victorinus claims that Paul "denies that James is an apostle" when he calls him the Lord's "brother." According to Victorinus, Paul had a "different conception of the gospel" than James, who "may have been in heresy."[55] Later, under the lemma to Gal 2.12–13, Victorinus explicitly asserts that this same James, the "brother of the Lord," is the progenitor of the Symmachians, a Jewish-Christian heretical sect.[56] Such judgments would be shockingly immature, not to say sub-Christian, from St. Jerome's Catholic perspective. They fundamentally misunderstand the nature of Paul's relations with the other apostles and the theological coherence of the New Testament.

---

53. *Paul,* pp. 409–10.
54. For instance, Jerome assumes that Luke's Gospel was circulating during the period of Paul's ministry activity; cf. *Commentary on Philemon* 22–25.
55. Cooper, *Marius Victorinus' Commentary on Galatians,* p. 266.
56. Ibid., p. 278.

Victorinus's English translator, Stephen Cooper, follows Harnack's lead in presenting Victorinus as a "proto-Luther" figure.[57] Cooper sees this connection especially in view of the strong "solafidian" (justification by faith alone) tendency in some of Victorinus's statements, which, of course, is also found in Luther's writings. The phrase *sola fide* (by faith alone) appears in Victorinus's commentary on Gal 2.15; 3.2; 3.7; 3.21; 3.22; 6.10. It seems reasonable, however, to question whether Victorinus and Luther really meant the same thing when they spoke of justification by faith alone. In calling attention to Victorinus's alleged resemblance to Luther, it is odd that Cooper overlooks what clearly appears to be the deepest link between Victorinus and Luther, namely Victorinus's disparagement of St. James and his depiction of him as a proto-heretic. Luther's similar animosity toward James is well known.[58]

Finally, in assessing Jerome's dismissal of Victorinus, it may also be relevant to notice that when he comments on Gal 4.4, Victorinus appears to speak as if the perpetual virginity of the Blessed Virgin Mary were still an open question: "cum Virgo Maria sit *vel* fuerit," "Because Mary is, or was a virgin." Thus does Cooper translate *vel* as a genuine alternative. Although the passage is not completely clear, and Cooper's theological conclusions may lay too much stress on a single word, it should be obvious that Jerome, following Origen, would attribute even the suggestion that Mary was not perpetually a virgin both to impiety and to the profoundest ignorance of Holy Scripture.[59]

From St. Jerome's standpoint, these are precisely the kinds of immature judgments that one might expect of a teacher of rhetoric, con-

---

57. Ibid., pp. 285, 327.

58. In his preface to the book of James, Luther writes: "He does violence to Scripture, and so contradicts Paul and all Scripture. He tries to accomplish by emphasizing law what the apostles bring about by attracting men to love. I therefore refuse him a place among the writers of the true canon of my Bible." J. Dillenberger, *Martin Luther: Selections from His Writings* (New York: Doubleday, 1961), p. 36.

59. Jerome wrote the first great defense of Mary's perpetual virginity, *Against Helvidius* (NPNF2 6.334–46). Origen described as an impious opinion the view that Mary did not remain a virgin. Cf. Origen *Commentary on John* 1.23 (FOTC 80.38).

verted to Christianity in extreme old age, who was unfamiliar both with the Christian exegetical tradition and with the Scriptures themselves. Thus Jerome's seemingly haughty dismissal of Victorinus's commentary actually has the result of protecting Victorinus's reputation for posterity against more serious charges against his orthodoxy. Victorinus is less culpable precisely because of his late conversion and ignorance of the deeper principles of Christian exegesis. It is noteworthy that in a similar fashion, at *Commentary on Galatians* 4.6 Jerome attributes the deficiencies found in Lactantius's Trinitarianism to his unfamiliarity (*imperitiam*) with the Scriptures.

Jerome's Interpretation of Galatians

Jerome's is the lengthiest and most learned of the ancient patristic commentaries on Galatians. His work occupies 130 columns in Migne, which compares with 43 columns for Augustine's commentary, 51 for Victorinus's, 36 for Ambrosiaster's, and 19 for Pelagius's.[60] He dictated the work hurriedly to a stenographer, and in the preface to book 3 he apologizes for the way the work lacks polish. In spite of this we are dealing with a formidable piece of exegesis. The patristic scholar C. P. Bammel considered Jerome the first "scholarly" (*wissenschaftlich*) Latin commentator on Paul.[61] In the nineteenth century, the great Protestant Scripture scholar J. B. Lightfoot assessed St. Jerome's *Commentary on Galatians* in these words:

> Though abounding in fanciful and perverse interpretations, violations of good taste and good feeling, faults of all kinds, this is nevertheless the most valuable of all the patristic commentaries on

---

60. These calculations were given in Plumer, *Augustine's Commentary on Galatians*, p. 33.

61. "Die Pauluskommentare des Hieronymus," in *Cristianesimo Latino e cultura Greca sino al sec. IV*, 187–207 (Rome: Institutum Patristicum Augustinianum, 1993), 206; cited by Cooper, *Marius Victorinus' Commentary on Galatians*, p. 109, n. 99.

the Epistle to the Galatians: for the faults are more than redeemed by extensive learning, acute criticism, and lively and vigorous exposition.[62]

Lightfoot, whose reflections are based on a careful study of Jerome's work, seems to have been one of the last "modern" exegetes to have read Jerome carefully and to have taken him seriously as an interpreter of St. Paul.[63]

On the other hand, J. N. D. Kelly dismisses Jerome's commentaries on Ephesians and Galatians as disappointing works, due to "Jerome's failure to understand, much less present adequately, the profound theological issues with which these letters are concerned."[64] This criticism resembles Martin Luther's, which will be discussed below.

The Main Argument

Jerome summarizes the argument of the Epistle to the Galatians in the preface. The subject is the same, he says, as that found in the Epistle to the Romans, with this difference: Romans is more exalted and profound, reasoned and persuasive, whereas Galatians contains a rebuke of the converts and shows Paul making use of his authority by means of blunt speech. The basic message is that the burdens of the old law have been set aside through the grace of the gospel. All that came before in types and images has ceased, because the law is now fulfilled through the believer's faith. These two epistles, Romans and Galatians, thus focus on the theme of the termination of the old law and the inauguration of the new. Yet Galatians is unique in that it was written to converts from paganism, not former Jews. Paul's audience in Galatians were guilty of backsliding after being terrified by certain men who

---

62. Lightfoot, *The Epistle of St. Paul to the Galatians*, p. 232.

63. For example, in contrast with Lightfoot, the commentaries by Burton (ICC), Ridderbos (NICNT), and Longenecker (WBC) contain no real engagement with Jerome's exegesis.

64. Kelly, *Jerome*, p. 147.

claimed that Peter, James, and all the churches had mixed the gospel of Christ with the old law. They also thought that Paul mingled the old and the new in his own missionary work. So Paul treads softly between the concerns of Jewish and Gentile Christians, not wanting to betray the grace of the gospel nor do injury to his predecessors while he defends grace. In the preface Jerome mentions Porphyry's interpretation, that Peter had been impudently rebuked by Paul for error, and that the early leaders of the Christian churches were at variance with each other. Jerome will combat this interpretation throughout the commentary.

Free Will, Foreknowledge, and Predestination

Jerome sustains his usual polemic against the heretics Marcion, Valentinus, Manicheus, Arius, and others, which is a trademark of all his exegesis.[65] It is particularly the anti-Gnostic material that is largely drawn from Origen, as Harnack's valuable study has called attention to.[66] In opposition to heretical ideas, Jerome insists upon the identification of the God of the Old Testament with the God of Jesus. Under the lemma to Gal 5.12 Jerome exposes serious inconsistencies in Marcionite exegesis of Scripture using arguments borrowed from Origen. A very significant byproduct of the anti-Gnostic polemic is Jerome's strong defense of the freedom of the human will in the process of salvation.[67] Jerome repeatedly says that the human being contributes something to his salvation and that obedience or disobedience lay within the power of his choice (5.8). God's work is to invite; man's is to believe or not believe (5.8). Paul does not remove personal choice from us (5.17). Moreover, Jerome explains that the divine predestination or choosing, of Jacob and Esau, for instance, is explained by God's

---

65. For a more detailed discussion of these heresies, see the introduction of my translation of *St. Jerome's Commentary on Matthew*, FOTC 117.

66. I have endeavored to integrate Harnack's insights into the footnotes. Harnack admitted that his research only scratched the surface of Jerome's assimilation of Origen.

67. Precisely the same emphasis is found in Origen's Pauline exegesis. See his *CRm*, Preface1.

foreknowledge of their future merits (1.15–16), not by their inborn nature or by any sort of pre-birth divine decree. It is the heretics who assert that there are different kinds of natures in men, some destined to perish, others to be saved, apart from the free choice of the will.[68] The proof Jerome offers for his defense of freedom is found in the scriptural witness to the human being's mutability, or capability of conversion in both directions (2.15).[69]

Jerome's approach to predestination is found prominently in the Greek theological tradition and in the early Augustine. It differs strikingly, however, from the late Augustine. Eric Plumer notes that the early Augustine held the same view as Origen, Chrysostom, and Jerome, that God chooses certain people for salvation on the basis of his foreknowledge of their free decision of faith.[70] Later on, however, Augustine became dissatisfied with this position and viewed it as endangering the sovereignty of divine grace. He continued to move further and further in the direction of religious determinism, without, however, ever abandoning the idea that human beings freely cooperate in conversion and always retain the power to resist divine grace. It is probably St. Jerome's support for the Greek understanding of predestination that led Erasmus of Rotterdam (1466–1536) to conclude that Augustine was isolated in his opposition to the idea that God chooses based on his foreknowledge of foreseen merits.[71] W. Fremantle confirms this when he says of Jerome's *Dialogue against the Pelagians,* "[I]t cannot fail to appear that Jerome is not like Augustine, a thorough-going predestinarian, but a 'synergist,' maintaining the co-

---

68. Once again, consider *CRm* 7.16.4; 7.17.7.

69. Cf. *CRm* 1.3.3.

70. *Augustine's Commentary on Galatians,* p. 182, n. 150, referring to lemma 4.7; *Expositio quarundam propositionum ex epistula ad Romanos* 52 (60).

71. Cf. Erasmus's words in *Hyperaspistes II,* addressed to Martin Luther: "Only Augustine excludes foreknown merits as the reason why Jacob was chosen and Esau rejected, and his interpretation makes original sin the cause of the hatred. For my part, Augustine is a man to whom anyone may grant as high a status as he likes; but I would never attribute so much to him as to think he sees further in Paul's epistles than the Greek interpreters"; Erasmus, *Controversies,* 77.535.

existence of free will, and that he reduces predestination to God's fore-knowledge of human determination (see the *Dialogue,* especially 1.5, 2.6, 3.18)."[72] This observation indicates that for Jerome the repudiation of Pelagianism did not entail the endorsement of Augustine's views on predestination.

John Ferguson confirms this when he writes with respect to Jerome's views articulated in his *Dialogue against the Pelagians:*

> But Jerome does not hold the extreme predestinarian views of Augustine. He is rather a synergist,[73] holding that God's grace and man's free will come together in the work of salvation, and equating predestination with prescience, that is to say, interpreting the doctrine not in terms of an arbitrary fiat of the Almighty that A shall be saved and B damned, but to mean that God having in His Almighty perfection complete knowledge of past, present and future, fore-knows that A will so live as to be saved, and B will so live as to be damned.[74]

Jerome's understanding of predestination and free will is more in line with the emphasis of the Greek theologians than with late-Augustinian views.

The Relation of Faith, Works of the Law, and Love

On the crucial question of justification by faith, Jerome presupposes that it is apart from the merit of works that our former sins are forgiven in baptism and that peace with God is granted after the pardon. He interprets Paul as being firmly opposed to those who think we can be

---

72. "Hieronymus," DCB 3.46.

73. Synergism is merely a transliteration of the Greek term, συνεργέω, which means "cooperation" (from *cooperor*) or "working together." The term is scriptural (cf. Mk 16.20; Rom 8.28; Jas 2.22) and indicates that God and man collaborate or work together in the process of salvation.

74. John Ferguson, *Pelagius* (Cambridge: W. Heffer & Sons, 1956), pp. 79–80.

justified by works (Gal 1.3). But Jerome makes a fundamental distinction between pre- and post-baptismal works, as well as pre- and post-baptismal merit. By no means does Jerome reduce Christ's benefits to the forgiveness of sins. Jerome says that Christ became a curse for us for our glory (3.13–14). He died that we might live; he descended to the underworld that we might ascend to heaven; he became foolishness that we might become wisdom; he emptied himself that the fullness of divinity might dwell in us; he was hung on the tree that our sins might be blotted out (3.13–14). To be sure Christ brought us the forgiveness of sins, but he brought us much more than that.

Jerome does not separate faith from love, grace from works; nor does he view "law" as a purely negative and condemnatory term (6.2). The *old* law of Moses is one thing, the *new* law of Christ is something else. Jerome thinks that St. Paul's principal polemic in Galatians is directed against "works of the law," not against good works or law in a general sense and certainly not against Christ's command of love and obedience. The "works of the law" refer to the works of Judaism, such as circumcision, Sabbaths, rituals, sacrifices. In the Christian dispensation no one is justified by these works, since they have been abolished by the advent of the grace of the gospel (2.3–5). However, ceremonial works are not identical with the good works of Christian discipleship that are demanded by Jesus of his disciples. On the contrary the law of Christ, the law of love, must be obeyed and fulfilled as a precondition of final salvation. This is according to Christ's own threats and promises (6.2). The law of the Spirit is that we love one another (6.3). We will be judged by whether or not we keep this law (6.5). Love alone cleanses the heart (5.13–14).

Natural Law and Knowledge of God

Jerome insists that the knowledge of God is present in everyone by nature; no one is born apart from Christ (Gal 1.15–16). All people can do some things wisely and virtuously for which they will be held responsible at the judgment. The principles of the virtues and the seeds of God are sown within all men. The Old Testament saints were justified in part by natural law. The justice of the old law, when fulfilled spiritually, can increase the justice of the law of nature (3.2). Cornelius the centurion received the Spirit by the hearing of faith *and* by works of natural law, but not by "works of the law," that is, Judaistic works, with which he was unacquainted (2.16; 3.2). The works of natural law were not adequate in themselves; rather Cornelius was saved by those works *and* by the hearing of faith (3.2). Without faith the works of natural law, though good, are reckoned as dead (5.6). But when faith is put first, this is not done in order to destroy the works of the law, or to give Christians a license to sin (3.2).

No License to Sin

Like Origen and St. Paul himself, Jerome does not believe that the purity of Christian faith requires the repudiation of morality and asceticism.[75] On the contrary he views the Christian life as a combat initiated at baptism.[76] Thus he insists that freedom to transgress does not arise from faith in Christ, but the will for good works is increased by the love that springs from faith (Gal 3.2). Indeed, Jerome says that in order to be saved one must have both faith and love, or rather, faith working through love (5.6).[77] The whole burden of the old law has not so much been *excluded* through the grace of the gospel as *abbreviated* into the one word of love (5.17). Therefore we must live according to the spiritual law and not fulfill the lusts of the flesh (5.17). The one who gives himself to the flesh and its passions is not alive in the Spirit (5.25). Far from being contrary to law, grace causes us to be restrained all the more by the law of nature. True freedom from the abolished law comes when we have put to death the deeds of the flesh (5.17). The Holy Spirit is always given to the worthy (3.5; 6.18). One must advance in the

---

75. Cf. 1 Cor 10; Gal 6.7. The interpretation of Paul's doctrine found in the new book by C. VanLandingham, *Judgment and Justification in Early Judaism and the Apostle Paul* (Peabody: Hendrickson, 2006), chap. 3, is strikingly consonant with Jerome's.

76. Cf. de Lubac, *History and Spirit*, 209–13.

77. Cf. Levy, "*Fides qua per caritatem operatur.*"

virtues and bring faith to completion in love (3.5), for works adorn faith (3.5). With the good thief we must nail the trophy of our own mortification to the wood of the Lord's suffering (2.19). For any one of the works of the flesh can equally exclude us from the kingdom of God (5.19–21).

Glorying in the Cross

Jerome states that "glorying solely in the cross of Christ" does not *negate* Christian asceticism and discipleship, but is *fulfilled* in the one who takes up the cross to follow the Savior. Thus there is no opposition between the teaching of Jesus, who demands the good works of obedient discipleship, and the teaching of Paul, who repudiates the Judaizing "works of the law." Paul's words in Gal 6.14 about glorying solely in the cross apply precisely to the one who has crucified his own flesh with its lusts and desires and who has died to the world. Thus according to St. Jerome, Paul does not exclude all "glorying" absolutely, but only that kind of glorying that boasts in the Judaistic works of the law.[78] The Christian's glorying in his weaknesses and mortifications *is* the glory of the cross, since anything worthy that is done in respect to the virtues is done for the sake of the Lord's passion (6.14).

Overall Jerome's exegesis of St. Paul represents a deeply Catholic synthesis of faith and post-baptismal good works, wherein paschal grace is seen as the source of the grace that enables the merits and achievements of Christian asceticism and discipleship. He supports fundamental themes in the Catholic interpretation of St. Paul, such as the distinction between pre- and post-baptismal works; pre- and post-baptismal merit; the claim that love, as a complement to faith, is equally necessary for salvation and is intrinsic to the process of the human being's justification; that St. Paul's polemic against "works of the law" is

---

78. The resemblance to Origen's categories of interpretation is remarkable. Cf. Origen, *CRm* 3.9.6–7; 8.6. In the former passage Origen says: "The only just boasting then is based upon faith in the cross of Christ, which excludes all boasting that derives from the works of the law."

directed primarily at the ceremonial works of the old law, not at law or good works in general; and finally that the good works that issue from faith formed by love have meritorious value before God, as an outworking of paschal grace. These themes will retain a firm place in Catholic theology in subsequent centuries.

Paul's Rebuke of Peter at Antioch

One of the more well-known interpretations advanced in Jerome's commentary is the way he mitigates the conflict between Paul and Peter that is described in Gal 2.11–14.[79] A pagan opponent of the Church, Porphyry, thought that Paul and Peter were adversaries. Porphyry interpreted Paul's threatening words in Gal 5.10, "he who is troubling you will bear his judgment," as being directed against Peter. Following Origen, Jerome answers that Paul would not have spoken with such an offensive malediction against the ruler of the church (5.10).

There is not complete consistency or clarity in the Jerome's interpretation of the Paul/Peter conflict at Antioch. In fact Jerome's remarks under 2.6 and 2.14, for example, seem to assume that the conflict was real.[80] Moreover, Jerome apparently did not wish to dogmatize on this subject, as he makes clear in his explanatory letter to St. Augustine, which will be discussed further below. However, the general outline of Jerome's view is this: in a very strong reaction against Porphyry's exaggerated portrayal of the dispute between the apostles, Jerome suggests that both Peter and Paul were behaving under a spontaneous (not planned) pretense for the sake of their respective audiences, Jewish and Gentile Christians. Peter knew full well that the Jewish ceremonial law was no longer binding after Christ's death and resurrection. In Antioch Peter temporarily withdrew from fellowship with Gentile

---

79. Cf. P. Auvray, "Saint Jerome and saint Augustin: La controverse au sujet de l'incident d'Antioche," *Recherches de science religieuse* 29 (1939), pp. 594–610.

80. Cf. *Commentary on Philemon*, 8–9. M. Wiles, *Divine Apostle*, p. 22, n. 1, suggests that Jerome may have been following different sources.

Christians for the sake of Jewish Christians. But the Gentile Christians misinterpreted Peter's policy and inferred that ceremonial law was binding on them. Paul saw that these Gentile Christians were now in danger of being led astray. To prevent them from falling away, he pretended to rebuke Peter, knowing full well Peter's good intentions. According to Jerome, when Paul states that Peter was "in the wrong" (2.11), he is expressing not his own opinion but only that of the Gentile believers. Jerome likens Peter and Paul to two orators who feign fictitious lawsuits for the sake of their respective clients. Jerome also offers examples of Old Testament kings of Israel who adopted public pretences in order to accomplish various purposes.

The gist of Jerome's interpretation is that Peter and Paul did not have a substantive disagreement over the question of whether the old law continued to be in force for Christians. Both were aware that the law was no longer binding on them. St. Peter's apparent backsliding was a tactical measure temporarily adopted to win Jews over to Christianity. St Paul's rebuke, similarly, was not seriously intended or taken as such. Jerome invites anyone who thinks that Paul truly opposed Peter for the sake of the truth of the gospel to explain Paul's own similar behavior, insofar as Paul circumcised Timothy,[81] participated in Jewish ceremonies,[82] and in general "became as a Jew in order to win the Jews," according to 1 Cor 9.20. By what effrontery, then, would he dare to rebuke Peter for such behavior, when he himself has done the very same things? Jerome thinks that, in Paul's argument in the epistle to the Galatians, the publicly contrived "polemic" with Peter is continued by Paul down to Gal 2.21.

Most modern exegetes dismiss Jerome's explanation of the incident at Antioch out of hand. It is alleged to be a ridiculous and forced interpretation. What is interesting to observe, however, is that these same modern exegetes, who think that Paul and Peter were indeed at loggerheads with each other over their basic understanding of the gospel, nevertheless claim that Paul, without any indication, abandons his

---

81. Cf. Acts 16.3.
82. Cf. Acts 21.26.

polemic against Peter in 2.15. Longenecker, for example, following Betz, asserts that Gal 2.15–21 "should not be considered just as part of Paul's speech to Peter, though it springs from that, but as the summary of all that Paul has argued in 1:11–2:14 and as the introductory transition to 3:1–4:11."[83] Likewise, Ridderbos says that 2.15–21 should be regarded as a "transition from the historically occasioned to the generally considered aspects."[84] In other words, both Longenecker and Ridderbos, as well as many others, want to mitigate the severity of Paul's words in 2.15–21 and deflect them from being interpreted as an attack against Peter. Yet there is not the slightest textual basis for reading these verses as a "transition." This idea has been introduced into the text by the modern interpreters.

Jerome thinks, on the contrary, that the "polemic" against Peter continues until the very end of chapter 2, but that it is a contrived or feigned polemic, not sincere. This does not mean that Jerome thinks that Paul and Peter had planned and staged the confrontation; rather, they had spontaneously feigned the dispute for the sake of others. What this shows is that even modern scholars agree with Jerome in denying that Gal 2.15–21 is directed purely and sincerely against Peter.

Scholars who are familiar with Jerome's interpretation usually do not find Jerome's particular explanation of the conflict at Antioch plausible, nor do I find it entirely satisfying. However, in my judgment Jerome's explanation deserves more careful consideration than it has hitherto received. He is usually rejected on the basis of hearsay and not as a result of careful consideration of his exegetical arguments. Many of the questions Jerome raises, modern exegetes simply refuse to answer. It seems that the unavailability of this commentary in translation has hindered scholars from fully engaging these issues. Jerome asks important questions of interpreters who support variations of the Porphyrian interpretation of the conflict. One query is found under the lemma to 2.14a: What consequences follow from Paul's reproving in

---

83. *Galatians*, WBC, pp. 80–81.

84. H. Ridderbos, *The Epistle of Paul to the Churches of Galatia*, NICNT (Grand Rapids: Eerdmans, 1953; repr. 1981), p. 98.

Peter what he himself had done? It appears to me that this question needs to be answered before Jerome's exegesis is utterly dismissed. It is no solution to simply set aside Luke's portrait of Paul in Acts as a fictional construction, since the evidence from Paul's own letters points to the same reality: that Paul became as a Jew and as one under the law in order to win to faith in Christ Jews who were under the law (cf. 1 Cor 9.20). In any case I. H. Marshall has demonstrated the historical plausibility of Luke's portrait of Paul.[85]

The Reaction of St. Augustine to Jerome's Explanation

Before he had been made a bishop, the forty-year-old Augustine wrote Ep. 28 to Jerome[86] in 394/95 in which, among other things, he took issue with Jerome's interpretation of the incident at Antioch, which he found unsatisfactory and even dangerous.[87] This letter never reached Jerome, and so Augustine penned Ep. 40 (Jer. 67) in late 398 or early 399, repeating much of what he said in Ep. 28 and offering his own exposition of the Galatians passage. Jerome's response to Augustine was written in Ep. 112 to Augustine[88] (Aug. 75) in the year 404, thus some ten years after the initial letter of Augustine. Augustine's criticism of Jerome's interpretation shows that the African doctor equates pretense with mendacity. He consequently accuses Jerome, and by implication those who agree with Jerome, of defending the use of lying for the sake

---

85. See his *Acts*, TNTC (Grand Rapids, Mich.: Eerdmans, 1989), pp. 246–47. Even with regard to Luke's claim that Paul took the step of circumcising Timothy (Acts 16.4), Marshall writes (p. 260): "To Haenchen it is impossible that the Paul who wrote 1 Corinthians 7:17–20 should have acted thus; why did he not go on to make Timothy keep the whole law of Moses (Gal 5:3)? But Haenchen has confused circumcision as a means of salvation with circumcision as a legal act to remove a stigma from Timothy, and his objections are without force."

86. CSEL 34.1, pp. 103–13. This is Jerome, Ep. 56.

87. I have used the edition of the Jerome-Augustine correspondence in White, *The Correspondence*.

88. CSEL 55, pp. 367–93.

of expedience. What Jerome had described as Peter and Paul's contrived or feigned public dispute, Augustine interprets as Jerome's advocacy of outright deception and lies. But if the Bible condones lies, then nothing in the sacred writings can be trusted.

It appears to me that Augustine is probably correct in finding some inadequacies in Jerome's particular explanation of the incident at Antioch. However, he does not seem to have fully grasped the nature of Jerome's explanation, and he draws defective inferences when he equates feigning with mendacity. Whereas Jerome is willing to admit that Paul made use of pretense and even lost his temper at times,[89] Augustine is at pains to safeguard the authority of Paul. Plumer has observed that this leads Augustine to casuistry and to some very tortured exegesis at times.[90]

Epistle 112 to Augustine is Jerome's response to Augustine's criticisms. Before he composes his defense of his own exegesis, Jerome offers two arguments that serve as preliminary rebuttals of Augustine's accusations. First Jerome clarifies the source of his interpretation as coming from the Greek Fathers. He reiterates his words from the preface of the commentary concerning his sources and reminds Augustine not only that Origen was the first to offer the interpretation that Jerome has transmitted, but that all subsequent Greek exegetes adopted Origen's explanation, including John Chrysostom in his *Homilies on Galatians*. Jerome then comments:

> If then you considered anything in my explanation worthy of criticism, it was up to your learning to find out whether what I had written was to be found in the writings of the Greeks, so that if they had not said them, then you could justifiably condemn my opinion, especially since I openly confessed in my preface that I had followed the commentaries of Origen and had dictated either my own or other people's ideas.[91]

---

89. See on Gal 5.12.
90. *Augustine's Commentary on Galatians*, pp. 92–93.
91. White, *The Correspondence*, p. 116.

Jerome's tactical maneuver demonstrates that the Greek exegetical tradition was a closed book to Augustine. Further, Jerome seems to presuppose that Origen's exegesis of Scripture is not to be accused of
heresy when it has been adopted by subsequent orthodox writers. Thus
Augustine should tone down his accusations of the senior scholar,
since the same charges would inevitably land not merely on Jerome but
on all the exegetes of the Greek tradition who followed Origen.

The second preliminary argument in refutation of Augustine's
criticism is preceded by another lengthy verbatim citation of his own
words in the commentary on Gal 2.14a. In this argument Jerome proposes an attactive model for scriptural interpretation. He says to Augustine: "I thereby made it clear that I was not defending unequivocally
what I had read in the Greek authors but had expressed the ideas that I
had read in such a way as to leave it to the reader to decide for himself
whether to approve these things or not."[92] In other words, Jerome reminds Augustine that he has not wished to dogmatize in his explanations, or to pretend to offer the final answer to every problem raised in
Scripture. He does not claim to be the final authority in Pauline interpretation. Instead, his method of exegesis aims to provide the reader
with multiple interpretations that are present in the ancient tradition
and to leave to the reader the freedom to adopt the view he deems best.
These two rebuttals are succeeded by a very detailed answer to Augustine's specific criticisms of the exegesis.

Unfortunately, in his lengthy response to Augustine, Jerome shows
himself equally guilty of drawing defective inferences of Augustine's
proposed interpretation of the issues. For example, Jerome concludes
that Augustine is espousing the idea that all who have been converted
from Judaism *have an obligation to keep the law*. In reality Augustine
had merely said that there was a period of time when this was *permitted*, in light of the fact that circumcision is an indifferent matter. Circumcision only threatens faith if one places one's hope of salvation in
it.[93] In general, however, it seems fair to say that Jerome is the more

---

92. Ibid.
93. Ibid., p. 117.

liberal minded of the two interpreters of St. Paul. While Augustine's *Commentary on Galatians* is a great piece of exegesis, perhaps his greatest, very frequently, especially in his later theological works, Augustine has a strong tendency to force a dogmatic straightjacket on Paul's thoughts.[94] Jerome, on the other hand, imitating Origen, often offers multiple interpretations of given passages. He is more pleased to leave the reader the freedom to choose for himself the best interpretation.[95]

The Incident at Antioch

Most modern Scripture scholars presuppose that Paul was in the right and Peter in the wrong in the incident described in Gal 2.11–14. Allegedly Peter, out of his characteristic weakness, caved in to Judaizing pressures and truly compromised the principles of the gospel when he temporarily withdrew from table fellowship with the Gentiles in Antioch. I am not convinced that this judgment on Peter is correct. Paul himself tells us that Barnabas took Peter's side in the situation (2.13), which would suggest that Paul was isolated in his criticism of Peter. Unfortunately we do not have Peter's version of the story. David Wenham offers a reconstruction of Peter's perspective on the events that strikes me as very plausible.[96] It may be the case that neither Jerome nor Augustine, nor even a majority of modern exegetes, have understood the true complexity of the situation at Antioch.

Paul comments in Gal 6.12 that the Judaizers were doing what they were doing only "to avoid being persecuted for the cross of Christ." For Jews in Jerusalem, the mission of Paul and Barnabas had been a particular source of friction, since this mission had divided the Jewish communities throughout Asia Minor. It is possible that Peter had been warned by Jewish Christians that he was forfeiting all respect as leader

---

94. Cf. Scheck, *Origen and the History of Justification,* pp. 93–94; C. P. Bammel, "Augustine, Origen and the Exegesis of St. Paul," p. 351.

95. Consider, for example, the three interpretations Jerome offers of Paul's "weakness of the flesh" (Gal 4.13).

96. *Paul and Jesus,* pp. 49–59.

of the Church by his custom of having table fellowship with Gentiles, since this was something that was explicitly forbidden in the Mosaic law. When the Jews from Jerusalem came to Antioch, he may have felt that his and Barnabas's initiative in withdrawing from table fellowship with Gentiles, and thus in increasing the rigor of their (provisional) adherence to the Mosaic law, was necessary in light of the crisis that their Christian brothers and sisters were experiencing in Jerusalem.

Clearly by their temporary separation, Peter and Barnabas had no intention of "compelling the Gentiles to live like Jews," as Paul defectively infers in 2.14. On the contrary, their behavior did not have Gentile Christians in view. Peter and Barnabas were motivated by missionary concern. Their withdrawal did not represent some official change in policy that was of universal application. It is true that according to Galatians Paul condemned the behavior on principle, but it is difficult to understand why, when we consider Paul's own flexibility in relation to practicing Jewish customs and food laws, according to Rom 14.15, 14.20, and 15.1, and 1 Cor 9.20. When Paul claims that Peter "stood condemned" and that Barnabas too was in the wrong in this "hypocrisy," these appear to be Paul's private inferences and do not necessarily correspond with God's judgment of the situation. It is hard to understand how these accusations could not be turned against Paul for his adoption of Jewish customs and even for his circumcising Timothy (cf. Acts 16.3). Scholars who assert that the "real Paul" (as opposed to Luke's allegedly fictional portrait) need to explain Paul's stated principles in the texts from Romans and 1 Corinthians cited above.

We also recall that when the issue of the necessity of circumcision for Gentile converts was finally resolved by the Council of Jerusalem, a sort of compromise was reached (Acts 15.22–29). To be sure Gentiles were declared to be free from the obligation to be circumcised and to keep the law of Moses. However, the same Council decreed that unnecessary offense to the Jews was to be avoided by means of the Gentiles' abstaining from food sacrificed to idols, from blood, from meat of strangled animals, and from sexual immorality (Acts 15.29). This was, to be sure, an endorsement of Paul's unwavering mission policy of maintaining table fellowship with the Gentiles; but it did not give Gentiles license to offend Jewish sensibilities unnecessarily.

The upshot of this analysis is that Jerome (and Origen) may have had a more profound understanding of the larger issues involved in this situation than they themselves realized or than they are often given credit for. They seem to have been right in seeing that Peter and Paul were in basic agreement about the core principles of the gospel as they pertained to Jewish and Gentile believers. Where Peter and Paul differed was in the application of those principles. Jerome is unwilling to conclude that Paul's angry rebuke of Peter was unjustifiable. Instead, he suggests the idea that the two men feigned the public quarrel as a matter of diplomacy.

The situation in Antioch seems similar to Acts 15.36–41, which reports a dispute between Paul and Barnabas over the worthiness of John Mark for missionary work. Paul judged him unworthy for ministry, whereas Barnabas considered him worthy. In assessing this situation, are we obligated to side with Paul against Barnabas? Why should this be the case, either in Acts or in Galatians? Paul himself appears to have changed his mind respecting John Mark: see Col 4.10; Phlm 24; and 2 Tm 4.11. From Rom 14.15 and 15.1 it appears that Paul eventually reconciled himself with Peter's principles.[97]

Legacy of St. Jerome's Commentaries on St. Paul

In the Middle Ages the Catholic Church declared St. Jerome to be one of its four great Latin Doctors, alongside St. Augustine (354–430),

---

97. For an assessment of the Antioch incident that dissents widely from Wenham's and mine, see Raymond E. Brown and John P. Meier, *Antioch and Rome: New Testament Cradles of Catholic Christianity* (New York: Paulist, 1982). In this imaginative book that makes capital use of the argument from silence, Meier (pp. 39–40) concludes that Paul lost the argument in Antioch and, subsequently, divorced himself completely from the church of Antioch, the evidence being that Paul never mentions Antioch again in his surviving epistles. Meier presumes that if Paul had any further contact with that church, we would be reading about it in his subsequent letters. Meier distrusts the account given in the book of Acts and thinks that Luke was perhaps confused. It appears to me that many of Meier's own reconstructions are confused and run directly counter to the New Testament evidence.

St. Ambrose (d. 397), and Pope St. Gregory the Great (d. 604).[98] He had always been recognized as a preeminent scriptural commentator, and the Council of Trent spoke of him as "the greatest doctor in explaining the Sacred Scriptures."[99] In particular Jerome's commentaries on Galatians, Titus, and Philemon became standard works of exegesis in the Western Church. In his influential book *Institutiones,* Cassiodorus (490–583) commended them immediately after mentioning Augustine's *Commentary on Galatians.*[100] The venerable Bede (d. 735) cites Jerome's exegesis frequently in his own exegetical writings. Scores of other medieval and renaissance theologians adopted Jerome as the model exegete.

In the sixteenth century the Catholic priest Erasmus of Rotterdam published the first complete edition of Jerome's writings in nine folio volumes at the Froben Press in Basel in 1516. He wrote: "It is a river of gold, a well-stocked library, that one acquires who possesses Jerome and nothing else."[101] In a letter to Pope Leo X in 1515, Erasmus assessed St. Jerome's stature as a theologian more fully in these terms:

> I saw clearly that St Jerome is chief among theologians of the Latin world, and is in fact almost the only writer we have who deserves the name of theologian (not that I condemn the rest, but men who seem distinguished on their own are thrown into the shade by his brilliance when they are compared with him); indeed he has such splendid gifts that Greece itself with all its learning can scarcely produce a man to be matched with him. What Roman eloquence, what mastery of tongues, what a range of knowledge in all antiquity and all

---

98. This was formally ratified by Pope Boniface VIII on September 20, 1295.

99. *Doctor maximus in exponendis aacris acripturis;* cited by F. X. Murphy, "Saint Jerome," 7.759.

100. PL 70: 1121A.

101. Ep. 396. This letter forms the dedicatory epistle addressed to Archbishop William Warham in Erasmus's edition of St. Jerome (1516). For an English translation of the prefatory documents, see Desiderius Erasmus, *Patristic Scholarship: The Edition of St. Jerome,* ed. J. Brady and J. Olin, CWE 61 (Toronto: University of Toronto Press, 1992).

history! And then his retentive memory, his happy knack of combining unexpected things, his perfect command of Holy Scripture! Above all, with his burning energy and the divine inspiration in that amazing heart, he can at the same moment delight us with his eloquence, instruct us with his learning, and sweep us away with his religious force.[102]

Erasmus's edition contains the first biography of the saint that uses well-grounded historical and critical principles.[103] It would be difficult to point to a Catholic scholar who has ever equaled Erasmus in devotion to St. Jerome and in the faithful imitation of Jerome's ascetic lifestyle devoted to ecclesiastical scholarship.[104] In his *Paraphrases* on Matthew, Ephesians, Galatians, Titus, and Philemon, Erasmus assimilates Jerome's exegesis into his own,[105] even to the point of Erasmus's adoption of Jerome's interpretation of the conflict between Peter and Paul at Antioch. Moreover, Erasmus wrote formidable defenses of Jerome's exegesis against both Catholic and Protestant critics.[106] Erasmus deservedly occupies one of the peak moments in the history of Roman Catholic veneration of St. Jerome.

---

102. Desiderius Erasmus, CWE, Ep. 335:232–45.

103. Cf. Erasmus. *Patristic Scholarship*.

104. See A. Reese, "'So Outstanding an Athlete of Christ': Erasmus and the Significance of Jerome's Asceticism," *Erasmus of Rotterdam Society Yearbook* 18 (1998), pp. 104–17; and J. Olin, "Erasmus and Saint Jerome: The Close Bond and its Significance," *Erasmus of Rotterdam Society Yearbook* 7 (1987), pp. 33–53.

105. Cf. Desiderius Erasmus, *New Testament Scholarship: Paraphrases on Romans and Galatians,* ed. Robert D. Sider, trans. and ann. by John B. Payne, Albert Rabil Jr., and Warren S. Smith Jr., CWE 42 (Toronto: University of Toronto Press, 1984). The *Paraphrase on Titus* is found in CWE 44; the *Paraphrase on Matthew* is CWE 45.

106. For example, Erasmus's Ep. 844 to the Catholic theologian John Eck is a careful and cogent defense of Erasmus's preference of Jerome's exegesis and learning to Augustine's. Erasmus's *Hyperaspistes I and II* contain lengthy defenses of Jerome's exegetical insights in the face of Martin Luther's attacks.

Martin Luther's Animosity toward Jerome's Pauline Exegesis

The antithesis of Erasmus's veneration of St. Jerome is encountered in the radical repudiation of St. Jerome by the German reformer Martin Luther (1483–1546). Luther praised his colleague Phillip Melanchthon in terms that deliberately contrast him with Origen and Jerome:

> No one has expounded St. Paul better than you, Philipp [Melanchthon]. The commentaries of St. Jerome and Origen are the merest trash in comparison with your annotations [on Romans and Corinthians]. Be humble if you like, but at least let me be proud of you. Be content that you come so near to St. Paul himself.[107]

In his own *Commentary on Galatians* Luther sustains a polemic specifically against St. Jerome's exegesis of Galatians. Luther claims that Jerome simply did not understand the difference between the gospel and the law. He writes:

> Of this difference between the law and the Gospel there is nothing to be found in the books of the monks, canonists, school-divines; no, nor in the books of the ancient Fathers. Augustine did somewhat understand this difference, and shewed it. Jerome and others knew it not.[108]

Luther strongly reproached Jerome's interpretation of Gal 3.13, and he makes Jerome's exegesis of the Pauline epistles one of his principal targets in his famous work defending his doctrine of the enslaved will, *De servo arbitrio* (1525). In this work Luther claims that among ecclesiastical writers "no one has handled Holy Scripture more ineptly and

---

107. WA 10, 2, pp. 309–10.

108. Cf. J. Dillenberger, *Martin Luther: Selections from his Writings*, pp. 144–45.

absurdly than Origen and Jerome."[109] Luther responds to Jerome's interpretation of the divine choice of Jacob over Esau by saying that Jerome "does nothing but corrupt the Divine Scriptures and deceive the souls of the faithful with a notion hatched out of his own head and violently thrust upon the Scriptures."[110] As an interpreter of Scripture, Jerome is "a man quite without either judgment or application."[111] Jerome has "besmirched with Jewish filth" his interpretation of Paul.[112] The high point of Luther's criticism of Jerome is articulated in the following text.

> But they are in the habit of trying to get around Paul here, by making out that what he calls "works of the law" are the ceremonial works, which since the death of Christ are deadly. I reply that this is the ignorant error of Jerome, which in spite of Augustine's strenuous resistance—God having withdrawn and let Satan prevail—has spread out into the world and persisted to the present day. It has consequently become impossible to understand Paul, and the knowledge of Christ has been inevitably obscured. Even if there had never been any other error in the Church, this one alone was pestilent and potent enough to make havoc of the gospel, and unless a special sort of grace has intervened, Jerome has merited hell rather than heaven for it—so little would I dare to canonize him or call him a saint. It is, then, not true that Paul is speaking only about ceremonial laws; otherwise, how can the argument be sustained by which he concludes that all men are wicked and in need of grace?[113]

Luther does not display an accurate knowledge of Augustine's conflict with Jerome here, which was not focused on the issue of law. In my

---

109. *DSA* WA 18: 703:27–8 / LW 33 167.

110. Martin Luther, *Bondage of the Will;* cited from *Luther and Erasmus: Free Will and Salvation,* trans. P. S. Watson with B. Drewery, Library of Christian Classics (Philadelphia: Westminster, 1969), p. 249.

111. Ibid., p. 267.

112. Ibid., p. 269.

113. *DSA* WA 763–69; trans. P. Watson in *Luther and Erasmus,* pp. 302–3.

study of the legacy of Origen's *CRm,* I have analyzed Luther and Melanchthon's decadence theory of Christian theology and noticed that in spite of some inconsistencies and contradictory statements, they equally faulted St. Augustine for failing to measure up to these key themes of Pauline theology.[114] Cornelis Augustijn confirms that Luther was diametrically opposed both to Jerome's and Erasmus's understanding of the "gospel." He writes: "In Luther's view the center of the Gospel is at stake here. Jerome is the quintessence of all theology which Luther detests."[115]

On the other hand Jerome's interpretation of St. Paul was admirably defended against Luther's accusations by Erasmus in his *Hyperaspistes I and II,* which was his two-volume refutation of Luther's *De servo arbitrio.*[116] For our purposes it has been important to note that Jerome's Pauline exegesis provoked a firestorm of controversy when it

---

114. *Origen and the History of Justification,* chap. 6. In an interesting article, Josef Lössl reports on the "sensational" discovery in 1988 of a handful of marginal annotations, written in Luther's own hand, in his personal copy of Erasmus's *Edition of St. Jerome.* Cf. Josef Lössl, "Martin Luther's Jerome: New Evidence for a Changing Attitude," in *Jerome of Stridon: His Life, Writings and Legacy,* ed. Andrew Cain & Josef Lössl, pp. 237–51 (Aldershot: Ashgate, 2009). In these marginalia Luther expressed approval of a handful of exegetical comments made by St. Jerome, namely, those which seemed to agree with several of Luther's own idiosyncratic interpretations of St. Paul. At the same time Luther vilifies Erasmus, as an atheist and a heretic, for questioning the accuracy of these particular insights of St. Jerome, in the scholarly annotations he had appended to his *Edition of St. Jerome.* Erasmus had questioned these particular comments of Jerome because they appeared to stand in tension with statements found elsewhere in Jerome's writings, and because they tended to set Jerome at odds with the broader consensus of the Greek and Latin exegetical tradition. Lössl's evidence shows that Luther, in some private unpublished marginalia, did apparently seek confirmation of his own views in the writings of St. Jerome, and also that he vilified Erasmus on these particular occasions. However, such evidence scarcely negates Luther's global repudiation of St. Jerome found in his *De servo arbitrio* (a work that Lössl never mentions or discusses).

115. Cornelis Augustijn, *Erasmus: Der Humanist als Theologe und Kirchenreformer* (Leiden: Brill, 1996), p. 251.

116. *Hyperaspistes I and II.*

was engaged during the first phase of the Protestant Reformation. This makes the work all the more interesting.

St. Jerome's Text and the Scripture Citations

The translation in this volume of Jerome's *Commentary on Galatians* has been made from the new critical text edited by Giacomo Raspanti, *Commentarii in Epistulam Pauli Apostoli ad Galatas,* S. Hieronymi Presbyteri Opera, Pars I Opera Exegetica 6, CCSL 77A (Turnhout: Brepols, 2006). For the *Commentary on Titus* and the *Commentary on Philemon,* I have used the new edition by Federica Bucchi, *Commentarii in Epistulas Pauli Apostoli ad Titum et ad Philemon,* S. Hieronymi Presbyteri Opera, Pars I Opera Exegetica 8, CCSL 77C (Turnhout: Brepols, 2003). These new critical editions represent the first activity in at least two centuries on Jerome's works, apart from the reprint by Migne in the latter half of the nineteenth century. Migne (PL 26) had reprinted the edition published by Vallarsi in Venice in 1766–72.

Scripture citations are given according to their location in the RSV, Catholic edition. I have tried to conform the wording of my translation to that of the RSV, as much as possible. The reader should be aware, however, that Jerome usually cites the Old Testament according to the Septuagint version, which does not have an identical versification as the RSV. The Septuagint was also the version that his main exegetical source Origen followed.

Commentary on
Galatians

BOOK ONE

Preface

It has been only a few days since I moved on to Galatians after interpreting Paul's letter to Philemon (going from back to front and bypass-
ing many [of his letters] that come in between). And now, all of the
sudden, a letter reaches me from Rome[1] with the news that the venerable elderly woman Albina[2] has been recalled to the presence of the
Lord, and that the saintly Marcella,[3] who is bereft of the company of
her mother, is demanding more than ever such solace as you can give,

---

1. Lit. "from the City."

2. This Albina (not to be confused with Albina, the daughter-in-law of Melania, the friend of Rufinus, and mother of St. Melania) was the mother of Marcella.

3. Marcella was a Roman lady descended from the illustrious family of the
Marcelli and of great wealth. She heard of Anthony from Athanasius, who came as
an exile to Rome in 340. Widowed after seven months of marriage, she refused a
marriage offer by the distinguished and wealthy Cerealis. She became a friend of Jerome and adopted strong ascetic tendencies while continuing to live with her mother
in the palatial residence on the Aventine. Jerome wrote for her some fifteen different

O Paula[4] and Eustochium.[5] And because this is impossible at present on account of the great distances that would need to be traversed by sea and land, she wishes at least to treat the wound so suddenly inflicted with the medicine of the Scriptures. I know full well her burning zeal, I recognize her faithfulness and how a fire is always burning in her heart. I know how she rises above her sex, and, forgetful of human nature itself, she crosses the Red Sea of this world to the drumbeat of the inspired books.[6] Certainly when I was in Rome, she never visited me, for however short a time, without interrogating me about some Scriptural matter. In fact, she did not, in Pythagorean fashion, consider correct whatever I had said in response;[7] nor did authority independent of the judgment of reason lead her to prejudge the matter; but she examined everything[8] and weighed the whole matter so intelligently that I felt that I had not so much a pupil as a judge.

And so, convinced that my labors will be very acceptable to her who is absent and useful to you who are present, I will tackle a work not previously attempted by any writers in our language before me. In-

---

treatises on difficult passages of Scripture and Church history. She was responsible for persuading Pope Anastasius (400–413) to condemn Origen and his adherents. Of this "glorious victory," Jerome says, "Marcella was the origin."

4. St. Paula (347–404) was a noble and wealthy Roman lady, the mother of four daughters and one son. In 382 during the synod held at Rome that followed on the council of Constantinople, she hosted in her house the bishops Epiphanius of Salamis and Paulinus of Antioch. Through them Jerome became intimately acquainted with her. After her husband's death in 384, she accompanied Jerome to Palestine in 385 and lived the rest of her life in Bethlehem. The chief facts of her life were given by Jerome in Ep. 108 to Eustochium.

5. St. Eustochium (370?–418) was the third daughter of Paula who accompanied her mother to Palestine and presided over the hospice and convent in Bethlehem after Paula's death. She had taken a vow of perpetual virginity, and Jerome wrote his famous Ep. 22 to confirm her in this resolution.

6. Cf. Ex 15.20.

7. For the proverbial reference to Pythagoras, cf. Origen, *Contra Celsum* 1.7; Philo, *Questiones in Genesin* 1.99; Clement, *Stromateis* 11.24.3; Cicero, *De natura deorum*. 1.5.10; Quintilian, *Institutio Oratoria* 2.1.27; Gregory of Nyssa, *Adversus Eunomium* 1.225.

deed, scarcely any of the Greeks themselves have undertaken it in a manner demanded by the dignity of the subject. It is not that I am unaware that Gaius Marius Victorinus,[9] who taught me rhetoric in Rome when I was a boy, published a commentary on the apostle;[10] but he did so while he was occupied by the task of instructing in secular literature and he was completely ignorant of the Scriptures. And no matter how eloquent someone is, he cannot discuss a subject well that he does not know. What then? Am I so foolish or rash as to promise what that man was unable to do? Hardly. But instead, being aware of the feebleness of my own abilities, I have (rather cautiously and hesitantly in my opinion) followed the commentary of Origen. For he wrote five books of his own on Paul's epistle to the Galatians, and in addition to his exposition he completed the tenth book of his *Stromateis* on it in the style of a commentary.[11] Moreover he composed various treatises and *Excerpts*,[12] which could stand in their own right. I need not mention Didymus my seer,[13] and the Laodicean[14] who recently left the church, and

8. Cf. 1 Thes 5.21.

9. For a discussion of Marius Victorinus, see the introduction to this volume.

10. "The Apostle," ὁ ἀπόστολος, is the regular phrase for the corpus of Pauline epistles and dates back to the end of the second century. Cf. *HE* 5.17, 18, 27; Clement, *Stromateis* 7.14; *Adv Haer* 27.4.

11. The *Stromateis*, or *Miscellanies*, were a collection of higher-level questions to pose and resolve among a group of Origen's advanced students. It was written in Alexandria before 231. Eusebius knew of this work (cf. *HE* 6.24.3), but it is now completely lost except for fragments. Jerome translates a section from *Stromateis* 10 under Gal 5.13. Cf. Jerome, *Ep.* 70.4.

12. Origen's *Excerpts*, or *Scholia*, are his more detailed commentary notes. They do not survive except for some passages assimilated into Rufinus's translation of Origen's *Homilies on Numbers*.

13. Didymus the Blind (313–398) was a celebrated exegete who taught in Alexandria and depended closely on Origen, both in exegesis and in doctrine. Jerome studied with him briefly in 386. Rufinus of Aquileia spent about eight years with him. Early on, Jerome admired Didymus so much that he translated his work *On the Holy Spirit*.

14. Apollinaris, bishop of Laodicea, had been one of Jerome's teachers during his sojourn in Antioch in 378; see *Ep.* 84.3. His faulty understanding of the Incarnation, according to which Christ's human and divine natures were integrated into one, was later condemned by the Council of Ephesus (431) and Chalcedon (451).

the Alexandrian, the heretic of old.[15] I also leave out Eusebius of Emesa[16] and Theodorus of Heraclea,[17] who have all left behind brief commentaries of their own on this subject. If I were to pluck a few flowers out of these gardens, the resulting commentary would not be something that could be completely despised. And so, I openly admit that I have read all these works and have accumulated more things in my mind. After summoning my secretary, I dictated either my own thoughts or the ideas of these others. As I do this, sometimes I do not keep to either the order or the wording or even the meanings. Now it is a gift of the Lord's mercy that things well spoken by others should not be lost through our lack of skill, and that things that are pleasing among their own people should not fail to please among outsiders.

And so, I will summarize the argument of this epistle briefly in this preface. I advise you to be aware that the subject of Paul's Epistle to the Galatians is the same as that found in the letter written to the Romans. But there is this difference between them: in the latter epistle he has made use of loftier meaning and more profound arguments, whereas in Galatians he writes as to those of whom he says in what follows, "Oh foolish Galatians,"[18] and, "so you are foolish?"[19] He has restrained himself by using this sort of language in which he is rebuking rather than teaching, using words that fools could understand. Thus he dresses common opinions in common speech, and authority recalls those whom reason was unable to persuade. Indeed, the apostle does not utter a single word, either by epistle or in person, in which he does not strive to teach that the burdens of the old law have been set aside,

---

15. Possibly the Valentinian heretic with whom Tertullian entered into controversy over the incarnation.

16. Eusebius of Emessa (300–359) was a pupil of Eusebius of Caesarea. He turned down the see at Alexandria when it was offered to him after Athanasius was expelled. Afterward he was elected bishop in Emesa. Jerome considered him an Arian but valued his learning (*Vir Ill* 91).

17. Theodore was an anti-Nicene bishop of Heraclea in Thrace in the fourth century and died in 355. Cf. Jerome, *Vir Ill* 90.

18. Gal 3.1.

19. Gal 3.3.

and everything that came before in types and images (Sabbath rest, the injury of circumcision, the returning cycle of the calendar and of the three annual solemn feasts, the scrupulous observance of foods, and the daily washing of things that are destined to be defiled again) have ceased rather suddenly through the grace of the gospel. It is fulfilled not in the blood of victims but in the faith of the believing soul. It is true that in his other letters this question presented itself to some extent and was discussed tangentially, and almost in passing, as if by one who was occupied with something else; but, as I said, these two epistles in particular contain the subject matter of the cessation of the old law and the inauguration of the new.

But the letter to the Galatians has this unique characteristic, that he is not writing to those who had believed in Christ from the Jews and who thought that the ancestral ceremonies had to be observed, but instead is writing to those from the Gentiles who had received the faith of the gospel and who were guilty of backsliding, terrified by the authority of certain men who were claiming that Peter, James, and all the churches of Judea had intermingled the gospel of Christ with the old law. Moreover, they thought that Paul himself likewise did one thing in Judea while preaching something else among the nations. And so they believe in vain in the crucified if they think that they can neglect what the leaders of the apostles were observing. This is why he treads so cautiously among the two [peoples], so that he will neither betray the grace of the gospel, as one overwhelmed by the weight and authority of the elders, nor do injury to his predecessors while he defends grace. But obliquely and as one secretly entering through hidden passages, he would show that even Peter acts in a way that is expedient for the people of the circumcision who have been entrusted to him.[20] For if a too sudden revolt takes place from their ancient mode of life, they might be scandalized by the cross and not believe. Moreover, Paul wants to show, inasmuch as the evangelization of the Gentiles had

---

20. Cf. Gal 2.7. The image of Paul entering through hidden passageways is found in *CRm* 5.1.9; 6.7.16.

been entrusted to himself,[21] that he is justified in defending as true that which the other[22] feigned as a matter of policy (*pro dispensatione*). That Batanean-born[23] wretch Porphyry[24] scarcely understood this. In the first book of the work that he wrote against us, he raises the objection that Peter was rebuked by Paul for not walking uprightly[25] as an evangelical teacher. Porphyry's aim was to brand the former with error and the latter with impudence, and, in more general terms, to raise the false accusation of fabricated teaching, on the ground that the leaders of the churches were at variance among themselves. Now we have briefly touched upon these things at this time for you who are praying that we might speak meaningfully about these matters. We will pursue these things more fully in the relevant passages. But now it is time to expound the details by setting forth the words of the apostle himself.

The First Book

1.1.   *Paul an apostle not from men nor through a man, but through Jesus Christ and God the Father who raised him from the dead.* It is not from arrogance, as some think, but by necessity that he proposes that he is an apostle "not from men nor through a man, but through Jesus Christ and God the Father." Thus by this authority would he confound those who alleged that Paul was outside the twelve apostles and somehow or other had suddenly burst on the scene, or that he had been

---

21. Cf. Gal 2.7.

22. That is, Peter.

23. In *Vita Plotini* 8, Porphyry calls himself a Tyrian. Therefore, even if Jerome and John Chrysostom (*Homily 6 on 1 Cor*), are correct, that he was actually born in Batanea, which is in Syria, he was no doubt of a Tyrian family. Some suppose that Batanea was a colony of Tyre.

24. Porphyry (232–305) was a Neoplatonist philosopher, pupil, and biographer of Plotinus, and opponent of Christianity who composed a work in fifteen books, *Against the Christians,* which survives only in fragments. It was refuted by Apollinaris of Laodicea and Eusebius of Caesarea.

25. Lit. "on the right foot."

ordained by the elders. But the statement can also be understood obliquely of Peter and the others, that the gospel was handed down to him not by the apostles, but by the same Jesus Christ who had also chosen those apostles.[26] But the reason he prepares all this in advance is so that no one can object to him as to one who is arguing against the burdens of the law on behalf of the grace of the Gospel: "But Peter said this"; "but the apostles have established that"; "but your predecessors decreed something different." To be sure, what he now is hinting at with concealed speech, he makes more clear in what follows when he relates of those who seem to be something, that they are nothing compared with himself,[27] and when he writes that he resisted Peter himself to his face,[28] saying that he was compelled by no necessity to yield to the hypocrisy of the Jews.[29] But if some think it seems rash that he contradicted the apostles, although privately[30]—this man who had reached Jerusalem for the very purpose of discussing the gospel with them, "lest perchance he should be running or should have run in vain"[31]—let us transfer the understanding in the following way. Until the present day, apostles are sent from the patriarchs of the Jews by whom even then, I think, the Galatians were led astray, and they begin observing the law; or, at least, others from the Jews who believed in Christ reached Galatia, who claimed that Peter too, the prince of the apostles, and James the brother of the Lord were observing the ceremonies of the law.

And so, to distinguish between those who are sent from men and he himself, who was sent by Christ, he commenced the letter in the following manner: "Paul an apostle, not from men, nor through a man." Now "apostle," that is, "one sent," is a uniquely Hebrew word that is expressed as well by the name "Silas," which derives from sending and

---

26. Cf. Mk 3.14; Jn 6.70.
27. Cf. Gal 2.6.
28. Cf. Gal 2.11.
29. Cf. Gal 2.13.
30. Cf. Gal 2.1–2.
31. Gal 2.2.

was given to him when he was sent.[32] The Hebrews say that some among them are apostles and holy men who are both prophets and apostles; but there are others who are merely prophets.[33] After all, Moses and Isaiah are both apostles and prophets. This is shown when Moses is told, "And I will *send* you to Pharaoh,"[34] and he himself answers, "Provide someone else whom you may *send*."[35] Also, God says to Isaiah, "Whom shall I *send* and who will go to this people?"[36] This is why we can also understand that John the Baptist too should be called both prophet and apostle, for indeed the Scripture says: "There was a man *sent* from God whose name was John."[37] And in the Epistle to the Hebrews, the reason Paul did not first record either his own name or the word apostle, in accordance with his usual custom, was because he was about to say of Christ, "Therefore since we have a high priest and *apostle* of our confession, Jesus."[38] For it would not have been fitting for "Paul an apostle" to be recorded in a letter in which he had to speak of Christ as an apostle.

Now there are four kinds of apostles. The first is "not from men nor through a man, but through Jesus Christ and God the Father"; the second is indeed from God, but through a man; the third is from man and not from God; the fourth is neither from God nor through a man nor from a man, but from himself. It is possible that Isaiah is one of the first sort, as well as the other prophets and the apostle Paul himself, who was sent neither "from men nor through a man, but from God the Father and Christ." Joshua (*Iesus*) son of Nun was of the second sort, who was appointed an apostle, to be sure, but through the man Moses.[39] The third kind is the person who is ordained by the favor and zealous

---

32. Cf. Acts 15.22; Jn 9.7.
33. This passage, based in Origen, is particularly important for the origin of the Christian apostolate. Cf. Harnack, *Der kirchengeschichtliche Ertrag,* p. 150.
34. Ex 3.10.
35. Ex 4.13.
36. Is 6.8.
37. Jn 1.6.
38. Heb 3.1.
39. Cf. Nm 13.2, 17; Dt 34.9.

striving of men, as we now see very many who are caused to be chosen for the priesthood in place of others, by the purchased favor of the mob, but not by God's judgment. The fourth kind is comprised of the false prophets and false apostles of whom the apostle says: "such are the false apostles, workers of iniquity, transforming themselves into *apostles* of Christ."[40] They say, "thus says the Lord," and the Lord has not sent them.[41] But Paul was not this kind. He was not sent "from men nor through a man," but from "God the Father" through "Jesus Christ."

From this the heresy of Ebion[42] and of Photinus[43] is likewise shown to be refuted. For our Lord Jesus Christ is *God,* since the apostle, who was sent by Christ to preach the gospel, denies that he was sent by a *man.*[44] Other heresies sneak in with claims that are based upon this

---

40. 2 Cor 11.13.

41. Cf. Ezek 13.6.

42. Jerome appears to be following the mistaken late tradition of an historical Ebion. According to Irenaeus (*Adv Haer* 1.26.2), the Ebionites were a Judaizing heresy that used only Matthew's Gospel, repudiated Paul as an apostate from the law, rejected the virgin birth of Christ, and insisted that the law of Moses (including circumcision) had to be kept in order to achieve salvation. See also Eusebius (*HE* 3.27), who says they believed that Christ was a plan and ordinary man. They probably were named from the Hebrew word for "poor" (*ebion*), because of their physical poverty or their attachment to the beatitude "Blessed are the poor" (though Eusebius says that their name arose "because of the poor and mean opinions they held about Christ"). Later heresiologists (Tertullian, *De praescriptione haereticorum* 33; Epiphanius, *Panarion* 30.17; Rufinus's Origen, *CRm* 3.11.2) adopted the mistaken view that the sect was founded by a heretic named Ebion.

43. Photinus of Sirmium, a deacon and disciple of Marcellus of Ancyra, was bishop of Sirmium (Pannonia) when Easterners first associated him with his teacher and condemned him. Westerners subscribed to his condemnation at Milan (345). Jerome, *Vir Ill* 107 says that he wrote much. Cf. Epiphanius, *Panarion* 71. He affirmed a rigid monarchianism in which the Logos was conceived as a mere impersonal power of the Father. Like Marcellus he made the Son of God to be born of Mary, in the sense that the Logos became Son only by being incarnate in the man Jesus and taking up his dwelling in him.

44. Cooper, *Marius Victorinus' Commentary on Galatians,* p. 251, invokes the same phrase of Paul's greeting as a means of refuting certain unnamed "heretics and

passage and say that Christ's flesh is putative, that Christ is God, but not man.[45] And besides these there is the new heresy that asserts that Christ's dispensation is divided in half. So it is that the faith of the church is set in between two great shipwrecks of false doctrines: if it admits that Christ is man, Ebion and Photinus sneak in; if it contends that he is God, Manicheus,[46] Marcion,[47] and the author of a new doctrine start babbling. And so, let them universally hear that Christ is both God and man. It is not that there is one God and another man, but he who was always God deigned to be man for the sake of our salvation.

---

blasphemers." In *Apology for Origen* 109, Pamphilus preserves an excerpt from Origen's *Commentary on Galatians* with strong parallels to Jerome's exposition here: "From what the apostle has said: 'Paul an apostle, not from men nor through a man, but through Jesus Christ,' it is given to be understood clearly that Jesus Christ was not a man but was a divine nature. For if he were a man, Paul would not have said what he says: 'Paul an apostle, not from men nor through a man.' For if Jesus had been a man, and Paul was received into the apostolate through him, surely he would have become an apostle through a man; and if he had been an apostle through a man, he would have never said, 'nor through a man.' But by these words Paul clearly separates Jesus from human nature; for it is not sufficient for him to have said, 'nor through a man,' but he goes on to say, 'but through Jesus Christ.' For surely he knew that he was of a more eminent nature, and for that reason he said that he himself had not been chosen 'through a man.'"

45. Harnack, *Der kirchengeschichtliche Ertrag*, p. 148, concluded that this passage most certainly derives from Origen.

46. Manicheus, or Mani/Manes (215–276), is the founder of the Manichaean heresy. He came from Persia and is reported to have died of torture in prison while chained up by the wrists. The sect threatened the Church for many centuries and even claimed the young Augustine as one of its adherents. The founder desired to blend Christianity, Zoroastrianism, and elements of Buddhism together. He preached an extreme dualism of two independent and absolutely opposed eternal principles of good and evil. Like Marcion he denied that Jesus was prophesied in the Old Testament, and said that the good God was characterized by light while the material world was inherently dark and corrupt. Manicheus believed that Jesus and other teachers came to release souls of light from prison in material bodies. The Old Testament was the product of the forces of darkness. Manicheus also denied the free choice of the will in salvation.

47. Marcion of Sinope in Pontus was reputedly the son of the bishop of Sinope, who came to Rome and founded a heretical sect in the 140s. Scandalized by the

One should know as well that in Marcion's *Apostle* it is not written, "and through God the Father." For he wanted to set forth a Christ who was raised, not by God the Father, but by himself,[48] as is said in the following: "Destroy this temple and in three days I will raise it";[49] and besides elsewhere: "No one takes my life from me, but I lay it down of my own accord. I have the power to lay it down and I have power to raise it up again."[50]

1.2.   *And all the brothers who are with me, to the churches of Galatia.* In other epistles Sosthenes, Silvanus, and sometimes Timothy are set down first in the opening.[51] Only in this letter, because the authority of more [people] was essential, the term "all the brothers" is used. They were perhaps themselves of the circumcision and were not regarded as contemptible by the Galatians. For generally the agreement of many on one matter and verdict is effective in correcting people.

Now regarding the words, "to the churches of Galatia," one should note that only here does he write generally, not to a single church of one city, but to the churches of a whole region, and he calls the churches

---

problem of evil and other philosophical issues, he responded by rejecting his prior faith and forming a doctrinal system based on the irreconcilability of justice and grace, law and gospel, Judaism and Christianity, the God of the Old Testament and the Father of Jesus. He posited two deities: a good nonjudgmental God (the Father of Jesus), who is not to be feared; and a just but inferior god (the Creator of the world, who is the God of the Old Testament and of the Jews), in whom resides the grounds of fear, anger, severity, judgment, vengeance, and condemnation. Marcion so emphasized the absolute newness of the dispensation brought by Jesus that he repudiated the Old Testament in its entirety and denied that it predicted the coming of Jesus or spoke about the good Father proclaimed by Jesus. Moreover, he taught his followers that the received form of the New Testament had been corrupted by Judaizing Christians, whom he identifies as the Catholics of his day.

48. Cf. Harnack (1919), *Der kirchengeschichtliche Ertrag,* p. 148: "The one who wrote this not only had a Marcionite Bible in hand but he also knew Marcionite exegesis." He traces the source to Origen.

49. Jn 2.19.

50. Jn 10.18.

51. Cf. 1 Cor 1.1; 2 Cor 1.1; 1 Thes 1.1; 2 Thes 1.1; Phil 1.1.

"corrupted" that he will later convict of error.[52] From this one should know that there are two ways in which "church" can be named: the one that does not have spot or blemish[53] and is truly the body of Christ, and the one that is gathered in the name of Christ without the virtues in their fullness and perfection. Just as the wise are named in a twofold sense, so are both those who possess full and perfect virtue, and those who are just starting out and are making progress. (Of the perfect it is said, "I shall send among you wise men";[54] of beginners it says, "Rebuke the wise man and he will love you";[55] for the one who possesses full and complete virtue does not need correction.) One can understand the other virtues as well in accordance with this sense, namely, those may be understood as strong, prudent, pious, chaste, just, and temperate, sometimes in the full sense of the term, sometimes in an improper sense.

1.3.   *Grace to you and peace from God the Father and our Lord Jesus Christ.* He does not record, as in the other epistles, "*grace* and *peace* of God the Father" and "of our Lord Jesus." Through both, apart from the merit of works, our former sins have been forgiven us and peace after pardon has been granted. But wisely he is already pleading his case against those who had been anticipated by the law and who thought that they could be justified by works. Thus they should know that they must persevere in their salvation by means of the grace in which they had begun.

1.4–5.   *Who gave himself for our sins to rescue us from the present evil age, in accordance with the will of our God and Father, to whom is the glory in the ages of ages. Amen.* The Son did not "give himself for our sins" without the Father's will,[56] nor did the Father hand over the Son

---

52. Cf. Gal 1.7.
53. Cf. Eph 5.27.
54. Lk 11.49.
55. Prv 9.8.
56. Cf. Jn 4.34.

without the Son's will; but this is the will of the Son: to fulfill the will of the Father, as he says in the Psalm, "I want to do your will, my God."[57] Now the Son "gave himself" that he himself, as *justice*,[58] might overthrow the injustice that is in us. *Wisdom*[59] handed itself over to sweep away foolishness; *sanctity*[60] and *fortitude*[61] offered themselves to blot out filth and weakness. And so, it is not merely in the future age in accordance with the promises and hopes in which we believe, but here as well that he delivered us "from the present age," provided that we have died together with Christ[62] and are being transformed in the renewal of our mind,[63] and provided that we are not "of this world"[64] and do not deserve to be loved by it.[65]

It is asked how the "present age" may be said to be "evil." For the heretics customarily seize upon this passage as an occasion to assert that there is one creator of light and of the future age, another creator of darkness and of the present age.[66] But we say that he is not so much calling the age itself evil—which runs on day and night, through years and months—as he is referring to the things that happen in the age using a homonym.[67] It is similar to the way it is said: "the *day's* own evil suffices";[68] and the *days* of Jacob are recorded to be few and very bad.[69] It is not that the time period in which Jacob lived was evil, but that the things that he endured through various trials trained him. After all, at

---

57. Ps 40.8.

58. Cf. 1 Cor 1.30.

59. Cf. 1 Cor 1.30.

60. Cf. 1 Cor 1.30.

61. Cf. 1 Cor 1.24.

62. Cf. 2 Tm 2.11.

63. Cf. Rom 12.2.

64. Cf. Jn 15.19.

65. Cf. Jn 15.18–19.

66. Marcionite exegesis is represented here. Cf. Harnack, *Der kirchengeschichtliche Ertrag,* p. 148.

67. A different term of the same name. Jerome uses the Greek ὁμωνύμως.

68. Cf. Mt 6.34.

69. Cf. Gn 47.9.

that time when he was serving for his marriage[70] and was afflicted by many troubles, Esau was at rest.[71] And thus the same period of time was good for one, evil for another. Nor would it have been written in Ecclesiastes, "Do not say that my former days were better than these,"[72] unless there was a distinction in the term evil. This is why John says, "The whole world lies under evil."[73] It is not that the world itself is evil, but that evils are done in the world by men who say, "Let us eat and drink, for tomorrow we will die."[74] And the apostle himself says, "Redeeming the time, for the days are evil."[75] Even forests receive a bad reputation when they are full of thieves. It is not that the earth and the forests commit sin, but that the locales too attract the bad reputation of murder. We are accursed, as is the sword by which human blood is shed and the cup in which poison is mixed. This is not by a sin of the sword and cup, but because those persons deserve hatred who use these things in an evil way. So also the age, which is a period of time, is not good or evil in itself, but it is called either good or evil because of those who are in it. For this reason the delusions and fables of Valentinus[76] must be rejected, who invented his thirty aeons[77] from the fact that Scripture

---

70. Cf. Gn 29.20.

71. Cf. Gn 28.9.

72. Lit. "good beyond these." Cf. Eccl 7.10.

73. 1 Jn 5.19.

74. Is 22.13; 1 Cor 15.32.

75. Eph 5.16.

76. Valentinus was an Egyptian heretic of the second century who spread Alexandrian Gnosticism in Rome between 135 and 160. He rejected the traditional identification of the Christian God with the Creator God of the Old Testament and taught a sort of natural predestination that divided humanity into three categories. The redeemer, Jesus, saves people from the world by giving them saving knowledge, or gnosis (from which Gnosticism derives its name), which is available only to the "spiritual" (*pneumatikoi*). The second kind of nature is the "soulish" (*psychikoi*) and refers to ordinary members of the Church, who can achieve some kind of salvation by faith and good works. The third group is the rest of mankind, or the "natural" (*hylikoi*) who have no chance at redemption.

77. This is the Greek word for "ages."

speaks of "ages."[78] He said that they are aerial (*animalia*)[79] and he put forth, in groups of four, eight, ten, and twelve, as many numbers of ages as Virgil's sow bred piglets.[80]

We also need to investigate what he means by "age," "age of age," or "ages of ages." When does this term refer to a brief period of time, when does it mean eternity? For in Hebrew "age," that is, *olam*, when it has the letter *vau*, signifies eternity, but when it is written without the *vau*, it means the fiftieth year, which they call the Jubilee year.[81] For this reason the Hebrew [slave] who loves his master on account of his wife and children may be subjected to his service by having his ear pierced and is commanded to serve "unto the age" (that is until the fiftieth year).[82] And Moabites and Ammonites do not enter the assembly (*ecclesiam*) of the Lord until the fifteenth generation and until "in the age."[83] For every hard condition is dissolved by the coming of the Jubilee. Some say that the meaning of "in the ages of ages" is the same as "in the holies of holies," "in the heavens of heavens," in the "works of works," in the "canticles of canticles." The difference the heavens have is the same. It is being compared with those to whom the heavens belong; and [they say that] the holies are holier in comparison with holy things; and works are better in comparison with works; and songs excel among all songs. And ages are ages by comparison with ages. Consequently, they explain "present age" in such a way that they say that it must be counted from that time when heaven and earth were created and it runs on until the consummation of the world, when Christ will judge all things.[84] They also look beyond this and move a step back to

---

78. Cf. *Adv Haer* 1.1–8, 11–12, 13–21; Hippolytus, *Refutatio omnium haeresium* 6.29–36; Tertullian, *Adversus Valentinianos*.

79. Harnack, *Der kirchengeschichtliche Ertrag*, p. 148, reports that the question of whether the *aeons* were *animalia* was itself controversial within the Valentinian school. He traces Jerome's source to Origen.

80. Cf. Virgil, *Aeneid* 3.390–91.

81. Cf. Lv 25.8–11.

82. Cf. Ex 21.5–6.

83. Cf. Dt 23.3.

84. Cf. Mt 25.32; Rom 14.10.

consider the former things. They discuss the past and future ages, whether there was or will be good or evil. And they fall into such profound questions that they have even produced books and infinite volumes upon this theme.[85]

Paul's prefatory remarks conclude with the Hebrew word "Amen." The seventy[86] translated "amen" as γένοιτο, that is, "so be it." Aquila[87] translated the word πεπιστωμένως, "truly" or "faithfully." In the Gospel as well the Savior always confirms his own words by employing the word "amen."[88]

1.6–7. *I am amazed that thus you are so quickly being transferred from him who called you in the grace of Christ Jesus to another gospel, which is not another; except if there are some who are confounding you and want to convert the gospel of Christ.* The first occurrence of "transferred"[89] is in Genesis where we read that God "transferred" Enoch and "he was not found."[90] It occurs again later in the books of Kingdoms[91] when Ahab's wife Jezebel "transferred" him from the worship of God to the veneration of idols, so that he acted "in accordance with everything that the Amorite did, whom the Lord utterly destroyed

---

85. Jerome must have in mind Origen's *De Principiis.*

86. According to a Jewish historical tradition, the Alexandrian Greek translation of the Hebrew Old Testament, known as the Septuagint (LXX), was carried out by seventy Jewish scholars. In Origen's *Hexapla,* the Septuagint occupied the fifth column.

87. Aquila was a second century AD Jew who published a slavishly literal Greek translation of the Hebrew Old Testament that was intended to replace the Septuagint that was in use by the Christians. He was a native of Sinope in Pontus and lived under Emperor Hadrian. Jerome and Origen admitted the fidelity of his translation to the Hebrew. Aquila's text occupied the third column of Origen's *Hexapla.*

88. Cf. Mt 5.18; Jn 1.51; 5.24, et passim.

89. The verb in question in Gal 1.6 is μετατίθημι and means "change," "transpose," "transfer." Jerome's discussion, which probably derives from Origen, traces some of the occurrences of this word in the Septuagint.

90. Gn 5.24.

91. In the Septuagint, "1–4 Kingdoms" refers to the books 1 and 2 Samuel and 1 and 2 Kings.

from the presence of the sons of Israel."[92] But although both are forms of "transference," one is of God, the other is of the devil. The one who is "transferred" by God is not found by his enemies, nor can an intruder sneak up on him[93]—for I think that this is the significance of the words "he was not found."[94] But the one who is "transferred" by the devil is transferred to what seems to be but is not. Also, the wise men of the age call those who are transferred from dogma to dogma "those who have transferred." For example, consider Dionysus,[95] whose former opinion was that "suffering is not an evil," but after he had been overwhelmed by calamities and tormented by suffering, he began to assert that suffering was the greatest of all evils. Because of this he was named "the transferred" or "the renegade," namely, because by drawing back from his former resolution, he had fallen into the opposite position.[96]

And so, Paul is "amazed," first, because they have been "transferred" from the freedom of the gospel to the servitude of works of the law; then because they have "so quickly" been transferred. For it is not the same charge "to be transferred" from something with difficulty and "to be transferred quickly." Thus in the case of martyrdom the same penalty is not inflicted upon the one who with no struggle and apart from torture has rushed out to deny [his belief], and the one who has been mangled in the midst of tortures, the rack and fire, and has been compelled to deny what he believed. The proclamation of the gospel

---

92. 1 Kgs 21.5–26.

93. Cf. Wis 4.10–15; Sir 44.16.

94. Gn 5.24.

95. Dionysius of Heraclea on the Pontus (c. 328–248 BC) was a pupil of Zeno (the founder of Stoicism), who wrote philosophical works, and also poetry. According to the OCD, 3rd ed.: "An attack of illness in old age led him to abandon the Stoic position that pain, because not morally bad, is not an evil. Subsequently he went over to the Cyrenaic position that pleasure is our final end; hence his nickname 'the Renegade.'" He committed suicide at the age of 80. Cf. Cicero, *Tusc* 2.60; *Fin.* 5.94; Ath 7.281.

96. Harnack, *Der kirchengeschichtliche Ertrag,* p. 153 traces the source of this passage to Origen.

was still recent, there had been no great length of time from when the apostle turned the Galatians from idols to Christ.[97] Consequently, he is amazed at how they have "so quickly" drawn back from him in whose name they had a little while ago been made Christians. But this passage contains a hyperbaton,[98] which in its proper order can be read thus: "I am amazed that thus so quickly you are being transferred" from Christ Jesus "who called you in grace," when he said, "I came not to call the just but sinners to repentance."[99] For we have been saved by grace[100] and not through the law.

Now he says, "You have been transferred to another gospel which is not another." For nothing that is false subsists, and what is contrary to truth does not exist, as [it says in] the following: "Do not give your scepter, O Lord, to those who are not."[101] And God called "things that were not" in order to cause "what was not" to exist.[102] But if this is said of those who believed in the same God and who had the same Scriptures, that they were transferred "to another gospel, which is not the gospel," what should we think of Marcion and the other heretics who spit upon the Creator and pretend that Christ belongs to another god?[103] What of those who slip and fall, not in the interpretation of the law and quarrels over the letter and the spirit, but who disagree with the entire law of the Church?

Now he makes a fine statement when he says: "Except[104] there are some who are confounding you and want to convert the gospel of Christ." He says, "they want to convert the gospel of Christ," to change it, to disturb it; but they are not able to, because it is of such a nature

---

97. Cf. 1 Thes 1.9.

98. A transposition of the order of the words.

99. Lk 5.32.

100. Cf. Eph 2.8.

101. Est 14.11. Notice that Jerome here (following Origen) quotes as Scripture the "deuterocanonical" portion of Esther.

102. Cf. 1 Cor 1.28.

103. Harnack, *Der kirchengeschichtliche Ertrag,* p. 148 says that this passage most certainly derives from Origen.

104. The lemma had: "Except if. . . ."

that it cannot be other than true. Everyone who interprets the gospel in another spirit and mind than was written disturbs believers and "converts the gospel of Christ." Thus he causes what is in the front to be behind the back, and he turns what is behind the back to the front. If someone follows the letter only, he puts backside things in the front; if someone caves in to the interpretations of the Jews, he sends to the back things that by their nature were constituted to be in the front.

Furthermore, even this word "transfer" has been fitted suitably to the Galatians, for in our language Galatia denotes "transfer."

1.8–9.   *But though we or an angel from heaven should preach a gospel to you besides what we preached to you, let him be anathema! Just as we said before and now I say again: if anyone preaches a gospel to you besides that which you have received, let him be anathema!* This could be understood as a hyperbolic statement in the sense that he does not mean that an apostle or an angel *could* preach otherwise than they had once spoken, but, even if this could happen, that even an apostle or an angel should be changed, nevertheless one must not depart from that which he had once accepted, especially since the apostle himself in another passage shows the constancy of his faith when he says, "I know that neither death nor life nor angels nor rulers nor things present nor things future nor strength nor height nor depth nor another creature can separate us from the love of God that is in Christ Jesus our Lord. I speak the truth, I am not lying, since my conscience bears witness with me."[105] For these things were not said of one who was ever capable of departing from the faith and love of Christ. But those who do not want this to be said καθ᾽ ὑπόθεσιν [hypothetically] but truly—namely, [those who think] that both apostles and angels are capable of being converted to the worse—raise the objection that Paul himself knew that he was capable of falling, if he would have behaved negligently. For he said: "But I subject my body and reduce it to slavery, lest in preaching to others I myself might be found rejected."[106] [They also

---

105. Rom 8.38–9.1.

106. 1 Cor 9.27. Origen appeals to this passage to make a similar point in *CRm*, Preface of Origen 3, 6; 1.3.3; 7.8.6.

object that] angels too are mutable, "who did not keep their own ruler-ship, but left their proper domicile and are held under the gloom in eternal chains for the judgment of the great day."[107] [They say that] only God's nature is immutable of whom it is written, "But you are the same";[108] and he says of himself, "I am your God and I am not changed."[109] But "Lucifer, who rose in the morning, fell, and the one who once sent to all the nations was trampled on the earth."[110] The very learned man Tertullian writes eloquently on this passage against Apel-les and his virgin Philumene, whom some angel of deceit had filled with a diabolical spirit.[111] He writes that this is the angel to whom the "anathema" applies through the apostle's prophecy, by a prediction of the Holy Spirit, well before Apelles was born.[112]

Furthermore, "anathema" is a word peculiar to the Jews and is re-corded both in Joshua son of Nun and in Numbers, when the Lord commanded everything in Jericho to be considered as an execration of the Midianites and as anathema.[113] Let us ask a question of those who claim that Christ and the apostle Paul are the son and slave, respec-tively, of the good God, who was still unknown at that time, who is un-acquainted with cursing and who does not know how to condemn anyone. How is it that his apostle uses a word of the Jews, that is, a word that comes from the Creator, and wants his angel and apostle to perish, when he is unaccustomed with taking vengeance?

---

107. Cf. Jude 6.

108. Ps 102.27.

109. Mal 3.6. Cf. Origen, *Contra Celsum* 1.21; 4.14; 6.62.

110. Is 14.12.

111. Apelles was the most famous and original of Marcion's disciples. Accord-ing to Tertullian, *De praescriptione haereticorum* 30 (cf. *De carne Christi* 1), he had to "withdraw from the presence of his most holy master," evidently at Rome, owing to an act of incontinence, and went to Alexandria. After some years, he returned and attached himself to a virgin named Philumene, who subsequently became a prosti-tute. Tertullian's aspersions on her character are not confirmed by Hippolytus.

112. Cf. Tertullian, *De praescriptione haereticorum* 6.

113. Cf. Nm 21.3; Jos 6.17.

Now in what he added, "as we said before and now I say again," he shows that at the beginning he had warned those to whom he was in any case going to preach to beware of an anathema. And now, after he has first spoken, he decrees the anathema that he had previously spoken about. So the reason he pronounced an anathema against himself, whom they were accusing of doing one thing in Judea and of teaching something else among the Gentiles, and against an angel, which it was agreed is greater even than his apostolic predecessors, is so that the authority of Peter and John should not be held in excessive regard. For it was permitted neither to himself, who had previously taught them, nor to an angel, to preach otherwise than they had once learned.

And so, he has recorded himself and the angel by name, but the others without a name. He says, "If anyone preaches a gospel to you," in order not to injure his predecessors by a general designation, and yet still to imply their names in a hidden way.

1.10. *For do I now persuade men, or God? Or am I seeking to please men? If I were still pleasing men, I would not be a servant of Christ!* We are not to think that we are being taught by the apostle that by his own example we should think nothing of the judgments of men. For he himself said in another passage, "Knowing the fear of the Lord, then, we persuade men, but we are manifest to God";[114] and this, "Be without offense to Jews and Gentiles and the church of God, just as I please everyone in every way, not seeking what is advantageous to myself but to the many, that they may be saved."[115] But if it can happen that we may equally please God and men, one should please men too; but if we may not please men otherwise than by displeasing God, we should instead please God rather than men.[116] In any case he himself reports why he pleases everyone in every way when he says, "not seeking what is advantageous to myself but to the many, that they may be saved."[117]

---

114. 2 Cor 5.11.
115. 1 Cor 10.32–33. Cf. *CRm* 9.20; 10.6.6.
116. Cf. 1 Thes 2.4.
117. 1 Cor 10.32–33.

Now assuredly, the one who pleases everyone based upon that love that seeks not what is its own, but what is another's,[118] in order that they be saved, pleases God in the first place, to whom the salvation of human beings is precious.

But the word "now" is added specially here, to show that men are to be pleased or displeased according to circumstance. For example, one who is not pleasing *now* for the sake of the truth of the gospel[119] was at one time pleasing for the sake of the salvation of more.[120] Paul had once pleased the Jews, when, as a zealot for the ancestral traditions,[121] he lived under the law without reproach.[122] Moreover, he had such great faith and burning zeal for the ceremonies of the elders that he participated in the killing of Stephen.[123] And he went as far as Damascus to arrest those who had abandoned the law.[124] But after he was transformed from a persecutor into a vessel of election,[125] and began to preach the faith that he had once fought against,[126] he began to displease equally the Jews, whom he had formerly pleased. So this is what he says: "Am I seeking to please" the Jews whom I pleased by displeasing God? For "if I were to please" them, "I would not still be a servant of Christ." For I would have asserted the law and would have destroyed the grace of the gospel. But now the reason I am not prosecuted even for the pretence of observing the law is because I cannot equally please God and the Jews, whom someone pleases by displeasing God.

Also the very word "persuade" is taken from human usage, when someone tries to introduce to others the very thing he himself possesses and has already absorbed. It is found in many passages in the Scriptures, including the following: "The *persuasion* is not from him

---

118. Cf. 1 Cor 10.24; 13.5.
119. Cf. Gal 2.5.
120. Cf. 1 Cor 9.19.
121. Cf. Gal 1.14.
122. Cf. Phil 3.6.
123. Cf. Acts 7.57–58.
124. Cf. Acts 9.2–3.
125. Cf. Acts 9.15.
126. Cf. Gal 1.23.

who called you."[127] And besides, it is found in the Acts of the Apostles: "So then many Jews came to him at his lodging. He expounded the matter to them until evening, testifying to them about the kingdom of God and *persuading* them about Jesus from the law of Moses and the prophets."[128] Now all this happened because it had been spread abroad about him that he secretly keeps the law and that he had mixed company in Jerusalem with those who were Judaizing.

1.11–12.   *For I make known to you, brothers, the gospel which was preached by me, that it is not according to man; for I did not receive it from a man nor did I learn it, but by a revelation of Jesus Christ.* On the basis of this passage the doctrine of Ebion and Photinus is crushed, since Christ is God and not merely man.[129] For if Paul's gospel "is not according to *man,* nor did he receive it or learn it from a *man,* but by a revelation of Jesus Christ," then assuredly Jesus Christ is not a man, who revealed the gospel to Paul. But if he is not a man, then logically he is God. It is not that we are denying that he assumed humanity, but we deny that he is merely man.[130]

It is asked whether the churches of the whole world received the gospel *of God* or *of a man.* For how much has each of us learned by a revelation of Christ and did not know it by a man's preaching? We will

---

127. Gal 5.8.

128. Acts 28.23.

129. On Ebion and Photinus see nn. 42–43 under 1.1 above.

130. Pamphilus, *Apology for Origen* 111, preserves a fragment from Origen's *Commentary on Galatians* that is parallel with Jerome's text here: "Pay attention to what he writes. For the one who adds these things to the former things is able adequately to show those who deny the deity of Jesus Christ and who declare him to be a mere man that Jesus Christ the Son of God is not a man but God. For if the apostle says that "the Gospel that I preached to you is not according to man" but according to Jesus Christ, he shows plainly that Christ Jesus is not a man; and if he is not a man, doubtless he is God [or rather, he will be nothing other than man and God]. And again if what Paul says is true, that 'I have not received the Gospel from a man but through a revelation of Jesus Christ,' it is certain that Jesus Christ who revealed it is not a man." See my new translation of Pamphilus in FOTC 120.

respond to this that those who are able to say, "Or do you seek proof of him who speaks in me, Christ?"[131] and, "But I live no longer, but Christ lives in me,"[132] show that it is not so much they themselves as God in them. He says to the saints, "I said, You are all gods and sons of the Most High";[133] and immediately of sinners, "But you will die as men and you will fall as one of the princes."[134] So then, when Paul and Peter speak, who neither die as men nor fall as one of the princes, it is clear that they are "gods." But those who are "gods" deliver the gospel *of God* and not *of a man.* Marcion and Basilides[135] and other heretical pests do not have the gospel *of God,* since they do not have the Holy Spirit, without whom the gospel that is taught becomes human. Nor should we suppose that the gospel is in the words of the Scriptures; rather it is in the meaning, and not the surface meaning, but the innermost.[136] It is not on the foliage of the words but in the root[137] of reason. In the prophet it is said of God: "His words are good with him."[138] The Scripture is profitable[139] to those who hear at that time when it is spoken not without Christ, when it is set forth not apart from the Father, when the one who preaches introduces it not without the Spirit.[140] Otherwise,

---

131. 2 Cor 13.3.

132. Gal 2.20.

133. Ps 82.6.

134. Ps 82.7.

135. Basilides was a Gnostic theologian who taught in Egypt in the first half of the second century. According to Clement, *Stromateis* 3, his followers did not lead upright lives but claimed to have authority "actually to commit sin because of their perfection, or that they will in any event be saved by nature, even if they do sin, because of their ingrained election" (FOTC 85:257, trans. John Ferguson). It is quite probable that Basilides, like Marcion, subjected this gospel to revision and alterations favorable to his preconceived dogmatic aims. Harnack, *Der kirchengeschichtliche Ertrag,* p. 148, tags Jerome's pairing of Marcion and Basilides as material that very certainly derives from Origen.

136. *In medulla;* cf. Heb 4.12.

137. Cf. Mt 13.6.

138. Mic 2.7.

139. Cf. 2 Tim 3.16.

140. Notice the Trinitarian structure of this thought.

even the devil speaks from the Scriptures; and according to Ezekiel all the heresies sew together pillows for themselves from it.[141] They place these on the bed of the whole age.[142] I myself too, who am speaking, if I have Christ in me, I do not have the gospel of a man; but if I am a sinner, it is said to me, "God said to the sinner: why do you narrate my justices and take my covenant on your lips? But you hated discipline and cast my words behind you,"[143] and the other things that follow. In the church, speaking entails great danger. For sometimes by a perverse interpretation the gospel of Christ becomes the gospel of a man, or what is worse, of the devil.

The difference between "receiving" and "learning"[144] is that the one to whom the gospel is first introduced "receives" it, and he is led to faith in it, so that he believes that the things that are written are true. But one "learns" it who knows that those things that are prefigured in it have been set forth and discussed by means of enigmatic figures and parables. And he knows this not by human revelation but by Christ revealing it, who revealed it to Paul,[145] or by means of Paul in whom Christ speaks.[146]

And this very word, ἀποκαλύψεως, "of revelation," is peculiar to the Scriptures and was employed by none of the wise men of the age[147] among the Greeks. This is why it appears to me that the seventy translators, just as they did for the other words that they translated from Hebrew into Greek, and for this one too, vigorously attempted to express the unique force of the foreign word and fashioned new words for new things. And when something is shown covered and veiled, they expressed it by removing the cover from the top and bringing it out into

---

141. Cf. Ezek 13.18, 21.

142. Origen's *Homilies on Ezekiel* 3.3–4 unfolds this idea. The latter work was translated into Latin by Jerome himself. See my new translation, Ancient Christian Writers 62 (Paulist Press).

143. Ps 50.16–17.

144. Cf. Gal 1.12.

145. Cf. Gal 1.12.

146. Cf. 2 Cor 13.3.

147. Cf. 1 Cor 1.20.

the light. To make this clearer, consider this example: When Moses spoke with God, [he did so] with an open and revealed face, that is, without the veil.[148] But when he spoke to the people, since they were not able to gaze at his face,[149] he put a veil on his face.[150] Also, a veil was spread out before the Ark of the Covenant.[151] Once it had been withdrawn, it betrayed things that were previously hidden and, if I may use the very word, they were "revealed." And so, if those who are accustomed to read eloquent men of the age should begin to ridicule us for the novelty and triviality of our language, let us send them to the books of Cicero, which take their titles from questions of philosophy. Let them see there the great necessity that compelled him to bring forth such great verbal monstrosities, which no Latin ear had heard before. This was because he was translating into our language from Greek, which is a cognate language. What do they endure who try to express the unique meanings from Hebrew difficulties? And yet, there are fewer things by far in so many volumes of the Scriptures that would sound novel than those that Cicero heaped up in that brief work.

Now as we said at the beginning when we were explaining "Paul an apostle not from men nor through a man,"[152] so also in the present passage it is possible for this to be understood obliquely of Peter and his other predecessors. For the one who has Christ alone as teacher of the gospel should not be moved toward the law by any man's authority. Furthermore he signifies that "revelation" when he was going on the journey to Damascus and merited hearing Christ's voice[153] and beheld the true light of the world[154] with blinded eyes.[155]

---

148. Cf. Ex 34.4.
149. Cf. Ex 34.30; 2 Cor 3.7.
150. Cf. Ex 34.35; 2 Cor 3.13.
151. Cf. Ex 40.3.
152. Gal 1.1.
153. Cf. Acts 9.2–4.
154. Cf. Jn 1.9; 8.12; 9.5.
155. Cf. Acts 9.8.

1.13–14.   *For you have heard of my former life in Judaism, since be-*
yond measure I persecuted the church of God and fought against it and
was advancing in Judaism beyond many who were of the same age in
my race, being a very great zealot for my ancestral traditions. This narrative is very beneficial to the Galatians. It explains how Paul, a onetime destroyer of the church and a very keen defender of Judaism, was
suddenly converted to faith in Christ. And this took place at that time
when Christ was first being proclaimed as crucified in the world, when
a new doctrine was being advanced by Gentiles and Jews to the ends
of the whole world. For the Galatians could have said: if the one who
was instructed from his youth in the training of the Pharisees,[156] who
surpassed all his contemporaries in the Judaic tradition, now defends
the church, which he once persecuted very severely, and wants to have
the grace and newness of Christ, together with the ill will of everyone,
rather than the oldness of the law accompanied by the praise of the
multitude, what should we do who have begun to be Christians from
the Gentiles? Indeed, he has nicely added, "I was persecuting the
church of God beyond measure." Thus from this fact too admiration
should arise. For he was converted to the faith not as one of those who
lightly persecuted the church, but as one who surpassed everyone else
in the field of persecution. And while recounting something else, he
prudently inserts that he served not so much God's law as the "ancestral traditions," that is, those of the Pharisees, who teach doctrines, the
commandments of men, and reject the law of God to set up their own
traditions.[157]

But how elegant is the usage and balance of the words! He says,
"You have heard of my former life in Judaism." "Life," not grace; "former," not current; "in Judaism," not in the law of God. "For I persecuted the church of God beyond measure and was destroying it." He
did not persecute like the rest, but "beyond measure"; nor did persecution suffice, however violent it was, but he was like some sort of bully
and robber destroying the church. He does not say he persecuted the

---

156. Cf. Acts 22.3; 23.6; Phil 3.5.
157. Cf. Mk 7.7–8.

"church of Christ," as he thought of it at the time, since he held it in contempt. But he speaks as he now believes, "the church of God." This indicates both that Christ himself is God, and that the church is of the same God who once gave the law. He says, "I was advancing in Judaism beyond many who were of the same age in my race, being a very great zealot for my ancestral traditions." On the other hand, he calls himself advanced, not in the law of God, but "in Judaism"; not beyond all, but "beyond many"; not beyond the old men, but "beyond those of the same age." Thus he refers to his own zeal for the law and declines to boast about it. Now when he mentions "ancestral traditions," not commandments of the Lord, he has indicated both that he was a Pharisee from the Pharisees,[158] and that he had zeal for God, but not according to knowledge.[159] But until today those who understand the Scriptures in a Judaic sense persecute the church of Christ and devastate it, not by zeal for the law of God, but as those who have been perverted by the "traditions" of men.

1.15–16a.   *But when it pleased him who set me apart from my mother's womb and called through his grace to reveal his Son in me, that I might preach him among the Gentiles.* Not only in this passage but also [in the letter] to the Romans, Paul writes that he was "set apart" for the gospel of God.[160] And Jeremiah asserts that he was known to God and sanctified before he was formed in the womb and conceived in his mother's womb.[161] And it is said under the persona of the just man, or as some think, of the Savior: "I was cast forth upon you from the womb, from my mother's womb, you are my God."[162] On the other hand David sings concerning sinners, "For behold I was conceived in iniquities and in transgressions did my mother conceive me";[163] and in another

---

158. Cf. Acts 23.6.
159. Cf. Rom 10.2.
160. Rom 1.1.
161. Cf. Jer 1.5; *CRm* 1.3.1.
162. Ps 22.10.
163. Ps 51.5.

passage, "Sinners are estranged from the womb."[164] And in both respects, before the little children were born, "God loved Jacob, but he hated Esau."[165] Heretics find room here, who allege that there are different kinds of natures, namely, spiritual, animal, and earthly.[166] They claim that one kind is saved, another perishes, the third is between the two. For unless there were different natures of those who will perish and of those who will be saved, the just man would never be chosen before he did anything good, nor would the sinner be hated before he committed transgression. A simple response can be given to this. This happens by the foreknowledge of God, so that the one whom he knows will be just, he "loves" before he comes forth from the womb; and the one whom he knows will be a sinner, he "hates," before he sins. It is not that there is iniquity in God's love and hate, but that he ought not regard otherwise those whom he knows will be either sinners or just. But we, as men, judge only from present things; but he to whom the future has already been done passes sentence from the end of things, not from the commencement.[167] And let these things be said rather simply and, one way or another, they can placate the reader without a deeper discussion.

In spite of this, [the heretics] strive to assert that God is unjust as a consequence of what we recorded a little while ago: "Sinners are estranged from the womb." They also bring up the rest that follows this: "they have gone astray from the womb, they have spoken lies."[168] And they say: how is it that, immediately from the womb, sinners have gone astray and have spoken lies, who were able to have neither speech nor sense? Or, where is the justice in God's foreknowledge, to love and protect one person before he is born, but to detest the other? And they refer the causes of this matter to the prior life, because each one who is

---

164. Ps 58.3.

165. Mal 1.2–3; Rom 9.13.

166. *Choicam* = χοϊκος; cf. 1 Cor 15.47. There is a close parallel in *CRm* 1.3.1–4. Cf. Harnack, *Der kirchengeschichtliche Ertrag*, p. 148. See note 76 above on Valentinus.

167. Cf. *CRm* 7.7–8.

168. Ps 58.3. Cf. *CRm* 1.3.2.

born is assigned immediately from the start either to good or evil angels in view of his own merit. And they wave about this whole passage about Jacob and Esau that we have mentioned now, written thus [in the letter] to the Romans.[169] Thus one cannot respond to them without the sweat and hellebore[170] of Chrysippus.[171]

Now the words "he revealed his Son *in* me" do not mean the same thing as if he had said, "he revealed his Son" *to* me. For with respect to the one *to whom* something is revealed, only that can be revealed to him which was not *in* him before; but that which is revealed *in him* was previously in him and is later revealed. It is like the following in the Gospel, "In your midst stands one whom you do not know";[172] and elsewhere, "He was the true light which enlightens every man coming into the world."[173] It is clear from this that the knowledge of God is present in everyone by nature, and no one is born apart from Christ, without having the seeds of wisdom and justice and of the rest of the virtues within himself. This is how it comes about that many, apart from faith and the gospel of Christ, do some things wisely and in a holy manner, for example, by obeying their parents, reaching out to the needy, refraining from oppressing their neighbors, not stealing what belongs to someone else. And all the more do they become responsible for this at the judgment of God.[174] For while they have the principles of the virtues within themselves and the seeds of God, they do not believe in him apart from whom they cannot exist.[175]

---

169. Cf. Rom 9.13.

170. Hellebore (Lat. *veratrum*) was a plant used as a remedy for madness. Cf. Pliny the Elder, *Historia naturalis* 25.5.21; Horace, Ep. 2.2.137; Vergil, *Georgics* 3.451.

171. Harnack, *Der kirchengeschichtliche Ertrag,* p. 153, traces this passage to Origen, who frequently cites Chrysippus in *Contra Celsum*. Chrysippus of Soli (280–207 BC) succeeded Cleanthes as the head of the Stoics.

172. Jn 1.26.

173. Jn 1.9.

174. Cf. Rom 2.5–7; 3.19.

175. Cf. Rom 1.20.

The words, the "Son" of God was "revealed" in Paul, can also be understood in another way, that when Paul preaches, the one whom they did not know before is recognized by the nations.

1.16b. *Immediately I did not find repose* (acquievi) *in flesh and blood;* or, as the Greek renders it better, "I did not discuss (*contuli*) with flesh and blood." I am aware that very many are of the opinion that this was said about the apostles. For even Porphyry raises the objection that after the revelation of Christ, he [Paul] did not deign to go to men and discuss with them in words, namely, in order that he would not be instructed by "flesh and blood" after [having received] the teaching of God. But far be it from me to imagine that Peter, John, and James are "flesh and blood," which cannot possess the kingdom of God.[176] If spiritual apostles are "flesh and blood," what should we think of the earthly?[177] Clearly Paul did not "discuss with flesh and blood" after the revelation of Christ, because he did not want to cast pearls before swine and give what is holy to the dogs.[178] Consider what is written about sinners: "My Spirit will not remain in these men, because they are flesh."[179] The apostle did not discuss the gospel that had been revealed to him with such [men], who were "flesh and blood," which also did not reveal the Son of God to Peter.[180] Instead, he gradually turns them from "flesh and blood" into spirit, and only then did he entrust the hidden mysteries (*sacramenta*) of the gospel to them.[181]

---

176. Cf. 1 Cor 15.50.
177. *Choicis;* see note 166 above.
178. Cf. Mt 7.6.
179. Gn 6.3.
180. Cf. Mt 16.17.
181. Cooper, *Marius Victorinus' Commentary on Galatians,* p. 265, also says that Paul would not have had enough time to learn his knowledge of God from Peter. Ibid., p. 265, n. 72, notes that both Victorinus and Jerome "share the odd sensibility that the extent of Paul's knowledge can be accounted for only by a divine revelation of such immensity that such a short (!) period of fifteen days would not suffice for it to have been transmitted humanly." Cooper also correctly observes (p. 264, n. 69) that Jerome's exegesis here "smacks of Origen."

Someone may say: If he "did not" at once "discuss" the gospel "with flesh and blood," yet it is understood that after a short while, he did "discuss with flesh and blood," then the sense here cannot stand, according to which the apostles are exempted from being "flesh and blood." For the one who at first "did not discuss with flesh and blood" afterward, as I said, did discuss with flesh and blood. This proposal compels us to make the following distinction: we should not link "at once" or "immediately" with "flesh and blood," but we should have it go with what is higher up. Thus it should be read, "but when it pleased him who separated me from my mother's womb," and then, "to reveal his Son in me," and at the end, "that I should proclaim him among the nations immediately." Thus the words "I did not discuss with flesh and blood" should start their own new section. And it should rather be thought that the sense stands as follows, that the one who was sent at once after the revelation of Christ did not stay to announce the gospel to the nations, nor did he protract the time by means of certain delays, by going to the apostles and discussing the Lord's revelation with men. Instead he went off into Arabia and again returned to Damascus after three years and preached the gospel. And only then did he go to Jerusalem to see Peter, John, and James.

1.17a.   *Nor did I go to Jerusalem to the apostles [who were] my predecessors.* If it were concerning the apostles that he had said "I did not discuss with flesh and blood," why was it necessary for him to repeat the same thing by saying: "nor did I go up to Jerusalem to the apostles who were my predecessors"? And so, the interpretation that we explained above should be retained.

1.17b.   *But I went into Arabia and returned again to Damascus.* The historical order does not seem to harmonize with what Luke relates in the Acts of the Apostles, that when Paul spoke the gospel boldly in Damascus for many days after [receiving] faith in Christ, plots were made against him. He was sent away during the night in a basket through the wall and went to Jerusalem, where he attempted to join himself with the disciples. When he was shunned by them and they were afraid to approach him, he was brought by Barnabas to the apostles.[182] Luke has also narrated there how Paul saw the Lord on the journey and he acted boldly in the name of Jesus. He says, "And he was with them, going in and out of Jerusalem and acting boldly in the name of the Lord. He also spoke and disputed with the Greeks, but they sought to kill him. When the brothers realized this, they brought him down to Caesarea and sent him off to Tarsus."[183] But here he claims that he first "went into Arabia and returned again to Damascus." After three years he went to Jerusalem, saw Peter, and stayed with him fifteen days. He did not meet with any other except James, the Lord's brother.[184] In order that these things may be believed as true (since they could have seemed doubtful to those who were not present), he confirms them by affirming them with an oath: "But what I am saying to you, behold before God that I am not lying."[185]

Therefore we can consider that Paul indeed went to Jerusalem according to Luke's account, not as if "to the apostles who were his predecessors," in order to learn something from them, but in order to avoid the onslaught of persecution that had been stirred up against him in Damascus on account of the gospel of Christ. Thus he went to Jerusalem as if to any other city. He immediately withdrew from there on account of plots and went to Arabia, or Damascus, and from there, after three years, he returned to Jerusalem "to see Peter." Or at least [it can be understood] as follows: immediately when he was baptized and strengthened after receiving food,[186] he was with the disciples who were in Damascus for some days, and at once he preached to all the amazed people in the synagogues of the Jews, that Jesus was the Son of God.[187] Then he went into Arabia and from Arabia returned to Damascus. He spent three years there, which the Scripture attests to as "many days" when it says, "But when many days were fulfilled, the Jews made a plan

---

182. Cf. Acts 9.19–27.
183. Acts 9.28–30.
184. Cf. Gal 1.18–19.
185. Gal 1.20.
186. Cf. Acts 9.19.
187. Cf. Acts 9.20–21.

to kill him. But their plot became known to Saul. And they guarded the gates day and night in order to kill him; so his disciples took him during the night and sent him away, lowering him in a basket through the wall. But when he came to Jerusalem, he tried to join himself to the disciples."[188] The reason in fact Luke omitted the part about Arabia is perhaps because Paul achieved nothing worthy of his apostolate in Arabia. In his brief narrative Luke preferred to report things that seemed worthy of the gospel of Christ.

This must not to be attributed to the apostle's laziness, if he was "in Arabia" to no effect, but so that a certain dispensation of God would teach him to be silent. For even after this we read that Paul, when he had left with Silas,[189] was hindered by the Holy Spirit from speaking the word in Asia.[190] Otherwise, how does this report help me—"but I went off into Arabia and again returned to Damascus"—if I read that Paul immediately went "into Arabia" after the revelation of Christ, and from Arabia he "returned to Damascus," if I do not know what he accomplished there or what advantage the journey and return held for him? The apostle himself offers me an opportunity for a deeper reflection in this same letter when he discusses Abraham, Hagar, and Sarah. He says, "Which things, of course, are said through allegory. For they are two covenants: one from Mount Sinai, giving birth in slavery, which is Hagar. For Sinai is a mountain in Arabia, which is joined to that which is the present Jerusalem."[191] And he shows that the Old Testament, that is, the son of the bondwoman, is established in Arabia (which is translated lowly and western).[192] And so, "immediately," when he believed, Paul turned to the law, to the prophets, and to the mysteries (*sacramenta*) of the old covenant, which was now located in the west, and he looked for Christ in them, the one whom he had been commanded to preach among the nations. And when he was found, he did not linger

---

188. Acts 9.23–26.
189. Cf. Acts 15.40.
190. Cf. Acts 16.6.
191. Gal 4.24–25.
192. Or, "sinking, setting."

there any longer but returned to Damascus, that is, to blood and to the passion of Christ. And from there, when he has been strengthened by reading the prophets, he goes to Jerusalem, the place of vision and peace.[193] This was not so much to learn anything from the apostles as to discuss with them the gospel that he had taught.

1.18a.   *Then after three years I went to Jerusalem to see Peter.* It was not to look at his eyes, cheeks, and face, to find out whether he was skinny or chubby, whether he had a straight or crooked nose, and whether he wore his hair in the front or had a bald spot (as Clement relates in his *Circuits*).[194] I do not think that it pertained to the apostolic dignity, after such a lengthy preparation of three years, to want to look upon anything human in Peter. Instead he looked at him with those eyes with which he is seen even now in his epistles. Paul "saw" Cephas with those eyes with which Paul himself is now perceived by the wise. But if this does not seem fitting to someone, he links all these things with the meaning given higher up, that the apostles did not discuss anything among themselves. For even the fact that he was seen to go to Jerusalem, it was not from a zeal to learn that he went to see the apostle. For he himself had the same authority to preach. Instead, he went to confer honor on the superior apostle.

---

193. "Vision of peace" is a popular etymology of Jerusalem found in Philo and Origen; cf. Origen *CRm* 3.5.2; *Homiliae in Jeremiam* 9.2; *Commentarius in Canticum* 2.1.

194. Grk. *periodis*. Περίοδοι Κλημέντος or περίοδοι Πέτρου was one of the Greek titles of the pseudo-Clementine work, *The Recognitions of Clement,* a fictional account originating in the early third century, that describes in a first-person narrative how Clement of Rome became Peter's travelling companion. The original existed in various versions and is lost. A passage from it is quoted by Origen in his *Commentary on Genesis,* written in 231; cf. *Philocalia* 22. One of the existing Greek forms was translated into Latin by Rufinus of Aquileia in 407; cf. ANF 8. The tradition about Peter's baldness reported by Jerome here is not extant in the surviving Latin translation. Smith and Wace, DCB 1.573, attribute this tradition to the common original of the *Clementine Homilies* and *Recognitions.*

1.18b.   *And I remained with him fifteen days.* He who had prepared himself for such a long time to see Peter did not need lengthy instruction. And, though it seems superfluous to some to investigate the numbers that are in the Scriptures, yet I do not think it is beside the point that the "fifteen days" that Paul dwelled with Peter signifies full knowledge and the perfect doctrine.[195] For indeed there are *fifteen* songs in the Psalter and *fifteen* degrees (*gradus*) by which the just man goes up to sing to God and to stay in his courts.[196] Hezekiah too earns the right to receive the sign for his life when a period of fifteen years was given in the degrees (*gradibus*).[197] Also the solemn feast days of God begin on the fifteenth day.[198]

And besides this (since we are following a twofold understanding) the reason he records "fifteen" days is to show that there was not much time for him to learn anything from Peter. Thus everything is related back to that meaning with which he began: Paul was not taught by man but by God.[199]

1.19.   *But I saw no other apostle except James, the Lord's brother.* I recall that when I was in Rome, at the instigation of the brothers, I published a book on the perpetual virginity of Saint Mary in which I had to discuss at length these men who were called the "brethren of the Lord."[200] So we ought to be content with whatever things we wrote

---

195. The number fifteen signifies the harmony between the two testaments, because it is made up of seven, a number characteristic of the Old Testament (the Sabbath was the seventh day), and eight, a number proper to the New Testament (the Resurrection occurred on the eighth day of the week). Cf. Augustine, *Ennarationes in Psalmos* 150.1 (CCL, 11.2191); cited by de Lubac, *Medieval Exegesis,* 1.258.

196. There are fifteen Psalms entitled ᾠδὴ τῶν ἀναβαθμῶν, or *canticum graduum,* "song of degrees": Ps 120–34.

197. Cf. 2 Kgs 20.6; Is 38.5–8.

198. Cf. Ex 12.2–6.

199. Cf. Gal 1.1.

200. He means *Against Helvidius,* NPNF 6.334–46. However, what he says in that work is not completely consistent with what he says here. See Lightfoot, *Epistle of St. Paul to the Galatians,* pp. 259–60.

there.[201] But for now, let this suffice, that on account of outstanding character, incomparable faith, and extraordinary wisdom, one may be called the "Lord's brother." It was also because he was first in charge of a church, which was the first to believe in Christ and was gathered from the Jews. Indeed they and the rest of the apostles are called the "Lord's brethren," as in the gospel, "Go, tell my brethren: I am going to my Father and to your Father, to my God and to your God";[202] and in the Psalm, "I shall tell of your name to my brethren; in the midst of the congregation (*ecclesia*) I will sing of you."[203] But mainly this one is called "brother" to whom the Lord had entrusted the sons of his own mother, when he was going to the Father.[204] And just as Job[205] and the other patriarchs were indeed called "servants of God," but Moses had a special distinction, as it were, so that it was written of him, "But not as Moses my servant,"[206] so also blessed James in particular is named "brother of the Lord" (as we said earlier).

That some, apart from the twelve, are called apostles is a consequence of the fact that all who had seen the Lord and subsequently preached him were called apostles. Thus it is written to the Corinthians: "For after this he was seen by those eleven; then he was seen by more than five hundred brethren together, many of whom remain until

---

201. Until Helvidius, the ancient Catholic Church (cf. Origen) was in consensus that James was not the Lord's uterine brother born of Mary. See J. McHugh, *The Mother of Jesus in the New Testament* (Garden City: Doubleday, 1975), and J. Redford, *Born of a Virgin: Proving the Miracle from the Gospels* (London: St. Paul's Publishing, 2007). David Hunter is seriously mistaken, therefore, when he claims that the orthodox doctrine of Mary's virginity has "only a fragile basis in the tradition of the first three centuries," and that the Helvidian position has a better claim to represent the mainstream of Christian tradition; see his "Helvidius, Jovinian, and the Virginity of Mary in Late-Fourth Century Rome," *Journal of Early Christian Studies* 1 (1993), pp. 47–71, esp. at 61, 69.

202. Jn 20.17.

203. Ps 22.22.

204. Cf. Jn 19.26–27.

205. Cf. Job 1.1.

206. Nm 12.7.

now, but some have fallen asleep; then he was seen by James, then by all the apostles."[207] But gradually, as time went on, others were ordained apostles by those whom the Lord had chosen, just as the words to the Philippians declare, saying, "But I consider it necessary to send to you Epaphroditus the brother, my co-worker and fellow soldier, but your apostle and servant of my need."[208] And to the Corinthians the following is written of such matters: "whether apostles of the churches, for the glory of God."[209] Silas too and Judas are named apostles by the apostles.[210]

This is why that person has erred gravely who thought that this James is the one from the gospel, the apostle and brother of John.[211] For it is an established fact, according to the reliability of the Acts of the Apostles, that he shed his blood for Christ after Stephen.[212] But this James was the first bishop of Jerusalem, surnamed Justus,[213] a man of such great sanctity and reputation among the people that they vied to touch the hem of his garment.[214] And he himself was later thrown from the temple headlong by the Jews.[215] He was succeeded by Symeon, whom tradition reports was himself crucified for the Lord.[216]

And so, he denies that he met with any of the apostles except these, lest a hidden objection should arise: "Even if you were not taught by Peter, you had other apostles as teachers." But he did not see them, not that he held them in contempt, but that they had been scattered throughout the whole world to preach the gospel.

---

207. 1 Cor 15.5–7.
208. Phil 2.25.
209. 2 Cor 8.23.
210. Cf. Acts 15.22, 27.
211. Cf. Mt 10.3.
212. Cf. Acts 12.2.
213. Cf. *HE* 2.1.
214. Cf. Mt 9.20; 14.36. Harnack, *Der kirchengeschichtliche Ertrag*, p. 152, notes that the tradition recorded here about vying to touch the hem of his garment is otherwise unknown and probably traces to Jerome's source in Origen.
215. Cf. *HE* 2.23.
216. Cf. *HE* 3.11, 22, 32.

1.20. *But what I am writing to you, behold before God that I am not lying.* Possibly this should be understood simply as, "the things I am writing to you" are true; and I affirm them with God as my witness, that they have not been fabricated by any craft of words, by any lie. Or perhaps this should be read in a deeper sense, that "what I am writing to you" is "before God," that is, worthy of God's sight. But why worthy of God's sight? "Because," of course, "I am not lying." And just as the eyes of the Lord are on the just,[217] but he turns his face away from the sight of the impious,[218] so now the things that are written are "before" the Lord, since I who am writing am not lying. If I were lying, these things would not be "before" the Lord. But this can be understood not only about these things which he is now writing to the Galatians, but also more generally about all the epistles. What he writes is not false, and there is no discord between his heart and his words.

1.21. *Then I came into the regions of Syria and Cilicia.* After the vision in Jerusalem[219] he went to "Syria," which among us means high and lofty, and from there he passed over to "Cilicia," which he longed to receive in the faith of Christ, preaching to it the call to repentance. For Cilicia translates as "reception" or "sorrowful calling."

1.22–24. *But I was unknown by face to the churches of Judaea which were in Christ Jesus. But they had heard only that the one who was formerly persecuting us is now preaching the faith which he once fought against; and they glorified God in me.* The "churches" that were in "Judaea" had known Paul only by reputation. The majority of them had seen more of the persecutor than the apostle. But possibly Syria and the regions of Cilicia, Arabia, and Damascus had known him by face too, since the teacher of the Gentiles preached the gospel of Christ not to the Jews but to the Gentiles. But all that he is doing is aimed to show that from his being a persecutor he would never have been able to arise as glorious among those very ones whom he had previously persecuted

---

217. Cf. Ps 34.15.
218. Cf. Ps 34.16.
219. Cf. Acts 22.17–21.

unless his preaching had been approved by the judgment of those who had previously known him badly. And he discreetly returns to the theme [of the letter], affirming that he had spent such a brief time in Judea that he was unknown even by face to the believers. This shows that he did not have Peter, James, and John as his teachers, but Christ, who had revealed his gospel to him.

But at the same time one should note that whereas above he is said to have fought against the "church,"[220] here it is against "the faith" (there the men, here the thing). Thus now it was introduced more appropriately: "he preaches the *faith* which formerly he fought against." For he could not express this similarly of the *church*.

2.1–2.   *Then after fourteen years I again went up to Jerusalem with Barnabas, taking Titus too. Now I went up in accordance with a revelation; and I discussed* (contuli) *with them the gospel which I preach among the gentiles, but apart, to those who seemed [to be something], lest perhaps I should be running or had run in vain.* What the Latin translator had rendered above as "find repose"—in that passage where it was written, "immediately I did not find repose with flesh and blood"[221]—in the present passage he translated as "I discussed" rather than "I found repose" (acquievi). And, to speak quite truthfully, the Greek word ἀνεθέμην is understood somewhat differently among us, namely, when we discuss the things we know with a friend and, as it were, pour into his bosom and awareness what we know, as things that must either be approved or disapproved by his equal counsel.

Therefore, he "went up to Jerusalem after fourteen years." The one who had first gone only to "see Peter" and had "stayed fifteen days with him,"[222] now claims that the reason he went was to discuss the gospel with the apostles. He took the circumcised Barnabas as well as Titus, an uncircumcised Gentile, in order to establish every word by the mouth of two and three witnesses.[223] Now to discuss is one thing, to learn is

---

220. Cf. Gal 1.13.
221. Cf. Gal 1.16b above.
222. Cf. Gal 1.18.
223. Cf. Dt 19.15.

something else. Among those who are discussing, there is equality; among the one teaching and learning, the one who is learning is inferior. At the beginning of the faith he sees the apostles in passing; after seventeen years[224] (as he himself says) he speaks with them fully and humbles himself and inquires "lest perhaps he was either running or had run in vain." There are two reasons for this inquiry: in order that Paul's humility should be manifested, who as teacher in the whole world of the gentiles already had "run" to his apostolic predecessors; and that the Galatians would learn that those too who were in charge of the churches in Judaea had not rejected his gospel. But at the same time he also shows that for the sake of faith in Christ and the freedom of the gospel, he dared to lead Titus, an uncircumcised man, to those who had known much about him (that he was breaking the law, destroying Moses, completely doing away with circumcision). And in the midst of such a great multitude of Jews and his own enemies, who on account of their zeal for the law desired to drain his blood, as it were, neither he himself nor Titus were overcome by any fear to yield to the compulsion that could have won them favor. At the same time they did not fail to endure a large measure of ill will on account of the location, the authority of the elders, the number of the churches that believed in Christ from the Jews, or for the sake of the circumstances.

Some say that the time when "after fourteen years he went up to Jerusalem" was when, in the Acts of the Apostles, dissension arose between the believers in Antioch concerning questions of observing and neglecting the law and it pleased him to go to Jerusalem and to await the judgment of the elders.[225] At that time Paul himself and Barnabas were sent. And this is what is read in the Latin manuscripts: "to whom we yielded in subjection for an hour, in order that the truth of the gospel would remain among you."[226] That is to say, the reason Paul and Barnabas allowed themselves to be sent to Jerusalem concerning this

---

224. Cf. Gal 1.18; 2.1.

225. Cf. Acts 15.1–2.

226. Gal 2.5. The omission of the negative particle is confined chiefly to Western witnesses. According to Metzger, *Textual Commentary*, 591, it seems to have

public issue, as if it were a doubtful matter, was so that, by a judgment of the elders too, the grace of the gospel would be proven to be confirmed to the believers and no further doubt would remain in anyone about omitting circumcision. For it was commanded in a letter from the apostles that the yoke of the law was to be removed from those who had believed in Christ from the Gentiles.[227]

But consider his words, "I discussed with them the gospel which I preach among the gentiles, but separately with those who seemed [to be something], lest perhaps I was running or had run in vain." This can also be understood to mean that he discussed in secret with the apostles the grace of gospel liberty and the oldness of the abolished law. He did so on account of the multitude of Jews who were not yet able to hear that Christ was the fulfillment and end of the law.[228] And these men, when Paul was absent, had boasted in Jerusalem that he "was running or had run in vain" when he supposed that the old law was not to be followed. It is not that Paul feared that he had preached a false gospel among the gentiles for seventeen years,[229] but that he might show his predecessors that he "was not running or had run in vain," as the ignorant had supposed.

2.3–5.   *But even Titus who was with me, though he was from the Gentiles, was not compelled to be circumcised. But because of false brethren secretly brought in, who secretly came in to spy out our freedom which he have in Christ Jesus, in order to reduce us to slavery; to whom we did not yield in subjection for an hour, that the truth of the gospel might remain among you.* "Titus, although he was from the Gentiles," was unable to be forced by any fear to be compelled to be circumcised in Jerusalem, the metropolis of the Jews. In this city Paul had been the

occurred "when certain scribes thought it necessary—in view of the apostle's principle of accommodation (1 Cor 9.20–23)—to find here an analogue to the circumcision of Timothy (Ac 16.3)." The Greek manuscripts decisively support the inclusion of the negative (οὐδέ).

227. Cf. Acts 15.23–29.
228. Cf. Mt 5.17; Rom 10.4; 13.10.
229. Cf. Gal 1.18; 2.1.

victim of such great ill will, even of the charge of committing blasphemy against Moses, that later on he was nearly killed by the Jews, at the time when he was set free by the tribune and sent to Rome in chains to Caesar.[230] If this is so, how is it that some think that the words "to whom we yielded in subjection for an hour, that the truth of the gospel might remain among you" are to be understood to mean that Titus himself, who previously was not able to be compelled to be circumcised, is again circumcised and subjected? Or what is this "truth of the gospel" that yields to the hypocrisy of Jews and observes things that previously you reckoned as dung[231] and despised as loss[232] and reckons them as something when they are nothing? Moreover, [this reading] completely contradicts the meaning of the epistle itself. In the entire text of his own discussion he summons the Galatians away from circumcision. He acts in order to show that he himself was a Hebrew from the Hebrews.[233] At one time he kept all the works of the law,[234] he was circumcised on the eighth day, according to the law he was a Pharisee.[235] And yet, in spite of this, he despises everything for the sake of the grace of Christ.[236] For when he went to Jerusalem and false brethren who had believed from the circumcision wanted to force him to circumcise Titus, neither he nor Titus yielded to the violent pressure, lest they fail to protect the truth of the gospel. But if he is saying that he was overcome by compulsion to circumcise Titus, how is it that he summons the Galatians away from circumcision from which he was unable to exempt Titus in Jerusalem, who had been with him from the Gentiles?

Consequently, either it should be read in accordance with the Greek manuscripts, "to whom we did *not* yield in subjection for an hour," so that "in order that the truth of the gospel might remain

230. Cf. Acts 21.31–32; 23.10.
231. Cf. Phil 3.8.
232. Cf. Phil 3.7–8.
233. Cf. Phil 3.5.
234. Cf. Phil 3.6.
235. Cf. Phil 3.5.
236. Cf. Phil 3.8.

among you" may be understood as the consequence of this; or, if someone agrees to trust the Latin copies, we should understand it in accordance with the sense given above, that "yielded for an hour" refers not
to the circumcision of Titus but to his going to Jerusalem. That is to
say, the reason Paul and Barnabas "yielded in subjection" by going to
Jerusalem, when the sedition in Antioch was stirred up over the law,
was so that their own opinion would be strengthened by means of the
epistle of the apostles, and the "truth of the gospel" would be manifest
among the Galatians. This truth was not in the letter but in the spirit;[237]
it was not in the fleshly meaning, but in the spiritual understanding;[238]
it was not in the Judaism that is outward, but in secret.[239]

In fact one should know that the conjunction "but" that is recorded
in the present passage—"but on account of false brethren secretly
brought in"—is superfluous. If it is read, it would not have anything to
which it is replying and to which it is bringing a conclusion. But the
order of the reading and the sense is: "but not even Titus, who was with
me, though he was of the Gentiles, was compelled to be circumcised."
And at once he adds the reason for which he would have been compelled unwillingly to circumcision when he says, "on account of false
brethren secretly brought in who secretly came in to spy out our freedom that we have in Christ Jesus, in order to reduce us to servitude."
To those who wanted to turn us away from the freedom of Christ to the
servitude in the law by threats, terror, and the multitude, we did not
yield even for a moment so as to circumcise Titus. This is especially the
case since a certain necessity on account of peace in the church could
have excused us. And we did all this in order that there would be no occasion for you to draw back from the grace of the gospel.

So then, while we were in Jerusalem amidst such eminent Jews, we
had false brethren threatening us from there, and those who were elders were holding things in check in some respects. Yet we were unable
to be compelled by any force or for any reason to observe circumcision.

---

237. Cf. 2 Cor 3.6.
238. Cf. 1 Cor 2.13.
239. Cf. Rom 2.29.

For we knew that it had come to an end. If this is the case, then you who are in Galatia, you to whom no force can be applied, by withdrawing from grace of your own accord, you are passing over to the oldness of the law that has already been abolished.[240]

2.6a.   *But by those who seemed to be something, what sort they were formerly does not matter to me: God does not accept the person of man.* Although, he says, the Lord had the apostles Peter and John with him and they saw him transfigured on the mountain,[241] and upon them the foundation of the church has been laid,[242] yet it is of no importance to me, because I am not speaking against them who followed the Lord at that time, but against those who now put the law ahead of grace. I do not detract from my predecessors, nor do I accuse the elders in any connection, but I say this, that "God does not accept the person of man."

For he did not accept [the person] of Moses,[243] he did not accept that of David,[244] he did not accept that of others; therefore, he will not accept theirs, who seem to yield to certain ones for a time,[245] even if they themselves agree with me. For Peter too says, "In truth I recognize that God is no acceptor of persons, but in every place the one who fears him and works justice is acceptable to him."[246] And so, the holy apostle Peter himself uses this argument against those who were scandalized by Cornelius, one of the Gentiles who was baptized, not circumcised.

---

240. Cf. Rom 7.6; 2 Cor 3.6.

241. Cf. Mt 17.1–2. Plumer, *Augustine's Commentary on Galatians,* p. 55, notes that Jerome seems deliberately to have omitted the name of James from his comment here, in order to avoid the mistake of confusing James the brother of the Lord (who was not present on the Mount of Transfiguration) with James the son of Zebedee (who was present there). Augustine and Ambrosiaster both confused these two men in their respective commentaries on Galatians.

242. Cf. Eph 2.20; Mt 16.18.

243. Cf. Dt 10.17.

244. Cf. 1 Sm 16.7.

245. Cf. Gal 2.5.

246. Acts 10.34–35.

And he placates them [by saying] that he could not refuse water to those who had received the Holy Spirit. With the same purpose in mind, the holy apostle Paul now uses this argument against Peter himself, that God is no acceptor of persons but judges each one for the truth. And so he treads lightly into the midst and step by step, between praise and scolding of Peter. Thus he both defers to the apostle who is his predecessor, and no less boldly resists him to his face when compelled by the truth.[247]

2.6b.   *For those who seemed [to be something] discussed* (contulerunt) *nothing with me.* Higher up he himself "discussed with them"[248] and related to them the many things that he had accomplished among the Gentiles. They "discussed nothing with him" but merely approved what he said, gave the right hand of partnership,[249] and confirmed that their own gospel and Paul's were one.[250] Once again it should be noted that the very word "discussed" (*contulerunt*), which we treated earlier, is itself Greek.

2.7–9.   *But on the contrary, when they saw that the gospel of uncircumcision was entrusted to me, just as that of circumcision [was entrusted] to Peter—for he who worked in Peter in the apostolate of circumcision worked also in me among the Gentiles—and when they recognized the grace which was given to me, Peter, James, and John, who seemed to be pillars, gave me and Barnabas the right hand of fellowship: that we among the Gentiles, but they among the circumcision.* This is a hyperbaton,[251] and when the many intervening words are removed, it may be briefly construed as follows: "For those who seemed (to be something) discussed nothing with me, but on the contrary gave the right hand of fellowship to me and Barnabas." Or, possibly, the sense is

---

247. Cf. Gal 2.11.
248. Gal 2.2.
249. Cf. Gal 2.9.
250. Cf. Gal 2.7.
251. A confusion in the order of the words.

hidden to avoid boasting of himself: those who seemed to be something discussed nothing with me, but on the contrary I discussed with them, until they become stronger in the grace of the gospel.

Now the gist of what he is saying is this: One and the same [God] entrusted to me the gospel of uncircumcision and to Peter the gospel of circumcision. He sent me to the Gentiles, he placed him in Judaea. The Gentiles, who were already of a mature age, were unable to be tormented by the unprofitable suffering involved in circumcision and to abstain from foods that they had always heartily enjoyed and that God had created to be used.[252] Those who had believed from the Jews and who had been circumcised, and who by custom, as if by second nature, reckoned that they had more than the other nations, were unable easily to despise the things in which they boasted. And so, by the providence of God, one of [these two] apostles was given to the circumcised, the one who seemed to be finding repose in the shadows of the law. The other was given to those who were in the condition of uncircumcision, namely, the one who did not reckon that the grace of the gospel was servitude but the free faith, lest by some pretext a hindrance to the faith might arise and on account of circumcision or uncircumcision someone would not believe in Christ. In the Acts of the Apostles, Peter himself testified that no man is common.[253] By means of that object that he saw being let down from heaven by four corners, he is taught that it doesn't matter if someone is a Jew or a Gentile.[254] We are not saying that it is as if he had forgotten these former things and thought that the law had to be observed over and above the grace of the gospel. On the contrary, we are saying that by feigning to keep the law he too was gradually leading the Jews out of their old way of life; for they were unable all of the sudden to despise as offscourings and loss[255] such a great effort of observance and the extremely conservative manner of

---

252. Cf. 1 Tm 4.3–5.
253. Cf. Acts 10.34–35.
254. Cf. Acts 10.11; 11.5.
255. Cf. Phil 3.7–8.

their old life (*veteris vitae cautissimam conversationem*). From this we perceive that the reason Peter, James, and John gave Paul and Barnabas the right hand was not that the gospel of Christ should be thought to be diversified into various observances, but that there would be one communion of both the circumcised and of the uncircumcised.

He has laid the foundation for this nicely by saying, "for he who worked in Peter in the apostolate of circumcision." This was to prevent anyone from thinking that he was detracting from Peter. On the contrary, Peter was to be understood from [Paul's] praises of him previously mentioned. The reason he accepted circumcision to some extent was in order to gain those who had been entrusted to him from the Jews and to keep them in faith in Christ and in the gospel. [Paul] wants it to be understood as well that [Peter] was without blame in doing this, when he observed for a time what was not permitted. For he had done this to keep from losing those who were entrusted to him. All the more so should [Paul] do for the sake of the truth of the gospel what was entrusted to him among the uncircumcised and prevent the Gentiles from withdrawing allegiance from their faith and belief in Christ, terrified by the burden and difficulty of the law.

An obscure question arises here: What then? If Peter had found some Gentiles, would he not have led them to the faith? Or if Paul had come across some of the circumcision, would he not have summoned them to the baptism of Christ? We can solve this problem by saying that for each of them there was a primary command that applied among the Jews and Gentiles: those who defended the law should follow what they had; those who placed grace ahead of the law should not lack a teacher and leader for them. But they had this purpose in common: to gather a church together for Christ from all nations.[256] For we read both that saint Peter baptized the Gentile Cornelius[257] and that Paul repeatedly preached Christ in the synagogues of the Jews.[258]

---

256. Cf. Mt 28.19.
257. Cf. Acts 10.47–48.
258. Cf. Acts 9.20; 17.1–2; 2 Cor 11.24.

2.9. *Peter and John and James, who seemed to be pillars.* Three times up above we read that this is said of the apostles, "But separately to those who *seemed* [to be something]";[259] and, "by those who *seemed* to be something";[260] and, "For those who seemed (to be something) discussed nothing with me."[261] And so, I was anxious to investigate why on earth it was that he says, "those who *seemed.*" But now he has delivered me from all doubt by adding, "those who *seemed* to be pillars." Therefore, the apostles *are* the "pillars" of the church, and above all Peter, James, and John. Two of them deserve to go up on the mountain with the Lord.[262] One of them introduces the Savior in the Apocalypse saying, "He who has overcome I shall make him a *pillar* in the temple of my God."[263] This shows that all believers who overcome the enemy can become pillars of the church. In fact when writing to Timothy Paul says, "that you may know how you should live in the household of God which is the church of the living God, the *pillar* and support of the truth."[264] And we are instructed by these others that both the apostles and all believers, as well as the church itself, are named *pillar* in the scriptures. There is no difference between what is said of the body or of the members[265] because the body is divided into members and the members belong to the body.[266]

And so, "Peter, James, and John, who seemed to be pillars, gave to Paul and Barnabas the right hand of fellowship." But to Titus, who was with them, they did not give the right hand. For he had not yet attained to that measure, that they could entrust Christ's wares[267] to him equally with the elders, and that he should hold the same place of business which Barnabas and Paul held, "that we among the Gentiles, but they among the circumcision."

---

259. Gal 2.6.
260. Gal 2.6.
261. Gal 2.6.
262. He means Peter and John. Cf. Mt 17.1–8.
263. Rv 3.12.
264. 1 Tm 3.15.
265. Cf. Acts 9.4.
266. Cf. 1 Cor 12.12–27.
267. Cf. Mt 25.14–30; Lk 16.10–13; 19.12–28.

2.10.   *Only that we should be mindful of the poor, which was the very thing I was anxious to do.* The holy "poor," care for whom is specially committed to Paul and Barnabas by the apostles, are those believers from the Jews who brought the proceeds of their possessions to the feet of the apostles to be given to the needy.[268] Or it may refer to those who were regarded as accursed and sacrilegious by their own kinsmen, relatives, and parents, as apostates from the law and believers in a crucified man.[269] The amount of labor the holy apostle expended in ministering to these people his letters bear witness, as he writes to the Corinthians, to the Thessalonians,[270] and to all the churches of the Gentiles,[271] that they should prepare this gift to be taken to Jerusalem, either through himself or through others who were pleasing to them.[272] For this reason he now says confidently, "which is the very thing I was anxious to do."

But "the poor" can also be understood in another way, of those of whom it is said in the Gospel, "Blessed are the poor in spirit, for theirs is the kingdom of heaven."[273] For such people deserve to be remembered by the apostles. And moreover, there are those poor of whom it is written in Solomon, "The redemption of a man's soul, his own wealth; but a poor man does not bear a rebuke."[274] For he cannot hear about the coming terror of punishments, [since he is] poor in faith, poor in grace, lacking spiritual riches and the knowledge of the Scriptures, which is compared with gold and silver and precious stone.[275] Since the healthy do not need a physician, but those who are sick,[276] therefore, it was befitting for the apostles, in the offering of the right

---

268. Cf. Acts 4.34–35.
269. Cf. Lk 21.16–17.
270. Cf. 1 Thes 2.9; 4.9; 5.12.
271. Cf. Rom 16.4.
272. Cf. 1 Cor 16.1–4; 2 Cor 8.1–4.
273. Mt 5.3.
274. Prv 13.8.
275. Cf. Ps 119.72; 1 Cor 3.12.
276. Cf. Mt 9.12.

hand, not to spurn the "poor," not to look down on sinners. On the contrary, they should always remember them, as Paul does when he remembers that Corinthian man. It is true that in the first epistle he had caused him grief for a time, in order that, with his body exerting itself through penance, his spirit would be saved.[277] Yet in the second letter, he calls him back to the church, lest he be overwhelmed by excessive grief. And he asks everyone to confirm love to him and to forgive their brother.[278] Thus he fulfills the agreement that he had made in Jerusalem, that he should always be mindful of the "poor."

2.11–13.   *But when Peter came to Antioch, I opposed him to his face, because he was blameworthy. For before certain men came from James, he was eating with the Gentiles; but when they came, he drew back and separated himself, fearing those who were of the circumcision. And the other Jews consented to his pretence, so that even Barnabas was led by them into this pretence.* From the fact that "Peter, before certain men came to Antioch" from Jerusalem, "ate with the Gentiles," it is shown that he had not forgotten the precept "Do not call any man common or unclean."[279] Now on account of those who thought that the law still had to be observed, Peter "withdrew" himself a little from association with the Gentiles (so that the "others" as well who were of the Jews did likewise, and "Barnabas," who with Paul had preached the gospel among the Gentiles, was compelled to do this). Because of this those who had believed in Antioch from the Gentiles and had not been circumcised were compelled to overstep in a move toward the burdens of the law. For they did not understand Peter's policy (*dispensationem*), whereby he longed for the Jews to be saved. Instead they thought that this was the guiding principle of the gospel. And so, when the apostle Paul saw that the grace of Christ was endangered, Christ's fighter made use of a new kind of fighting: he himself corrected the policy of Peter,

---

277. Cf. 1 Cor 5.5.
278. Cf. 2 Cor 2.6–10; *CRm* , Preface of Origen 5.
279. Acts 10.28.

whereby he was longing to save the Jews by a new policy of contradiction, and he "opposed him to his face." He does not expose his purpose, but it is as if he is publicly contradicting him. Thus from the fact that Paul offered opposition by exposing him, those who had believed from the Gentiles would be saved.

But if anyone thinks that Paul truly opposed the apostle Peter, and that for the sake of the truth of the gospel he boldly inflicted an injury on his predecessor, this will be contradicted by the fact that Paul himself "became a Jew to the Jews in order to gain the Jews."[280] And he will be held guilty of the same pretense when he shaved his head in Cenchrea,[281] and having become bald when he made an offering in Jerusalem.[282] Moreover, he circumcised Timothy[283] and he took part in the procession (*exercuit*) with bare feet.[284] Assuredly these are things that very openly derive from the ceremonies of the Jews. And so, if the one who had been sent to preach to the Gentiles did not think of saying groundlessly, "Be without offense to the Jews and to the church of God, just as I please everyone in all things, not seeking what is useful to myself, but what is useful to the many, that they may be saved";[285] and if he did certain things that were contrary to the freedom of the gospel in order not to scandalize the Jews; then by what authority, by what effrontery, does he dare to rebuke this in Peter, who was the apostle of the circumcision? For he himself, the apostle of the Gentiles, is convicted of having done the very same thing. But, as we have already said earlier, he opposed Peter and the others with his public face, in order that the hypocrisy of observing the law, which was harming those who had believed from the Gentiles, would be corrected by the

---

280. Cf. 1 Cor 9.20.

281. Cf. Acts 18.18.

282. Cf. Acts 21.23–26.

283. Cf. Acts 16.3.

284. Jerome must be referring to Jewish religious processions in which Paul allegedly took part. *Nudipedalia* is the same word used in Tertullian, *On Fasting* 16 and *Apologeticus* 40 to describe (pagan) religious processions of persons with bare feet.

285. 1 Cor 10.32–33.

hypocrisy of correction. Thus both peoples would be saved, as those who praise circumcision follow Peter, and those who do not want to be circumcised preach the freedom of Paul. Now by his words "he was blameworthy," he has softly tempered [his rebuke]. Thus we should understand that he was not so much blameworthy to Paul as to those brothers from whom he subsequently separated himself, after formerly eating with them.

In fact let the example of Jehu king of Israel show us that a pretence is useful and should be adopted on occasion. He would not have been able to kill the priests of Baal had he not pretended that he wanted to worship the idol, saying, "Gather to me all the priests of Baal. For if Ahab served Baal a little, I shall serve him a lot."[286] And David did this when he altered his face before Abimelech, who dismissed him and he went away.[287] It is no wonder, however, that just men feign some things just the same to suit the occasion on account of their own salvation and that of others, since even our Lord himself, who had no sin[288] nor the flesh of sin, adopted the pretence of sinful flesh[289] so that by condemning sin in the flesh[290] he would make us the justice of God in himself.[291]

Surely Paul had read the Lord's command in the Gospel,[292] "But if your brother sins against you, go and correct him between you and

---

286. 2 Kgs 10.18–19.

287. 1 Sm 21.13–15 speaks of David feigning madness before Achish, the king of Gath. However, the title words of Ps 34 refer to this episode in connection with Abimelech.

288. Cf. Jn 8.46; 2 Cor 5.21; Heb 4.15.

289. Cf. Rom 8.3.

290. Cf. Rom 8.4.

291. Cf. 1 Cor 1.30; 2 Cor 5.21.

292. It is possible that Paul could have encountered this command in written form in an early Aramaic or Hebrew version of Matthew's Gospel. However, even if one were to assume that Jerome is mistaken in his claim here, since Paul at his early date could not have known the written text of the Gospels, which were allegedly written down later, it is nevertheless certain that he was intimately acquainted with the Gospel traditions orally. Wenham, *Paul,* pp. 210–13, demonstrates, for instance, that Paul in his letters follows the procedure for church discipline outlined by Jesus in Mt 18.15. Cf. 1 Cor 5.3–5. Thus Jerome's premise is valid.

100 St. Jerome's Commentaries on Galatians, Titus, and Philemon

him alone; if he listens to you, you will have gained your brother."[293] How is it, then, when he likewise commands this to be done for the least brothers,[294] that he has dared with his public face to convict the greatest of the apostles, so impudently and so persistently, unless it be the case that Peter was pleased to be convicted like this? And Paul would not have injured him of whom he had previously already said, "I went to Jerusalem to see Peter and remained with him fifteen days; but I saw none of the other apostles";[295] and again, "For he who worked in Peter in the apostolate of circumcision";[296] and after this, "Peter, James, and John, who seemed to be pillars";[297] and the other things that he says in summation in praise of him.

Many times when I was a young man, I practiced public speaking in Rome and trained myself for true disputations by means of fictitious lawsuits. I would run to the judges' tribunals and watch the most eloquent of orators contending among themselves with such great bitterness that often they would leave business on the side and turn to private insults, ridicule, and biting one another with their teeth. If they do this without incurring any suspicion of collusion with the defendants and fool the people who are standing around, what do we think such great pillars of the church ought to have done, Peter and Paul, such great vessels of wisdom, in the midst of Jews and Gentiles who were at odds with each other? What else but a feigned dispute between them that would bring peace to the believers and bring the faith of the church into harmony by means of a holy quarrel between them?

There are those who think that the "Cephas" of whom Paul writes here, who he "resisted him to his face," is not the apostle Peter, but one of the seventy disciples[298] who was designated by that name. They say that Peter could never have "drawn back" from association with the

---

293. Mt 18.15.
294. Cf. Rom 14.15, 20–21.
295. Gal 1.18–19.
296. Gal 2.8.
297. Gal 2.9.
298. Cf. Lk 10.1.

Gentiles, since he had baptized Cornelius the centurion.[299] Moreover, when he had gone up to Jerusalem—after he told the story of the vision to those who were of the circumcision who argued with him and said, "Why did you go to uncircumcised men and eat with them?"[300]—he concluded the speech with this summary: "'Therefore, if God gave the same grace to them as he also gave to us, who believed in the Lord Jesus Christ, who was I to be able to hinder God?' When they heard this they were silent and praised God saying, 'so then, God has granted even to the Gentiles repentance unto life.'"[301] [Such interpreters] think this most of all because Luke, the writer of history, makes no mention of this conflict and does not say that Peter was ever in Antioch with Paul. Thus they give Porphyry an opportunity to blaspheme, if one believes either that Peter had gone astray or that Paul had impudently rebuked the chief of the apostles.

In response one should first say to them that we do not know of any other whose name is Cephas except for him who, both in the Gospel and in the other letters of Paul, is written sometimes in this way, as Cephas, and sometimes as Peter.[302] It is not that Peter signifies one thing and Cephas something else, but what we would call in Latin and Greek *petra,* both the Hebrews and Syrians[303] (because of the affinity of their languages) call *cephas.* Secondly, the whole argument of the letter is against this interpretation, in that he speaks indirectly of "Peter, James, and John." Nor is it surprising that Luke was silent on this matter, seeing that there are many other things that Paul claims to have suffered[304] that Luke omits, making use of his freedom as an historian. And it is not immediately a contradiction if what one person thought was worthy to relate for some reason, someone else leaves out. After all,

299. Cf. Acts 10.48.

300. Acts 11.2.

301. Acts 11.17–18.

302. For a study of the use of Cephas in the New Testament, see M. Miguens, *Church Ministries in New Testament Times* (Arlington: Christian Culture Press, 1976), pp. 88–96.

303. That is, Aramaic.

304. Cf. 2 Cor 11.23–27.

we accept that Peter was the first bishop of the church of Antioch and from there was transferred to Rome, but Luke has altogether omitted any mention of this. Finally, if on account of Porphyry's blasphemy we need to fabricate another Cephas in order that it not be thought that Peter erred, there will be countless things in the holy Scriptures that will have to be erased, which that man complains about, since he does not understand them. But we will do battle against Porphyry in another work, if Christ commands. For now let us pursue what remains.

2.14a. *But when I saw that they were not proceeding on the right foot* (recto pede) *toward the truth of the gospel, I said to Peter before everyone.* Just as those ones do not have a defect in their feet who have sound steps but pretend to limp, yet there is some reason for their limping, so too in the case of Peter. He knows that circumcision and uncircumcision are nothing, but keeping God's commands is what matters.[305] To be sure he ate previously with the Gentiles, but to suit the occasion he drew back from them, lest the Jews be lost from faith in Christ. This is why Paul too, by the same contrivance by which Peter himself was feigning, resisted him to his face and says "before everyone," not so much to convict Peter as to correct those for whose sake Peter had feigned. But if this interpretation displeases anyone, whereby neither Peter sinned nor is Paul shown to be impudent in having accused his superior, he should explain what the consequences are of Paul's reproving in another what he himself has done.

2.14b. *If you, being a Jew, live after the manner of the Gentiles and not as the Jews do, how is it that you compel the Gentiles to Judaize?* With an inextricable argument he binds Peter, or rather, through Peter, those who were compelling him to create clashes among themselves. "If you," O Peter, he says, "a Jew" by nature, circumcised as a child and keeping all the precepts of the law, now know, owing to the grace of Christ, that those things are not useful in themselves, but are examples

---

305. Cf. 1 Cor 7.19.

and images of things to come,[306] and if you receive food along with those who are from the Gentiles, not by any means in a superstitious way as before but living with freedom and indifference, "how is it" that you compel those who have believed from the Gentiles to "Judaize," by now drawing back from them and by separating and severing yourself from them, as if from those who are defiled? For if those from whom you are drawing back are unclean (but the reason you draw back is because they are not circumcised), you are compelling them to be circumcised and to become Jews, since you yourself, born a Jew, "live in the manner of the Gentiles." And in a hidden way he shows the reason why he has quarreled with him, namely, because he was compelling Gentiles to Judaize by his pretense, so long as they desire to imitate him.

2.15.   *We by nature [are] Jews and not of the Gentiles, sinners.* The heretics sneak in at this point, those who fabricate certain ridiculous and inept ideas and say that a spiritual nature is not capable of sinning and that an earthly nature cannot do anything justly.[307] Let us ask them why the branches were broken off from the good olive tree, and why they were grafted from the wild olive into the root of the good olive tree,[308] if no one can either fall from the good or rise up out of evil. Or how is it that Paul formerly persecuted the church, if he was of a spiritual nature? How did he become an apostle subsequently, if he was generated from earthly slime? But if they contend that he was not earthly, let us cite his own words: "We were by nature sons of wrath, just as the rest."[309] He is a "Jew by nature" who is of Abraham's race

---

306. Cf. Heb 10.1.

307. Cf. *CRm* 8.11.1–5. According to Clement, *Stromateis* 3 (FOTC 85:257), Basilides' followers did not lead upright lives but claimed to have the authority "actually to commit sin because of their perfection, or that they will in any event be saved by nature, even if they do sin, because of their ingrained election." Harnack, *Der kirchengeschichtliche Ertrag*, p. 148, traces Jerome's discussion to Origen.

308. Cf. Rom 11.17,24.

309. Eph 2.3.

and has been circumcised by his parents on the eighth day. He is not a "Jew by nature," who has become one later from the Gentiles.

But that I may summarize the whole argument in a few words, the sense of the text is as follows: "We," that is, you and I, Peter, (for he includes his own person lest he should seem to do him injury), "though we are Jews by nature," he says, doing those things that were instructed from the law "and not sinners from the Gentiles"—either in the sense of those who are sinners generically, because they serve idols, or those whom we now regard as unclean—we know that we were not able to be saved by the work of the law, but by faith in Christ we have believed in Christ. Thus the faith that we had in Christ has bestowed upon us what the law had not given us. But if, by drawing back from the law by which we could not be saved, we pass over to faith, in which is sought not the circumcision of the flesh but the pure devotion of the heart, and if by now drawing back from the Gentiles, we act in such a way that whoever is not circumcised is unclean, is not faith in Christ, then, in which we previously supposed we were saved, in the service of sin rather than in the service of the righteousness that takes away circumcision, which makes unclean the one who lacks it? But may it never be that I should once again vindicate what I once destroyed and knew was of no profit to me. By once and for all withdrawing from the law, I died to the law[310] so that I might live in Christ.[311] And having been fastened to his cross[312] and renewed in the new man,[313] I take my stand by faith rather than by the flesh,[314] and with Christ to leave the world.[315] What I have once undertaken, I hold on to; Christ did not die for me in vain (*gratis*). I have believed in him in vain (*frustra*), if I am able to be saved by the old law apart from faith in him.

---

310. Cf. Rom 7.4; Gal 2.19.
311. Cf. Gal 2.20.
312. Cf. Gal 2.20.
313. Cf. 2 Cor 4.16; Col 3.10.
314. Cf. Gal 2.20.
315. Cf. 1 Cor 5.10; Lk 23.43.

2.16a. *But knowing that a man is not justified by works of the law, but*
by faith in Jesus Christ, we also have believed in Christ Jesus, that we
may be justified by faith in Christ and not by works of the law. Some
say, if what Paul claims is true—that no one "is justified by the works
of the law" but "by faith in Jesus Christ"—then the patriarchs and
prophets and saints who lived before the coming of Christ were imperfect. We should warn such people that those who are said here not to
have obtained justice are those who believe that they can be justified
only by works. But the saints who lived long ago were justified "by faith
in Christ." For indeed Abraham saw Christ's day and rejoiced.[316] And
Moses "reckoned that the reproach of Christ was greater wealth than
the treasure of the Egyptians; for he was looking to the repayment."[317]
Also Isaiah saw Christ's glory, as the evangelist John records.[318] Moreover, Jude speaks in general terms of everyone, "I want to warn you,
who once knew all things, that Jesus, in saving the people from the
land of Egypt, did afterwards destroy them that did not believe."[319]

Therefore, it is not so much works of the law that are condemned
as those who trust that they can be justified *only* from works. For the
Savior too says to the disciples, "Unless your justice abounds beyond
that of the Scribes and Pharisees, you will not enter into the kingdom
of heaven."[320] On this passage one should assemble the many precepts

---

316. Cf. Jn 8.52.

317. Heb 11.26.

318. Cf. Jn 12.41.

319. Jude 5. Jerome's reading of "Jesus" here is extremely well attested in ancient manuscripts, and critical principles seem to require its adoption. In spite of
this, the reading was rejected in favor of "the Lord" by the divided translation com-
mittee for the Nestle-Aland Greek New Testament. See Metzger, *Textual Commen-*
tary, pp. 723–34; A. Wikgren, "Some Problems in Jude 5," in *Studies in the History*
and Text of the New Testament in Honor of Kenneth Willis Clark, ed. B. Daniels and
M. Suggs, Studies and Documents 29; (Salt Lake City, 1967), pp. 147–52. The ancient reading "Jesus" is a witness of fundamental importance to the early (first century) Christian belief that Jesus was preexistent. Cf. S. Gathercole, *The Pre-Existent*
Son: Recovering the Christologies of Matthew, Mark, and Luke (Grand Rapids: Eerdmans, 2006), pp. 36–41.

320. Mt 5.20.

of the law that no one can fulfill, and on the other hand, one should say that some matters of the law are done even by those who do not know it. But those who perform it are not therefore justified, because this happens without "faith in Christ." For instance, [they do this] by not sleeping with a man as one sleeps with a woman,[321] by not committing adultery, by not stealing, but rather by honoring father and mother, and by doing the other things that are commanded. But if they produce for us examples of holy men and say that they lived under the law and achieved the things that pertained to the law, we will say that "the law is not laid down for the just man, but for the unjust and insubordinate, for the impious and sinners, for the polluted and unclean."[322] But the one who is taught by God does not need this. Thus let him at least learn about love from Paul, who says, "But concerning love I do not need to write to you; for you yourselves are taught by God to love one another."[323]

2.16b.   *Because by works of the law no flesh will be justified.* The flesh that is not justified "by works of the law" is that of which it is written, "All flesh is grass and all its glory is like the flower of grass."[324] But that flesh is justified through faith in Jesus Christ of which it is said in a figure (*sacramento*) of the resurrection: "All flesh shall see the salvation of God."[325] Moreover, according to a lower level of understanding, there was a time when "no flesh was justified from the law," but only those men who were in Palestine; but now "all flesh" is justified by faith in Jesus Christ, while his churches are being established throughout the whole world.

2.19a.   *For through the law I died to the law that I may live to God.* It is one thing to die *through* the law and something else to die *to* the law. The one who dies *to* the law was alive to it before he died, by keeping

---

321. Cf. Lv 18.22; *CRm* 4.4.9.

322. 1 Tm 1.9.

323. 1 Thes 4.9.

324. Is 40.6. Origen's interpretation is strikingly similar in *CRm* 3.6.7.

325. Is 40.6. Cf. *CRm* 2.13.36.

Sabbaths and new moons and feast days,[326] and the curious types of sacrificial victims and Jewish fables and genealogies.[327] But after Christ came and the law of which it is written, "But we know that the law is spiritual,"[328] the soul "died to the" former "law through the law" of the gospel. According to what is written to the Romans, the soul would have been labeled an adulteress if it had married while the husband was alive; but when its husband died, that is, the old law, it married the spiritual law in order to bear fruit for God.[329] This is also why in Hosea it is said to the soul, "From me is your fruit found."[330] The following beautiful mystery is related to this: "Who is wise and will understand these things? Or understanding, and will know them?"[331] Therefore, the one who "dies through the" spiritual "law to the law" of the letter "lives to God," though he is not without God's law, but is under the law of Christ.[332] But the one who dies to the law on account of sins is dead, to be sure, but what comes next cannot be said of him, that "he lives to God."

But elsewhere as well the apostle shows that there is another spiritual law apart from the law of the letter when he says, "And so, the law indeed is holy, and the commandment is holy and just and good."[333] And Ezekiel says under the persona of God, "I have led them," that is, the people of the Jews, "out of the land of Egypt, and I have brought them into the desert and given them my precepts and shown them my justifications, which a man will do and will live in them."[334] But concerning this law, which works wrath,[335] to which the apostle has died, it relates later on, "And I gave them precepts that were not good and

---

326. Cf. Col 2.16.
327. Cf. 1 Tm 1.4; Ti 1.14.
328. Rom 7.14.
329. Cf. Rom 7.2–4.
330. Hos 14.9.
331. Hos 14.10.
332. Cf. 1 Cor 9.21.
333. Rom 7.12.
334. Ezek 20.10–11.
335. Cf. Rom 4.15.

justifications in which they will not live in them."[336] The very same thing is indicated in the Psalter: "Because I have not known learning, I will enter into the strength of the Lord."[337]

2.19b. *With Christ I am nailed to the cross.* Since he had said that he had died to the law through the law, he shows how he died: "With Christ I am nailed to the cross." He takes up his own cross and follows Christ.[338] And united in the same suffering, he pleads, "Remember me, when you come into your kingdom."[339] And immediately he hears, "Today you will be with me in paradise."[340] If anyone is conformed to the death of Jesus Christ,[341] who is dead to the world[342] and whose members have been put to death on earth,[343] he is crucified with Jesus.[344] He nails the trophy of his own mortification to the wood of the Lord's suffering.[345]

2.20a. *But I live no longer, but Christ lives in me.* The one who once lived in the law, who persecuted the church, does not live; but "Christ lives in him," wisdom, strength, speech, peace, joy, and the other virtues.[346] The one who does not have these cannot say, "But Christ lives in me." But he discusses all this concerning Peter under his own persona against Peter.

---

336. Ezek 20.10–11.
337. Cf. Ps 71.15–16. See the Vulgate version.
338. Cf. Mt 16.24.
339. Lk 23.42.
340. Lk 23.43.
341. Cf. Phil 3.10.
342. Cf. Col 2.20.
343. Cf. Col 3.5.
344. A similar interpretation of the mortification of the good thief is found in *CRm* 5.9.7; cf. 4.12.4; 7.3.4.
345. Cf. 2.14.
346. Cf. 1 Cor 1.18–24; Eph 2.14; Gal 5.22–23. This understanding in which being in Christ is defined as being in possession of his virtues and operations is found throughout *CRm*. See, e.g., 5.8.10; 5.10.18; 6.9.2.

2.20b. *But what I now live in the flesh.* It is one thing to *be* in the flesh and [something else] to *"live* in the flesh." For "those who are in the flesh cannot please God."[347] This is why it is said to those who are living well, "But you are not in the flesh."[348]

2.20c. *I live in faith in the Son of God, who loved me and handed himself over for me.* To the Romans he says of God that he "did not spare his own Son but handed him over for us."[349] But now he says of Christ that he "handed himself over," "who loved me and handed himself over for me." In fact in the Gospel, when the apostles are listed, it is related, "And Judas Iscariot, who *handed him over*";[350] and again in the same Gospel, "Behold the one who will *hand me over* has drawn near."[351] Indeed of the chief priests and elders of the people the Scripture records that they condemned Jesus to death and, after binding him, led him and *handed him over* to Pilate the governor.[352] And then it says of Pilate: "He released Barabbas to them, but Jesus he scourged and *handed over* to them to be crucified."[353] Therefore, both the Father "handed over" the Son and the Son "handed himself over"; and Judas and the priests together with the rulers "handed him over"; and finally, Pilate himself "handed over" the one who had been "handed over" to himself. But the Father "handed over" to save a lost world; Jesus "handed himself over" to do his own and the Father's will.[354] But Judas and the priests and elders of the people and Pilate unwittingly "handed over" life to death.[355] Since this very life handed itself over for our salvation, blessed and very happy is the one who has Christ living within

---

347. Rom 8.8.
348. Rom 8.9.
349. Rom 8.32.
350. Mt 10.4.
351. Mt 26.46.
352. Cf. Mt 27.1–2.
353. Mt 27.26.
354. Cf. Jn 6.38.
355. Cf. Acts 3.15–17.

himself in all his thoughts and works and can say, "I live in faith in the Son of God, who loved me and handed himself over for me."

2.21.   *I do not cast away the grace of God; for if justice be through the law, then Christ died in vain* (gratis). The one who "casts aside the grace of God" is both he who after the gospel lives in the law, and the one who is defiled by sins after baptism.[356] But he who is able to say with the apostle, "His grace did not become vain (*vacua*) in me,"[357] is the one who says this confidently, "I do not cast away the grace of God."

But what follows is very necessary in refutation of those who think that after faith in Christ the precepts of the law need to be kept. For one should say to them, "If justice is through the law, then Christ died in vain." Or at least let them show how Christ did not "die in vain" if works justify. But, although they may be stupid, they will not dare to say that Christ died without reason (*sine causa*). Consequently, in the partial syllogism that is here proposed, namely "for if justice is through the law, then Christ died in vain," we ought to assume that the consequence that follows cannot be denied, "But Christ did not die in vain"; and to conclude, therefore, justice is not through the law.[358]

Up to this point he is speaking against Peter. Now he returns to the Galatians.

3.1a.   *O senseless Galatians, who has bewitched you?* This passage can be understood in two ways: either he has called the Galatians "senseless," a people who are going from greater things to inferior things, because they began in the spirit and are finishing in the flesh;[359] or, he

---

356. Cf. *CRm* 3.9.4.

357. 1 Cor 15.10.

358. Marius Victorinus follows precisely the same logic in his *Commentary on Galatians.* Cooper, p. 286, n. 150, refers to the source in what Quintilian calls *enthymeme ex pugnantibus,* an enthymeme "from denial of consequents" (*Instituto Oratoria* 5.14.24–6; Loeb ed., ii.362).

359. Cf. Gal 3.3.

says this owing to the fact that each province has its own unique characteristics. The apostle approves as true the saying of the poet Epimenides, "Cretans are always liars, evil beasts, lazy gluttons."[360] A Latin historian stamps the Moors as vain and the Dalmatians as savage.[361] All the poets scourge the Phrygians as cowards (*timidos*).[362] Philosophers boast that the finer minds are born in Athens. And with Caesar, Cicero suggests that Greeks are fickle, when he says, "either of the fickle Greeks or of savage barbarians," and in *Pro Flacco* he says: "inborn levity and learned vanity."[363] All Scripture convicts Israel of having hard hearts and stiff necks.[364] In this manner, then, I think the apostle too has stamped the Galatians as possessing a unique characteristic of their region.

It is true that some involve themselves in very deep questions, as if under the pretext of avoiding the heresy that introduces diverse natures [of souls]. They say that the Tyrians, the Sidonians, the Moabites, Ammonites and Idumeans, the Babylonians, Egyptians, and all the nations that are named in the Scriptures have certain unique characteristics that derive from antecedent causes and from the merit of their former works. Otherwise, they say that the justice of God would come into doubt, when each nation is claimed to have a good or evil that another does not have. But let us stay away from these profundities and pursue better things.[365] We say either that the Galatians are convicted

---

360. Cf. Ti 1.12.

361. Cf. Cicero, *Pro Ligario* II; Livy, *Ab urbe condita* 38, 37, 3.

362. Cf. Cicero, *De divinatione* 1.41.92; *De legibus* 2.13.33; Pliny the Elder, *Historia naturalis* 8.48.74. Compare the ancient adage *Sero sapiunt Phryges*, "The Phrygians learn wisdom too late." According to Erasmus, *Adages* I.i.28 (CWE 31), this "fits those people who repent too late of the stupidities they have committed. The Trojans, for instance, after so many disasters, only began to think of giving back Helen when nearly ten years had elapsed; whereas if they had handed her back at the very beginning when Menelaus asked for her, they would have saved themselves from innumerable calamities."

363. Cicero, *Pro Flacco* frg. 9.

364. Cf. Ex 32.9; Lk 24.25; Acts 7.51.

365. This seems to refer to Origen's speculations in *De Principiis*.

of foolishness through which they are unable to judge the spirit and letter of the law, or through a vice of their nation they are unable to be corrected because they are not teachable; they are stupid and sluggish in respect to wisdom.

But we must expound what follows, "Who has bewitched you?" in a way that is worthy of Paul (who, even if he is "unskilled in his speech, but not in knowledge"[366]). It is not that he is recognizing the existence of witchcraft, which is commonly supposed to do harm. On the contrary he has used words from the street and, as elsewhere, so in this passage too, he has adopted a word from everyday speech. We read in Proverbs, "The gift of an envious man torments the eyes."[367] The word for "envious" [*invidus*] in our language is recorded more meaningfully in Greek as "bewitched."[368] And in the Wisdom that is ascribed to Solomon it says: "The bewitching of malice obscures good things."[369] By these examples we are shown either that the envious man is tormented by the happiness of another, or he in whom there are some good things suffers harm by another who bewitches, that is, by the one who envies. In particular it is said that witchcraft harms infants and small children and those who do not yet leave a solid footprint behind. This is why one of the pagans said, "Some eye bewitches my tender lambs."[370] God will see whether or not it be true, since it is possible that even demons are in service to this sin, turning away from good works those who they recognize have begun or have made progress in the work of God. We think that the reason he has now taken this example from popular thinking is that, just as the tender age is said to be harmed by witchcraft, so also the Galatians, recently born in the faith of Christ and nourished with milk, not solid food,[371] have been injured. It is as though

---

366. 2 Cor 11.6.

367. Sir 18.18. Notice that Jerome (who is probably translating Origen here) quotes from the deutero-canonical Sirach as "Proverbs."

368. In Gal 3.1 Paul uses ἐβάσκανεν. In the Septuagint, Sir 18.18 has βασάκανου.

369. Wis 4.12 (Βασκανία).

370. Virgil, *Eclogues* 3.103.

371. Cf. 1 Cor 3.2; Heb 5.12.

someone has cast a spell on them and they have vomited out the food of the Holy Spirit. For they are sick to their stomachs in respect to faith. But if someone contradicts this explanation, let him explain how one can understand on the basis of common opinions the "valley of the Titans" in the book of Kingdoms;[372] the "sirens and satyrs" in Isaiah;[373] "Arcturus, Orion, and Pleiades" in Job;[374] and other similar things. Assuredly these things derive their names, causes, and sources from pagan fables.

But with respect to this passage let us ask Marcion, who repudiates the prophets, how he interprets what follows.

3.1b. *Before whose eyes Jesus Christ has been written before as crucified among you.* Christ has rightly been "written before" us. For the whole chorus of the prophets predicts his gallows and passion, his blows and scourging. Thus we know about his cross not only from the Gospel, in which his crucifixion is narrated, but well before the one who was crucified deigned to come down to earth and assumed humanity. Nor is it a trivial praise of the Galatians that they believed in the crucified, as it was previously written for them in such a manner. For by continually reading the prophets and by becoming familiar with all the mysteries of the old law, they came in due course to belief.

In some manuscripts it reads: "Who has bewitched you not to believe the truth?" But we have omitted this, since it is not found in the copies of Adamantius.[375]

3.2. *This only would I learn from you: Did you receive the Spirit by works of the law or by the hearing of faith?* There are indeed many

---

372. Cf. 2 Kgs 23.13.

373. Cf. Is 13.21–22; 34.13–14.

374. Cf. Job 9.9.

375. This is the nickname of Origen and means "man of adamant." According to *HE* 6.14.10, he was known by this name even during his lifetime, and it referred to the firmness with which he stood like a rock against the heretics. Jerome, Ep. 43, thought it signified his unwearied industry in producing innumerable books.

things, he says, which could under interrogation compel you to prefer the gospel to the law; but since you are senseless and are by no means able to hear these things, I should speak with simple words to you. I should ask about what is at hand: whether it was works of the law, observance of the Sabbath, the superstition of circumcision and new moons[376] that gave you the Holy Spirit that you received? Or was it the hearing of faith through which you believed from the Gentiles? But if it cannot be denied that the Holy Spirit and the virtues that followed at the commencement of faith were received not by works of the law, but were given by faith in Christ, then it is plain that you have begun to fall from better things into worse things.

Let us consider carefully that he does not say, "I want to learn from you" whether you "received the Spirit" by *works,* but instead "by the *works of the law.*" For he knew that even Cornelius the centurion had received the Spirit by *works* but not by "works of the law," with which he was unacquainted.[377] But if, on the other hand, it is said: well then, the Spirit can be received even without the "hearing of faith," we will respond that he [Cornelius] did indeed receive the Spirit, but by the "hearing of faith" *and* by natural law, which speaks within our hearts the good things that must be done and the evils that must be avoided. We have related that long ago Abraham, Moses, and other saints were justified through the natural law. From then on the observance of works and the justice of the law can increase the law of nature; but we are not speaking of the justice of the carnal law, which passes away, but of the spiritual law; for "the law is spiritual."[378] But, when we put faith first, we neither destroy works of the law,[379] nor do we say, as some do, "Let us do evil until good things come, whose damnation is just."[380] But we place grace ahead of servitude, and we say that what the Jews do out

---

376. Cf. Col 2.16.
377. This distinction between "works" and "works of the law" is fundamental in the Catholic exegetical tradition. Cf. *CRm* 8.7.6
378. Rom 7.14.
379. Cf. Rom 3.31; Mt 5.17.
380. Rom 3.8

of fear, we do out of love. They are slaves, we are sons; they are compelled to the good, we receive the good of our own free will. Freedom to transgress does not therefore arise from faith in Christ, but the will for good works is increased by the love that springs from faith, provided that we do good things, not because we dread the judge, but because we know the things that are pleasing to him in whom we believe.

Someone may ask: if there is no "faith" except "by hearing,"[381] how can those who are born deaf become Christians? For someone can understand God the Father "from the greatness and beauty of creatures,"[382] and the creator is known as a consequence "from the things that have been made."[383] But the birth of Christ, the cross, death, and resurrection, cannot be known except by hearing. Either the deaf, therefore, are not Christians, or, if the deaf are Christians, what is said by the apostle elsewhere is false: "And so faith is from hearing, but hearing is through the word of God."[384] One who is content with a simple response to this says that he did not say universally, "the faith *of everyone* is from hearing," but "faith is from hearing." This can be understood both in respect to the part and to the whole, namely the "faith from hearing" of those who hear, who believe. But the one who tries to satisfy this objection will first attempt to assert the following, that the deaf are able to learn the gospel by nods of assent, by everyday manner of life, and by the speech, so to speak, of the bearing of the whole body. Secondly, what the word of God says, to which nothing is deaf, is spoken more to those ears of which he himself says both in the Gospel, "Who has ears to hear, let him hear,"[385] and in the Apocalypse, "He who has an ear, let him hear what the Spirit says to the churches."[386]

---

381. Cf. Rom 10.17.
382. Wis 13.5. Notice the quote from the "deuterocanical" book of Wisdom.
383. Rom 1.20.
384. Rom 10.17.
385. Mt 11.15.
386. Rv 2.11.

Also, Isaiah says, "The Lord has also given hearing to me"[387] (that is the other man to whom God speaks in secret, who calls out in the heart of the believer, "Abba, Father"[388]). And, as we have frequently explained, just as the body has all the members and senses, so too the soul has all the senses and members; and among the rest it has ears too. The one who has them will not be too much in need of those ears of the body in order to become acquainted with the gospel of Christ.

At the same time, pay attention to the fact that here the Spirit whom we attain as a gift, and not from man, is understood without any adjective "Holy." Elsewhere it is written of him, "An incorruptible Spirit is in everyone";[389] and, "the Spirit himself bears testimony with our spirit";[390] and in another passage, "No one knows the things that are of a man, except the spirit of the man which is in him";[391] and in Daniel, "Bless the Lord, spirits and souls of the just."[392]

3.3.   *Are you so foolish? Having begun with the Spirit, are you now ending with the flesh?* If the Galatians had received the Holy Spirit, how were they "foolish"? But at once this is resolved: they "began with the Spirit," to be sure, but when they "ended with the flesh," the Spirit was taken from them.[393] This is why it was "in vain" (*sine causa*) that they suffered such great things that they suffered.[394] It was to prevent this from happening to himself that David, after his sin, prays and says, "Take not your Holy Spirit from me."[395]

Pay careful attention to what is being said: the one who follows the Scriptures according to the letter is said "to end with the flesh." This is

---

387. Is 50.5

388. Cf. Rom 8.15; Gal 4.6.

389. Wis 12.1.

390. Rom 8.16.

391. 1 Cor 2.11.

392. Dn 3.86. Notice the citation from the deuterocanonical portion of Daniel. This may be an indication that Jerome is copying Origen's exegesis.

393. Cf. *CRm* 6.7.6.

394. Cf. Gal 3.4.

395. Ps 51.11.

why what is written to the Corinthians, "Though we live in the flesh we do not war according to the flesh,"[396] can be better understood to mean that those ones may be said to "war in the flesh" who have analyzed fully the Old Testament in a lowly manner. On the other hand, those who follow the spiritual understanding are indeed "in the flesh" because they have the same letter that the Jews have, but they do not "war according to the flesh" because they pass beyond the flesh to the Spirit. Suppose you see someone who first believes from the Gentiles, who puts his hand to the plow of Christ,[397] with another prudent teacher leading the way. He is traveling down the road of the law toward the gospel in such a way that he understands everything that is written there—about the Sabbath, unleavened bread, circumcision, sacrificial victims—in a manner that is worthy of God. And suppose that later, subsequent to the reading of the gospel, he is persuaded by some Jew or by a friend of the Jews, that he should interpret the Scriptures just as they are written, and that he should abandon the cloudy shadows of allegory. Of this man you can say, "Are you so foolish? Having begun with the Spirit, are you not ending with the flesh?"

3.4.   *Have you suffered such great things in vain* (sine causa)? *If it be yet in vain!* Were we to consider the wretched Jews, under what great superstitions they live among the rest of the nations and the effort of their observances, as they say, "Do not touch, do not taste, do not handle,"[398] we would also prove that what is said is true: "Have you suffered such great things in vain?" But the statement is not immediately applied to them; it becomes doubtful, "if it be yet in vain," because this is being said of those who are able to return to the gospel after the law.

But it can be understood better in the following way: those in Galatia who first believed in the crucified endured many reproaches, both from the Jews and from the Gentiles, and suffered tremendous persecutions. These are exposed as having been suffered in vain, if they draw

---

396. 2 Cor 10.3.
397. Cf. Lk 9.62.
398. Cf. Col 2.21.

back from the grace of Christ, on account of which they suffered "such great" things. And at the same time that hope [is in vain], because whoever labors on account of faith in Christ and afterwards falls away into sin, just as the former [hope] is said to have been "in vain" when he sins, so he does not again lose these things, if he returns to his original faith and to his old zeal.

Here is another way to interpret this: if, he says, you think that one must follow circumcision after grace, then all that you have suffered, you who have lived without circumcision until the present time, has been done pointlessly (*in irritum*). These are the things that you see in my case have not been endured in vain. For I know that the law does not avail after the gospel.

Or possibly it may be understood in this way: it would have been no trivial loss, if by following circumcision you would have lost only the original effort of faith; but now the penalty of collusion is added to this loss as well. Thus you both underwent the past things "in vain," and you will be tormented in the future.

Some people somewhat force the interpretation in this way: consider the original freedom of grace and the burdens of the present observation in the law. You will then see how many things you have done with pointless zeal, although the fruit of that error is not entirely to be despaired of, while you are brought by the zeal of God to this very thing. For pardon can be granted to the ignorant, if, having converted to better things, you learn that it was your knowledge that wavered, not your zeal.

3.5.   *Well then, does he who gives the Spirit to you and who works the virtues in you [do this] by works of the law or by the hearing of faith?* He "gives," that is, administers. One should read: in the present time. Thus it is shown that during all hours and moments the Holy Spirit is always administered to the worthy.[399] And to the extent that someone advances in the work and love of God, so much the more does he have

---

399. Cf. on Gal 6.18.

the "virtues" of the Spirit in himself, which the "hearing of faith," and not the "works of the law," bring to completion. It is not that the works of the law are to be despised and one should seek simple faith apart from them, but that the works themselves are adorned by faith in Christ. For the following judgment of a wise man is well known: "the faithful lives not from justice, but the just lives from faith."[400] At the same time it is shown that the Galatians, having received the Holy Spirit after their faith, had the gifts of the virtues, that is prophecy, kinds of tongues, healing of diseases, and the other things that are listed among the spiritual gifts in the letter to the Corinthians.[401] And yet, after such great things (perhaps because they lacked the grace of discerning the spirits),[402] they were trapped in the net of false teachers.

One should observe as well that the "virtues" are said to be inoperative in those who do not hold fast to the truth of the gospel, as for example in those who did not follow the Lord, though they did signs in his name. It was John who especially complained about this: "Teacher, we saw someone expelling demons in your name and we hindered him, because he does not follow with us."[403] This is directed against the heretics who think that the fact that they do some sign is a proof of their faith.[404] Those who, although they ate and drank in the Lord's name[405] (for they also have a sacrilegious altar), boast that they have done many signs and have invoked the Savior, will merit hearing on the Day of Judgment: "I do not know you; depart from me, you who work iniquity."[406]

---

400. Cf. Hab 2.4; Rom 1.17; Gal 3.11; Heb 10.38.

401. Cf. 1 Cor 12.4–11, 29–30.

402. Cf. 1 Cor 12.10.

403. Lk 9.49.

404. Harnack, *Der kirchengeschichtliche Ertrag*, p. 149, comments on this passage, "We do not know to which heretics this applies, but it cannot be attributed to Jerome."

405. Cf. Lk 13.26.

406. Mt 7.23.

3.6.   *Just as Abraham "believed God and it was reputed to him unto justice."* Marcion made a deletion from "his apostle,"[407] from this passage to the place where it is written, "Those who are of faith will be blessed with the faithful Abraham."[408] But what good did it do him to have published this, since the other things he left behind refute his madness?

Now "Abraham believed God" by leaving his homeland to go to a land he did not know;[409] by trusting that Sarah, who was ninety years old and sterile, would give birth;[410] and by offering Isaac as a sacrifice,[411] after he had heard God's promise that in Isaac his seed would be called,[412] and yet without doubting the Lord's promise.[413] To such a man faith is rightly reputed for justice[414] because, having gone beyond the works of the law, he earned God's approval (*Deum promeruit*), not from fear but from love.[415]

3.7.   *You know, therefore, that those who are of faith are sons of Abraham.* He discusses this in greater detail in the epistle to the Romans, that faith was reputed to Abraham for justice, not in circumcision but in uncircumcision.[416] By paying careful attention to this, he shows that whoever believes with that mind by which Abraham believed while he was uncircumcised, who "exulted to see the day" of the Lord and "saw it and rejoiced,"[417] are sons of Abraham. This is also why it is said to unfaithful Jews, "If you were sons of Abraham, you would do the works

---

407. See note 10 in this book.

408. Gal 3.9. Harnack, *Der kirchengeschichtliche Ertrag*, p. 149, attributes this passage with certainty to Jerome's source in Origen.

409. Cf. Gn 12.1–8; Heb 11.8.

410. Cf. Gn 17.15–21; 18.9–14.

411. Cf. Gn 22.1–14.

412. Cf. Gn 21.12; Heb 11.17–18.

413. Cf. Heb 11.19.

414. Cf. 1 Mc 4.52.

415. Cf. Heb 13.6.

416. Cf. Rom 4.9.

417. Cf. Jn 8.56; Heb 11.13.

of Abraham."[418] But what other works was the Lord demanding from them at that time when he said these things, if not belief in the Son of God whom the Father had sent, the Son who says, "He who believes in me, believes not in me, but in him who sent me"[419]? This is also why in another passage, an answer is given to those who were applauding the antiquity and nobility of their race: "And do not say that we have father Abraham; for God is able to raise up sons of Abraham from these stones."[420] No one doubts that stones there signify the hard hearts of the Gentiles, which were later softened[421] to receive the seal of faith.[422] Diligent reader, enumerate Abraham's virtues by which he pleased God before his circumcision, and let anyone you discover with similar works be called sons of Abraham, who was justified in uncircumcision, who received circumcision not on account of the merit of works, but as a sign of his prior faith.[423]

For since Christ was to descend from his seed, in whom the blessing of all the nations had been promised,[424] and many ages were to pass from Abraham until Christ, God provided that the offspring of chosen Abraham should not be mixed with other nations. For gradually his family would have become uncertain. He marked out the Israelite flock with a brand, as it were: circumcision. Thus while they lived among the Egyptians, Assyrians, Babylonians, and Chaldeans, they were distinguished by this sign. After that no one was circumcised in the wilderness for forty years. They lived in isolation, without any intermixing with other nations.[425] As soon as the people crossed the bank of the Jordan and the multitude poured into the land of Judea in Palestine, a necessary circumcision provided against the future error of miscegenation with the Gentiles. But the fact that the people are recorded to

---

418. Jn 8.39.
419. Jn 12.44.
420. Mt 3.9.
421. Cf. Ezek 36.26.
422. Cf. Rom 4.11.
423. Cf. Rom 4.11.
424. Cf. Gn 12.3; 18.18.
425. Cf. Jos 5.5–6.

have been circumcised a second time by the leader Jesus[426] signifies both that circumcision had ceased in the wilderness, which was practiced in Egypt for good reason, and that believers must be cleansed by our Lord Jesus Christ through a spiritual circumcision.[427]

3.8–9.   *But the Scripture, foreseeing that God justifies the Gentiles by faith, announced in advance to Abraham that "All nations will be blessed in you."*[428] *Therefore, those who are of faith will be blessed with faithful Abraham.* It is not that the Scripture itself, that is, the ink and parchments (which are insensible), could know in advance what was coming, but that the Holy Spirit and the meaning that lies hidden in the letters predicted things that were coming after many ages.

Furthermore, the example that is taken from Genesis is found as follows in the original text: "And all nations of the earth will be blessed in your seed."[429] The apostle interprets this of Christ and says, "It is not written 'and to seeds,' as unto many, but as of one, 'and to your seed,' who is Christ."[430] But we need to pay attention to the fact that in nearly all the testimonies that are adopted into the New Testament from the old books, the evangelists or apostles trusted their memory. They often changed the order and expounded merely the sense. Sometimes they removed or added words. In fact, no one supposes that all the nations were blessed in Isaac and Jacob, or in the twelve patriarchs and the rest who descend from the stock of Abraham. Rather, it was in Christ Jesus through whom all the nations praise God and a new name is blessed on the earth. But the apostle can employ an example about "seed" from even another passage of Genesis, where it is written, "But God led him outside" (doubtless Abraham is intended) "and said to him: 'Look at the sky and count the stars, if you are able to count them'; and he said to him, 'So shall your seed be.' And Abraham believed God and it was

---

426. Heb. Joshua. Cf. Jos 5.2–3.
427. Cf. Rom 2.29; Col 2.11.
428. Gn 12.3.
429. Gn 12.3.
430. Gal 3.16.

reputed to him for justice."[431] Therefore, whoever believes "will be blessed with faithful Abraham," the one who on account of his outstanding faith in God is said to be the first to have *believed* in him. Similarly, Enosh is recorded to have *hoped* to call on the Lord God[432] on account of his fundamental hope in God which was eminent even among the others. It is not that Abel did not also hope to call on God, of whom the Lord says, "The voice of your brother's blood cries out to me,"[433] and the others from that point on; but that each one is named from that quality that he possesses especially much.

---

431. Gn 15.5–6.
432. Cf. Gn 4.26 in the Septuagint version; *CRm* 5.1.20.
433. Cf. Gn 4.10.

Commentary on

Galatians

BOOK TWO

Preface

It seems that now in the second book of the *Commentary on Galatians* I need to return to things I left untouched in the first book, when I was discussing the unique characteristics of the nations: Who are the Galatians? Where did they come from and migrate to? Did the land they now inhabit produce them as natives, or did it receive them as foreigners? Did they lose their language by intermarriage, or learn a new one and lose their own?

Marcus Varro,[1] a very careful investigator of all antiquities, and others who have imitated him have handed down many things about this nation that are worthy of remembrance. But because it is not our purpose to introduce heathen writers[2] into the temple of God, and

---

1. Marcus Terentius Varro (116–27 BC) was known as Rome's greatest scholar. Of his almost five hundred books, only fifty-five titles are known. He wrote on nearly every branch of inquiry: history, philosophy, music, medicine, architecture, literary history, religion, agriculture, and language. The achievements of the Augustans are scarcely conceivable without the foundation that Varro laid.

2. Lit. "uncircumcised men."

because, as I freely confess, it has now been many years since I stopped reading such things, let us record the words of our Lactantius.[3] In the third volume to Probus,[4] he has conjectured the following about this nation when he says:

> The ancient Gauls were named Galatians from the whiteness (*candore*) of complexion of their bodies. Also the Sibyl[5] calls them this. The poet wanted to indicate this when he said: "their milky-white necks are entwined with gold,"[6] though he could have said "bright" (*candida*). Surely the province of Galatia is derived from this, into which the Gauls once came and settled among the Greeks. This is why that region was named first Gaulo-Graecia, and afterwards Galatia.

It is not surprising that he should say this about the Galatians and record that the western peoples settled in the region of the east, having passed over such great stretches of land in between. For it is an established fact that throngs from the east and from Greece had reached the limits of the west. The Phocians founded Massilia[7] whom Varro says were trilingual, because they spoke Greek, Latin, and Gaulic. Colonists

---

3. Lactantius (260–330) was a well-known Christian apologist of the beginning of the fourth century. His most famous work was *The Divine Institutes*. Cf. *Vir Ill* 80. V. Loi, *EEC* 1.470, writes: "But despite the deficiencies of a theological thought which is neither acute nor systematic, despite the limits imposed on stylistic and linguistic originality by his deliberate imitation of Cicero, Lactantius has great importance in the history of Western literature and culture: he was the first Western writer who attempted a systematic exposition of Christian doctrine addressed to the cultivated classes of the Roman world."

4. In *Vir Ill* 80 Jerome reports that Lactantius wrote four books of epistles to Probus. They are not extant.

5. The name first used in Hellenistic Greek of an inspired prophetess, who was localized in several places, until its use became generic. Varro lists ten Sibyls. The most famous was the Sibyl of Cumae in Campania, who tells Aeneas in Aeneid 6 how to enter the Underworld.

6. Virgil, *Aeneid* 8.660–61.

7. A Greek colony on the southern coast of Gaul (modern Marseilles).

from Rhodes established the town of Rhoda from which the Rhone river took its name.[8] I pass over the founders of Carthage, the Tyrians,[9] and the city of Agenor.[10] I omit mention of Liber's[11] Thebes, which he founded in Africa. This city is now called Thebestis. I leave out that region of Lybia that is full of Greek cities. I pass over to Spain: Did not Greeks who had set out from the island of Zacynthus found Saguntum?[12] And is it not reported that Greek men from Ionia founded the town of Tartessos, which is now called Carteia?[13] Do not the Greeks point out the significations of the words for the mountains of Spain too, for Calpe, Hydria, Pyrene? Likewise for the islands of Aphrodite and Gymnasia, which are called Baleares? Italy itself, when she was occupied by Greek peoples, was once called Greater Greece. Of course it cannot be denied that the Romans were generated from the stock of an Asian man, Aeneas. From him it came to pass that even in the West, minds of Greek acumen may often be found, and in the East minds are redolent of barbaric stupidity. We do not say this to deny that diverse minds are born in both regions, but because the rest, who are not similar, are named from the majority. And so, it is not surprising that the Galatians have been called foolish and slow to understand, since even Hilary,[14] a man of the Rhone, himself a Gaul and a native of Poitiers, says in a poem found among his hymns that the Gauls are stupid.[15] It is true that they are now producing orators, but this has to do

---

8. Cf. Pliny the Elder, *Historia Naturalis* 3,4,5.33.

9. Cf. Virgil, *Aeneid* 1.20.

10. Agenor was a son of Belus, king of Phoenicia, father of Cadmus and Europa and ancestor of Dido. Hence the city of Agenor is Carthage; cf. Virgil, *Aeneid* 1.338.

11. An old Italian deity who presided over planting and fructification; afterwards identified with the Greek Bacchus.

12. A city on the east coast of Spain which Hannibal attacked, thus bringing on the First Punic War. Cf. Liv 21.7, 18; Juv 15.114

13. Cf. Pliny the Elder, *Historia Naturalis* 3,1,3.7.

14. St. Hilary, bishop of Poitiers (315–68), was a great opponent of Arianism. See *Vir Ill* 100.

15. This work is mentioned by Jerome in *Vir Ill* 100. Only three incomplete hymns of Hilary are extant.

not so much with the diligence of the region as with the clamor for rhetoric, especially since Aquitania boasts a Greek origin, and the Galatians did not originate from that part of the region but from the fiercer Gaulish tribes.[16]

Do you want to see, O Paula and Eustochium, how the apostle identifies each province by its own unique characteristics? Until the present day the same vestiges remain, whether of virtues or of errors. He praises the faith of the *Roman* people.[17] Where else do crowds frequent the churches and the tombs of its martyrs with such great zeal?[18] Where else does the Amen resound so loudly, like heavenly thunder, and shake the empty idol-temples? It is not that the Romans have a different faith than what all the churches of Christ have; but devotion is greater among them and the simplicity of their faith. On the other hand they are convicted of levity and arrogance; of levity in the following passage: "I ask you, brothers, to look out for those who cause dissensions and stumbling blocks contrary to the teaching which you have learned; turn away from them; for they are not serving our Lord Christ in this way, but their own belly, and through sweet words and blessings they seduce the hearts of the innocent. For your obedience has been spread abroad in every place; therefore I rejoice over you and I want you to be wise in the good and simple in respect to evil."[19] He accuses them of arrogance here: "Do not be high-minded but fear";[20] and, "I do

---

16. Lightfoot, *Epistle of St. Paul to the Galatians,* pp. 242–43 comments on this passage: "Though betraying the weakness common to all ancient writers when speculating on questions of philology, this passage taken in connection with its context implies a very considerable knowledge of facts; and if Jerome agreed with the universal tradition in assuming the Galatians to be genuine Gauls, I can hardly doubt that they were so."

17. Cf. Rom 1.8.

18. Jerome himself followed this practice of visiting the tombs of the martyrs while he was in Rome; cf. his *Commentariorum in Ezechielem libri XVI* 40.5 (PL 25.375).

19. Rom 16.17–19.

20. Rom 11.20.

not want you to be ignorant, brothers, of this mystery, that you not be wise in your own selves";[21] and in what follows, "For I say through the grace which was given to me to all who are among you: do not be wiser than is fitting, but be wise in moderation";[22] and more openly, "Rejoice with those who rejoice, weep with those who weep. Think the same thing mutually, and be not mindful of lofty things, but be in agreement with the lowly. Do not be prudent in your own selves."[23] He takes note of the *Corinthians* too, that their women have uncovered heads[24] and their men attend to their long hair[25] and they eat indifferently in temples[26] and, being puffed up in their secular wisdom,[27] they deny the resurrection of the flesh.[28] Anyone who visits Achaia cannot doubt that these things remain to some extent to the present day. The *Macedonians* are praised for their love, hospitality, and reception of the brethren. This is why he writes to them: "But concerning love of the brethren, we do not have need to write to you; for you yourselves have learned from God to love one another; for you are also doing this among all the brothers throughout Macedonia."[29] But they are rebuked because inactive men go around to homes expecting to eat someone else's food, while they desire to please everyone and run about here and there telling what everyone is doing. For this is what follows: "But we ask you, brethren, to abound all the more and strive to be quiet and mind your own business and work with your hands, as we commanded you, and that you live decently among those who are outside and do not long for anything from anyone."[30]

---

21. Rom 11.25.
22. Rom 12.3.
23. Rom 12.15–16.
24. Cf. 1 Cor 11.13.
25. Cf. 1 Cor 11.14.
26. Cf. 1 Cor 11.20–21.
27. Cf. 1 Cor 4.6, 18.
28. Cf. 1 Cor 15.12.
29. 1 Thes 4.9–10.
30. 1 Thes 4.10–12.

Lest anyone think this admonition is reflective of the duty of a teacher rather than a defect of the race, he drives it home and repeats it in the second letter when he says: "For when we were among you, we warned you that if anyone does not want to work, neither should he eat. For we hear there are some among you walking in a disorderly fashion. They are not working but are curiously meddling. Now we warn those who are like this, and we beseech them by the Lord Jesus Christ to work in silence and eat their own bread."[31] It would take too long if I were to take note of the virtues and vices of each of the nations from the apostle and from all the Scriptures, since from there we might have spun off to these very things that we have said, that the *Galatians* are declared to be foolish and senseless. Anyone who has seen by how many schisms the city of Ancyra, the metropolis of Galatia, is rent and torn, and by how many varieties of false doctrines the place has been violated, knows this as well as I do. I say nothing of Cataphrygians,[32] Ophites,[33] Borborites,[34] and Manichaeans;[35] for these are now familiar

---

31. 2 Thes 3.10–12.

32. This is another name of the Montanists, a sect named after Montanus, a native of Ardabau, a village in lower Phrygia, in the late second century (155–160). He originated a schism that spread far and wide and even won Tertullian for an adherent in 207. Montanus claimed to be a prophet and a mouthpiece of the Holy Spirit. Prisca and Maximilla were two of his female disciples who outdid him in prophesying. Both had been previously married and left their husbands. The sect initiated new fasts after Pentecost, to which Jerome alludes in his *Commentary on Matthew* 9.15. In his Ep. 55.3 to Marcella, Jerome summarizes the teachings of the Montanists and says that they keep three Lents in the year, as opposed to Catholics, who have one.

33. A Gnostic sect of the second century described by Clement of Alexandria, Origen, Hippolytus, and Epiphanius. The name derives from the Greek word for serpent, to whom the sect's adherents evidently paid honor for his opposition to the Creator God and for showing himself a friend of the human race by offering to teach our first parents knowledge. See DCB 4.80–88.

34. This is one of the names given to the Ophite Gnostics, derived by Epiphanius (*Panarion* 1.85A) from Βόρβορος, "mire," as expressing their unclean living. It may be coincidental that Clement of Alexandria, *Stromateis* 2, describes certain unworthy Nicolaitans as "sunk in the mire of vice," ἐν βορβόρῳ κακίας.

35. See under Gal 1.1, p. 56, n 46.

names of human woe. Who ever heard in any part of the Roman Empire of the Passaloryncitae,[36] and the Ascordrobi,[37] and the Artotyritae,[38] and other portents—I can hardly call them names. The traces of this ancient foolishness remain to this day.

One remark we must make, and so fulfill the promise with which I started. Besides Greek, which is spoken throughout the East, the Galatians use as their native tongue a language that is almost identical with that of the Treveri;[39] and if through contact with the Greek language they have acquired a few corruptions, it is a matter of no moment, since even the Africans have to some extent changed the Phoenician language, and Latin itself is daily undergoing changes because of differences of place and time. But now let us return to our theme.

The Second Book

3.10.   *For as many as are of the works of the law are under a curse. For it is written: "Cursed is everyone who does not remain in everything that is written in the book of the law to do them."*[40] I have this custom, that whenever the apostles take anything from the Old Testament

---

36. Epiphanius, *Panarion* 48.14, mentions them in his article on the Montanists. He derives their name from πάσσαλος and ῥύγχος and states that these people were so called because in prayer they put their forefinger on their nose, an expression of downcast humility. They are also referred to by Philaster, *Diversarum haereseon liber* 76.

37. Under the name *Ascodrugitae*, Philaster, *Diversarum haereseon liber* 75, describes a sect in Galatia who set up and "covered" an inflated wine-skin in their churches and danced wildly around it in Bacchanalian fashion, "like pagans dancing to father Liber." Epiphanius, *Panarion* 416, states that the *Tascodrugitae* was a name for either the Cataphrygians (Montanists) or the "Quintilliani," the Cataphrygians again under another title.

38. Philaster, *Diversarum haereseon liber* 75 names this group next to the *Ascodrugites*.

39. This is Lightfoot's correction of Jerome's *Treviri* (Treves); *Epistle of St. Paul to the Galatians*, p. 243.

40. Dt 27.26.

(*Instrumentum*), I consult the original books and carefully examine how they are written in their own passages.[41] And so, I have found in Deuteronomy this passage recorded as follows by the seventy translators: "Cursed is every man who does not remain in all the words of this law to do them; and all the people will say: 'So be it.'"[42] But in Aquila[43] it is recorded as follows: "Cursed is he who does not establish the words of this law to do them; and all the people will say: 'truly.'" Symmachus[44] has: "Cursed is he who does not fortify the words of this law to do them; and all the people will say: 'amen.'" Furthermore Theodotion[45] has translated as follows: "Cursed is he who does not stir up the words of this law to do them; and all the people will say 'amen.'" From this we understand that the apostle, as elsewhere, has recorded the sense of the testimony rather than the words. And we consider it uncertain whether the seventy interpreters have added "every man" and "in everything," or whether it was thus in the old Hebrew and subsequently deleted by the Jews. Now what makes me suspect the latter is that the apostle, a man skilled in Hebrew and very learned in the law,

---

41. Even in seemingly autobiographical first-person passages like this one, Jerome still appears to be translating and adapting Origen's original discussions. Bardy, "Jérôme," argued, for example, that Jerome took from Origen all of what he claimed to know firsthand from the Jews. J. Gribomont follows this judgment in Quasten, *Patrology*, 4 vols. (Allen, Tex.: Christian Classics, n.d.; repr. of Utrecht: Spectrum, 1964–66), 4.235.

42. Dt 27.26.

43. See above on 1.4–5.

44. Symmachus was the second-century Jewish translator of the Hebrew Bible into Greek, whose version occupied the fourth column of Origen's *Hexapla*. *HE* 6.16ff. states that he was an Ebionite, but Epiphanius says he was a Samaritan who became a Jewish proselyte.

45. Theodotion was the author of a Greek version of the Old Testament written in the reign of Commodus (180–92), probably at Ephesus. Irenaeus makes him a proselyte at Ephesus (*Adv Haer* 3.21.2); Jerome calls him an Ebionite (*Vir Ill* 54); Ephiphanius says he was a disciple of Marcion (*De mensis et ponderibus* 17). His version is of singular importance for the book of Daniel because it contains the deuterocanonical part of the book. Theodotion's version constitutes the sixth column of Origen's *Hexapla*.

would never have added the word "every" and "in everything," as if these words were necessary to his meaning in order to prove that "as many as are of the works of the law are under a curse," unless they were found in the Hebrew copies. Therefore, reading over the Hebrew copies of the Samaritans, I found the word *chol* written, which means "every" or "in everything." This harmonizes with the seventy translators. In vain, therefore, have the Jews suggested this, lest they should seem to be under a curse if they are not able to fulfill *everything* that is written. For writings that are older than the other nation also testify that it was recorded.

But because no one could fulfill the law and do everything that was commanded, the apostle testifies elsewhere, saying, "For what was impossible for the law, in that it was weakened through the flesh, God in sending his own Son, in the likeness of the flesh of sin, concerning sin condemned sin in the flesh."[46] But if this is true, then the question can be raised to us: Are then Moses, Isaiah, and the other prophets, who were under the "works of the law," "under a curse"? The one who reads what the apostle says will not be afraid of assenting to this: "For Christ redeemed us from the curse of the law, having become accursed for us."[47] He will respond that each of the saints became accursed for the people during his own time. Attributing this to just men as well will not seem at once to detract from the Savior, as if there were nothing excellent or unusual in his "having become accursed," since the others too became accursed for others. For none of those others, however much they became the very curse, liberated anyone from the curse, save only the Lord Jesus Christ, who by his own precious blood redeemed from the curse of the law both all of us and them (I mean Moses, Aaron, all the prophets, and the patriarchs). You should not suppose that this has been said by my own interpretation. The Scripture is witness that "Christ, by the grace of God," or, as it reads in some copies, "apart from God," "died for all."[48] But if [he died] for all, [he

---

46. Cf. Rom 8.3.

47. Gal 3.13.

48. Heb 2.9 has "tasted death for all" and the textual variant. Cf. 2 Cor 5.15, "died for all."

died] both for Moses and for all the prophets, none of whom was able to blot out the ancient handwriting that had been written against us and nail it to the cross.[49] "All have sinned and lack the glory of God."[50] Ecclesiastes also affirms this verdict: "There is no just man on earth who does good and does not sin."[51] Finally, a statement of the apostle lower down also shows manifestly that neither Moses nor any other illustrious man of old could be justified before God through the law. For he continues:

3.11–12. *But that in the law no one is justified with God is manifest, since "the just lives by faith."*[52] *But the law is not of faith but "he who does these things will live in them."*[53] From Habakuk the prophet he has taken the example by which it is proved that "the just lives by faith" and not by works. The seventy translators published it this way: "But the just lives by *my* faith." Aquila and Theodotion read: "But the just lives by *his* faith," that is, God's.

And so, one should consider that he did not say a *human being* or a *man* "lives by faith," lest he should provide an occasion for despising works of virtue. Rather, he says "the *just* lives by faith." Thus whoever was faithful and "will live through faith" could not come to "faith" or "live in these things" in any other way unless he has first been "just," and by the purity of his life has ascended to faith, as if by certain stages. Therefore, it is possible for someone to be "just," and yet not to "live," apart from "faith" in Christ. If someone becomes uneasy upon reading this, let him take up Paul's words in which he says concerning himself, "according to the justice which is in the law, without reproach."[54] Therefore, at that time Paul was "just" in the law, but he was not yet able to "live," because he did not have Christ speaking in him, "I am the

---

49. Cf. Col 2.14.
50. Rom 3.23.
51. Eccl 7.21.
52. Hab 2.4.
53. Lv 18.5.
54. Phil 3.6.

life."[55] It was by believing in him later that he began also "to live." Let us also do something similar to what is said, "the just lives by faith," and say, the chaste lives by faith, the wise lives by faith, the strong lives by faith. And let us bring forward a similar judgment in respect to the other virtues, in confrontation of those who, while not believing in Christ, suppose that they are strong and wise, temperate and just. They need to know that no one lives apart from Christ, without whom every virtue is a vice.[56]

The present testimony can also be read as follows: "since the just by faith," so that one introduces "lives" after that. But his words, "the law is not by faith, but he who does these things will live in them," demonstrate very clearly that he is not speaking of life in an unqualified sense but of "life" that is related to something. For "the just lives by faith," and it is not added "in these things" or "in those things." But of the one who lives in the law, it says, "he who does these things will live in these things"; that is, in those things which he has done, which he thought were goods, having a reward for his own effort only in the works that he performed. This would refer either to a long life (as the Jews think) or to the avoidance of the punishment for which the transgressor of the law is killed.

But let us not imagine that the words "live in these things" are the apostle's. On the contrary they come from Ezekiel the prophet, who says, "And I led them into the desert and gave them my precepts and I showed to them my justifications, which a man will do and will live in them."[57] When he had said that they will "live" if they walk in his precepts and justifications, he added, "And I gave them precepts [that were] not good and justifications in which they will not live in them."[58] How much there is to consider in these words! When he said, "I gave them precepts and justifications," in which they would have lived in them, he did not add "good"; but when he recorded, "in which they will

---

55. Jn 11.25; 14.6.
56. Cf. *CRm* 5.10.18.
57. Ezek 20.10–11.
58. Ezek 20.25.

not live in them," he added, "and I gave them precepts [that were] not good and justifications in which they will not live in them." But these things [are found] in more detail in Ezekiel; let us now return to the arrangement of the epistle.

3.13a.   *Christ redeemed us from the curse of the law, having become a curse for us.* On this passage Marcion sneaks in some things concerning the power of the Creator, whom he slanders as a blood-thirsty, cruel judge. He claims that we have been redeemed by Christ who is the son of another good God.[59] Had he understood the difference in meaning between "buy" and "redeem" (namely, that the one who "buys," buys what belongs to another, but the one who "redeems," buys precisely what was his own and stopped being his own), he would never have twisted the simple words of the Scriptures into the misrepresentation of his own doctrine. Therefore, "Christ redeemed us from the curse of the law," which was established for those who sin. He himself rebukes them through the prophet, saying, "Behold you have been sold for your sins, and for your iniquities I have dismissed your mother."[60] And the apostle reflects this very thing when he says, "But I am carnal, sold under sin."[61] The "curses" of the law as well, which are recorded in Leviticus and Deuteronomy, are not carried out with God as their author, but by the spirit of prophecy things that are coming are announced to those who were going to sin. But if he [Marcion] wants to press us by the testimony of the apostle when he says, "As many as are of the works of the law are under a curse. For it is written: 'Cursed is everyone who does not remain in all the things that are written in the book of the law, to do them'"; and if he asserts that all who were under the law were accursed, we should ask him whether those who are under the gospel of Christ and do not carry out his commands are cursed or not. If he says that they are cursed, he will have what we have

---

59. Harnack, *Der kirchengeschichtliche Ertrag,* p. 149, identifies this passage as most certainly deriving from Origen.

60. Is 50.1.

61. Rom 7.14.

in respect to the law; if he denies that they are cursed, then the commands of the gospel are recorded in vain, and those who fulfill them will be without reward.[62] And so, both [curses] are resolved in this manner: just as Christ Jesus freed us from the "curse of the law," by "having been made a curse for us," so too he rescued us from the curse of the gospel, which is appointed over those who do not carry out his commands, by "having himself become a curse for us" and by knowing not to forgive the least portion of a talent[63] and to exact the very last penny.[64]

3.13b–14. *For it is written: "Cursed is everyone who hangs on a tree,"*[65] *so that the blessing of Abraham might come on the Gentiles in Christ Jesus, that we may receive the promise of the Spirit through faith.* Before we discuss the apostle's meaning and words, it seems right to reflect on the testimony from Deuteronomy from which the apostle has taken these few things and to compare it with the other versions. Well then, the seventy translators rendered this passage as follows: "But if there be sin in any one (*aliquo*), the judgment of death, and he is killed, and you hang him on a tree, his body shall not sleep upon the tree, but you will by all means bury him on that day, for everyone that hangs on a tree is cursed *by God;* and you will not defile your land (*terra*) which

---

62. Reward is a major emphasis in the theology of St. Jerome, as it is in Origen's anti-Marcionite theology. J. P. O'Connell, in *The Eschatology of Saint Jerome*, 102–18, has identified the unifying thought of Jerome's teaching on heaven to be the idea of reward. He notes the significant fact that Jerome never presents the beatific vision of God (cf. 1 Cor 13.12) as the cause of heavenly happiness. Jerome seems to have considered this vision, which is so fundamental to Augustine's conception of heaven, and subsequently to that of Thomas Aquinas, as one of the less important elements of the heavenly life. Jerome's concept of heavenly life is intimately linked to his concept of the Christian's earthly life. Jerome recognizes that the theme of God's rewarding and punishing according to one's deserts is a major emphasis in the proclamation of Jesus.

63. Cf. Mt 25.28.
64. Cf. Mt 5.26.
65. Dt 21.23.
66. Dt 21.22–23.

the Lord your God will give you for an inheritance."[66] Aquila has: "And
when there is sin in a man (*vir*), the judgment of death, and he is killed
and you hang him on a tree, he will not linger on the tree for the car-
rion, but you will by all means bury him on that day, because he who
has been hanged is a curse *of God;* and you will not defile your soil
(*humus*) which the Lord your God will give you for an inheritance."
Symmachus has: "But if there is sin in a man (*homo*) leading to the
judgment of death and he is killed and you hang him on a tree, his
corpse will not spend the night on the tree, but you will bury him with
a burial on that day, because he has been hanged on account of blasphemy *of God;* and you will not defile your land (*terra*) which the Lord
your God will give you for an inheritance." Theodotion has: "And since
there will be sin in a man (*vir*), the judgment of death, and he will die
and you hang him on a tree, he will not sleep on the tree for his car-
rion, for you will bury him with a burial on that day, because the one
hanged is a curse *of God;* and you will not defile your earth (*adama*)
which the Lord your God gave you as an inheritance." Moreover, in
the Hebrew language the earth (*terra*) or soil (*humus*) is called *adama*.
But in that passage where Aquila and Theodotion have translated similarly and said, "for the one hanged is a curse *of God*," in Hebrew it is
recorded as follows: *chi klalat eloim talui.* Ebion, that half-Christian,
half-Jewish heresiarch, translated these words thus: ὅτι ὕβρις θεοῦ
κρεμάμενος, that is, "he who is hanged is an affront of God." I recall
having found in the *Debate of Jason and Papiscus,*[67] which is recorded
in the Greek language, the following: λοιδορία θεοῦ ὁ κρεμάμεος, that

---

67. Harnack, *Der kirchengeschichtliche Ertrag,* p. 149, cites this passage as most
certainly deriving from Origen, since Celsus and Origen are the only Easterners to
know about this obscure ancient dialogue. Aristo of Pella (who is mentioned in *HE*
4.6) is the supposed author of this dialogue between Jason (a Christian) and Papiscus (a Jew). The dialogue was known to Celsus, whose mockeries of it are criticized by Origen, *Contra Celsum* 4.52. It was referred to by John of Scythopolis (sixth
century), in a passage preserved in the scholia on *The Mystical Theology* of Dionysius the Areopagite attributed to Maximus the Confessor. Cf. DCB 1.160–61; Eusebius, *The History of the Church,* trans. G. Williamson, glossary, p. 348. Jerome
mentions it here and in *Quaestionum hebraicarum liber in Genesim.*

is, "he who has been hanged is a curse of God." The Hebrew who instructed me in some measure in the Scriptures told me that it could also be read as follows: "God has been outrageously hanged."

The reason we have compiled these things is because of a very well-known problem. In order to slander us, the Jews customarily raise the objection that our Lord and Savior was under *God's* curse. In the first place, then, one should consider that it is not whoever hangs on a tree that is accursed by God, but the one who sins and on account of a wicked deed is condemned to death and taken away to the cross. He is not accursed because he has been crucified but because he fell into the kind of guilt that merited crucifixion. In the second place, the following should be said in reply: that the lesser reason for the gallows may be explained more fully when the Scripture relates that he was crucified on account of cursing and blaspheming God. Symmachus has translated this very clearly when he says, "Because on account of blasphemy of God he has been hanged." In the last place, let us ask them this. Suppose Ananias, Azarias, and Mishael had been "hanged on a tree" for refusing to worship the idol of Nabuchodonosor;[68] or even the ninety-year-old Eleazar during the reign of Antiochus the Syrian;[69] or the glorious mother with her seven sons.[70] Would they be reckoned as accursed or as completely worthy of every blessing? Surely if Mordecai himself had mounted the unmerited cross that Haman had prepared for him,[71] Mordecai would have ascended it, I think, not as an accursed man but as a saint. And along with these other similar cases it is proven that one is accursed who has committed a crime worthy of the gallows, not one who was crucified by the wickedness of his judges, by the power of his enemies, or by the outcry of the mob,[72] envy of his virtues,[73] or

68. Cf. Dn 3.16–18.
69. Cf. 2 Mc 6.18–31.
70. Cf. 2 Mc 7.
71. Cf. Est 7.9–10.
72. Cf. Lk 23.23.
73. Cf. Mt 27.18.

the wrath of a king.[74] The whole city of Jezreel once condemned Naboth to death in accordance with Jezebel's letter.[75] But many generations later this man's blood is vindicated as a type of Christ, when the Lord says to Hosea, "Call his name Jezreel, for yet a little while and I will avenge the blood of Jezreel on the house of Jehu."[76] This is directed against the Jews.

However that may be, let the discussion come back to us. I cannot determine why the apostle has either subtracted or added something, in respect to what is written: "Cursed *by God* is everyone who hangs on a tree."[77] For if he once and for all followed the authority of the seventy translators, he should have attached the name "of God," just as they published it. But if, as a Hebrew of Hebrews,[78] he supposed that what he had read in his own language was the truest, he should not have adopted the words "all" or "on a tree," which are not found in the Hebrew. Therefore, it appears to me either that the ancient Hebrew books read differently than they do now, or that the apostle, as I have already said previously, recorded the sense, not the words, of the Scriptures. Or we must instead suppose that after the passion of Christ, both in the Hebrew manuscripts and in our own, the name "of God" was added by someone in order to introduce grounds for slandering us, who believe in a Christ who was cursed *by God*. And so, I proceed to this contest with a reckless pace. I appeal to the manuscripts, that in no passage is it written that anyone was cursed "by God"; and wherever the word "curse" is recorded, the name "of God" is never added. It is said to the serpent, "Cursed are you from all the beasts";[79] and to Adam, "Cursed is the land in your works";[80] and to Cain, "Cursed are you on the earth";[81] and elsewhere, "Cursed is Canaan, he will be a slave boy to his

---

74. Cf. Dn 3.19.
75. Cf. 1 Kgs 21.8–22.
76. Hos 1.4.
77. Dt 21.23.
78. Cf. Phil 3.5.
79. Gn 3.14.
80. Gn 3.17.
81. Gn 4.11.

brothers."[82] And besides these passages, in another passage it says: "Cursed is their fury, because it is reckless; and their anger, because it is cruel."[83] It would take too long to list all the curses that are recorded in Leviticus, Deuteronomy, and Joshua son of Nun; and yet in none of them is the name "of God" added. So much so is this the case that when Satan himself promised that Job would blaspheme, once he had been overwhelmed by huge difficulties, he signified this by a more favorable sense, saying, "if he does not *bless* you to your face."[84] And in the books of kingdoms Naboth is said to have been stoned because he *blessed* God and the king.[85]

Now no one should be disturbed by the fact that "Christ became a curse for us,"[86] since even God himself, who is said to have made him the curse, made him sin for us, though Christ did not know sin.[87] And the Savior emptied himself of the fullness of the Father, taking the form of a slave.[88] "The life"[89] died, and the "wisdom of God"[90] was called stupid, so that what was God's foolishness might become wiser with men.[91] And in the sixty-eighth Psalm he says of himself, "God, you know my foolishness, and my transgressions are not hidden from you."[92] And so, the Lord's affront is our glory;[93] he died that we might live;[94] he descended to the underworld that we might ascend to heaven;[95] he

---

82. Gn 9.25.
83. Gn 49.7.
84. Job 1.11.
85. Cf. 1 Kgs 21.13.
86. Gal 3.13.
87. Cf. 2 Cor 5.21.
88. Cf. Phil 2.7.
89. Cf. Jn 14.6.
90. Cf. 1 Cor 1.24.
91. Cf. 1 Cor 1.25.
92. Ps 69.5.
93. Cf. Gal 6.14.
94. Cf. 2 Cor 5.15.
95. Cf. Eph 4.9–10. For Jerome, Christ descended into hell in soul only while his body remained in the tomb. He did so as a victor, in contrast to all others who had gone there vanquished. His purpose was to free the souls of the saints held there

became foolishness that we might become wisdom;[96] he emptied himself of the fullness and form of God, taking the form of a slave,[97] that the fullness of divinity might dwell in us,[98] and that we might become lords from being slaves.[99] He was hung on a tree[100] in order to blot out the sin that we had committed,[101] having been suspended on the tree of knowledge of good and evil.[102] His cross has turned bitter waters sweet to the taste.[103] He has raised the lost axe that was submerged in the depths[104] upon the released floodwaters of the Jordan.[105]

Finally, he "became a curse": *became,* I say, not *was born.* Thus the blessings that had been promised to Abraham himself, the source and leader, were transferred to the Gentiles, and the "promise of the Spirit" that came through that man's faith was fulfilled in us. We should interpret this promise in a twofold way, either in the spiritual gifts of the virtues[106] or in the spiritual understanding of the Scriptures.[107]

3.15–18.   *Brothers, I speak according to man: yet no one despises or adds to*[108] *a man's testament that has been confirmed. The promises were*

---

by the bonds of sins. See: *Commentariorum in Osee libri III* 13.14 (PL 25.937); *Tractatus in Psalmos* 15, 107, 87; *Commentariorum in Epistulam ad Ephesios libri III* 4.9; Ep. 60.3. For a discussion, see O'Connell, *The Eschatology of St. Jerome,* pp. 134–38. For a nice dossier of early patristic discussions of Christ's descent into hell, see J. Wicks, "Christ's Saving Descent to the Dead: Early Witnesses from Ignatius of Antioch to Origen," *Pro Ecclesia* 17.3 (2008), pp. 281–309.

96. Cf. 1 Cor 1.30.
97. Cf. Phil 2.6–7.
98. Cf. Col 2.9–10.
99. Cf. Jn 15.14–15.
100. Cf. Acts 5.30; 10.39.
101. Cf. 1 Pt 2.24.
102. Cf. Gn 2.9; 3.1–7.
103. Cf. Ex 15.22–25.
104. Cf. 2 Kgs 6.1–7.
105. Cf. Jos 4.19.
106. Cf. 1 Cor 12.7–11.
107. Cf. Col 1.9.
108. *Superordino* is also found in Tertullian, *Adversus Marcionem* 5.4.

spoken to Abraham and to his seed.[109] *He does not say: "and to seeds," as of many, but as of one: "and to your seed," which is Christ. But I say this: a testament confirmed by God is not nullified by the law that came four hundred and thirty years later, to make the promise of no effect. For if the inheritance is of the law, it is no longer of the promise. But God gave [it] to Abraham by a promise.* The apostle, who "became all things to all men" in order to "gain them all,"[110] who became a debtor to the Greeks and barbarians, to the wise and the foolish,[111] has also become a fool to the Galatians, whom a little while before he had called fools.[112] For with them he does not employ the arguments that he used with the Romans, but more frank ones, practically street talk, arguments that even fools could understand. Lest it should seem that he has done this by inexperience rather than by craft, he first appeases the prudent reader and qualifies what he is about to say with prefatory remarks: "Brothers, I speak according to man." For what I am about to say I say not according to God; I do not speak in accordance with the "hidden wisdom"[113] and with those who can eat "solid food,"[114] but in accordance with those who feed on drops of milk because of the sensitivity of their stomachs.[115] By no means can they hear the great things. This is why he even says to the Corinthians,[116] among whom there was rumor of fornication, and such kind of fornication that is not even among the Gentiles: "I say and not the Lord."[117] And to the same persons he says in the second letter, "What I am speaking, I do not say according to the Lord, but as it were in foolishness."[118]

---

109. Cf. Gn 12.7.
110. Cf. 1 Cor 9.22.
111. Cf. Rom 1.14.
112. Cf. Gal 3.3.
113. Cf. 1 Cor 2.7.
114. Cf. 1 Cor 3.2; Heb 5.12–14.
115. Cf. 1 Tm 5.23.
116. Cf. 1 Cor 5.1.
117. 1 Cor 7.12.
118. 2 Cor 11.17.

Some think that since he was about to discuss a man's testament, the death of the testator, and the other examples of human comparison, he said, "Brothers, I speak *according to man.*" But to me it seems that he uses this expression both for that reason, to be sure, which they think, but chiefly it has been said in anticipation in view of what follows, namely, "he does not say 'and to seeds' as if to many, but as if unto one 'and to your seed,' who is Christ." When I run with my mind and memory through all the Scriptures, I have nowhere found "seeds" written in the plural, but always in the singular, whether it is used in a good or bad sense. And besides this, consider what he further introduces: "but I say this, a testament confirmed by God." If anyone carefully compares the Hebrew volumes and the other versions with the translation of the seventy translators, he will find that where "testament" is written, what is meant is not "testament" but "covenant," which is expressed in the Hebrew language by the word *berith.* Whence it is clear that the apostle has done what he promised. He has not used hidden meanings among the Galatians, but everyday and common ones, which might have displeased the prudent, had he not said beforehand, "I am speaking *according to man.*"

It is no easy matter for the one who does the addition to determine whether the years referred to in this passage come out to "four hundred thirty," from the time when the Lord spoke to Abraham, saying, "And in your seed all nations will be blessed,"[119] to the lawgiver Moses; or, as the Lord in Genesis promises to Abraham himself, that after *four hundred years* his sons will come out of the land of slavery.[120] Although this has been investigated by many, I do not know whether the answer has been found. Likewise I do not know whether what is read in the same book agrees with the present passage, namely the story about Tamar and her two infants (the first, called Zerah, put out his hand, and the midwife tied a scarlet thread on it and then it drew back its hand inside; and afterward the one called Perez stretched forth).[121] For Israel shows

---

119. Gn 22.18.
120. Cf. Gn 15.16.
121. Cf. Gn 38.27–30.

its *hand* in the work of the law and *withdraws* it, when it has been polluted by the blood of the prophets and of the Savior himself. But afterward the people of the Gentiles break forth. For their sake the fence
and the dividing wall that stood between the Jews and the Gentiles is
said to be destroyed.[122] It is demolished so that there may be one flock
and one shepherd,[123] and so that there may be glory and honor and
peace for everyone working the good, for the Jew first and for the
Greek.[124] Now the simple meaning that is woven into this passage has
the following force. The apostle is showing that the promises that were
previously made to Abraham cannot be destroyed by the law, which
was given later, and the later things cannot prejudge the former things.
For the promises to Abraham were given four hundred thirty years
earlier, that all nations would be blessed in him, but the observance of
the law, which the one who had done it would live in those things,[125]
was given to Moses on Mount Sinai[126] four hundred thirty years later.

But on the other hand it could be said here: What then was the
need for the law to be given such a long time after the promise? For
once the law was given, a suspicion could arise that the promise had
been destroyed; and while the promise remains, a law has been given
that will not be beneficial.

Foreseeing this question, the apostle himself proposes it to himself
in what follows and explains it when he says:

3.19–20.   *What then? The law was laid down on account of transgressions, until the seed should come to whom it had been promised, ordained through angels by the hand of a mediator. But the mediator is
not of one, but God is one.* Because the law that was given later through
Moses seemed to have been published in vain, while the promise that
had been made to Abraham remains, he explains why it was given and

---

122. Cf. Eph 2.14.
123. Cf. Jn 10.16.
124. Cf. Rom 2.10.
125. Cf. Ezek 20.21.
126. Cf. Ex 34.

says, "on account of transgressions." For after the offense of the people in the desert, after the worship of the calf[127] and the murmuring against the Lord,[128] the law came in to prohibit "transgressions." "For the law is not laid down for the just, but for the unjust and insubordinate, for the impious and sinners."[129] And, that I might reflect more deeply on this, [it was laid down] after the idolatry to which they had been transferred in Egypt so that they forgot the God of their fathers and said, "These are your gods, Israel, who led you forth from the land of Egypt."[130] The rite for worshiping God and the penalty for transgressors was sanctioned "by the hand of a mediator," Christ Jesus. For "all things were made *through* him and without him nothing was made,"[131] not merely the heaven, earth, sea, and everything we perceive, but also those matters of the law which were imposed like a yoke through Moses upon the hardened people. It is also written to Timothy, "For there is one God and one mediator of God and men, the man Christ Jesus."[132] Later, for the sake of our salvation he deigned to be born from the virgin's womb. Christ Jesus is called a trustee of God and a man of men. But before he assumed a human body and was God the Word with the Father in the beginning,[133] he is called merely a "mediator," without the addition "of man," which he had not yet assumed, to all the saints to whom the word of God came (namely to Enoch, Noah, Abraham, Isaac, and Jacob, and later to Moses and all the prophets whom Scripture mentions).

But consider what he says, "the law ordained through angels." This should be understood to mean that in the entire Old Testament, where an angel is first reported to be seen, and afterward an angel is brought in, as if God is speaking, it is truly one of his many attendants, which-

---

127. Cf. Ex 32.
128. Cf. Ex 15.24; 16.2; 17.3; Nm 14.2.
129. 1 Tm 1.9.
130. Ex 32.4.
131. Jn 1.3.
132. 1 Tm 2.5.
133. Cf. Jn 1.1–2.

ever one is seen. But with regard to him, the mediator speaks who says, "I am the God of Abraham, the God of Isaac, and the God of Jacob."[134] It is not surprising that God speaks in "angels," since the Lord also speaks in the prophets through the angels who are in men, as Haggai says, "And the angel who spoke in me says."[135] And then he says, "Thus says the Lord Almighty."[136] For the angel who had been said to be in the prophet did not dare to say under his own persona, "Thus says the Lord Almighty." We should interpret "hand of a mediator" of the power and virtue of him who, though according to God is himself one with the Father, but according to the office of mediator, he is understood to be different from him.

But because the order of the reading is confused and is disturbed by a hyperbaton,[137] we apparently need to render it in this way: "The law was laid down through angels by the hand of a mediator, on account of transgressions, ordained through angels, until the seed should come to whom the promise was made." It is hardly doubtful that the "seed" signifies Christ. He is shown to be the son of Abraham from the beginning of Matthew too, when the Scripture records, "The book of the generation of Jesus Christ, the son of David, the son of Abraham."[138]

3.21–23.   *Was the law, then, against the promises of God? Certainly not. For if a law had been given that could give life, truly justice would be from the law; but Scripture has shut up everything under sin that the promise from faith in Jesus Christ would be given to those who believe. But before faith came we were kept under the law, shut up in that faith that was to be revealed.* Just as the mediator of God and men was in the

---

134. Ex 3.6.

135. Hg 2.14 (Septuagint).

136. Hg 2.14 (Septuagint).

137. A confusion of the order of the words. See Quintilian, *Training of an Orator* 8.6.62–7; 9.3.91. Origen points out Pauline *hyperbata* in *CRm* 1.13.1 and 6.7.6.

138. Mt 1.1.

middle between the one giving and the one receiving the law, so the law itself, which was given after the promise, snuck in between the promise and its fulfillment. It must not be supposed that it excludes the promise, since having followed later it seems to abolish what was former; but from the fact that it was unable "to give life" and to bestow what the first promise pledged, it is plain that it was given to guard, not subvert, the pledge of the promise. "For if a law were given that could" offer life and exhibit what the promised had pledged, "truly the promise" would be thought to be excluded through the law. But now, having been "laid down" instead "on account of transgressions," as we said above, it convicts those sinners to whom it was given after the promise, who were under guard and, so to speak, in prison. Thus since they were unwilling through freedom of choice to wait innocently for the promise, they were shackled by legal chains and reduced to slavery to the commandments. They are guarded until the advent of the faith that was coming in Christ that brought the end of the promise.

But one must not suppose that "Scripture" is responsible for sin, since it is said to have "shut up all things under sin."[139] For the command, which is prescribed by right, points out and exposes sin rather than is the cause of sin. In the same way a judge is not the author of crime because he locks up bad men; but he shuts them up and indicts those who do harm, by the authority of his own verdict, so that afterward an imperial pardon may absolve those who are resigned to punishment, if he wills.[140]

3.24–26.   *And so the law was our pedagogue in Christ Jesus so that we might be justified by faith. But when faith came, we are no longer under*

---

139. Gal 3.22.

140. This passage resembles *Adversus Jovinianum* 2.32. O'Connell, *The Eschatology of St. Jerome*, p. 130, explains the latter passage as follows: "Here all that seems to be common to all the saints is the opportunity to win a place in heaven. However, the passage was written in the heat of controversy when Jerome was not careful of his expression. Moreover, it is figurative, and it would be unfair to Jerome to push his figures to their ultimate implications." It seems doubtful, however, whether O'Connell's clarification can be applied to the present text.

a pedagogue. For you are all sons of God through the faith which is in Christ Jesus. A "pedagogue" is assigned to small children to rein in an age full of passion and to restrain hearts prone to vice while tender youth is being instructed by studies and prepared for the more important disciplines of philosophy and government, coerced by the fear of punishment. Yet the "pedagogue" is not a teacher and father, and the one who is instructed does not expect the inheritance and knowledge of the "pedagogue." Instead the "pedagogue" guards another person's son. He will take leave of him when the son arrives at the lawful time for receiving the inheritance.[141] After all, even the name "pedagogue"[142] denotes this exact thing and is composed from the fact that he "leads boys," that is, he escorts them. And thus also the law of Moses was appointed for a lascivious people as a very severe "pedagogue" to guard them and prepare them for the coming faith. After faith "came" and we believed in Christ, "we are no longer under a pedagogue": the tutor and guardian leaves us. And upon entering the legal age of life, we are truly named "sons of God," for whom it is not the abolished law that gives us birth, but our mother is "faith which is in Christ Jesus."[143]

But if someone wants to be "under the pedagogue" after this period of his life has been completed, when he is already named heir and free and a son, he should know that he cannot live by the laws of childhood. For when can the following now be fulfilled: "Three times a year every male will appear in the presence of the Lord your God"?[144] For Jerusalem has been overthrown and the temple has been demolished and turned to ashes. Where are the saving sacrifices for sin? Where is the perpetual fire of the burnt offerings[145] in the image of stars of heaven, seeing that the altar has been completely destroyed? Indeed what penalty can be decreed against the guilty, since the Scripture says, "You shall remove the wicked from your midst,"[146] seeing that the Jews

---

141. Cf. *CRm* 3.11.4.
142. Παιδαγωγός = παιδὸς ἀγωγός, a boy-ward.
143. Cf. Jn 1.12
144. Ex 23.17. Cf. *CRm* 6.7.11.
145. Cf. Lv 6.12.
146. Dt 13.5.

are slaves and the Romans are in charge? And thus it will be that while one lives neither under a father nor "under a pedagogue," even the law cannot be fulfilled after the succession of faith. And faith is not grasped, so long as the law is sought after by means of a pedagogue.[147]

3.27–28.   *For as many of you who have been baptized in Christ have put on Christ. There is neither Jew nor Greek; there is neither slave nor free; there is neither male nor female. For you are all one in Christ Jesus.* He shows how we are born "sons of God through faith which is in Christ Jesus" when he says, "for as many of you who have been baptized in Christ have put on Christ." Christ is proven to be a garment not only from the present passage but also from another when the same Paul exhorts, "Put on the Lord Jesus Christ."[148] If, therefore, those "who have been baptized in Christ" have "put on Christ," it is obvious that those who have not put on Christ have not been baptized in Christ. For to those who were thought to be faithful and to have achieved the baptism of Christ, it is said, "Put on the Lord Jesus Christ."[149] If someone has received only this bodily washing in water and what is seen by the eyes of the flesh, he has not "put on the Lord Jesus Christ." For even that man Simon of the Acts of the Apostles had received the washing in water,[150] but because he did not have the Holy Spirit, he had not "put on Christ." Moreover, the heretics, or hypocrites, and those who live filthy lives appear to receive baptism, but I do not know whether they have Christ as their garment. And so, let us consider whether perhaps even among us someone may be discovered who, in view of the fact that he does not have Christ as his garment, is exposed as not having been baptized in Christ.[151]

---

147. Compare Origen's very similar interpretation of "pedagogue" in *CRm* 3.11.4–5.

148. Rom 13.14.

149. Rom 13.4.

150. Cf. Acts 8.13.

151. Compare *CRm* 5.8.2: "[I]f someone has first died to sin, he has necessarily been buried with Christ in baptism. But if the person does not die to sin beforehand, he cannot be buried with Christ. For no one who is still alive is ever buried. But if one is not buried with Christ, he is not validly baptized."

But when someone has once and for all put on Christ, and having been cast into the fire,[152] glows with the ardor of the Holy Spirit, it is not understood whether he is gold or silver. As long as the heat takes over the mass, there is one fiery color, and all diversity of race, condition, and body is taken away by such a garment. For "there is neither Jew nor Greek." For "Greek" we should understand Gentile; since ῞Ελλην signifies both Greek and pagan. That is why the "Jew" is not better off because he is circumcised, and the Gentile is not inferior because he is uncircumcised. Instead, a "Jew" or "Greek" is better or worse in view of the quality of his faith. Also, "slave" and "free" are not separated by this condition, but by faith, because a "slave" can be better than a "free" and a "free" can outstrip the "slave" by the quality of his faith. Likewise, however much "male" and "female" may be separated by the strength and weakness of their bodies, faith is assessed in view of the devotion of one's mind, and it often happens that the woman becomes the cause of salvation for the man,[153] and the man excels the woman in religious devotion.

Now since this is the reality and the entire distinction between race, condition, and body is removed by Christ's baptism and being clothed in him, then "we are all one in Christ Jesus." Thus just as Father and Son are one in themselves,[154] so also we are one in them.[155]

3.29. *But if you are Christ's, then you are Abraham's seed, heirs according to the promise.* Since the promises were made to Abraham and to his seed, which is Christ Jesus,[156] consequently those who are Christ's sons, that is, his seed, are also called seed of Abraham. They are his (Abraham's) seed from the seed. But whenever our Lord Jesus Christ is called Abraham's seed, this must be understood in the bodily sense of his generation from the stock of Abraham. But whenever it is applied to us who, by receiving the Savior's word, believe in him and

---

152. Cf. Dn 3.23; Mt 3.11; Mk 9.22; Lk 12.49; 1 Cor 3.13.
153. Cf. 1 Cor 7.16; 1 Pt 3.1.
154. Cf. Jn 10.30; 17.11.
155. Cf. Jn 17.11, 21.
156. Cf. Gal 3.16.

assume the dignity of Abraham's race, to whom the promise was made, then we should understand "seed" spiritually, as that of faith and preaching.

Next, we must also consider that, when he speaks about the Lord, he records "promises" in the plural: "but the *promises* were made to Abraham and to his seed,"[157] that is, to Christ Jesus. But when he speaks of those who through Christ are the "seed" of Abraham, "promise" is referred to in the singular, as in the present passage: "so then you are Abraham's seed, heirs according to the promise." For it was befitting that what was spoken in the plural in respect to the one Christ should be recorded in the singular in respect to many men. It follows:

4.1–2.   *Now I say: For as long a time as the heir is a child, he does not differ from a slave, though he is lord of all, but he is under tutors and governors until the time pre-appointed by the father.* This "heir," the "child who does not differ from a slave, though he is lord of all," but is even "under tutors and governors until the time pre-appointed by the father" signifies the whole human race until the coming of Christ, and to speak more broadly, until the consummation of the world.[158] For just as all not yet born die in the first-formed[159] Adam, so all, even those who were born before Christ's advent are made alive in the second Adam.[160] And thus it is that we served the law in the fathers and they are saved by grace in the sons. This understanding agrees with the Catholic Church, which maintains a single providence in the Old and New Testament and does not distinguish in time those whom it has associated by condition. We are all built upon the foundation of the apostles and prophets,[161] with our Lord Jesus Christ the cornerstone holding us together. He made the two one by destroying the middle wall of enmity between the two peoples.[162] He destroyed it in his own

---

157. Gal 3.15.
158. Cf. Mt 28.20.
159. Cf. Wis 10.1.
160. Cf. 1 Cor 15.22.
161. Cf. Eph 2.20.
162. Cf. Eph 2.14.

flesh and changed the difficulty of the ancient law by the soundness of the doctrines of the gospels. Truly we are all one loaf in Christ,[163] and the two agree on earth.[164] And just as we are founded upon the prophets, so too the patriarchs were established on the foundation of the apostles.

Now "tutors and governors" could be taken to refer to the prophets. By their words we have been educated daily in the coming of the Savior, just as the law of Moses is described above as a pedagogue. Also they could refer to the angels of children who daily see the face of the Father[165] and who intercede for them.[166] Of them it is said, "The angel of the Lord will encircle those who fear him and will rescue them."[167] Rightly are they said to be "under tutors and governors," who have the spirit of fear and have not yet merited receiving the Spirit of freedom and adoption.[168] For the age of infancy dreads sins, it fears the pedagogue and does not believe in its own freedom, even though it is "lord" by nature. And in accordance with both understandings, whereby we said that "tutors and governors" are either prophets or angels, that one is a child for as long a time as he is under "governors and tutors," until he has fulfilled the lawful time of the perfect man.[169]

Now the lawful time is terminated within the space of twenty-five years, just as it is in Roman law. Thus is the coming of Christ reputed for the perfection of the human race. As soon as he comes and we all grow into a perfect man, the pedagogue and tutor leave us. Then we enjoy the authority of the Lord and the possession of the inheritance in which, though we were born first, in some way we were thought to be aliens.

---

163. Cf. 1 Cor 10.17.
164. Cf. Mt 18.19.
165. Cf. Mt 18.10.
166. Cf. Tob 12.15.
167. Cf. Ps 34.7.
168. Cf. Rom 8.15.
169. Cf. Eph 4.13.

4.3.   *So we also, when we were children, were serving under the elements of this world.* He has used the term "elements of the world" to designate the same ones whom he called "tutors and governors" above.[170] For at first we were constituted under these very guardians. Incapable of receiving the coming of the Son of God to us, we were being educated in the world. Some hold that these are angels who preside over the four elements of the world (namely, earth, water, fire, and air). They say that before someone believes in Christ, he is necessarily governed by those mediators. Many think that it is the heaven and earth and the things that are within them that are called the "elements of the world," namely, because the wise men of Greece, the barbarian nations, and the Romans, the dregs of all superstition, worship the sun, the moon, the seas, and the gods of the forests and mountains. We are liberated from these by Christ's coming and understand them to be creatures, not divinities.

Others interpret the "elements of the world" as the law of Moses and the utterances of the prophets, because, by them, as it were by the beginning and the ABCs, we receive the fear of God, which is the beginning of wisdom.[171] After all, in the Epistle to the Hebrews the apostle writes the following to those who already should have been perfect but who neglected the truth and were still cleaving to the elementary instruction: "For indeed, although you ought to be teachers on account of the time, you have need again to be taught the elements of the beginning of the words of God."[172] On the other hand, what the apostle Paul writes to the Colossians could be cited as an objection to us. He names another kind of "elements of the world" and says, "See to it that no one takes you captive through philosophy and vain deceit according to the tradition of men, according to the *elements of the world* and not according to Christ."[173] But in what he added, "according to the tradition of men" and "vain deceit," he shows that he is not speaking of the same

---

170. Cf. *CRm* 7.2.1; 7.5.3.
171. Cf. Prv 1.7.
172. Heb 5.12.
173. Col 2.8.

"elements" to the Colossians and to the Galatians. For from the latter "elements" we are redeemed after the fullness of time comes. And advancing to greater things, we receive the adoption of sons.[174] But from the former elements nothing like that is said to follow. Instead the elements are simply understood for letters. Therefore, as we said, the law of Moses and the prophets can be taken as the elements of writing because, through them, syllables and names are joined together. They are learned not so much for their own sake as for their usefulness to others in order that we can read a composed speech in which we consider more the sense and the order of words than the elements of the letters.

But with respect to our interpretation of the "elements of the world" as the law and the prophets, "world" is customarily taken to signify those who are in the world. For the same Paul says, "God was in Christ reconciling the world to himself."[175] And in the Gospel it says, "And the world was made through him and the world did not receive him."[176] Some wander about even more freely in these things. They ask whether, since the law has the shadow of the good things to come,[177] we were first constituted as "children" and "under the elements" of beginners in another world of which the Savior says, "I am not of this world."[178] They think that we gradually advance to the summit and receive the place of adoption that we once lost.[179]

4.4–5.   *But when the fullness of time came, God sent his Son, made of a woman, made under the law, that he might redeem those who were under the law, that we might receive the adoption of sons.* Pay careful attention that he did not say "made *through* a woman," which Marcion and other heresies want, which pretend that Christ had putative flesh;

---

174. Cf. Gal 4.4–5.
175. 2 Cor 5.19.
176. Jn 1.10.
177. Cf. Heb 10.1.
178. Jn 8.23.
179. This sounds like Origen's speculations about the preexistence of souls.

but "*of* a woman."[180] Thus one should believe that he was born not *through* her but *of* her.[181] But because he has named the holy and blessed mother of the Lord a "woman," not a virgin, this same thing is also written in the Gospel according to Matthew, when she is called the "wife" of Joseph.[182] Also she is rebuked as a "woman" by the Lord himself.[183] For it was not necessary always to be so cautious and timid about saying "virgin," since woman signifies gender more than union with a man. And according to the understanding of the Greek, γυνή may be validly translated both "wife" and "woman." But, to pass over everything, just as "he was made under the law to redeem those who were under the law," so he wanted to be born of a woman for the sake of those who were born of a woman. For that is why he also received baptism in the waters of the Jordan, as a penitent, though he was free from sins, so that he would teach others of the need to be cleansed through baptism and to be born as sons by the new adoption of the Spirit. By no means did John the Baptist understand this. For he hindered him from approaching the washing and said, "I ought to be baptized by you."[184] And at once the mystery is shown: "Allow it for now, for thus it is fitting for us to fulfill all justice."[185] For he who had come for the sake of the salvation of men would not omit anything from the manner of life of men.

Someone might raise a question and say: If the reason "he was made under the law to redeem those who were under the law" was, namely, because it was impossible for those who were under the law

---

180. Cf. *CRm* 3.11.5.

181. Marcion was a docetist, a term that derives from the Greek word, *dokein,* "to seem or appear." Docetists denied the incarnation of Christ, saying that he only appeared to be human. Some docetists taught that Jesus passed *through* Mary, but did not receive a human nature *from* Mary. Others claimed that Christ simply appeared from heaven as a full-grown human being. This heresy is combated in the New Testament itself. Cf. 1 Jn 4.2.

182. Cf. Mt 1.18; Lk 2.5.

183. Cf. Jn 2.4.

184. Mt 3.14.

185. Mt 3.15.

to be redeemed, had he himself not been made under the law; or [if the reason] he was made "without law"[186] was to redeem those who were not under the law; or if he had not been made "without the law,"[187] he would not have redeemed those who were not under the law; because, if it was possible for those who were without the law to be redeemed, so that he himself would not have become without the law, then it is superfluous that he was "made under the law to redeem those who were under the law." Briefly one will resolve this problem if one makes use of that citation, "and he was reckoned with those who were *without the law*."[188] For granting that in the Latin manuscripts, on account of the simplicity of the translators, it was rendered badly: "and he was reckoned with the wicked," nevertheless one must know that in Greek ἄνομος signifies one thing, which is the word used here, but ἄδικος signifies something else, which is found in the Latin texts. For ἄνομος describes one who is without law and is constrained by no sense of right; ἄδικος, on the other hand, means wicked or unjust. This is why the apostle himself says in another passage: "When I was *without the law* of God, but I was in the law of Christ."[189] And certainly in this citation too ἄνομος is written in the Greek. The same word that has been well translated here could also be translated there in a similar way, had not the ambiguity deceived the translator.

But someone else will consider the word "redeem" more closely and will say that by the "redeemed" are meant those who were once on God's side and later ceased to be so, whereas those who were not under the law are not so much redeemed as purchased. This is also why to the Corinthians among whom there was rumor of fornication, and such a kind of fornication that was not even among the Gentiles,[190] it is written, "You were bought," not redeemed, "for a price."[191] For they had not been under the law.

---

186. Cf. 1 Cor 9.21a.
187. Cf. 1 Cor 9.21b.
188. Is 53.12; cf. Lk 22.37.
189. 1 Cor 9.21.
190. Cf. 1 Cor 5.1.
191. 1 Cor 6.20; 7.23.

Therefore, "we receive the adoption of sons," and redeemed by Christ we cease being under the slavery of the "elements of the world" and in the power of "tutors." But just as we have shown the difference between "redeem" and "purchase," so we should take into consideration that between "taking" and "receiving" the adoption of sons.

4.6.   *But since you are sons of God, God sent the Spirit of his Son into our hearts, crying: "Abba, Father."* Manifestly the apostle Paul names three spirits: "the Spirit of the Son" of God, as in the present passage, "he sent the Spirit of his Son into our hearts"; the Spirit of God, as in the following, "As many as are led by the Spirit of God, these are sons of God";[192] and the Holy Spirit, as here, "Your bodies are a temple of the Holy Spirit who is in you."[193] Now, that the Holy Spirit is different from the Son of God is manifestly proven in the Gospel: "Whoever speaks a word against the Son of man, it will be forgiven him. But whoever speaks against the Holy Spirit, it will not be forgiven him either here or in the future."[194] Since, therefore, many assert this through their lack of familiarity with the Scriptures[195] (which even Firmianus[196] does in the eighth book of his letters to Demetrian[197]), that the Holy Spirit is often named the Father, often the Son, and since we clearly believe in the Trinity, by removing the third person, they do not want his essence to exist, but his name. But to make a long story short (for I am writing a commentary, not a dialogical treatise), I will show briefly

---

192. Rom 8.14. Cf. *CRm* 1.1.1.

193. 1 Cor 6.19.

194. Mt 12.32.

195. Jerome says this of Marcus Victorinus in the Preface.

196. This is another name of Lactantius (260–330). See n. 3 in this portion of Jerome's commentary.

197. Apparently Jerome regarded Lactantius's four books of letters to Probus, two books to Severus, and two to Demetrian as eight consecutive books. Here Jerome accuses Lactantius of doubting whether the Holy Spirit was the third Person, and of having confounded him with the Son and sometimes with the Father. Elsewhere, on the other hand, Jerome refused to be debarred from reading Lactantius's *Institutiones* on this account. This seems to imply that he judged his language to be more at fault than his faith. Cf. Ep. 84.7 to Pammachius and Oceanus; Ep. 62.2 to Tranquillinus; *Commentariorum in Epistulam ad Ephesios libri III, Praefatio.*

from the fiftieth Psalm that three Spirits are named, when the prophet says: "Create in me a clean heart, God, and renew a right spirit in my inner being. Do not cast me from your face and do not remove your Holy Spirit from me. Restore to me the joy of your salvation and strengthen me by your principal Spirit."[198] He calls the Father the "principal Spirit," because the Son is from the Father[199] and not the Father from the Son; but he signifies Christ the Lord as the "right Spirit" of truth and justice,[200] since the Father has given all judgment to the Son.[201] "God, give your judgment to the king and your justice to the son of the king."[202] Furthermore, he calls the "Holy Spirit" by his well-known name. Although they do indeed differ in their designations and persons, they are united in essence and nature. On account of the association of his nature, the same Spirit is now said indifferently to be "of the Father" and now "of the Son."

But he completes the argument that he is endeavoring to make, that we are no longer under the law but under the grace of the Lord Jesus, with the following conclusion. Above he had said that "we received the adoption of sons"; now he proves that we are "sons of God" by the "Spirit" whom we have in us. For, he says, we would never dare to say, "Our Father who art in heaven, hallowed be thy name,"[203] except from the awareness of the "Spirit" who dwells in us and by the great sound of meanings and doctrines calling out, "Abba, Father." "Abba" is a Hebrew word and signifies the same thing as Father. And Scripture preserves this usage in many places, when it records the Hebrew word together with its own interpretation: "Bartimaeus, son of Timaeus";[204] "Asher," wealth;[205] "Tabitha, Dorcas";[206] and, in Genesis, "Mesech," the home-born slave;[207] and others similar to these.

---

198. Cf. Ps 51.10–12; *CRm* 7.1.2.
199. Cf. Jn 16.27–28.
200. Cf. Eph 4.24.
201. Cf. Jn 5.22.
202. Ps 72.1.
203. Mt 6.9.
204. Cf. Mk 10.46.
205. Cf. Gn 30.13.
206. Cf. Acts 9.36.
207. Cf. Gn 15.3.

But seeing that "Abba Father" is said in the Hebrew and Syrian language, and our Lord commands in the Gospel that no one should be called father except God,[208] I do not know by what license we either address others by this name or allow ourselves to be called by it. And certainly the one who commanded this was the very one who had said that one should not swear.[209] If we do not swear, we should not even name anyone father; if we offer a different interpretation of "father," we will also be compelled to think otherwise about swearing.

One should also note that "cry" in the Scriptures should be understood not of the emission of a loud voice, but of the greatness of knowledge and doctrines. For even in Exodus the Lord answered Moses, "Why do you cry to me?"[210] when absolutely no voice of Moses had preceded. Scripture has called a "cry" a truly contrite heart that tearfully groans on behalf of the people. Therefore, just as the one who has the "Spirit of the Son" of God is a "son of God," so in reciprocity the one who does not have the Spirit of the Son of God cannot be called a son of God.

4.7.   *And so, now he is not a slave but a son; but if a son, also an heir through God.* He says, having the Spirit of the Son of God crying in you, "Abba, Father,"[211] you have begun to be not "slaves" but "sons," since previously you differed in no respect from a slave, though you were by nature lords.[212] Instead you spent your time as children "under tutors and governors."[213] But "if you are sons," the inheritance is owed to you as a consequence.[214] Thus just as you have received the Spirit of the Son of God and have been made sons of God, so you have been changed from slavery to freedom[215] into "heirs" with the heir of the

---

208. Cf. Mt 23.9.
209. Cf. Mt 5.34.
210. Ex 14.15.
211. Cf. Gal 4.6.
212. Cf. Gal 4.1.
213. Gal 4.2.
214. Cf. Rom 8.17.
215. Cf. Rom 8.21.

Father, Christ Jesus.[216] In the Psalm he says under the persona of his assumed humanity: "The Lord said to me: You are my son, today I have begotten you. Ask of me and I will give the nations to you, your inheritance, and your possession, the ends of the earth."[217]

But what we say in respect to this passage we should also observe in respect to the others, that the discussion concerns the whole human race under a single number. For all we who believe are one in Christ Jesus and members of his body.[218] Having been made into a perfect man,[219] we have that head, since Christ is the head of man.[220]

4.8–9.   *But indeed at that time, since you did not know God, you served those who by nature were not gods; but now, since you know God, or rather are known by him, how do you convert again to weak and destitute elements, which you want to serve again?* He accuses the Galatians, whom he had converted from the worship of idols to faith in the true God of this: How is it that, having forsaken the idols, which "by nature were not gods," and "knowing God, or rather known by him," having also received the Spirit of adoption, do they return again, as if they desire to be children and under tutors and a pedagogue, to the weak and poor elements? These were given to the people of weak and poor understanding in the desert precisely because they were not able to receive and sustain greater things. These same elements that he has now styled "weak and destitute," he called above merely the "elements of the world." And where "elements of the world" were spoken of, there it was not added "weak and destitute." Here, on the other hand, where they are called "weak," the term "of the world" is unmentioned, as we said above. And so I think that so long as someone is a child[221] and has not completed the time appointed by the father to be able to be called

---

216. Cf. Rom 8.17.
217. Ps 2.7–8; cf. Heb 1.5; 5.5.
218. Cf. Rom 12.5.
219. Cf. Eph 4.13.
220. Cf. 1 Cor 11.3.
221. Cf. Gal 4.1.

son and heir,[222] he is under the elements of the world, namely, the law of Moses. But when, after [receiving] the freedom and adoption and inheritance due to a son, he has again returned to the law and desires to be circumcised and to follow the whole letter of Judaic superstition, then those things that were merely the elements of the world to him before are now said to be "weak and destitute" beginnings. For so much so do those things not profit their worshipers, they are not even able to offer them what they previously gave, since the temple of Jerusalem and the altar have been destroyed.

Should someone respond and say: If the law and commandments which are recorded in the law are "weak and destitute elements," and those who "knew God, or rather were known by him," are not obligated to observe the law (lest they begin not so much to worship God by whom they "were known" as to revert to those "who by nature are not gods"), then either Moses and the prophets observed the law and "did not know God" and were not "known by him," or, if "they knew God," they hardly fulfilled the commands of the law. It is dangerous to say either of these things, that they did not do the things that are of the law and thus "knew God," or that they did not "know God" while they are keeping the "weak and destitute elements" of the law. This can be resolved if we say the following: Paul "became a Jew to the Jews to gain the Jews."[223] He cut his hair under a vow at Cenchreae,[224] and took part in a religious procession (*exercuit*), shaven and with bare feet, in the temple of Jerusalem.[225] He did all this in order to appease the ill will of those who had been taught about him that he acted against the law of Moses and the God of the prophets. In like manner those holy men did certain things that were of the law, but they followed the sense of the law rather than the letter. They were those who, with an unveiled face,[226] desired no less than Abraham to see the day of Christ[227] and saw

---

222. Cf. Gal 4.2.
223. Cf. 1 Cor 9.20.
224. Cf. Acts 18.18.
225. Cf. Acts 21.21–26.
226. Cf. Ex 34.33; 2 Cor 3.15.
227. Cf. Mt 13.17.

it and rejoiced.[228] They were made weak for the weak people, in order to gain the weak.[229] And for those who were under the law, they acted as if they were themselves under the law, in order to separate those people from the idols that they were accustomed to in Egypt. For it is absurd that Moses and the other conversation partners of God[230] were not in that condition, so that we should not believe that the time pre-ordained from the Father had come to them, and that they were re-deemed from legal servitude and had attained to the adoption of sons[231] and had received the inheritance with Christ.[232] For whatever the wisdom of God offered to the whole human race, as if to one son, it has always given these same things to each of the saints in their own order[233] and dispensation.

When we speak of the law of Moses as "weak and destitute ele-ments," the heretics find an occasion to disparage the Creator who founded the world and sanctioned the law. We will respond to them with what we said above: the "elements" are "weak and destitute" to those who revert to them after the grace of the gospel. But before the time pre-ordained from the Father came,[234] the "elements" were not so much called "weak and destitute" as "of the world."[235] After all, before the gospel of Christ flashed throughout the whole world, the com-mands of the law had their own radiance. But after the greater light of the grace of the gospel shined, and after the sun of justice[236] revealed it-self to the whole world, the light of the stars was concealed and their rays were veiled in darkness. Thus it is that the apostle said in another

---

228. Cf. Jn 8.56.

229. Cf. 1 Cor 9.20.

230. Cf. Ex 33.11. *Confabulator* is used in Ambrose, *In Canticis Canticorum* 4.39; Jerome, *Commentariorum in Epistulam ad Ephesios libri III* 2.

231. Cf. Gal 4.4–5.

232. Cf. Gal 4.7.

233. Cf. 1 Cor 15.23.

234. Cf. Gal 4.2.

235. Cf. Gal 4.3.

236. Cf. Mal 4.2.

passage: "For what was glorified has not been glorified in this aspect on account of the surpassing glory."[237] He is now expressing this in different words. Thus he is saying: The law of Moses, which before was rich, affluent, and illustrious, was diminished after Christ's advent, as if it were "weak and destitute" in comparison with him. It was destroyed by him who was greater than Solomon,[238] than the temple,[239] and than Jonah.[240] For in my opinion what is written, "He must increase, but I must decrease,"[241] was said not so much under the persona of John as of the law. For lesser things always yield to greater things, and what is perfect has priority over the beginning stages.

But in any case we will prove that the "weak and destitute elements" [are] the traditions of the Jews and their base understanding according to the letter, which are the "justifications that are not good and the commandments that are not good."[242] For the spiritual understanding of the law is robust and rich, so that it should either not be called an "element" at all, or it is an "element" in comparison with the coming age and the life in Christ Jesus by means of which angels and the celestial powers now live. But compared with the Judaic sense, it is not so much called an "element," that is, the beginning, as the perfection.

But as for what he says, "But now since you know God, or rather are known by him," this shows that after they had worshiped idols, the Galatians understood God, or rather, they were judged worthy of the knowledge of him. It is not that God, the Creator of all things, does not know anything, but that he is said to know only those who have exchanged error for piety: "The Lord knows those who are his."[243] Also

---

237. 2 Cor 3.10.

238. Cf. Mt 12.42.

239. Cf. Mt 12.6.

240. Cf. Mt 12.41.

241. Jn 3.30.

242. Cf. Ezek 20.25. Origen gives a similar interpretation of this passage in *Contra Celsum* 7.20.

243. 2 Tm 2.19. Cf. *CRm* 7.7.5; 7.8.3.

the Savior says in the Gospel, "I am the good shepherd and I know mine and mine know me."[244] In contrast he says to the impious, "I do not know you; depart from me, workers of iniquity";[245] and to the foolish virgins, "I do not know who you are."[246]

4.10–11. *You observe days and months and times and years! I am afraid of you, lest perhaps I labored among you without reason.* The one who does not worship the Father in spirit and truth[247] does not know that a Sabbath rest is reserved for the saints, of which God says, "If they entered into my rest."[248] It is not recorded of those times of which it is written, "Remember the days of the age,"[249] and elsewhere, "I remembered the ancient days and I held the eternal years in mind."[250] That person is observing Judaic "days and months and times and years."

The "days" refer to things like Sabbaths and new moons, and from the tenth to the fourteenth [day] of the first month for which a corporeal lamb is reserved as a [sacrificial] victim,[251] and from the fourteenth to the twenty-first [day] of the same month, when unleavened bread is consumed,[252] not that of sincerity and truth,[253] but that which has the old yeast of the malice and wickedness of the Pharisees.[254] Also on the seventh "day" of the seventh month, which by Judaic ritual he computes after the feast of unleavened bread, he celebrates the "days" of the Israelite Pentecost.[255] And besides, they observe Judaic "days" in the seventh month, on the first "day" of the month, in the blast of

---

244. Jn 10.14.
245. Mt 7.23; Lk 13.27.
246. Mt 25.12.
247. Cf. Jn 4.23–24.
248. Ps 95.11; cf. Heb 4.3.
249. Is 46.9.
250. Ps 77.5. Cf. *CRm* 5.1.41.
251. Cf. Ex 12.3–6.
252. Cf. Ex 12.18–20.
253. Cf. 1 Cor 5.8.
254. Cf. Mt 16.12.
255. Cf. Lv 23.15–21; Dt 16.9–12.

trumpets;[256] also on the tenth "day" of the same month, in the atonement, the fast[257] and the customary fabricating of tabernacles.[258]

But they keep "months" who observe the first and seventh "month" without understanding the mystery of the truth. They celebrate "times" too who three "times" each year go to Jerusalem and think that they are fulfilling the Lord's command who says: "Three 'times' a year you will celebrate a feast to me: the solemnity of unleavened bread, the solemnity of the harvest of the first-fruits, and the solemnity of consummation at the end of the year."[259] And elsewhere it says: "Three 'times' a year your males shall appear in the presence of the Lord your God."[260] By "years" I think he means the seventh "year" of release,[261] and the fiftieth, which they call the jubilee.[262]

The apostle explains this passage in more detail when he says to the Colossians, "Let no one judge you, then, in respect to food or drink or in part of a feast day or of a new moon or of Sabbaths, which are a shadow of things to come."[263] He has recorded here "part of a feast day" in distinction from the perpetual feast. Thus we do not have a brief period of our life and, so to speak, some tiny little portion of the whole body, but we have the entire period of our life as a continuous solemnity in Christ. And in order that I might link the former things with what comes later, he immediately supplies in this same letter what he means by the law of Moses and the superfluous pursuit of foods. For he says, "For if you died with Christ from the elements of this world, why, as those still living in this world, do you decree: 'Do not touch, do not taste, do not handle'? These things lead to destruction by their very use, according to the commands and doctrines of men."[264]

---

256. Cf. Lv 23.23–25.
257. Cf. Lv 23.27–32.
258. Cf. Lv 23.34–36.
259. Ex 34.14–16.
260. Ex 23.17; 34.23.
261. Cf. Dt 15.1.
262. Cf. Lv 25.10.
263. Cf. Col 2.16–17.
264. Col 2.20–22.

Someone may say: If it is not permissible to "observe days and months and times and years," then we too commit a similar offense by observing the fourth day of the week,[265] Good Friday,[266] the Lord's day, the forty-day fast and festival of Passover, the joyous day of Pentecost, and the different times that are established in various regions for honoring the martyrs.[267] One simple response to this will be to say that the days of Judaic observance are not identical to ours; for we do not celebrate the Passover of Unleavened Bread,[268] but of the cross and resurrection. Nor do we count seven weeks until Pentecost according to the custom of Israel,[269] but we venerate the coming of the Holy Spirit.[270] And to prevent a disorderly assembly of people from threatening faith in Christ, some days have been appointed for all of us to come together on equal terms. It is not that that day on which we come together is more celebrated, but that greater joy springs forth when we see one another on whichever day one must come together.

But one who tries to respond more penetratingly to the question posed in opposition to us will affirm that all days are equal, and Christ is crucified not merely on Good Friday,[271] and he rises not merely on the Lord's day; but for a saint it is always the day of resurrection and he always feeds on the Lord's flesh.[272] But fasts and assemblies have been appointed amidst the days for their sake by prudent men. The former have more time for the world than for God, and they are unable, or rather unwilling, to come together in the church for the entire time of their life and to offer the sacrifice of their prayers to God in preference to their human activities. For how few they are who always practice at least these few things which are appointed, whether as times of prayer

---

265. Wednesday.

266. That is, Parasceve, the preparation of the Passover; cf. Jn 19.14.

267. Harnack, *Der kirchengeschichtliche Ertrag,* p. 154, concludes that Jerome is copying Origen in this passage.

268. Cf. Ex 12.15.

269. Cf. Tb 2.1; 2 Mc 12.32.

270. Cf. Acts 2.1–4.

271. Parasceve.

272. Cf. Jn 6.53–56.

or of fasting! And so, just as for us it is allowed both to fast always and to pray always, and unceasingly to celebrate the Lord's day by receiving the Lord's body with rejoicing; so also it is not right for the Jews to sacrifice a lamb at all times, to celebrate Pentecost, to set up tabernacles, and to fast daily.

He has qualified his words quite carefully between the authority of an apostle and the mildness of a saintly man, by concluding, "I am afraid of you, lest perhaps I labored among you without reason." For had he wanted to condemn them sharply, he would have assuredly said, "I am afraid of you: for I have labored among you without reason." But now, seeing that they have "zeal for God but not according to knowledge,"[273] he has not completely lost hope for their salvation, since they had been deceived by a pious error. And yet, on the other hand, he has not left them blameless. Otherwise, he would offer an occasion both for them to continue in the error and for others to err in a similar fashion. He has recorded, "I am afraid *of* you," in place of, "I am afraid *for* you." A teacher "labors without reason" when he himself challenges his disciples to greater things, and they fall and roll backwards toward inferior lowly things.

4.12a.   *Be as I [am], because I also [am] as you.* He is saying something like this: Just as "I" became weak for you who are weak,[274] and I could not speak to you as to those who are spiritual but as to those who are carnal and infants in Christ; and because you were not yet capable of eating solid food,[275] I gave you only gospel-milk, being unwilling that you ever abide in the age of infancy, but gradually [I wanted] to lead [you] to adolescence and manhood, so that you could become capable of receiving solid food;[276] so also you should be "as I am." That is to say, you should understand the more perfect things, leaving behind the milk for the stronger food and passing on to greater things as your

---

273. Rom 10.2.
274. Cf. 1 Cor 9.22.
275. Cf. 1 Cor 3.1–2.
276. Cf. Heb 5.12–14.

food. Now he says this as an imitator of the Savior, who "thought it not robbery to be equal to God, but emptied himself, taking the form of a slave, being found in appearance as a man."[277] This was done in order that we might become gods from being men,[278] that we might no longer die; but rising up together with Christ,[279] we should be called his friends[280] and brothers.[281] Thus would the disciple be like the teacher[282] and the slave as the Lord.[283]

But it can also be understood as follows: I entreat you, brothers, he says, that you despise the Judaic observance of days, months, times, and years, which are a shadow of the things to come,[284] and imitate me, who lived without reproach under the law and reckoned everything as offscourings and refuse that I might gain Christ.[285] For I was "also as you" now are, when I was held fast by those same observances and laid waste and persecuted the church of Christ,[286] because it was not doing these things.

4.12b–14.   *Brothers, I entreat you. You have not injured me at all; but you know that through infirmity of the flesh I preached the gospel to you long ago and you neither spurned nor rejected your temptation in my flesh, but you received me as an angel of God, as Christ Jesus.* In order to make this clearer, join what follows to the sentence above. Then the order of what we are fashioning would be this: "I entreat you, brothers, be as I am, since I also am as you are." It is similar to this: "We ask you for Christ's sake, be reconciled to God."[287] And besides, elsewhere it

---

277. Cf. Phil 2.6–8.
278. Cf. 2 Pt 1.4; Ps 82.6–7.
279. Cf. Col 3.1.
280. Cf. Jn 15.15.
281. Cf. Jn 20.17.
282. Cf. Mt 10.24–25.
283. Cf. Jn 15.15.
284. Cf. Col 2.17; Heb 10.1.
285. Cf. Phil 3.6–8.
286. Cf. Phil 3.6; Gal 1.13.
287. 2 Cor 5.20.

says: "First of all I ask for intercessions, prayers, requests, and thanks-givings."[288] Consider also the words of Peter when he says, "I request of the elders among you, I myself being a fellow elder and witness of Christ's sufferings."[289] These things indeed exhort us to humility. They also strike at the arrogance of bishops, who, as if they are stationed on some lofty summit, scarcely deign to look upon mortals and speak with their fellow slaves.[290] Let them learn from the apostle that the erring and foolish Galatians are called "brothers." Let them learn that after his rebuke come the winsome words of one who says, "I entreat you." And what he "entreats" is that they be his imitators, just as he is of Christ.[291] Or rather, that I might follow the present passage, what he asks is no great thing: that just as he became less from being greater on account of them, so they should ascend to greater things from lesser ones.

He says, "You have not injured me at all." A disciple "injures" his teacher if he squanders his commands and effort by his own negli-gence. The Galatians had not "injured" the apostle, because they had observed his gospel and his commands right up to the present time. Or else [he means] this: Recall when I first "preached the gospel" to you and I preached to you as if to children,[292] on account of the "weakness of your flesh." For since you were not able to receive greater mysteries, I pretended to be weak, that I might gain you in your weakness.[293] Did you not "receive me as an angel, as Christ Jesus"? Since, therefore, you did not "injure" me at that time, and you thought that for your sake I was humble and downcast, like the Son of God,[294] why do you injure me when I challenge you to greater things? You do this by ruining my labor and that policy by which I pretended to be a child. I am now in mourning over my pointless work.

---

288. 1 Tm 2.1.

289. 1 Pt 5.1.

290. Harnack, *Der kirchengeschichtliche Ertrag,* p. 154, identifies this passage as one that certainly derives from Origen.

291. Cf. 1 Cor 4.16; 1 Cor 11.1.

292. Cf. 1 Cor 3.1.

293. Cf. 1 Cor 9.22.

294. Cf. Mt 11.29.

Paul proclaims to the Galatians "through weakness of the flesh." He does not mean his own flesh but that of the hearers. They were unable to subject the flesh to the Word of God, but as fleshly[295] people they by no means received the spiritual understanding. To make this clearer let us cite an example: He teaches "through weakness of the flesh" who says, "If they cannot control themselves, let them marry,"[296] and, "The woman is free if her husband dies; let her marry whom she wants, only in the Lord."[297] But by no means does he teach "through weakness of the flesh" who records this: "Are you released from a wife? Do not seek a wife,"[298] and, "It is time that those who have wives be just as those who do not have."[299] For some precepts are given for the spiritual, others for the fleshly;[300] and what is given as a command is one thing, but what is prescribed as a concession is something else.[301]

"And you did not spurn your temptation in my flesh." This is an obscure passage and demands closer attention. "Long ago I preached the gospel to you," he says, as if to little children and suckling infants, "through the weakness of your flesh." I began with lesser things and, so to speak, I practically stammered among you. This policy, and my pretense of weakness in preaching, was indeed my manner of leadership. But it was "your temptation," whether the things would be pleasing to you that both seemed great but that were rather small in view of their condition, and were presented by me as of little account. You admired these things, to be sure, and received them not as small things but as great, to such an extent that you received me who spoke these things as an "angel" and, to say more, as the Son of God. So then, this "temptation" of yours, whereby I tempted you in the fleshly proclamation of my words, was not lowly and contemptible, but had more worth than I was reckoning.

---

295. Cf. 1 Cor 3.3.
296. 1 Cor 7.9.
297. 1 Cor 7.39.
298. 1 Cor 7.27.
299. 1 Cor 7.29.
300. Cf. 1 Cor 3.1.
301. Cf. 1 Cor 7.6.

The passage can also be explained in another way. When I came to you, I did not come in words of wisdom,[302] but as a lowly and despised man declaring nothing great: the crucified.[303] Therefore, when you saw that I was subject to weaknesses in the body, you did not ridicule the one promising a heavenly kingdom, and you did not reckon him to be worthy of your contempt. For you understood that the lowliness of my flesh and the plainness of my dress were for "your temptation," namely, whether you would despise him who was considered wretched by unbelievers. But on the contrary you received that lowly, plain, and contemptible man as an angel, and more than an angel. Or, we might suppose that the apostle was sick when he first came to the Galatians and had not ceased being in the grip of some bodily infirmity; and yet he did not suppress his voice in silence to keep him from preaching the beginning of the gospel. For tradition records that he often suffered from severe headaches,[304] and that this is the angel of Satan that was appointed for him, to buffet him in the flesh lest he become puffed up.[305] This weakness and illness of the body among those to whom the gospel was being proclaimed was a "temptation," whether they would despise the one promising lofty things, one whom they saw was subject to illnesses of the body. And certainly this can also be said, that at the commencement of his arrival among the Galatians, he endured abuse, persecution, and physical beatings from the adversaries of the gospel. And this was a "temptation," indeed the greatest one of all: for the Galatians to see an apostle of Christ being beaten.

Now his words, "You received me as an angel, as Christ Jesus," show that Christ is greater than an angel, whom the Psalmist had celebrated as lesser, according to the dispensation of the body, when he said, "You have lowered him a little less than angels."[306] And so much

---

302. Cf. 1 Cor 2.1.

303. Cf. 1 Cor 2.2.

304. Cf. Tertullian, *De pudicitia* 13.16; Chrysostom, *Homily 26 on 2 Cor* (NPNF 12.400).

305. Cf. 2 Cor 12.7.

306. Ps 8.5.

so does he demonstrate that his own words were in force in the beginning that they were reckoned to be those of an angel and of Christ.

4.15–16.   *Where then is your blessedness? For I bear you witness that if it could have been done, you would have plucked out your eyes and given them to me. Have I therefore become your enemy by speaking the truth to you?* Blessed is the one who walks in the way of the virtues,[307] but only if he attains to the virtues; for it is no benefit to withdraw from vices unless you apprehend what is best, since it is not so much the commencement of striving after the good that is to be praised, as the outcome. For it is the same situation as in a vineyard, where there are many stages of the grapes leading up to the winepress. It is first necessary that the vine sprouts its tendrils and promises hope in its flowers. Then, when the flower has been removed, the outward appearance of the future grape changes form. It swells gradually, then the grape sprouts, so that the press may exude the sweet juice that has been pressed out from the winepress. In the same way, in doctrine there are individual stages of progress in beatitude: as someone hears the word of God, as one conceives it, as it grows in the womb of his soul and reaches the point of birth, and when it gives birth, nurses, and feeds, as it attains to the perfect man through infancy, childhood, adolescence, and youth. Therefore, since as we have said each stage has a blessedness according to its own progress, if the outcome and, so to speak, the finishing touches are missing from the work, the whole effort will be wasted and it will be said, "Where then is your blessedness?" Although, he says, I called you blessed at that time when you had received the gospel according to the flesh, since at the beginning you were fervent, nevertheless now, since I do not see a roof placed on the building,[308] and the foundations have been laid almost pointlessly, I am compelled to say, "Where is that beatitude of yours" by which previously I praised you when I regarded you blessed?

---

307. Cf. Ps 1.1.

308. This image is found frequently in Jerome. Cf. *Commentariorum in Isaiam libri XVIII* 1.5 (PL 24: 154); *Commentariorum in Amos libri III* 3.9.6 (PL 25: 1090 B); *Commentariorum in Matthaeum libri IV, Praefatio* 5.

For I truly confess that at the beginning you so esteemed me, as I preached lowly things to you and was afflicted by persecution, that, "if it could be done" (what is said here has to be understood as hyperbole), "you would have plucked out your eyes and given them to me," that I might see more than the lights of all of you.[309] For you wished to be blind through inexpressible love for me, that the light of the gospel might arise more in my heart.[310] You wanted to increase my benefit by your losses, and this at that time when, either on account of the weakness of your flesh, I was proclaiming small and lowly things to you, as if to little children and nursing babes, or on account of injuries to my flesh I did not seem worthy of credence. But now, because I began to summon you away from the elements and syllables and childish reading to greater pursuits, that you might hold the books in your hands, that you might learn the fullness of the words of instruction and of their meaning, you are kicking back, you are angry. The perfection of doctrine seems burdensome to you, and to such an extent have you changed to different feelings that you now regard me as an "enemy," the man whom you once received as an angel and as Christ, to whom you wanted to hand over your eyes. This is because I proclaim the full "truth to you."

But he has finished his statement elegantly when he says, "So then, I have become your enemy by speaking the truth to you." He says this to show that the beginning of his preaching was not so much truth as shadows and an image of truth. Similar to this is that statement of the poet who is famous among the Romans: "Compliance (*obsequium*) wins friends, but the truth engenders hatred."[311] But consider how much better this is than that: For the apostle qualified this statement of those whom he called fools,[312] whom he has identified as children.[313] And he made it unique when he directed it to a particular situation and

---

309. Cf. Phil 2.15.
310. Cf. 2 Pt 1.19.
311. Terence, *Andria* 68.
312. Cf. Gal 3.3.
313. Cf. Gal 4.3.

to the Galatians in person. But [the poet] has gone wildly astray by making a general pronouncement, that things are this way with everyone. For the compliance by which he thought friends are made when truth has been obliterated is not so much compliance as flattery and agreement, which plainly should be called clandestine hostility rather than "friendship."

But at the same time, the following should be considered: Today too, so long as we explain the Scriptures according to the letter, to children and nursing babes and to those in whose hearts Christ has never developed or "increased in stature, wisdom, and grace with God and men,"[314] we are praised, we are respected, we are held in admiration.[315] But when we make a small attempt to challenge them to pass on to greater things, they stop acclaiming us and become our enemies. They prefer to follow the Jews rather than the apostles. The latter withdrew from the teaching and traditions of the Pharisees and moved toward Christ himself, the propitiatory[316] and perfection of the law.[317] They do not consider it fitting to receive the divine word, which commands teachers of the church to "go up" to higher doctrines and to "lift up their voice" with all their "strength."[318] It commands them "not to fear" the racket of the little children barking around them, when it says, "Go up on the high mountain, you who preach the gospel to Zion; lift up your voice with strength, you who preach the gospel to Jerusalem. Lift it up, do not fear."[319]

4.17–18. *They are zealous for you, not properly, but they want to exclude you, so that you should be zealous for them. But be zealous for the good in a good thing always and not only when I am present with you.* "They are properly zealous" who, when they see that there are graces,

---

314. Cf. Lk 2.52.

315. This passage does not appear to be autobiographical to Jerome, as much as to Origen, whom Jerome is translating and adapting.

316. Cf. Rom 3.25.

317. Cf. Mt 5.17; Rom 13.10.

318. Cf. Is 40.9.

319. Is 40.9.

gifts, and virtues in others, desire to be like them themselves, and they strive to imitate their faith, life, and diligence by means of which they earned these things. Thus they may be able to attain these things too, which are good things worthy of their zeal. The apostle also says of these things, "Be zealous for spiritual things, but mostly that you should prophesy";[320] and then, "And so, since you are zealots for spiritual things, seek to abound in the edification of the church";[321] and again, "And so, brothers, be zealous to prophesy, and do not prohibit speaking in tongues."[322] On the other hand, "they are zealous not well" who do not so much desire to be better themselves, so as to imitate those who are worthy of zeal, as to want to make them worse and drag them backwards by a perverse zeal. For instance, let it be said: Someone is a Christian, he reads Moses and the prophets. He knows that everything came before for that people in shadow and in image,[323] but they were written for our sake upon whom the ends of the ages have come.[324] He understands circumcision not so much of the foreskin as of the ears and heart.[325] He has resurrected with Christ, he seeks the things that are above.[326] He is freed from the burden and legal servitude of the one who commands, "do not touch, do not taste, do not handle."[327] If anyone wants to persuade this person with the words of the Scriptures, that he should understand what is written not by tropology[328] but by the letter that kills,[329] with the result that he becomes a

---

320. 1 Cor 14.1.
321. 1 Cor 14.12.
322. 1 Cor 14.39.
323. Cf. Col 2.17.
324. Cf. 1 Cor 10.11.
325. Cf. Jer 4.4; 6.10; Rom 2.29.
326. Cf. Col 3.1.
327. Cf. Col 2.21.
328. Tropology refers to a deeper and more figurative interpretation. Referring to Jerome, *Commentary on Matthew* 9.1–2, M. Simonetti, *Matthew 1a*, p. 173, observes: "The term *tropologia* originally meant an allegorical interpretation in general. From the late fourth century, however, it came to mean specifically a moral allegory, as in this example from Jerome."
329. Cf. 2 Cor 3.6.

Jew openly and not in secret,[330] he is zealous for him "not well." Instead he is hastening to drag back one who is proceeding at top speed toward greater things, in order that the one who is going backwards should be zealous for himself, or at least in order that he not make any further headway.

And so, he addresses the Galatians, who had been induced by champions of the law to imitate them, when instead they should have imitated the Galatians (since it is natural to go from lesser to greater, not the other way around), and he says, "Be zealous for the good in a good thing"; that is to say, do not imitate the champions of Judaic observance but imitate things which are "goods." For just as the one who imitates someone's wealth, power, or dignity is not so much zealous for good things as for things from which one ought to flee, so also you, on the contrary, "be zealous for the good in the good" by seeking spiritual things rather than carnal. Thus it is not they who should teach you to be Jews, but you who should teach them to be Christians.

But do this "always," so that by persistent steps you can reach the end of the good work. For indeed, "you were zealous for the good in the good" previously, when I was with you. But after I departed from you, you ruined everything that I had handed down. You withdrew from the fixed position and safe harbor onto a wave that was flowing out again into the deep. It is no wonder if the Galatians were changed when the apostle departed, who was the vessel of election[331] and the one in whom Christ was speaking.[332] For even now we witness the same thing happening in the churches. Whenever there happens to be some teacher in the church who is distinguished in speech and life, who moves his hearers toward the virtues, as if with certain pricks, we see all the fervent people scampering about and hastening after almsgiving, fasting, moral purity, relief of the poor, taking care of graves, and other similar things. But when he departs we see that they gradually waste away and, since their food source has been removed, they grow thin,

---

330. Cf. Rom 2.28–29.
331. Cf. Acts 9.15.
332. Cf. 2 Cor 13.3.

pale, and languid. Then follows the death of all that had previously been flourishing. Therefore, since the "harvest is plentiful, but the workers are few,"[333] let us ask the Lord of the harvest to send workers into the harvest, who may reap the crop of the Christian people, which is standing in the church, having been previously prepared as the wheat of the future.[334] May they gather and bring them into barns[335] and by no means allow them to perish.

This concerns that zeal and perverse form of envy of which another passage has said, "Do not be envious (*aemulari*) of wrongdoers."[336] Here it says, "they are improperly zealous (*aemulantur*) for you." Now we have found another zeal by which the sons of Jacob were jealous of their brother Joseph,[337] and Miriam and Aaron were jealous of Moses, the friend of the Lord.[338] For neither the former nor the latter were incited to "jealousy" (*zelum*) in order that they might be better than Joseph and Moses; but it was because it pained them that they were better. That "jealousy" (*zelum*) is near to being envy. It would take too long if I wanted to bring forth from the treasure trove of Scripture everything it says in general about zeal, whether good or bad. We read of a good zeal in the case of Phineas,[339] Elijah,[340] Mattathias,[341] and the apostle Judas (not the betrayer) who on account of the remarkable virtue of zeal within him even received the name "Zealot."[342] But the bad kind is Cain's against Abel[343] and that of the rest against others; and there is the zeal of the man of whom it is written, "And a spirit of jealousy came on him,"[344] unless possibly this is the indifferent zeal and

---

333. Mt 9.37; cf. Jn 4.35–38.
334. Cf. Jn 4.38.
335. Cf. Mt 6.26.
336. Ps 37.1.
337. Cf. Gn 37.11.
338. Cf. Nm 12.1.
339. Cf. Nm 25.7,11,13; Ps 106.30–31; Sir 45.23.
340. Cf. 1 Kgs 19.10.
341. Cf. 1 Mc 2.26–27.
342. Cf. Lk 6.15–16; Acts 1.13.
343. Cf. Gn 4.8.
344. Nm 5.14.

can be understood neither in a good sense nor in a bad, but should rather be called a type of jealousy that is between the two. Here is another possibility: When those who were of the circumcision see that the Gentile Galatians are abounding in the virtues of the Holy Spirit, whereas they themselves do not speak in tongues and do not have gifts of healings and the grace of prophecy, they are incited by the goads of jealousy and longed to transfer them to the burdens of the law, in order that they might begin to become like themselves.

4.19.   *My little children for whom I am in labor again, until Christ is formed in you.* The first curse shows the great hardships and pain involved in bringing babies forth from the womb when it says, "In grief you will bear sons."[345] So when Paul wanted to show the solicitude of teachers for their disciples, what feelings they experience, lest their followers fall away from salvation, he says, "My little children, for whom I am in labor again." For he who in another place had spoken like a father, "If you have ten thousand pedagogues in Christ, but not many fathers,"[346] now speaks not like a father but like a mother in Christ, so that they may recognize in themselves the dutiful anxiety of both parents. Moses said something like this concerning the people: "Have I not conceived this entire people?"[347] Which of us, do you suppose, is so anxious over the salvation of his disciples that he is in agony, not for a few hours or, as in many cases, for two or three days, but for the entire length of his lifetime "until Christ is formed in them"?

The example of a pregnant woman conceiving and forming seeds within herself deserves our close attention, so that we can understand what is being said (nature is nothing to be ashamed of but is to be revered). For it is likened to the seed that is unformed when first sown into the woman's body. It cleaves to her like glue, as if in a furrow of some piece of farmland. (The prophet recalls this subject when he describes his own origin and says: "Your eyes saw my unformed

---

345. Gn 3.16.
346. 1 Cor 4.15.
347. Nm 11.12.

substance.")[348] Then, over a period of nine months, when the blood has been restricted, the future human being coagulates, is formed into a body, is nourished and made distinct. Thus, after it moves about the uterus, at the appointed time it issues into the light and is born with difficulties as great as those with which it is later nourished, in order to keep it from dying. In the same manner, when the seed of Christ's word falls[349] into the soul of the hearer, it grows by its proper stages and (to pass over much, since it is not difficult to convert the bodily description into the spiritual understanding) it remains in jeopardy so long as the one who has conceived it is in labor. But the work does not end as soon as it emerges, but this is merely the beginning of another kind of labor. Thus she brings up the nursing infant, by constant nourishment and attention, to the full maturity of Christ.[350]

And just as in marriage, often it is the man's seed that is the reason children are not produced, though sometimes a sterile wife does not retain the seed, and frequently neither is fit to reproduce; and on the other hand, both may be fertile. In the same way, in those who sow the word of God, this four-fold division[351] is preserved: The teacher may indeed fulfill his duty, but the hearer may be sterile; or the hearer may have a natural capacity for good, but through the teacher's ignorance the seed of the word may perish; or possibly the one being taught may be as senseless as the one giving the instruction. And seldom does it happen that both the teacher and the disciple have minds that match each other, that is to say, that the one teaches as much as the other is able to take in, or that the one taught can receive as much as the teacher can pour out. But these days we are all judges; we do not know what is a Psalm, what is a portion of prophecy, what is a chapter of the law. And we loquaciously and recklessly interpret what we scarcely understand. It does not matter to us to see "Christ formed" in the people, that

348. Ps 139.16.

349. Cf. Mt 13.3, 19.

350. Cf. Eph 4.13.

351. Jerome (Origen) is expounding the four kinds of responses to the seed sown in the Parable of the Sower (Mt 13.1–23).

each one should return to his home in possession of the seed of the word of God,[352] which, when he has conceived it, he would be able to say with the prophet, "From your fear, Lord, we have conceived and given birth, we have made sons of your salvation on the earth."[353] Disciples like this pass over to apostles and deserve to hear from the Savior, "Whoever does the will of my Father, he is my brother and sister and mother."[354] The diversity of the stages of progress is shown by the different terms. Also "Christ is formed" in the heart of believers when all the mysteries are revealed to them, and the things that seemed obscure become clear. Moreover, the following needs to be contemplated: that the one who because of sin had ceased existing, so to speak, is "conceived" by a teacher through repentance, and once again the formation of Christ within him is promised.[355] This refutes the Novatians[356] who are unwilling to see reformed those who have once been wiped out by sins.

4.20.　*But I would willingly be present with you now and change my voice because I am confounded in respect to you.* Holy Scripture edifies even when read; but it is much more profitable if one is turned from a letter to a voice, so that the one who had taught through an epistle may instruct the hearers in person.[357] For indeed the "living voice" has great

---

352. Cf. Lk 8.11.

353. Is 26.17–18.

354. Mt 12.50.

355. Cf. *CRm* 4.6.9; 7.7.4; 8.10.7.

356. The Novatianists were a sect founded by the followers of Novatus, or Novatian (d. 258), who was a learned Roman priest and author of an important book, *On the Trinity*. Disappointed in the election of pope St. Cornelius (d. 253) after the Decian persecution, he took a rigorist line over the treatment of those who had lapsed in the persecution. He denied the possibility of a second repentance after an act of apostasy and became an anti-pope. According to the church historian Socrates, he suffered martyrdom in the Valerian persecution. He is not to be confused with the Novatus who led the opposition to Cyprian in North Africa. Cf. *HE* 6.43, 45f.; 7.4.7f.; Jerome, *Commentariorum in Matthaeum libri IV*13.21; Ep. 42 to Marcella.

357. 2 Cor 10.9–11.

force: the voice of the author resounding with his own mouth, a voice which is brought forth with that delivery and is distinguished in such a way that it is produced in the very heart of the man. And so, knowing that speech has greater force when addressed to those who are present, the apostle longs to change the epistolary voice, the voice confined to a letter, into actual presence; and since this was more expedient for those who had been seduced by error, he desires to draw them back to the truth by "living words."

So this, then, is why he is "confounded" over them, which is more properly said in Greek; for ἀπορούμαι means not so much "confusion," which among them is called ἀισχύνη or συγχύσι, as "indigence" or "scarcity." And so the sense is this: "I want to be present" now "among you," and in person bring forth the voice of the letter, because I am in need "in respect to you." For I do not have the fruit that teachers customarily have from their disciples, and the seed of doctrines has been cast[358] in vain,[359] since I am experiencing complete poverty "in respect to you," so that I could burst forth with the voice of Jeremiah: "I have not helped, nor has anyone helped me."[360]

This passage can be interpreted in another way as well. The apostle Paul "became a Jew to the Jews to win the Jews";[361] and "to those who were under the law," he became as if he himself were "under the law";[362] and to the weak he "became weak, to win the weak."[363] This was in view of the characteristics of those whom he desired to save. He "changed his voice," and like an actor (since indeed he has become a "theater to the world, angels and men")[364] he changed his dress into different forms and voices. It is not that he was pretending to be what he was, but that he merely seemed to be what would have helped others. He perceives

---

358. Cf. Mt 13.3.
359. Cf. Gal 3.4.
360. Jer 15.10 (Septuagint).
361. 1 Cor 9.20.
362. 1 Cor 9.20.
363. 1 Cor 9.22.
364. Cf. 1 Cor 4.9.

that the Galatians are in need of different teaching; they need to be saved by a different way,[365] not that way by which they had first been brought to faith in Christ from paganism. Thus he is compelled to say, "I would willingly be present with you now and change my voice." "In respect to you," he says, I see that I am not helping, if I repeat the same things that I said at first. Therefore, since I do not know what to do and since I am drawn in different directions, I am torn, "I am confounded" and am being torn to pieces. And just as doctors, when they see that the force of their craft is not at first effective by means of medicine, they pass to other means and keep experimenting with what might help, making use of many different methods, until they attain to the cure. Thus what some soft poultice was ineffective in healing might be healed by a more pungent powder and a more severe form of healing. In the same way, since "I am confounded in respect to you" and am torn here and there, "I would willingly be present" to offer the "voice" of my letter with my mouth, that I might correct you more severely than usual. For an epistle cannot express the tone of the one scolding; it does not have the ability to resonate the loudness of the one who is angry and to exhibit in the shape of the written characters the grief of one's heart.

However, this passage can be understood more simply: I used coaxing words "with you now" when I said, "brothers, I beseech you" and "my little children, for whom I am again in labor until Christ is formed in you"; but I who spoke to you as a father am coaxing and gentle. In light of that love which prevents me from allowing my sons to perish and stray forever, "I would willingly now be present," if the chains of my confession did not constrain me,[366] and "change" my coaxing "voice" to words of scolding. It is not because of fickleness that I am coaxing one moment, irate the next. Love impels me, grief impels me to speak with different emotions. For I do not know into what words I should first burst forth and with what kind of medicine I ought to heal you, since "I am confounded in respect to you."

---

365. Cf. Mt 2.12.
366. Cf. Col 4.18; Eph 6.20; 2 Tm 1.16; 2.9.

4.21.　*Tell me, you who want to be under the law, have you not heard the law?* One should note that the historical narrative of Genesis is here called "law." It refers not, as is popularly thought, to what is to be done or what is to be avoided, but everything that is composed concerning Abraham and his wives and children is called "law." We read in another passage as well that the prophets too are called "law."[367] He "hears the law," then who, like Paul, looks not at its surface but into its marrow; he does not "hear the law" who, like the Galatians, follows only the outer shell.

4.22–23.　*For it is written that Abraham had two sons, one from a slave woman*[368] *and one from a free woman.*[369] *But the one from the slave woman was born according to the flesh; but he who was from the free woman was through a promise.* It is extremely difficult to show that Isaac alone, who was from Sarah, was born "from a promise," and not Ishmael too, who was born from the Egyptian slave woman Hagar. For the Scripture relates that the pregnant Hagar fled from Sarah, who was persecuting her.[370] An angel came to her in the desert and warned her to submit to the authority of her mistress.[371] The same angel also said the following: "I shall greatly multiply your seed and it will not be numbered ahead of the multitude."[372] And afterward the angel spoke what assuredly no one can doubt are words "of promise" concerning Ishmael: "He will be a rustic man; his hand will be upon all and the hands of all will be upon him, and he will dwell against the presence of all his brothers."[373] But a response can be given, that an angel's promise is of lesser authority than one from God himself; for just as stars do not shine after the sun rises, so too the words of an angel are darkened and disappear and count for nothing in comparison with the promise

---

367. Cf. 1 Cor 14.21.
368. Cf. Gn 16.4.
369. Cf. Gn 21.2.
370. Cf. Gn 16.6; *CRm* 6.12.9.
371. Cf. Gn 16.9.
372. Cf. Gn 16.10.
373. Gn 16.12.

of God. This response does indeed appear to have some force, but immediately it is obliterated by the authority of the Scripture that follows. For it is written, "But Abraham said to God: 'May Ishmael himself live in your presence'; and God responded to him thus: 'Behold Sarah your wife will bear a son to you and you will call his name Isaac and I will establish my covenant with him in an eternal covenant and with his seed after him'; but of Ishmael: 'Behold I have heard you and behold I have blessed him and I will increase him and I will multiply him exceedingly. He will become the father of twelve nations and I will make him a great nation; but I will establish my covenant with Isaac, whom Sarah will bear for you at this time next year.'"[374] From this it is evident by the words of God himself that Ishmael was born according to "promise." But even this is solved as follows: the "promise" is properly fulfilled in the giving of the covenant, and it is one thing to bless, increase, and multiply exceedingly, as is written in Ishmael's case, but it is something else to make an heir through a covenant, which is said of Isaac, "I will establish my covenant with him in an eternal covenant and with his seed after him";[375] and in what follows, "But I will establish my covenant with Isaac, whom Sarah will bear you."[376] And just as gifts are one thing, but the property is something else, so legacies are one thing, but the inheritance is something else (for we read that gifts were given to the sons of Abraham's concubines, but the inheritance of the whole property was left to Sarah's son); so, as we have said, blessing and legacies are one thing, but the covenant something else. Moreover the following can be said: concerning Ishmael after he was conceived, either an angel or God spoke; but concerning Isaac before he was conceived in Sarah's womb, God made a promise. For the time being let these things be said. They correspond to what the mediocrity of our intelligence allows. Otherwise, if anyone is able to figure out anything better as an explanation of how Ishmael, "who was born from a slave woman," is not a son of a promise, but Isaac, "who [was born] from a

---

374. Gn 17.18–21.
375. Gn 17.19.
376. Gn 17.21.

free woman," let that person be listened to instead of me.[377] And "if you think anything otherwise," the apostle says, "God has revealed even this to you."[378]

Now one must briefly turn attention to deeper things. Thus we may say that each one of us at first is not born according to a "promise," so long as one is instructed by the simple words of the Scriptures and is still enticed by the Judaic explanations. But when one moves on to the deeper matters and understands the spiritual law,[379] then he is begotten "of the promise," and, if I may speak quite plainly, those who do the works of Abraham[380] are being born daily from Abraham. But those who have the spirit of slavery again in fear[381] are born of the Egyptian slave woman; but those who have received the spirit of adoption[382] are from the free woman Sarah. Christ has gifted us with this freedom.[383] The Lord says to the Jews who still preferred to be sons of the slave woman, "If you abide in my words, you will truly be my disciples, and you will know the truth and the truth will make you free."[384] This is why those who do not understand that what was said is mystical say, "We are Abraham's seed and have never been enslaved to anyone. How is it that you say, 'You will be free?' Jesus answered them: 'Amen, amen, I say to you, that everyone who commits sin is a slave of sin. But a slave does not remain in the house for ever; the son remains forever.'"[385] If we are slaves of sin, the Egyptian Hagar bore us; if sin does not reign in our mortal body,[386] we are truly God's sons.

---

377. This kind of expression of humility is frequent in Origen (another indication that Jerome is probably translating Origen here). For example, in *CRm* 5.8.9 Origen says: "If, however, someone discerns something better, let the reader not feel reluctant to receive those things, leaving behind the things [I have said]."

378. Phil 3.15.

379. Cf. Rom 7.14.

380. Cf. Jn 8.39.

381. Cf. Rom 8.15.

382. Cf. Rom 8.15.

383. Cf. Gal 4.31.

384. Jn 8.31–32.

385. Jn 8.33–35.

386. Cf. Rom 6.12.

4.24.   *These things are indeed allegorical.* Allegory is properly a term from the art of grammar. How it differs from metaphor and other figures of speech we learn in school as children. It presents one thing in words and signifies something else in its meaning. The books of the poets and orators are filled with allegory. Holy Scripture too in no small part is composed in this way. The apostle Paul understands this, for the one who had some knowledge of secular literature also has used the very word of this figure of speech when he called it "allegory," just as it is called among his own people. By using (*abusione*)[387] precisely this Greek *word,* he points more strongly to the *meaning* of the passage.

Now Paul's own words bear witness that he knew secular literature (granted not perfectly):[388] "One of their own prophets has said, 'Cretans are always liars, evil brutes, idle bellies.'"[389] This is an epic line from the poet Epimenides,[390] who is mentioned by both Plato and other ancient writers. And when he was giving his apology on the Areopagus among the Athenians, Paul added this: "Just as some of your poets have said: 'For we are his offspring.'"[391] This half-verse is taken from Aratus,[392] who was writing about the sky and the stars. And besides there is this: "Bad company corrupts good morals."[393] This iambic

---

387. *Abusione* can also mean "misusing."

388. Harnack, *Der kirchengeschichtliche Ertrag,* p. 150, traces the classical knowledge that is displayed in what follows to Jerome's source in Origen.

389. Ti 1.12; Aratus, *Phaenomena* 5.

390. Epimenides of Crete, holy man of the late seventh century BC, was supposed to have been called in to purify Athens after the sacrilege of the Cylon affair (Aristotle, *Athenaion politeia* 1). Plato, however, puts him a century later (*Leges* 642d). Genuine traditions about him were quickly obscured by legends and miraculous tales. Many early epic works were attached to his name, including oracles, a *Theogony,* and an Argonautic poem.

391. Acts 17.28.

392. Aratus (c. 315–240 BC) was a Greek poet from Cilicia, who came to Athens, where he learned Stoicism from Zeno and became a friend of Callimachus. His most famous work was his *Phaenomena,* a long astrological poem on the fixed stars and constellations and the myths attached to them.

393. 1 Cor 15.33; Menander, fr. 187.

trimeter is taken from a comedy of Menander.[394] From these and other passages it is clear that Paul was not ignorant of secular literature. What he has here called "allegory" elsewhere he called the *spiritual* understanding, as for instance in this passage: "For we know that the law is spiritual."[395] This is said in view of the fact that the law is allegorical, or figured allegorically. And elsewhere he writes, "And all consumed the same *spiritual* food and drank the same *spiritual* drink. For they drank from the *spiritual* rock that followed them, but the rock was Christ."[396] Here there is no one who doubts that these things need to be interpreted allegorically: the manna, the sudden bursting forth of a spring, and the very rock that follows. I am aware that something could be objected to the contrary: "Brothers, if a man is taken in some transgression, you who are *spiritual* must instruct such a one with a spirit of gentleness";[397] and in another place: "But the *spiritual* man judges all things, but he himself is judged by no one."[398] This of course expresses something different from the word "spiritual" we spoke of above. But we call that man "spiritual," who "judges all things and is himself judged by no one," who, while knowing all the mysteries[399] of the Scriptures, understands these things loftily, and, while seeing Christ in the holy books, admits nothing of the Judaic tradition in them.

4.24–26.   *For these are two covenants, one from Mount Sinai, bearing unto slavery, which is Hagar. For Mount Sinai is in Arabia, which is adjacent to that which is the present Jerusalem, and it is enslaved with her sons. But the Jerusalem that is above is free, which is the mother of us all.* This is the explanation of nearly everyone on this passage: they interpret Hagar the slave woman as the law and the people of the Jews; but

----

394. Menander (341–290 BC) was the most distinguished author of Greek New Comedy, who wrote over a hundred plays of which only one survives, the *Dyscolus*, or *Bad-Tempered Man*. His Roman imitators were Plautus and Terence.

395. Rom 7.14.

396. 1 Cor 10.3–4.

397. Gal 6.1.

398. 1 Cor 2.15.

399. Cf. 1 Cor 13.2.

Sarah the free woman is the church that is gathered from the Gentiles, which is "mother" of the saints, since Paul says, "which is mother of us all." For a long time she did not give birth, before Christ was born of the virgin.[400] She was sterile, since the laughter of the world, Isaac, from a chosen father, was not yet resounding with the voice of lofty teachings. For indeed Abraham in our language is related in sound to "chosen father." But Hagar, which translates as παροικία, that is, "resident alien" or "wandering," gives birth to Ishmael without delay. He merely hears God's commands and does not do them, a rustic man, bloodthirsty, hunting in the desert, who is an adversary to all his own brothers who were born from the free woman and resists them with a hostile look. It is no wonder that the old covenant, which is on Mount "Sinai, which is in Arabia" and nearby to "that which is the present Jerusalem," is not constituted and recorded to be perpetual. For a resident alien is different from perpetual possession; and the name of "Mount Sinai" means "temptation." Arabia means "death" and, on the other hand, "the Jerusalem that is above," which "is free" and "mother" of the saints, shows that this Jerusalem, which is for the present, is from below and is submerged at the lowly bottom.

There are those who understand the "two covenants" in another way as well, as referring to holy Scripture, both the old and the new, in accordance with the difference in meaning. They interpret the meaning of those who read slave woman and free woman like this: they want those who are born from Hagar the Egyptian to refer to those who still serve the letter and have the spirit of fear in slavery.[401] On the other hand they understand those who ascend to higher things and who wish to understand what is written allegorically to be the sons of Sarah, which in our language translates ἄρχουσα, that is, ruler, a word that [in Greek] is feminine in gender. And they claim that they are forced to adopt this view out of necessity, since it would be unjust to understand Moses and all the prophets as children of the slave woman, but whoever comes from the Gentiles are from the free woman. This is why

---

400. Cf. Mt 1.18–25; Lk 2.26–38.
401. Cf. Rom 8.15.

they think that it is better not only that some of those who are in the church should be thought of as slaves, in view of the diversity of understandings (as we said above), and others as sons; but even he is a son of the slave woman who is from one and the same man, as long as he follows the history. But when Jesus opens the Scriptures,[402] his heart is set on fire,[403] and in the breaking of the bread he gazes on him whom previously he did not see.[404] Then he himself is called a son of Sarah.

Marcion and Manicheus[405] were unwilling to remove this passage from their codex, in which the apostle said, "these things are indeed allegorical," and the other things that follow. They imagined that they could leave it as a testimony against us, namely, that the law should be understood otherwise than as it has been written, though assuredly, even if it is to be taken allegorically (as we too confess and as Paul teaches), it was not so constituted for the sake of the will of the reader but for the authority of the writer. And in this very thing that they have seemed to have retained against us, they are obliterated. For Moses, the slave of the Creator,[406] wrote spiritual things, as their own "Apostle" teaches, whom they assert was a proclaimer of another Christ and of a superior God.

4.27.   *For it is written: "Rejoice, you barren one who does not give birth, break forth and cry, you who do not travail; for many are the sons of the desert, more than of her who has a husband."*[407] The synagogue "had a husband," the law, and according to the prophecy of Hannah too, it was once teeming with children.[408] But the church, while she was in the

---

402. Cf. Lk 24.27.

403. Cf. Lk 24.32.

404. Cf. Lk 24.30–31.

405. Harnack, *Der kirchengeschichtliche Ertrag*, p. 149, traces this passage with certainty to Origen, but asks whether Jerome may have added "and Manicheus" to the original. In *CRm* 2.13.27 Origen says that Marcion "takes no pleasure at all in allegorical interpretation."

406. Cf. Jos 1.2.

407. Is 54.1. Cf. *CRm* 6.7.9.

408. Cf. 1 Sm 2.5.

desert, was barren, without Christ as a husband, without any reassuring words of the groom's talk. But after she received the bill of divorce in her hands and turned all the husband's jewelry into an idol's adornment, then the husband, since the first girdle was rotten,[409] wove together another belt for his loins, another apron from the Gentiles. As soon as she was united with the husband, she conceived and gave birth. And in Isaiah the Lord cries out through the prophet: "Has a nation been born at once?"[410] referring to the time when in one day in the Acts of the Apostles three thousand and five thousand men believed.[411] I do not think it necessary to speak about the multitude of Christians versus the paucity of the Jews. For the banners of the cross are resplendent in the whole world and seldom does a rare and notable Jew appear in the cities.

4.28.   *But we, brothers, are sons of promise according to Isaac.* There is no difficulty in understanding how the apostle and those like him are "sons of promise according to Isaac." For Origen explained this passage and recorded the warning of the apostle in this way:

"But you, brothers, are sons of promise according to Isaac." It is asked: In what sense is he now calling the Galatians "sons of promise according to Isaac." For he had called them fools;[412] and he had said of them that they had "begun in the Spirit" and were "finishing in the flesh."[413] And so, we say that the apostle called them "sons of promise according to Isaac," because he did not completely despair of their salvation. He judges that they would return again to the Spirit, in which they had begun, and become sons of the free woman. But if they finish in the flesh, they would be sons of the slave woman.

409. Cf. Jer 13.7.
410. Is 66.8.
411. Cf. Acts 2.41; 4.4.
412. Cf. Gal 3.1.
413. Cf. Gal 3.3.

4.29–31.   *But just as at that time the one who was born according to the flesh persecuted him who was according to the Spirit, so also now. But what does the Scripture say? "Cast out the slave woman and her son. For the son of the slave woman will not be heir with my son Isaac."*[414] *And so, brothers, we are not sons of the slave woman, but of the free woman. With this freedom Christ has freed us.* I do not think we can find a place where Ishmael persecuted Isaac, but only the following: when the son of the Egyptian woman, who was older by birth, was playing with Isaac,[415] Sarah became indignant and said to Abraham, "Cast out the slave woman and her son; for the son of the slave woman will not inherit with my son Isaac."[416] Now assuredly simple play among children does not deserve expulsion and renunciation. But the apostle was a Hebrew from the Hebrews.[417] He had been taught at the feet of the teacher Gamaliel,[418] who had once come up with a plan to hold the Pharisees in check, when they were raging against the Lord.[419] The apostle understood from the words of Sarah, "For the son of the slave woman will not inherit with my son Isaac," that this had not been simple play. But perhaps it was because Ishmael, as the one who was older by birth and who had been circumcised at a time when he was already able to understand and sense what he had endured, was laying claim to the rights of the firstborn for himself. Therefore Scripture has called a quarrel between boys "play." Whence also Sarah refuses to put up with these words. She does not tolerate the practice of the slave woman's son, who as a mere youth is laying claim to the rights of the firstborn for himself. And she erupts into a voice: "Cast out the slave woman with her son; for the son of the slave woman will not inherit

---

414. Gn 21.10.

415. Gn 21.9. This reading corresponds with the Greek and Vulgate reading. The Hebrew lacks "with her son Isaac." See RSV ad loc. This is an indication that Jerome is translating Origen's exegesis, which was always based on the Septuagint reading.

416. Gn 21.10.

417. Cf. Phil 3.5.

418. Cf. Acts 22.3.

419. Cf. Acts 5.33–42.

with my son Isaac." Since this seemed harsh to Abraham (for greater things are always owed to the firstborn), not only to stop Ishmael from being the first, but that he would not even receive a portion that was equal to that of his younger brother, God confirms Sarah's words. For he wanted the free woman to be inside and the slave woman to be cast outside. He says to Abraham: "Let it not be a harsh thing before you concerning the boy and the slave woman. Listen to Sarah's voice in all the things that she has spoken to you; for in Isaac will your seed be called."[420]

Therefore, just as at that time Ishmael, the elder brother, persecuted Isaac who was still a nursing infant, and claimed for himself the prerogative of circumcision and the inheritance rights of the firstborn, "so also now" is Israel "according to the flesh" lifted up, puffed up, and incited against her younger brother, the Christian people from the Gentiles.[421] Let us consider the insanity of the Jews, who killed both the Lord and the prophets who persecuted the apostles, and who are opposed to the will of God.[422] We will see the degree to which even history teaches us that the persecutions incited by Jews against Christians are greater than those that have come from the Gentiles.[423] Do we wonder about the Jews? Even today those who are infants in Christ and live carnally[424] persecute those who are born of water and the Spirit,[425] and who, by rising with Christ, seek the things that are above, not below.[426] Let them do what they want, let them persecute Isaac along with Ishmael: they will be cast outside with their Egyptian mother, the slave woman; they will not receive the inheritance that only he who has been born of the promise will attain.

---

420. Gn 21.12.

421. Cf. *CRm* 6.12.9.

422. Cf. 1 Thes 2.15.

423. This statement would have been true of the New Testament period and for the second and third centuries up through Origen's lifetime, but it hardly seems to apply to Jerome's epoch. This would indicate that Jerome is drawing on Origen's exegesis here.

424. Cf. 1 Cor 3.1–2.

425. Cf. Jn 3.5.

426. Cf. Col 3.1–2.

But it is elegantly said that "he who was born according to the flesh" persecutes the spiritual. For the spiritual never persecutes the fleshly, but he pardons him as the rustic brother. He knows that [this brother] can make progress over time, and if ever he sees the angry son of the Egyptian woman, he recalls their one father who created both elephants and gnats. He remembers that "in a large house there are not only vessels of gold and silver, but of wood and clay."[427] And so, let us say with the apostle Paul, "We are not sons of the slave woman, but of the free." And renewed in Christ, let us listen to the words of the Lord when he is speaking to the Jews: "If you will remain in my words, you will know the truth and the truth will set you free."[428] By this freedom the apostle was liberated and said, "For though I am free from all."[429] "He who commits sin is a slave of sin."[430] That man, because he was free from all vices, because he knew that he was estranged from all concupiscence and error, rightly rejoiced in his freedom in Christ, and said, "We are not sons of the slave woman, but of the free. By this freedom Christ has freed us."

5.1.   *Stand, and do not be held again under the yoke of slavery.* From this it is shown that he does not "stand" who cleaves to the "yoke of slavery"; and also that he who has been gifted with freedom from Christ is "under the yoke" as long as he has the spirit "of slavery" in fear,[431] and has followed the beginnings of the law. Now his word "stand" encourages firm and stable faith in Christ, that the churches of Galatia might continue with their feet planted in the Savior. In another passage the just man speaks thus: "He has set my feet upon the rock,"[432] because they are upon Christ.[433] Thus they are not borne around by

---

427. 2 Tm 2.20.
428. Jn 8.31–32.
429. 1 Cor 9.19.
430. Jn 8.34.
431. Cf. Rom 8.15.
432. Ps 40.2.
433. Cf. 1 Cor 10.4.

every wind of teaching[434] and carried off in different directions. This is also why it is said to those who are "standing," "And let him who 'stands' look out lest he fall";[435] and in another passage, "'Stand,' act manfully, be strong."[436] Thus do they "stand" with him whom Stephen saw "'standing' at the right hand of the Father,"[437] when he persevered to the point of martyrdom; and with him who said to Moses, "But you, 'stand' with me."[438]

Now he calls the law a "yoke of slavery." It is hard, difficult, and laborious; it wears out its adherents with heavy work day and night.[439] This is just what Peter says in the Acts of the Apostles: "Why are you trying to place a heavy *yoke* upon the neck of the brothers, which neither we nor our fathers were able to carry?"[440] But he has added "do not *again*," not because the Galatians had previously kept the law, but because the "yoke" of idolatry is heavy, because the people of the Egyptians were overwhelmed and drowned like lead in the Red Sea.[441] In accordance with this meaning, he had said above, "How is it that you turn *again* to weak and impoverished elements, to which you want to be enslaved *again,* by observing days and months and times and years?"[442] For the Galatians, who abandoned idols upon hearing the preaching of the apostle Paul, and immediately converted to the grace of the gospel, did not return to the slavery of the Judaic law (which they had never formerly known). But in their desire to observe "times," to be circumcised in the flesh and to offer corporeal sacrifices, they were in a sense returning to the same forms of worship that they had previously served in the state of idolatry. For they say that neither the

---

434. Cf. Eph 4.14.

435. 1 Cor 10.12.

436. 1 Cor 16.13.

437. Cf. Acts 7.55.

438. Dt 5.31. It is striking that Origen, in *CRm* 5.9.14, links Acts 7.55 with Dt 5.31 and 1 Cor 10.12.

439. Cf. Ps 1.2.

440. Acts 15.10.

441. Cf. Ex 15.10.

442. Gal 4.9–10.

Egyptian priests nor the Ishmaelites nor the Midianites have circumcision; but would that we were unaware that the nations do observe "days, months, and years," so that there would never be a festival that mixed us with them.

5.2.   *Behold, I Paul say to you that, if you are circumcised, Christ is of no benefit to you.* In the Gospel the Savior says to his disciples, "He who hears you hears me, he who receives you receives me."[443] And the apostle testifies, saying, "But I no longer live, but Christ lives in me";[444] and elsewhere, "Or do you seek proof that he who speaks in me is Christ?"[445] From this it is clearly proven that what he has now said, "Behold, I Paul say to you," is to be received not merely as Paul's words, but as the Lord's. For since even in the first letter to the Corinthians he first said, "Now to those who are married, I give a charge, not I but the Lord";[446] and he immediately added, "But to the rest, I command";[447] but lest his own authority should be thought to be trivial, he says, "I think that I too have the Spirit of God."[448] Thus by the Spirit and by Christ speaking in him he should not be held in contempt, who could have said in imitation of the prophets, "Thus says the Lord Almighty."[449] But his statement, "Behold I Paul say to you that, if you are circumcised, Christ is of no benefit to you," will become more significant if it is linked to the first part where he says, "Paul an apostle not from men nor through a man, but through Jesus Christ,"[450] and the rest. Thus those who are listening are roused not so much by the authority of the one sent as by that of the one sending.

Someone can say: What is written to the Romans contradicts this passage, "Circumcision is indeed of benefit if you keep the law";[451] and

---

443. Lk 10.16.
444. Gal 2.20.
445. 2 Cor 13.3.
446. 1 Cor 7.10.
447. 1 Cor 7.12.
448. 1 Cor 7.40.
449. Cf. Jer 6.6; 9.7.
450. Gal 1.1.
451. Rom 2.25.

further down, "Then what advantage has the Jew, or of what usefulness is circumcision? Much in every way. To begin with, because the oracles of God were entrusted to them."[452] For if "Christ is of no benefit" to those who have been circumcised, how is circumcision "of benefit" to those who keep the law? This will indeed be resolved by the following response. We say that the letter that was written to the Romans was addressed to those who had believed from the Jews and the Gentiles. Paul pleaded this so that neither people would be offended, that is to say, that both peoples would possess their own privileges. Thus the Gentiles were not to be circumcised and the circumcised were not to introduce uncircumcision.[453] But when writing to the Galatians he argues differently. For they were not from the circumcision, but they had believed from the Gentiles. Circumcision was not able to "benefit" those who after the grace of the gospel again returned to the "elements" of the law. And in the Acts of the Apostles, history narrates that when certain ones arose from the circumcision and claimed that those who had believed from the Gentiles ought to be circumcised and to keep the law of Moses, the elders who were in Jerusalem and the apostles who were equally gathered together decreed through a letter that the yoke of the law was not to be placed upon them; nor were they to observe it any further except merely to keep themselves from things sacrificed to idols and from blood and from fornication,[454] or, as is written in some copies, from strangled things.[455] And to remove any doubt about circumcision being of no "benefit," but that it was for the sake of those who had believed from the Jews, he qualified the opinion about circumcision

---

452. Rom 3.1–2.

453. In *CRm* 2.14.1 Origen summarizes Paul's conduct in Romans in this way: "In this letter Paul, like an arbiter sitting between the Jews and the Greeks, that is, believing Gentiles, summons and invites both groups to faith in Christ in such a way as to not offend the Jews completely by destroying the Jewish ceremonies nor to cause despair in the Gentiles by affirming the observance of the law and of the letter. And whether he is recalling the promises or the punishments, he apportions the word to each people." Cf. *CRm* 2.13.3.

454. Acts 15.29.

455. See RSV note, Acts 15.29.

that is found in the letter to the Romans, gradually descending to later things of the same epistle. He showed that circumcision and uncircumcision do not have any effect when he says, "And so, circumcision is nothing and uncircumcision is nothing, but keeping God's commands."[456] For so much so is it the case that circumcision is nothing that it brought no benefit even to the member of the house of Israel who boasts about his circumcision, as the prophet records: "All the nations are uncircumcised in flesh, but the house of Israel is uncircumcised in heart."[457] Moreover, the uncircumcised Melchizedek blessed the circumcised Abraham.[458] For his words, "if you are circumcised," are just as if he had wanted to say, "If you are circumcised" in the flesh. In another passage he does not call it circumcision but mutilation, when he says, "Beware of the mutilation. For we are the circumcision, who serve the Spirit of God and glory in Christ and do not have confidence in the flesh."[459] He does not have confidence in the flesh who expects every benefit from Christ. And he does not "sow in the flesh," that "from the flesh he would reap corruption," but "in the Spirit," from whom eternal life is born.[460]

The statement needs to be considered more deeply: "If you are circumcised, Christ is of no benefit to you." For not only is that circumcision "of no benefit" to them, if they are circumcised in him, but even if they seem to possess the other virtues outside of circumcision in Christ, everything would perish, when they are circumcised after faith in Christ. What then? Was circumcision "of no benefit" to Timothy?[461] Much in every way.[462] For he was circumcised not so much be-

---

456. 1 Cor 7.19. Jerome seems to have misremembered this passage as coming from Romans, unless the memory slip was found in his source, Origen.

457. Jer 9.26.

458. Cf. Gn 14.18–19. But Abraham was not circumcised until later (cf. Gn 17.10).

459. Phil 3.2–3.

460. Cf. Gal 6.8.

461. Cf. Acts 16.3.

462. Cf. Rom 3.2.

cause he reckoned that he was able to attain to some benefit from circumcision itself, as in order to gain others, having become a Jew to the Jews,[463] in order to lead the Jews to faith in Christ by his own circumcision. For circumcision is indeed "of no benefit" whenever it is thought to bring some advantage in and of itself.

5.3.   *But I testify to every man who circumcises himself, that he is a debtor to do the whole law.* God, who commanded circumcision first to Abraham,[464] then through Moses in the law,[465] established not only circumcision but many other things to be observed: feast days to be attended in Jerusalem,[466] the burnt offerings of sacrificial victims every morning and evening,[467] the sacrifice of a lamb in one place only,[468] giving the land a rest in the seventh summer,[469] the fiftieth year of remission,[470] and the other things which it is easy for each reader to gather for himself from the Scriptures. And so we will keep Ebion[471] at bay and his followers, who think that believers in Christ need to be circumcised after the gospel. Let them practice both circumcision *and* the other things that are commanded in the law; or, if it is impossible to do *everything,* let circumcision also cease, which along with the other things has been omitted as unprofitable. But if they respond that they are obligated to do only the things that are possible to do (for God does not demand of us things that we are not able to do, but what we are able to fulfill), we will say to them that it does not befit the same God to want the law to be kept and to forsake those who keep the law (or how will he make them guilty of suspending the law who cannot fulfill everything, even though they want to?). But we follow the spiritual law

---

463. Cf. 1 Cor 9.20–21.
464. Cf. Gn 17.10; 21.4; Jn 7.22.
465. Cf. Lv 12.3.
466. Cf. Ex 23.14–17.
467. Cf. Lv 1; Ex 29.39–41.
468. Cf. Ex 29.38–42.
469. Cf. Lv 25.4.
470. Cf. Lv 25.9–10.
471. See p. 55, n. 42 above.

that says, "You will not put a bridle in the mouth of an ox that is tread-ing out the grain."[472] And we understand with the apostle, "Does God care about oxen? But surely he says this for our sake."[473] As for observ-ing frivolous Sabbaths, this is not in order that our ox and ass and common beasts might be glad on the Sabbath, but it refers to those men and beasts of which it is written "You will save men and beasts, Lord,"[474] that is, all rational human beings and spiritual men. But the animals are those who are of more sluggish mind. They are instructed by the spiritual to carry out the Lord's Sabbaths. What he said above, "If you are circumcised, Christ is of no benefit to you,"[475] and what fol-lows, "I testify to every man who circumcises himself, that he is a debtor to do the whole law," does not contradict what we have intro-duced here. For it is not the hearers of the law who are just before God, but the doers of the law will be justified.[476] For that one is a doer of the law who can say, "We are the circumcision"[477] and "the Jew is in se-cret,"[478] and, "We know that the law is spiritual."[479] But the one who would follow the mutilation[480] and the killing letter[481] is not a doer of the law, but an enemy of the true law. This is especially so after the coming of the Savior, who removes the veil from the heart of those who turn to him,[482] so that all of us, with an unveiled face, may con-template the Lord's glory and be transformed from the oldness of the letter into the newness of the Spirit.[483]

---

472. Dt 25.4; 1 Tm 5.18.
473. 1 Cor 9.9–10.
474. Ps 36.6.
475. Gal 5.2.
476. Cf. Rom 2.13.
477. Phil 3.3.
478. Rom 2.29.
479. Rom 7.14.
480. Cf. Phil 3.2.
481. Cf. 2 Cor 3.6.
482. Cf. 2 Cor 3.16; Ex 34.34.
483. Cf. 2 Cor 3.18.

5.4. *You who are being justified in the law have been made void of Christ, you have fallen away from grace.* Just as no one can serve two masters,[484] so it is difficult to fulfill both the shadow and the truth of the law at the same time. There is a shadow on the old law until day dawns and the shadows are removed.[485] The truth is in the gospel of Christ, "For grace and truth have come through Jesus Christ."[486] Therefore one who thinks that he "is justified" by some observance of the law destroys the grace of Christ and loses the gospel that he had held fast. And when he has lost "grace," he is destroyed from faith in Christ and stops in his work. For κατηργήθητε ἀπὸ τοῦ χριστοῦ does not mean, as it has been poorly translated into Latin, "you have been made void of Christ," but instead, "you have ceased in the work of Christ." Thus what he had commanded above in particular about circumcision, when he said, "if you are circumcised, Christ is of no benefit to you," now embraces the whole law universally: it does not contribute to the advancement in the works of Christ for those who believed that they must be justified by some observance of the law.

5.5. *For by the Spirit we await the hope of justice by faith.* He recorded "Spirit" in distinction from letter; but "hope of justice" must be understood of Christ. For he is truth,[487] patience,[488] hope,[489] justice,[490] and all virtues.[491] We "await" his second coming[492] when he will judge all things[493] and will be present not with patience but with justice, to repay to each one in accordance with his works.[494] While "awaiting" the

---

484. Cf. Mt 6.24.
485. Cf. Sg 2.17.
486. Jn 1.17.
487. Cf. Jn 14.6.
488. Cf. Gal 5.22.
489. Cf. Col 1.27.
490. Cf. 1 Cor 1.30.
491. Cf. Col 3.12–15; Heb 9.28.
492. Cf. Phil 3.20.
493. Cf. 2 Tm 4.1.
494. Cf. Ps 28.4; 62.12; Pr 24.12; Sir 35.19; Mt 16.27; Rom 2.6; Rv 22.12.

arrival of this day, the apostle and those who are like him say, "Thy kingdom come."[495] Thus when the Son hands over the kingdom to God the Father and is himself subjected to all things that are subject, then the head is subjected in the body and God is all in all.[496] For the one who is now in part through each individual will then begin to be the whole through all.

5.6.   *For in Christ Jesus neither circumcision is of any value nor uncircumcision, but faith that works through love.* The virtues need to be sought after by those who want to live "in Christ Jesus," and the vices must be shunned. But the indifferent things, which are between the virtues and vices, do not need to be shunned or sought after, such as "circumcision," "uncircumcision," and other things similar to these. To be sure "circumcision" is beneficial if you keep the law.[497] The reason it was useful to those who lived under the law was not because they had been circumcised, but because the oracles of God were entrusted to them,[498] by which they, by turning to works, were not estranged from salvation. We should not be disturbed by the fact that Zipporah took a flint knife and circumcised her son and hindered the strangling angel from her husband (or as it is related differently in the Hebrew).[499] For he has now attested not so much that circumcision is of no benefit absolutely as that it does not "have value in Christ Jesus." Indeed from that time when the gospel flashed forth into the whole world, the injury of circumcision is superfluous. Formerly it and other things of the law too "had value," when even carnal blessings were promised to those who kept the law, namely, that if they should fulfill it, they would be blessed in the city, blessed in the country, they would have full barns, and many other things that are contained among the promises.[500] But we want to "have value" and be strengthened "in Christ

495. Mt 6.10; Lk 11.2.
496. Cf. 1 Cor 15.28.
497. Cf. Rom 2.25.
498. Cf. Rom 3.2.
499. Cf. Ex 4.24–26.
500. Cf. Dt 28.3–14.

Jesus," that is, in the true circumcision and not in Judaic mutilation.[501] "For he who is in the open is not a Jew, and circumcision is not manifest in the flesh, but a Jew is in secret, and circumcision is of the heart in the Spirit, not the letter."[502] And so, in Christ it is not the circumcision of the flesh that benefits, but that of the heart,[503] and of the ears, which removes the reproach of the Jews: "Behold your ears are uncircumcised and you cannot hear."[504] Of benefit too is the circumcision of the lips, which Moses, in accordance with his humility,[505] did not yet claim to possess, as is written in the Hebrew, "But I am uncircumcised in lips."[506] Circumcision offers great advantage even in sexual matters, when unchastity is cut off by chastity.

Therefore "in Christ Jesus neither (bodily) circumcision nor uncircumcision has value," because they are indifferent, that is, they are placed between the vices and the virtues, "but faith which works through love." Thus both the faith which is reputed to Abraham as justice is proven,[507] and every work of faith in love is placed on those who hang by love from the whole law and the prophets. For indeed, the Savior claims that the law and the prophets "consist"[508] in these two commands: "You shall love your God and you shall love your neighbor."[509] And Paul says in another passage, "For 'you shall not commit adultery,' 'you shall not steal,' 'you shall not covet,' and if there is any other commandment, it is summarized in these words: 'You shall love your neighbor as yourself.'"[510] So, if every commandment is summarized in what is said, "You shall love your neighbor as yourself," but "faith working through love" has more value, then it is manifest that the

---

501. Cf. Phil 3.1–2.
502. Rom 2.28–29.
503. Cf. Jer 4.4.
504. Jer 6.10.
505. Cf. Nm 12.3.
506. Ex 6.12.
507. Cf. Gn 15.6.
508. Cf. Mt 22.40.
509. Cf. Mt 22.37, 39.
510. Rom 13.9.

working of faith through love contains the fulfillment of all the commands. But just as, according to the apostle James, faith without works is dead,[511] so without faith, works are reckoned as dead, even though they may be good. Consequently, do those who do not believe in Christ and who are of good character have anything more than virtuous works? That prostitute from the gospel may offer an example of "faith that works through love." When the Lord was reclining in the house of the Pharisee, she washed his feet with her tears, wiped them with her hair, and soothed them with ointment. When the Pharisee murmured about this, the Lord set forth the parable of the debtor of fifty and five hundred denarii[512] and added, "Therefore I tell you, her many sins are forgiven, for she loved much."[513] And turning to the woman herself he said, "Your faith has saved you: Go in peace."[514] For it is openly shown in this passage that this woman had "faith working through love," which "had" much "value in Christ."

So be it, someone may say. He has shown well that "circumcision is of no value in Christ," which he knew once had value. But was anyone in doubt about "uncircumcision," so that he is led to say, "nor uncircumcision"? But consider the fact that the majority of Christians, that is, of us, who were grafted from the wild olive tree into the root of the good olive, exult against the branches of the people of the Jews that were broken off.[515] We claim instead that uncircumcision, in which Abraham pleased God and his faith was reckoned to him for justice,[516] is of more value than circumcision. It was given as a sign of faith[517] and did not benefit Israel who had it. If we think about this, we will see that even this arrogant boast of certain people has now also been excluded with the greatest foresight.

---

511. Cf. Jas 2.26.
512. Cf. Lk 7.40–46.
513. Lk 7.47.
514. Lk 7.50.
515. Cf. Rom 11.17–19.
516. Cf. Gn 15.6; Gal 3.6.
517. Cf. Rom 4.11.

Commentary on

Galatians

BOOK THREE

Preface

We are hammering out a third book on Galatians, O Paula and Eustochium, well aware of our weakness and conscious that our slender ability flows in but a small stream and makes little roar and rattle. For these are the qualities that are now looked for even in the churches. The simplicity and purity of apostolic language is neglected, and we meet as if we were in the Athenaeum[1] or in auditoriums aiming to kindle the applause of the bystanders. What is now required is a discourse painted and decked out with spurious rhetorical skill, and that aims, like a public prostitute, not at instructing the people but at winning their favor. Like a stringed instrument or a sweet-sounding flute, it must soothe the ears of the audience. Thus the passage in the prophet Ezekiel can truly be applied to our times, where the Lord says to him, "You have become to them as a sweet-sounding and well-made lyre;

---

1. The Athenaeum was a famous institution founded by Emperor Hadrian (117–38) for the study of Greek rhetoric and literature in Rome. Its precise location is uncertain. In the fourth century AD it was the setting for public declamation in Latin as well. Cf. OCD, p. 202.

and they hear your words but do not do them."[2] But what should I do? Should I be silent? But it is written, "You shall not appear in the sight of the Lord your God empty."[3] And Isaiah groans (at least according to the Hebrew books[4]), "Woe to wretched me, for I have kept silent."[5] Should I speak? But the harsh sound of the Hebrew reading has ruined all the elegance of my words and the beauty of the Latin language. For you know well that it is now more than fifteen years since Cicero,[6] Virgil,[7] or any author of secular literature has even come[8] into my hands.[9] And if anything from those sources perchance sneaks in while we are speaking, we are remembering it as if through the fog of a dream of long ago. But what I have gained by my tireless study of Hebrew[10] I leave to others to decide; what I have lost in my own language, I can tell. In addition to this, on account of the weakness of my eyes and bodily infirmity generally, I do not write with my own hand. Moreover, I cannot compensate for my slowness of utterance by effort and diligence, as is said to have been the case with Virgil, of whom it is related that he treated his books as a bear treats her cubs, and licked them into shape.[11] But I must summon a secretary, and either dictate at once whatever comes into my head, or, if I wish to think a little bit in the hope of producing something better, my assistant silently reproves me, shakes his fist at me, wrinkles his brow, and plainly declares by all his bodily gestures that he has come for no reason. But a speech, though it has been set forth by a mind equipped with good natural ability and

---

2. Ezek 33.32.

3. Cf. Ex 23.15; Dt 16.16.

4. The Septuagint of Is 6.5 has "for I am pricked to the heart."

5. Is 6.5.

6. Tullius.

7. Maro.

8. Lit. "ascended."

9. This appears to be a reference to Jerome's famous dream; cf. Ep. 22.30 to Eustochium.

10. Lit. "of that language."

11. Cf. Suetonius, *frg* p. 59.12–16; Aulus Gellius 17.10.2–3; Jerome, *Commentariorum in Zachariam libri III, Praefatio* 12–14 (p. 848).

distinguished by originality and decorated by verbal flowers, neverthe-less, if it is not refined and polished by the hand of the author himself, it does not glisten, it does not combine dignity with charm; but in the manner of rich farmers, it is left to its own resources rather than adorned.

What is my point? Let this be my response to you and to others (who may perhaps want to read this): I am writing neither a panegyric nor a disputation, but a commentary. That is to say, my purpose is not that my words be praised but that things that were well said by some-one else may be understood just as they were spoken. My duty is to ex-plain what is obscure, to lightly touch upon what is clear, to pause over what is ambiguous. This is why the majority of people call the work of a commentary an explanation. If someone is looking for eloquence, or if someone delights in declamations, he has in the two languages Demosthenes[12] and Tullius (Cicero),[13] Polemon[14] and Quintilian.[15] The

---

12. Demosthenes (384–322 BC) was an Athenian orator and statesman, gener-ally considered to be the greatest of Greek orators and master of prose style. His *Olynthiacs* and *Philippics* are directed against Philip, and his most famous speech was entitled *On the Crown* (*De Corona*). "Philippics" as a title for speeches of invec-tive was adopted by Cicero for his own speeches against Mark Antony after the death of Caesar.

13. Marcus Tullius Cicero (143–106 BC) was the greatest of Latin orators and supreme master of prose style.

14. Marcus Antonius Polemon (c. 88–144) of Laodicea-Lycus was a prominent sophist who was chosen to deliver the inaugural oration for Hadrian's Olympieum at Athens in AD 130. His oratory was in the grand manner, his delivery passionate and excited. Extant are two declamations in which the fathers of two heroes of Marathon present their sons' claims for the prize of valor. The subjects of other dec-lamations are known from Philostratus.

15. Marcus Fabius Quintilianus (35–100) was a Roman rhetorician and teacher from Spain, appointed first professor of rhetoric at Rome by Emperor Vespasian. Tacitus and the younger Pliny were among his pupils, and he was admired by Juve-nal. His speeches are lost, but his most important work has survived complete in ten books, *Institutio Oratoria, Education of an Orator*.

church of Christ has not been gathered from the Academy[16] and the Lyceum,[17] but from the common rabble. This is why the apostle says, "Consider your calling, brothers, for not many were wise according to the flesh, not many were powerful, not many were well-born, but God chose the things that are foolish in this world in order to confound the wise; and God chose the weak things of the world and the contemptible things and the things that are not in order to destroy the things that are."[18] For since, from the order, variety, and constancy of created things,[19] the world did not know God through wisdom,[20] it pleased God, through the foolishness of the preaching, to save believers, not by the wisdom of the word, lest the cross of Christ be made void.[21] (For "where is the wise man, where is the scholar?"[22] Where are the investigators of natural causes?) This was done "not in persuasive words of wisdom, but in a manifestation of virtue and the Spirit, so that the faith of believers would not be in the wisdom of men, but in the virtue of God."[23] For this reason the apostle himself said to the same Corinthians, "And when I came to you, brothers, I came not with lofty words and wisdom, proclaiming to you the testimony of the Lord. For I decided to know nothing among you except Christ Jesus and him crucified."[24] And lest perchance it should be thought that in saying this he is a proclaimer of foolishness, with prophetic foresight he undermines that very objection that could have been raised and says, "But we speak

---

16. The Academy was the public gymnasium at Athens, sacred to the hero Academus, which gave its name to the school founded there by Plato in the early fourth century BC and maintained by an unbroken line of successors until the first century BC.

17. The Lyceum is the name of the school established by Aristotle in Athens in 335 BC.

18. 1 Cor 1.26–28.

19. Cf. Wis 13.5.

20. Cf. Rom 1.20; 1 Cor 1.21.

21. Cf. 1 Cor 1.17.

22. Cf. 1 Cor 1.20.

23. Cf. 1 Cor 2.4–5.

24. 1 Cor 2.1–2.

God's wisdom in a mystery, which is hidden, which none of the rulers of this world knew."[25] How few there are who now read Aristotle! How many there are who know the books, or even the name, of Plato? You may find here and there a few old men who have nothing else to do who study them in a corner. But the whole world speaks the language of our rustic fishermen, the whole world expresses itself thus.[26] And so, their simple words must be set forth with simple speech; words, I say, not meaning. However that may be, if, with the help of your prayers, I could, in expounding their epistles, have the same spirit that they had when they dictated them, you would then see that there was in the apostles as much majesty and breadth of true wisdom as there was arrogance and vanity in the learned men of the world. If I may briefly confess a secret of my mind: I should not like anyone who wished with my help to understand the apostle to find it difficult to understand my writings, and so be compelled to find someone to interpret the interpreter. But now the time has come to pursue the rest.

The Third Book

5.7.   *You were running well; who hindered you from obeying the truth?* What the Latin translator has recorded here as "from obeying the truth" and is written in Greek as τῇ ἀληθείᾳ μὴ πείθεσθαι is translated in a passage higher up as follows: "from believing the truth." Now we have noted that this is not found in its own place in the old manuscripts, though even the Greek copies have been confused by this error.

---

25. 1 Cor 2.7–8.

26. John Chrysostom, *Homily 4 on Acts* (NPNF 11.29), has a passage that resembles Jerome here: "And Plato, who talked a great deal of nonsense in his day, is silent now, while this man [Christ] utters his voice everywhere; not among his own countrymen alone, but also among Parthians, and Medes, and Elamites, and in India, and in every part of the earth, and to the extremities of the world. Where now is Greece, with her big pretensions? Where the name of Athens? Where the ravings of the philosophers? He of Galilee, he of Bethsaida, he, the uncouth rustic, has overcome them all."

But this is the meaning: you worshiped the Father in spirit and truth,[27] and by receiving from the fullness of Christ,[28] you knew that the law was merely *given* to the people through Moses, it was not *made* as well. But grace and truth were not only *given* but also *made* through Jesus Christ.[29] Since, therefore, "you were running well," while serving the "truth" rather than images, by what perverted teacher have you been obstructed, so as to follow the shadow of the law and to abandon the truth of the gospel? Then follows, "You should not have consented to anyone." But since we have not found this reading in the Greek manuscripts or in commentaries on the apostle, it is apparently to be omitted.

5.8.   *Your persuasion is not from him who called you.* In the Latin manuscripts it is found written as follows: "Your persuasion *is* from *God* who called you." Now I think that this was "from *him*," but over time it was not understood. It arose on account of its likeness to "from God," in view of the fact that it *is* "from him." But the meaning cannot stand this way. He had just accused them of not obeying the truth. This shows that both their obedience and disobedience lay within their choice. It cannot be the case, then, that he is now claiming the opposite: that their persuasion and obedience is not so much from themselves, who are being called, as "from him who called." Therefore, the superior and more accurate reading is the following: "your persuasion is not from him who called you." For the work of God is one thing, man's part is something else: God's work is to "call"; man's is either to believe or not believe.[30] And if the free choice of man is affirmed anywhere else in the Scriptures, as for instance here, "If you are *willing* and

---

27. Cf. Jn 4.23–24.

28. Cf. Jn 1.16.

29. Cf. Jn 1.16–17.

30. Consider the parallel thoughts in John Chrysostom's *Homily 2 on Rom 1.17* (NPNF 11.349); *Homily 9 on Rom 4.2* (NPNF 11.396); and *Homily 14 on Rom 8.24* (NPNF 11.446). Cf. also Augustine, *Expositio in Epistulam ad Galatas* 42; CSEL 84:114; Ep. 211.3; CSEL 57:357–58. The latter texts were indicated to me by one of the anonymous readers of the manuscript.

will listen to me";[31] and again, "And now, Israel, what does the Lord your God seek from you?"[32] it is proven especially much from this passage. But all those who are rather simple think that they are deferring to God [by saying] that our "persuasion" too is in his power. They have removed the word "not," which is the aspect of prayer; and they have rendered a sense that contradicts the apostle.

Therefore, the cause of either the good or the evil part is neither God nor the devil. For "our persuasion is *not* from him who called us," but from us, who either *consent* or do not consent to the "one who calls." Another possibility: this "persuasion" that we now follow "is not from" God, who "called" you in the beginning, but from those who have caused trouble for you afterward.[33]

5.9. *A little leaven leavens the whole lump.* This is rendered badly in our manuscripts: "a little leaven corrupts the whole mass." The translator has rendered his own meaning rather than the apostle's words. Now Paul uses this same thought also [in the letter] to the Corinthians, when he commands the man who has his own father's wife to be removed from the midst[34] and to be handed over to repentance, for the destruction and harassment of the flesh, through fasting and sickness. Thus his spirit may be saved on the day of the Lord Jesus Christ.[35] For he says: "Your boasting is not good. Do you not know that a little leaven corrupts the whole mass?"[36]—or, as we have already corrected it, "leavens the whole lump?" And he immediately added, "Purge out the old leaven, that you may be a new lump, just as you are unleavened. For Christ our Passover has been sacrificed. And so, let us feast not with the old leaven, nor with the leaven of malice and wickedness, but with the unleavened bread of sincerity and truth."[37]

---

31. Ex 19.5.
32. Dt 10.12.
33. Cf. Gal 5.10.
34. Cf. 1 Cor 5.1–2.
35. Cf. 1 Cor 5.5.
36. 1 Cor 5.6.
37. 1 Cor 5.7–8.

But now by means of the very same thought, he is showing that the spiritual bread of the church, which came down from heaven,[38] must not be violated by the Judaic interpretation. And the Lord taught precisely this to his disciples, to beware of the "leaven" of the Pharisees.[39] The evangelist made this plainer when he added, "But he had spoken to them about the teaching of the Pharisees."[40] Moreover, what is this different teaching of the Pharisees, if not the observance of the law according to the flesh? And so, this is the meaning: Do not think that the plots of the few "men coming from Judea"[41] who teach differently are to be disregarded. A spark is a small thing, and it is almost not seen when it is discerned. But if it lays hold of tinder and finds material to feed itself on, although it is a small fire, it consumes walls, cities, and the largest forests and regions. "Leaven" too seems to be "little," indeed, nothing at all. In fact a parable in the gospel has qualified another aspect of it.[42] But when it is sprinkled into flour, it corrupts the "whole mass" with its vigor. It transfers its force into all that is mixed. So also, perverse teaching begins with one person and finds scarcely two or three hearers at the beginning. But gradually the cancer grows in the body, and in accordance with the popular proverb, one sheep's mange infects the whole flock. Therefore, even a spark should be extinguished as soon as it appears; and "leaven" should be separated from proximity to the mass; rotten flesh should be cut out, and a mangy animal should

---

38. Cf. Jn 6.32–33, 51.

39. Cf. Mt 16.6.

40. Mt 16.12.

41. Cf. Acts 15.1.

42. Cf. Mt 13.33.

43. Arius (260–336) was a priest from Alexandria whose doctrine was condemned at the Council of Nicaea in 325. He asserted that the Son is a creature in the proper sense of that word, and as such does not share in the divine nature. Arius believed that the Father created the Son in time, and, therefore, the Son has not always existed. The notorious Arian affirmation was: "There was a time when he (the Son) was not (that is, did not exist)." Important modern studies of the Arian crisis include M. Simonetti, *La crisi ariana nel IV secolo* (Rome: Institutum patristicum Augustinianum, 1975); R. Williams, *Arius: Heresy and Tradition* (London: Longman and Todd, 1987).

be driven away from the sheepfold of the sheep. Otherwise, the whole house may burn, the entire mass might be corrupted, the whole body may contract gangrene, all the livestock might perish. In Alexandria Arius[43] was a single spark; but because he was not immediately put down, his flame devastated the whole world.[44]

5.10.   *I have confidence in you in the Lord that you will think nothing else.* It is not by conjecture, as some think, but through a prophetic spirit, that Paul declares that the Galatians will return to the way of truth that they had lost. For he who exhorted others to be zealous for the gifts, but above all to prophesy,[45] himself spoke while filled with the same grace. "We know in part and we prophesy in part."[46] Foreseeing in the spirit, therefore, that they would believe "nothing else" but what they were being taught through his epistle, he says, "I have confidence in you in the Lord that you will think nothing else." For the addition of the Lord's name also indicates this very thing; for if he thought this by conjecture, he could have said, "I have confidence in you," but now he adds "in the Lord," since he is confident by means of some kind of divine spirit, because he knew that he has prophesied what will happen.

5.10.   *But the one who is troubling you will bear the judgment, whoever he is.* They say that Paul is secretly attacking Peter,[47] of whom he writes above that he "opposed him to his face,"[48] since he was not "proceeding on the right foot toward the truth of the gospel."[49] But Paul

---

44. The Council of Nicea of 325 condemned Arius's teaching and describes God's Son as "begotten, not made, one in being (*homoousios*) with the Father." But after the death of Constantine in 337, Arianism regained ascendancy in the East and spread far and wide.

45. Cf. 1 Cor 14.1.

46. 1 Cor 13.9.

47. Harnack, *Der kirchengeschichtliche Ertrag,* p. 149, identifies "they" as "the Marcionites" and traces this passage with certainty to Origen.

48. Cf. Gal 2.11.

49. Cf. Gal 2.14.

would not have spoken with such an offensive malediction of the ruler of the church;[50] nor did Peter deserve to be blamed for "troubling" the church. Therefore, it must be supposed that he is speaking of someone else, who had either been with the apostles,[51] or had come from Judea,[52] or was one of the believing Pharisees,[53] or at any rate who was reckoned important among the Galatians. This is the one who "will bear the judgment" of the church he has "troubled, whoever he is."

Now to "bear judgment" is expressed in different words in what follows when he said, "Each one will bear his own burden."[54] And I think that "burden" in the Scriptures can be understood in both a good and bad respect, that is to say, it is both in those who are oppressed by serious sins and in those who support the "light burdens" of the virtues.[55] The penitent man in the Psalm speaks of sins this way: "My iniquities have risen above my head, as a heavy burden they weigh down upon me."[56] Of the virtues and the teaching of the virtues the Savior says, "For my yoke is gentle and my burden is light."[57] Now it is also clear in the gospel that "teaching" may be understood as a "burden." For the Pharisees "tie heavy burdens" and those "which cannot be carried" and they "place them upon men's shoulders," but they themselves "are unwilling to touch them with one finger."[58]

The words of the Savior to the apostles testify to how "heavy" it is, to "trouble" someone from a state of tranquility and to incite the calm hearts of men as if by waves, as it were, when he says, "Do not be troubled, let not your heart fear."[59] For it is better for one who "troubles"

---

50. Cf. Mt 16.18.
51. Cf. Gal 2.12.
52. Cf. Acts 15.1.
53. Cf. Acts 15.5.
54. Gal 6.5.
55. Cf. Mt 11.30.
56. Ps 38.4.
57. Mt 11.30.
58. Cf. Mt 23.4.
59. Cf. Jn 14.27.

and scandalizes someone in the church to have a millstone placed around his neck and to be cast with it into the sea, than to scandalize one of the least of these, who are warned by the Savior.[60] Thus the Galatians had been "troubled," not knowing what to do between the spirit and the letter,[61] circumcision and mutilation,[62] secret and manifest Judaism.[63]

But it can be understood more concisely as follows: "whoever he is" who drags you back to the teaching of the Pharisees and desires that you be circumcised in the flesh, although he may be eloquent and may boast of being learned in the law, I say nothing but this (which even you cannot deny), that he "will bear judgment" for this deed, and he will attain to a "reward" for his labor.[64]

5.11.   *But I, brothers, if I preach circumcision, why do I still suffer persecution? Therefore the scandal of the cross has been made void* (or, as it is better rendered in the Greek, *has ceased*). We read in the Acts of the Apostles, and the apostle Paul himself often records in his epistles, that he endured very frequent persecutions from the Jews[65] because he taught that those who had believed in Christ from the Gentiles did not need to be circumcised.[66] And so, those of whom he says above, "But he who troubles you will bear judgment, whoever he is," because they wanted to cause the Galatians to despair, added this as well: Not only Peter, James, John, and the other apostles in Judea observe circumcision and the other commands of the law; moreover, even Paul himself, who taught you differently than comports with the truth of the matter, circumcised Timothy[67] and frequently became a Jew to the Jews[68] as

---

60. Cf. Lk 17.1–2.
61. Cf. 2 Cor 3.6.
62. Cf. Phil 3.2–3.
63. Cf. Rom 2.28–29.
64. Cf. 1 Cor 3.8; Mt 16.27; Rom 14.10; 2 Cor 5.10.
65. Cf. 2 Cor 11.24; 1 Thes 2.15.
66. Cf. Acts 21.21; 1 Cor 7.18.
67. Cf. Acts 16.3.
68. Cf. 1 Cor 9.20.

the truth compelled him to do. This is the opinion that Paul now wants to remove from the minds of the Galatians when he says, "But I, brothers, if I preach circumcision, why do I still suffer persecution?" He is saying, all the ill will of the Jews against me, and the insanity by means of which they rage against me, is for no other reason than that I teach that Gentiles do not need to be circumcised and to keep the superfluous burdens of the law, which have already been abolished. But since "I suffer persecution," it is plain that I am not "preaching the circumcision" that I destroy. For I do not "suffer persecution" from the Jews so much because I preach the crucified and say that Jesus is the Christ, whom the law and the prophets predicted,[69] as because I teach that the law has been completed.

Now that the "cross" is a "scandal" to the Jews, foolishness to the Gentiles, our Lord himself shows who is called the stone of offense and the rock of scandal,[70] I think, for no other reason except that when the preaching proceeds with full sails among the hearers, as soon as it reaches the cross, it dashes against it and can proceed no further by a free course. But this "cross," which is a scandal among the Jews and foolishness among the Gentiles,[71] to us who believe is the power and wisdom. "For Christ is the power of God and the wisdom of God."[72] Thus for the sake of what was called folly, the foolishness of God becomes wiser than men; and for the sake of what was weakness and scandal, the weakness of God becomes stronger than men.[73] But since, he says, the "scandal of the cross" of Christ remains, and since "I suffer persecution," which I would not suffer if the scandal did not remain, in vain do certain ones claim that I "preach circumcision." For it is for my opposition to it that I endure persecution.

---

69. Cf. 1 Cor 1.23.
70. Cf. Mt 21.42–44.
71. Cf. 1 Cor 1.23.
72. 1 Cor 1.24.
73. Cf. 1 Cor 1.25.

5.12.   *Would that they would even be cut off who are troubling you.* It is asked how Paul, a disciple of him who said, "Bless those who curse you,"[74] and who himself says, "Bless and do not curse,"[75] and in another passage, "those who curse will not possess the kingdom of God,"[76] now both curses those who were "troubling" the churches of Galatia, and he curses them with a prayer of one expressing a wish: "Would that they would even be cut off who are troubling you." For the suffering of amputation is necessarily so abhorrent that even the one who inflicted it unintentionally is punished by the public laws, and the one who castrates himself is regarded as disgraced.[77] For, they say, as the following is true, "Christ lives in me";[78] and this, "Or do you seek proof that it is Christ who is speaking in me?"[79] then certainly the sound of cursing cannot be understood to be his who says, "Learn from me, for I am humble and meek and gentle of heart."[80] Rather, Paul's inability to control himself is attributed to Judaic fury and to some sort of unhinged madness rather than to his being an imitator of him who like a lamb before its shearer did not open his own mouth[81] and who did not curse back to those who curse.[82] But he handed himself over as one condemned to death.

The one who will respond on Paul's behalf to this will say the following: what he has said is not so much words of fury directed against enemies as words of love directed at God's churches. For he saw that the whole province was troubled by a sudden persuasion, a province that he himself had converted from idolatry to faith in Christ by his own blood and dangers. And from apostolic grief, from the grief of a father, he could not control himself. He changed his voice and became

---

74. Lk 6.28.
75. Rom 12.14.
76. 1 Cor 6.10.
77. Cf. Lv 21.18.
78. Gal 2.20.
79. 2 Cor 13.3.
80. Mt 11.29.
81. Cf. Is 53.7.
82. Cf. 1 Pt 2.23.

angry with those whom he had been flattering, in order at least to keep in check by scolding those whom he was unable to restrain by leniency. Nor is it any wonder if the apostle, as a man still enclosed in a frail vessel and one who sees the law in his own body taking him captive and leading him into the law of sin,[83] should have spoken like this once. For we observe such lapses frequently in holy men.

Moreover, the following can be said (though it may seem to be superfluous to some), that Paul has not so much cursed them as prayed for them, that they might lose those parts of the body through which they were being compelled to transgress. And just as in the gospel it is said to be better that someone should enter into the kingdom of heaven without an eye and without a hand and without a foot and any other part of the members, than to go whole into Gehenna;[84] so also now he desires for them to lose one part of the body rather than, through the occasion of the whole body, to be condemned to eternal fire. If this passage is ever reprehended by pagans, we are showing how one could respond to them.

Now let us confront the heretics, namely Marcion, Valentinus, and all who snarl at the Old Testament, by making known what method those who accuse the Creator of being a bloodthirsty, ruthless warrior and merely a judge, are able to excuse these words in the apostle of the good God.[85] Certainly I do not think that any statement in the old law against anyone is so savage and cruel as, "would that they be cut off, those who trouble you." Nor can they say that the apostle has prayed for Christ's enemies who "trouble" his churches. Nor is affection demonstrated in this mass of words that he has brought forth, seeing that he is full of indignation and rage. Therefore whatever excuse they produce for the apostle, we shall make this our defense for the old law.[86]

---

83. Cf. Rom 7.23.

84. Cf. Mt 18.8–9.

85. Harnack, *Der kirchengeschichtliche Ertrag,* p. 149, lists this passage among those that certainly trace to Jerome's source in Origen.

86. A similar argument against heretics is given in Jerome's *Commentary on Matthew,* 21.37.

5.13a.   *For you have been called to freedom, brothers; only do not [give] freedom an opportunity for the flesh.* The Latin translator recorded "give," since it is not found in the Greek. Because of the excessive obscurity of this passage, I have decided to translate word for word from the tenth book of [Origen's] *Stromateis*. It is not that the details could not be explained in their own passages and with their own meanings, but that when they are separated from the larger issue, they become one difficult unit and, if they are understood just as they sound, they may appear to be an outburst that is self-contradictory, incoherent and abrupt.

And so, here are the words of Origen:

> The passage is difficult, and thus seems to require an explanation from us. The one who is "free" and follows the spirit and truth by means of the deeper sense thinks little of the types and the letter that precede. He should not on that account think little of the lesser ones and "give occasion" to those who are not able to understand more deeply concerning that which causes absolute desperation to themselves. For though they are weak and are called "flesh" in comparison with spirit, they are still *Christ's* "flesh." For if he understands the mystery of the love that serves those who are weaker, he does something for the sake of the weak, lest a brother for whom Christ died should perish by his knowledge.[87] Therefore, from what follows pay careful attention to whether this meaning is woven in.

> He says, "You, brothers, were called unto freedom."[88] Perhaps the reason not all were able to receive the call to "freedom" is because of what you now hear: "only do not give freedom an opportunity for the flesh." For because of love the greater ones should serve the lesser, since the one who wants to be greater will be servant of all.[89] Therefore let not the spiritual [man] wound Christ's

---

87. Cf. 1 Cor 8.10–11.
88. Gal 5.13.
89. Cf. Mk 10.44.

"flesh" or offer them an opportunity to bite the one provoking them, lest they be devoured by one another.[90] Therefore, it is necessary that the one who walks by the Spirit[91] and who follows the words of the Scriptures by the Spirit does not "fulfill the desire of the flesh"[92] of those Scriptures.

But if we understand in a simple way what is said, "Walk by the Spirit and you will not fulfill the desire of the flesh,"[93] (as the majority think), Paul will suddenly be erupting in an outburst that is contrary to the argument and thesis of the whole letter. For it immediately follows, "But if you are led by the Spirit, you are not under law." Up to this point the words cohere with one another in some measure. But on the other hand, if we follow the simple understanding, he suddenly transfers us to ill-suited commands by discussing the flesh and the Spirit, that is, "But the works of the flesh are manifest,"[94] this and that; and on the other hand, "but the fruit of the spirit is love,"[95] and the rest.

But we should not despair of the consequence of the fact that the history of the divine books contains "works of the flesh" and does not really help those who understand it just as it is written. For who will not be taught to be a slave to "excess"[96] and to regard "fornication" as nothing,[97] when he reads that Judah went to a prostitute,[98] and that many of the patriarchs were polygamous?[99] How will someone not be provoked to "idolatry"[100] who thinks that the blood of bulls and the other Levitical sacrifices[101] signify

---

90. Cf. Gal 5.15.
91. Cf. Gal 5.16.
92. Gal 5.16.
93. Gal 5.16.
94. Gal 5.19.
95. Gal 5.22.
96. Cf. Gal 5.19.
97. Cf. Gal 5.19.
98. Cf. Gn 38.14–18.
99. Cf. Gn 25.1.
100. Cf. Gal 5.20.
101. Cf. Lv 1–7.

nothing more than what is expressed in the letter? But that the words of Scripture that are recorded may openly teach "enmity"[102] is proven from this passage: "Wretched daughter of Babylon, blessed is he who will repay you with your own repayment that you paid out to us. Blessed is the one who will take your infants and dash them against the rock";[103] and from this, "In the morning I killed all the sinners in the land."[104] And there are other things similar to these, namely concerning "strife, jealousy, wrath, quarrels, and dissensions."[105] If we do not understand something deeper here, the examples of history would provoke, rather than prohibit, these vices. "Heresies"[106] too have come into being more from the carnal understanding of Scripture than, as the majority think, from the work of our flesh. Surely we learn "jealousy" and "drunkenness"[107] through the letter of the law: After the flood Noah gets drunk,[108] as do the patriarchs with their brother Joseph in Egypt.[109] Moreover "revelry"[110] is recorded in the book of Kingdoms, when David danced and made noise on drums before the ark of God's covenant;[111] and there are other things like this.[112] It is asked how the simple words of divine Scripture, which is called its "flesh," do not invite us to commit sorcery and evil arts, unless we transcend them to the Spirit of the same Scripture. I think that this is the meaning of Daniel and the three young men being found "ten times wiser" than the Magi, the enchanters, the sorcerers

---

102. Cf. Gal 5.20.
103. Ps 137.8–9.
104. Ps 101.8.
105. Cf. Gal 5.20.
106. Gal 5.20.
107. Gal 5.20–21.
108. Cf. Gn 9.21.
109. Cf. Gn 43.34.
110. Gal 5.21.
111. Cf. 2 Sm 6.14–16.
112. Cf. 1 Sm 18.6.

(*gazarenis*), and the Chaldeans;[113] and of Moses being educated in all the wisdom and teaching of the Egyptians.[114]

The occasion of many evils, therefore, is when someone remains in the "flesh" of Scripture. Those who do this will not "attain to the kingdom of God."[115] For this reason let us seek the spirit of Scripture and the fruits that are not said to be "manifest." For by much effort and sweat, and by worthy training in the Scriptures, the fruit of the Spirit is found. This is why I think that Paul has carefully and cautiously said of the fleshly senses of Scripture, "But the works of the *flesh* are manifest."[116] But on the other hand, of the spiritual meanings he did not record, as he did there, "the fruit of the Spirit" is *manifest,* but this: "But the fruit of the Spirit is love, joy, peace," and so on.[117] But if we leave the types behind and move on to the truth of Scripture and the Spirit, at once, first, "love"[118] is opened up to us, and from there, by moving on to "joy," we reach "peace," through which we attain to "patience." But who would not be instructed in "mercy" and "goodness," when even the things that are thought of by some as grievous things in the law—I mean punishments, battles, the overthrow of nations, and the threats against the people by the prophets—are understood instead to be remedies more than punishments?[119] For the Lord "will not be angry forever."[120] When these things are opened up to us, then, we will have a more rational "faith," and "moderation" will be in the company of upright character. "Self-control" will follow this, as well as "chastity." And after all these things the "law" will begin to be *for* us.[121]

---

113. Cf. Dn 1.20; 2.2.

114. Cf. Acts 7.22.

115. Cf. Gal 5.21.

116. Gal 5.19.

117. Gal 5.22.

118. Here begins Origen's progression through the virtues listed in Gal 5.22–23.

119. A beautiful example of Origen's interpretation of such matters is found in his *Homilies on Joshua,* trans. B. Bruce, FOTC 105.

120. Is 57.16.

121. As opposed to "against"; cf. Gal 5.23.

Thus far [I have been translating] Origen.

We can add to these things and say that those who have been "called" from legal servitude "to the freedom of the gospel" (to whom it is said above, "Stand and do not again cleave to the yoke of slavery"),[122] even now are warned that those who follow the light yoke of Christ[123] and the delightful precepts of the gospel should be no means think that it is permitted to them to use this very "freedom" for living "as an occasion of the flesh"; that is to say, that they may live according to the flesh, be circumcised according to the flesh. On the contrary let them instead stand in the Spirit, let them by the Spirit cut off the uncircumcision of the flesh and hasten toward the loftier things of the Spirit, leaving behind the lowliness of the letter.

It can also be understood in another way. Should someone say: If I have ceased, O Paul, being under the law and "have been called" from slavery "to freedom," then I ought to live in such a way that corresponds to "freedom." I should not be held fast by any precepts, but should do, fulfill, and follow whatever pleases me and whatever pleasure suggests. The apostle's response to this is that they have indeed been "called unto the freedom" of the Spirit, but in such a way that that very "freedom" must not be at the service of the "flesh." Let us not imagine that everything is permitted to us, that everything is expedient. On the contrary, since we have ceased being slaves of the law, having become free, let us instead serve one another through love so that the precepts of the intricately complex (*laciniosus*)[124] law may be summarized in the one point of love.[125]

5.13b–14.   *But serve one another through love. For the whole law is fulfilled in one word: "You shall love your neighbor as yourself."*[126] The one who though he was free from all made himself a slave of all for the

---

122. Cf. Gal 5.1.

123. Cf. Mt 11.30.

124. *Laciniosus* is also found in Tertullian, *Adversus Marcionem* 4.29.

125. Cf. Mt 22.39–40; Rom 13.8–10.

126. Cf. Mt 22.39–40; Lv 19.18.

sake of love, in order to gain more,[127] rightly exhorts others as well to "serve one another through love," which seeks not what is its own but what is the neighbor's.[128] For the one who wants to be first will be slave of all.[129] Thus, just as the Savior, though existing in the form of God, did not regard it to be robbery to be equal to God, but he emptied himself, taking the form of a slave; and being found in appearance as a man, he humbled himself, having become obedient unto death, even the death of the cross;[130] so also with respect to whatever things we were seen to be doing previously by compulsion under of the law, let us now know that we should do these things as free persons more "through love."

But "love" is the only good, so that the "whole law" is recapitulated in it. The apostle enumerates the good things of love in another passage as well when he says, "It is not jealous, it does not act wrongly."[131] And after unfolding many things in between, he concludes at the end, "It hopes all things, endures all things, love never falls."[132] And in the Gospel the Savior says that the sign of his disciple is that he loves his neighbor.[133] Indeed, I think this applies not only to men but also to angels. The same thing is said in different words: "what you do not want done to you, do not do to another";[134] and "what you want men to do to you, do these same things likewise to them."[135] I do not want anyone to commit adultery with my wife, I do not want my property to be stolen, I do not want to be ruined by false testimony, and, that I might summarize everything with a few words, I am indignant when anything unjust is done to me. If I either do or will these same things to another, "the whole law is fulfilled," "through the love" that is "at work"[136] in me.

---

127. Cf. 1 Cor 9.19.
128. Cf. 1 Cor 13.5; Rom 15.2.
129. Cf. Mk 10.44.
130. Cf. Phil 2.6–8.
131. 1 Cor 13.4.
132. 1 Cor 13.7–8.
133. Cf. Jn 13.35.
134. Tob 4.16.
135. Mt 7.12; Lk 6.31.
136. Cf. Gal 5.6.

It is not difficult to show how the "whole" of the commands ("you shall not kill, you shall not commit adultery, you shall not steal, you shall not speak false testimony,"[137] and other things similar to these) may be kept by the one observance of love. What is hard is to show how the sacrifices commanded in Leviticus are recapitulated in the one command of love; or the absention from and allowance of foods, with some of them being called "clean," others "unclean"; or the continuous annual cycle of solemn festivals; unless perhaps someone at this point makes a transference, affirms that the law is spiritual,[138] and says that before the true high priest came we served images and a copy of the heavenly things.[139] After he had offered himself once as a sacrifice[140] and redeemed us by his own blood,[141] the "whole" variety and difficulty of the former law was fulfilled in his love for men. For the Father so loved the world that he gave his own very dear and only-begotten Son for us.[142]

But the law is no longer laid down[143] for him who, by living once and for all by the Spirit, has put to death the deeds of the flesh,[144] and whom the Savior calls a chosen friend, hardly a slave.[145] For "the law is appointed for the impious and sinners, and for the insubordinate and wicked."[146] But now, since we should do all things that are rather difficult, even in some small measure, we do not do that alone that is easier to do and apart from which everything that we do is pointless. Fasting feels like an injury to the body; vigils wear down the flesh; almsgiving is sought by effort; blood is not shed in martyrdom without fear and grief, even though one's faith may be fervent. There are those who do

---

137. Ex 20.13–16; Mt 19.18.
138. Cf. Rom 7.14.
139. Cf. Heb 10.1.
140. Cf. Heb 7.27.
141. Cf. Heb 9.12.
142. Cf. Jn 3.16.
143. Cf. 1 Tm 1.9.
144. Rom 8.13.
145. Cf. Jn 15.15.
146. Cf. 1 Tm 1.9.

all these things: love alone is without effort, and, since it alone makes the heart clean, the devil attacks it within us, in order to prevent us from seeing God with a pure mind.[147] For when I sit and speak against my brother and put a stumbling block in front of the son of my mother,[148] when I am tormented by someone else's piece of good fortune and make another's good my evil, is not what follows fulfilled in me: "If you bite and devour one another, take heed not to be consumed by one another"?[149] "Love" is a rare possession. Who wants to follow the apostle in being accursed from Christ for the sake of his brothers?[150] Who "grieves with those who grieve," "rejoices with those who rejoice,"[151] is wounded by another's wound? Who dies on the occasion of his brother's death? We are all lovers of ourselves rather than lovers of God.[152] Consider how great is the good of "love." If we build a martyr's grave in such a way that we are intending that our own remains be honored by men,[153] if we follow the opinion of the fickle crowd when we pour out our blood and give away our property to the point of private begging,[154] to these works is owed not so much reward as punishment, and they are more the torments of treachery than the crown of victory.

5.15. *But if you bite and devour one another, take heed that you are not consumed by one another.* This can be understood simply, that we are not to detract from one another, we should not think of avenging ourselves by cursing. When we are gloomy we should not long to make others gloomy and to devour and bite back like beasts, so that after the bite follows death and consumption.

---

147. Cf. Mt 5.8.
148. Ps 50.20.
149. Gal 5.15.
150. Cf. Rom 9.3.
151. Cf. Rom 12.15.
152. Cf. 2 Tm 3.4.
153. Cf. Mt 6.2; 23.29.
154. Cf. 1 Cor 13.3.

But it is better to understand this in such a way that we refer every-thing to circumcision and observation of the law. Otherwise Paul would be erupting suddenly into unusual commands that run contrary to the reasoning and logic of the whole epistle. He is saying: If others trouble you, but you are troubled. Suppose you read the whole of the old Scripture and understand it just as it is written: "an eye for an eye, a tooth for a tooth."[155] And wrath longs for vengeance, but vengeance imposes grief. For the law not only does not prohibit these things but even commands them, by restoring justice as compensation in kind. It follows that the one who has been stripped[156] strips, and the one who has been wounded[157] wounds back, and the one "eaten up" bites back, and what appears to be justice is consumption. It does not vindicate one but "consumes" both.

5.16.   *But I say: Walk in the Spirit and you will not fulfill the desire of the flesh.* This too should be understood in two ways in accordance with what comes above. Thus we tell those who "by the Spirit"[158] have put to death the works "of the flesh," and who have sown "in the Spirit" in order to reap eternal life "from the Spirit,"[159] whenever they sense that the desire of the flesh is stimulated, "not to fulfill its desire" (which indeed, if it is fulfilled, seems soothing at the time). Instead, we tell them to hold back "by the Spirit," and to live in accordance with the statement of the historian: "by the command of the mind, rather than by slavery to the body."[160] And besides, there is also the following in-terpretation: that since the law is spiritual,[161] and since the Jew is not the one who is outward but who is in secret, and circumcision is of the heart, in the Spirit not the letter,[162] we say that those ones "walk in the

---

155. Dt 19.21.
156. Cf. Lk 10.30.
157. Cf. Lk 10.34.
158. Cf. Rom 8.13.
159. Cf. Gal 6.8.
160. Cf. Sallust, *Bellum catalinae* 1.2.
161. Cf. Rom 7.14.
162. Cf. Rom 2.28–29.

Spirit and do not fulfill the desire of the flesh" who march out of Egypt spiritually and who draw spiritual food and drink from the spiritual rock.[163] They are not judged for food or drink, or in respect to a feast day or new moon and Sabbath.[164] On the contrary they "walk" in all things spiritually, not "fulfilling the desire" of the fleshly law and of the letter, but reaping the harvest of the spiritual understanding.[165]

A third interpretation too has been mentioned by some on this passage, but which is hardly discordant with the second. They claim that the "desire of the flesh" is in those who are infants in Christ,[166] but the journey "of the Spirit" is in perfect men.[167] And the sense is: "walk" as perfect men in the dignity, that is, the journey, of the Spirit, and "you will not carry out the desires" of infants.

5.17.   *For the flesh lusts against the Spirit, and the Spirit against the flesh. For these are opposed to each other, so that you do not do what you want.* The "flesh" takes delight in what is at hand and short-lived; the Spirit in what is perpetual and coming in the future. In the midst of this struggle the soul stands in the middle, having both good and evil in its power, both willing and not willing.[168] But it does not have this same willing and not willing forever, since it can happen that it consents to the "flesh" and carries out its works. On the other hand by biting back against itself through repentance it may be united with the Spirit and bring about his works. This then is what he says: "for these are opposed to each other," that is, the "flesh" and the "spirit," "so that you do not do what you want." It is not that he removes personal choice from us when we consent either to the "flesh" or to the "Spirit," but that what we do is not strictly ours, but the very work is attributed either to the "flesh" or to the "spirit." Now that the works of the flesh

---

163. Cf. 1 Cor 10.3–4.

164. Cf. Col 2.16.

165. Cf. Gal 5.22.

166. Cf. 1 Cor 3.1.

167. Cf. Eph 4.13.

168. Compare the remarkable parallels in *CRm* 1.18.5–10; cf. 4.8.3; 6.1.3, 4; 6.8.5; 6.9.11; 6.12.10; 7.6.4.

and of the spirit have been displayed, it is a matter of great effort and of a lengthy discussion to discover certain ones that are indifferent (*media*), which seem to pertain neither to the "flesh" nor to the "spirit." We are called "of flesh"[169] when we give ourselves totally to pleasures. We are called "spiritual" when we follow the lead of the Holy Spirit, that is, when we are mindful of his instruction, when we are taught by the author himself. I think that the philosophers are the "sensual" (*animales*)[170] who think that their own ideas are wisdom. It is rightly said of them, "The sensual man does not receive the things that are of the Spirit. For it is foolishness to him."[171] In order to make this clearer, let us offer an example. Let the "flesh" be called earth, let the soul be called gold, let "spirit" be called fire. As long as the gold is in the earth, it spoils its own name and is named from the earth with which it is comingled. But when it has been separated from the ground, it takes both the outward appearance and name of gold. It is indeed called gold, but it is not yet refined. But if it is tempered and purified by fire, then it receives the splendor of gold and the dignity of its own adornment. So also the soul exists between the ground and fire, that is between the "flesh and the spirit." When it hands itself over "to the flesh," it is called "flesh"; when it gives itself "to the Spirit," it is called "spirit." But if it believes in its own ideas and, apart from the grace of the Holy Spirit, thinks that it has discovered the truth, it will be stamped with the designation of "sensual man" as if it were impure gold.

This passage can thus be explained better and can become as it were one series and body mutually interconnected and not clashing with itself: brothers, you were called from servitude to the law to the freedom of the gospel. But I beseech you not to use (*abutamini*) freedom as a license and think that everything that is allowed is expedient to you, and that you may give opportunity to the flesh and to excess. But instead, learn that this freedom means greater service. Thus the

---

169. Cf. 1 Cor 3.3.
170. Cf. 1 Cor 2.14.
171. 1 Cor 2.14.

obedience that the law previously wrenched from the unwilling, now, through love, you should serve one another. For indeed the whole burden of the law and its manifold commands have not so much been excluded by the grace of the gospel as abbreviated into the one word of love, that we should "love our neighbor as ourselves."[172] For the one who loves his neighbor, by bestowing good things upon him, not inflicting evils, fulfills the whole law. But if love (*dilectio*) ceases and there is no love (*caritas*) by which the whole law is fulfilled, there will be public banditry among men, so to speak, when those who steal from each other and bite one another are consumed by one another. But you, brothers, for this reason you ought to live according to the spiritual law, so that you do not fulfill the desires that are of the flesh. For the "flesh" fears the cold, it spurns hunger, it is weakened by vigils, it burns with lusts, it desires everything that is soft and pleasant. It strives against the things "of the Spirit," which are contrary "to the flesh," and which can weaken it. Thus it happens that you should not consider yourselves to be free *because* you have ceased being under the servitude of the law; but rather, you should know that you are restrained all the more by the law of nature. For nature has not immediately ceased, if the law does not command, that is to say, to prevent works from following subsequent to your will; but frequently you are compelled to do things "which you do not want to do,"[173] with the "flesh" fighting "against the spirit." Therefore, brothers, I plead for this: that you not give your freedom an opportunity "of the flesh," but instead serve the "Spirit," so that you may begin "doing the things you want"[174] and owe nothing to the law, which means not being under the flesh. For in the gospel you can truly have freedom from the abolished law at that time when the "flesh" by no means compels you "to do the things you do not want," but, by serving the Spirit, you show that you are not under the law.

---

172. Rom 13.9. Cf. Origen, *CRm* 9.31.
173. Gal 5.17; cf. Rom 7.19.
174. Cf. Rom 7.15.

And since above we began to explain this passage in accordance with a twofold understanding, what we left out needs to be rendered. "The flesh lusts against the Spirit"; that is, the history and the fleshly understanding of Scripture fights against allegory and spiritual doctrine. "And the Spirit is against the flesh"; that is, the more elevated things are opposed to what is down low. Eternal things resist what is fleeting; truth thwarts shadow. And the fleshly sense of Scripture, since it cannot be fulfilled (for we cannot do all that is written), shows that we do not have it in our power to fulfill the law, since even if we wish to follow the letter, its impossibility does not allow this.

5.18.   *But if you are led by [the] spirit, you are not under law.* "Spirit" does not mean him of whom in another passage the apostle says, "The Spirit himself bears witness with our spirit that we are sons of God";[175] that is, [in the latter passage] he is not signifying the spirit of man who is in him, but the Holy Spirit, by following whom we become spiritual and cease being under the law. Therefore, one should note that he is called "spirit" here without the ἄρθρῳ [article] and without any added word. In other places it is called "spirit of meekness"[176] and "spirit of faith,"[177] but here it is simply called "spirit." Now these minutia, which have been noticed more on the basis of the Greek than in our language (since our language lacks ἄρθρα altogether) seem to have some importance.[178]

It is asked on the basis of this passage, if whoever "is led by spirit is not under the law," whether Moses and the prophets acted "by the Spirit" and lived "under the law" (which the apostle denies); or whether, though they had the Spirit, they were not "under the law" (which the apostle here affirms); or a third possibility, whether, though they lived "under the law," they did not have the "Spirit," which is wrong to

---

175. Rom 8.16.
176. Cf. Gal 6.1.
177. Cf. 2 Cor 4.13.
178. Origen discusses Paul's use and non-use of articles with the term "law" in *CRm* 3.7.9.

believe of such great men. We will briefly respond to this by saying that being "under the law" and being "as though under the law"[179] are not the same thing. Similarly, it is not the same thing to be "in the likeness of the flesh of sin,"[180] and to be "in the flesh of sin."[181] Nor do the true serpent and the likeness of the bronze serpent that Moses suspended in the desert denote the same thing.[182] So then, the holy prophets and Moses, while they walked "by the Spirit"[183] and lived "by the Spirit," were not "under the law," but they lived "as if under the law." Thus they *appeared* to be "under the law" but only in order to "gain those who were under the law,"[184] and to summon them away from the lowliness of the letter toward the heights of the "Spirit." For even Paul, who "became a Jew to the Jews" and "all things to all that he might gain all,"[185] did not say that he became "under the law" but "as if under the law."[186] This shows that he did not keep the truth of the law but its likeness. We seem to have resolved the question proposed. But what will we do about the point Paul makes when he says, "But when the fullness of time came, God sent his own Son, made of a woman, made under the law, in order to redeem those who were under the law"?[187] For if Christ was made "under the law," and not "as if under the law,"[188] the whole foregoing discussion will become null and void. But even this point of contradiction will be resolved from its own passage. For the one who was "made under the law" for this very reason, "to redeem those who were under the law," surely, though he was free from the law, submitted himself to the law voluntarily. And he was much more free than Paul, who testified that he was not "under the law" but "as if

179. Cf. 1 Cor 9.21.
180. Cf. Rom 8.3.
181. Cf. Rom 7.25.
182. Cf. Nm 21.4–9; Jn 3.14.
183. Cf. Gal 5.16.
184. Cf. 1 Cor 9.20.
185. Cf. 1 Cor 9.19–22.
186. Cf. 1 Cor 9.21.
187. Gal 4.4–5.
188. Cf. 1 Cor 9.20.

under the law." And just as he descended into the slimy pit of death for our sake, who were saying in prayer, "Who will liberate me from the body of this death?"[189] so also he wanted to be born from a woman and be under the law, in order to save those who had been born of a woman and under the law. And, of course, he was not born from a *woman,* that is, from a married woman, but from a *virgin;* but the *virgin* was called a *woman* improperly, for the sake of those who did not know she was a virgin. And so, just as *woman* is recorded for *virgin* for the sake of those who thought that Mary was married, so Christ himself is said to be "made under the law" for the sake of those who thought that he was "under the law," but who did not know that he became "as if under the law"[190] for those who were under the law.

5.19–21.   *But the works of the flesh are manifest, which are fornication, uncleanness, excess, worship of idols, sorcery, enmity, strife, jealousy, wrath, quarreling, dissension, heresies, envy, drunkenness, carousing,*[191] *and similar things. I warn you now as I warned you before that those who do these things will not obtain the kingdom of God.* Up above, when we were discussing flesh and spirit, we had spoken of three ways to understand this. First it can refer to those who are fleshly, who are infants and bodily in Christ; they are incapable of taking in solid food and the nourishment of the mature age of life.[192] Secondly, the flesh of the law refers to those who by Judaic custom have followed merely the history and the letter. Or [thirdly], perhaps in accordance with the simple meaning, flesh and spirit subsist in the formation of the human being, and in accordance with the diversity of substance, they are either works of the flesh or of the spirit. Now, then, the things that are here named "works of the flesh," "fornication, uncleanness, excess" and the other things that follow, seem to me to refer more to the simple understanding of flesh and spirit than to the flesh of the law and to infants in Christ, although anything that could likewise be perceived about these

---

189. Rom 7.24.
190. Cf. 1 Cor 9.20.
191. The works from "sorcery" onward are plural in the original.
192. Cf. 1 Cor 3.1–2; Heb 5.13–14.

[first and second interpretations] is articulated above in that passage where we translated word for word from the tenth [book of the] *Stromateis* of Origen.

Now his words, "But the works of the flesh are manifest," show either that these things are known to everyone, since they are exposed in and of themselves as being evils that must be avoided, insomuch as even those who do these things desire to conceal what they are doing; or, possibly, they are "manifest" only to those who have believed in Christ. For the majority of pagans boast in their disgraceful acts and think that if they have fulfilled some form of pleasure, they have attained to a victory of base actions. Moreover, the way he has spoken of "works" in respect to the "flesh" and "fruits" in respect to the Spirit,[193] is elegant. For vices come to nothing and perish of their own accord, whereas virtues bear fruit and abound. Let us not think that the soul is unnecessary, if vices are attributed to the flesh and virtues the spirit. For (as we said above)[194] the soul is placed in the middle, as it were: it is either joined to the flesh and it is said of it, "My spirit will not remain in these men, since they are flesh";[195] or it is united with the spirit and passes into the term of spirit, "For he who cleaves to the Lord is one spirit."[196]

And so, the first "work of the flesh" is "fornication." He has recorded "manifest" at the beginning lest we be in doubt about the intervening things. "For everything whatsoever a man does is outside the body; but the one who commits fornication sins in his own body."[197] And "we are not our own; for we were bought at a price; let us glorify and bear God in our body."[198] In that respect the fornicator is guilty of a greater sin because he "takes the members of Christ and makes them the members of a prostitute."[199] For "the two will be one flesh."[200] He

---

193. Cf. Gal 5.22.
194. See under 5.17.
195. Gn 6.3. Cf. *CRm* 1.18.5.
196. 1 Cor 6.17.
197. 1 Cor 6.18.
198. Cf. 1 Cor 6.19–20.
199. 1 Cor 6.15.
200. 1 Cor 6.16; Gn 2.24.

who is not faithful and does not believe in Christ makes *his own* members the members of a prostitute; he who believes and commits fornication makes *Christ's* members the members of a prostitute. On the other hand I do not know whether the unbeliever, in his act of fornication, violates or builds up the temple to his idol. For demons are especially worshiped by vices. This one thing I know,[201] that the one who commits fornication after [coming to] faith in Christ violates the temple of God.[202]

The second "work of the flesh" is called "uncleanness," and "excess" follows it as its companion. For in the old law, in connection with wicked crimes that are done in secret, it is very shameful even to name these things (lest even the mouth of the speaker and the ears of the hearers be defiled). Scripture in general has included them when it says, "Make the sons of Israel ashamed (or reverent[203]) of every uncleanness."[204] In the same way, in this passage he has named as "uncleanness" and "excess," the rest of the out-of-the-ordinary pleasures, including the marital act itself, if it is not done modestly and with uprightness, and, as it were, under the eyes of God, so that it serves only for [the procreation of] children.[205]

"Idolatry" holds the fourth place on the list of "works of the flesh." For the one who has once surrendered himself to "excess" and "pleasure" does not respect the Creator. And besides, all forms of "idolatry" delight in partying, gluttony, the belly, and in what is below the belly.

Now perhaps it was to prevent the arts of witchcraft and "sorcery" from appearing not to be prohibited in the New Testament that they too are named among the "works of the flesh." For often it is through magical arts that it comes to pass that pitiful people both fall in love and are loved.[206]

---

201. Cf. Jn 9.25.

202. Cf. 1 Cor 3.17; 6.19.

203. The Septuagint has εὐλαβεῖς.

204. Cf. Lv 15.31.

205. Cf. *CRm* 5.7.4.

206. In the New Testament "sorcery" refers to mixing of potions for secret purposes, such as to prevent or stop a pregnancy. J. F. Kippley, *Sex and the Marriage Covenant: A Basis for Morality,* 2nd ed. (San Francisco: Ignatius,1991), p. 328, notes

There is "enmity"[207] too, which is put after "sorcery." When it has become the cause of a manifest crime, it proves guilty anyone who has it. For "as far as it pertains to us," we ought to be no one's enemies but "have peace with everyone."[208] But if by speaking the truth we earn some enemies, we are not so much their enemies as they are enemies of the truth. For even what is said in Genesis to Abraham, "I will be an enemy to your enemies and an adversary to your adversaries,"[209] should be understood as above: it is not so much that Abraham was their enemy as they were enemies of Abraham's virtues and religion through which he trampled upon idols and worshiped the God who had become known to him. That too which is commanded to the people of Israel, that they are enemies of the Midianites by an everlasting hatred and a discord that is transmitted to later generations,[210] is said, as it were, to those who were under a pedagogue.[211] And in another place they deserved to hear, "You shall regard your enemy with hatred."[212] Or perhaps "dissension" is created not so much between the persons as between the morals. Thus God beneficially put "enmity" between the serpent and the woman,[213] namely, the "enmity" by means of which the serpent was cast out of Paradise, lest friendly relations between

---

the importance of this passage in Galatians for the modern birth control controversy. He observes that the typical translation of the Greek term φαρμακεία as "sorcery" may not reveal all of the specific practices condemned by the New Testament. In all three passages in which the term appears, it is in a context of condemning sexual immorality; two of the three passages also condemn murder (Gal 5.19–26; Rv 9.21; 21.8). He concludes: "Thus it is very possible that there are three New Testament passages condemning the use of the products of "pharmakeia" for birth control purposes." St. Jerome condemns drugs that procure abortion in Ep. 22.13 to Eustochium.

207. Singular here, but plural in the lemma.
208. Cf. Rom 12.18.
209. Ex 23.22 (Septuagint). This is said to Moses in Exodus.
210. Cf. Nm 31.1–38.
211. Cf. Gal 3.25.
212. Cf. Mt 5.43.
213. Cf. Gn 3.15.

them should be harmful to humanity. In the same way, between the Israelites and the Midianites, their dissimilar mode of life was condemned more than a single nation.

"Contention" holds the seventh place among the "works of the
flesh." It is located in the midst of the vices, as it were as a sacred and
eminent number. But "the Lord's servant should not be quarrelsome,
but be gentle to everyone, an apt teacher, patient, instructing with
meekness even those who contradict."[214]

After "contention" comes "jealousy" as the eighth, which in Greek
is identified more meaningfully and notably by the word "zelus." Indeed I do not know which of us is free from this. For even the patriarchs were jealous of their own brother Joseph, and Miriam and Aaron,
a prophetess of God and a priest, were misled by such a passion against
Moses[215] that it reached the point of the things described by Scripture,
which says, "But Miriam the prophetess, taking a timbrel,"[216] and the
rest. After she was cast outside the camp, she was defiled by the blemish of leprosy,[217] and she sealed her repentance by a separation that
lasted more than seven days.[218]

"Anger" comes next, which "does not bring about the justice of
God."[219] It is the outward form of fury.[220] Now between wrath and
anger there is this difference, that the wrathful man is always angry, the
angry man is stirred up for a time. I do not know who can "obtain
the kingdom of God," since the one who is angry is separated from the
kingdom.[221]

"Quarreling" too, which the Greeks signify differently and call
ἐριθείας (for a quarrel is call a μάχη), keeps one out of the kingdom of
God. Now an ἐριθεία exists when someone who is always ready to

---

214. 2 Tm 2.24–25.
215. Cf. Nm 12.1.
216. Ex 15.20 (Septuagint).
217. Cf. Nm 12.10.
218. Cf. Nm 12.15.
219. Cf. Jas 1.20.
220. Cf. *CRm* 2.6.6.
221. Cf. Mt 5.22.

contradict takes delight in someone else's tastes and contends with womanish wrangling and provokes his opponent. Among the Greeks this goes by a different name, φιλονικία.

And in addition, "dissensions" are "works of the flesh," when someone who is by no means perfect says with the same understanding and the same intention: "I am of Paul, I am of Apollos, I am of Cephas, and I am of Christ."[222] Moreover, this same "dissension" is found in homes, namely, between husband and wife, father and son, brother and brother, fellow slave and fellow slave, soldier and army buddy, craftsman and members of the same craft.

Sometimes it happens that "dissension" arises in the interpretation of Scripture, from which "heresies" too bubble over, which are recorded next among the work of the flesh. For if "the wisdom of the flesh is at enmity with God"[223] (and all false doctrines, being repugnant to God, are at enmity), "heresies" also, being at enmity with God, are logically included among the "works of the flesh." Now heresy comes from the Greek word for choice, because each one *chooses* that doctrine that seems to be better.[224] So then, whoever understands the Scripture differently than the understanding of the Holy Spirit demands, the understanding with which it was written down[, is called a heretic]. Granted, he may not have departed from the church, but he can still be called a heretic, and he is choosing things that are worse from the "works of the flesh."

"Envy" follows "heresies," which we should not think is the same thing as zeal (*zelum*).[225] For zeal[226] can be understood in a good sense, when someone strives to be zealous for the things that are better. But "envy" is tormented by the prosperity of another and is torn into a double passion, when either there is someone in that [thing] in which he does not want the other to be, or when he sees that another is better

---

222. 1 Cor 1.12.
223. Cf. Rom 8.7.
224. Cf. *CRm* 7.19.6; 6.1.2.
225. Cf. Cicero, *Tusculanae disputationes* 3.9.20–10.21; 4.7.16–8.17.
226. Or "jealousy."

and grieves that he is not like him. One of the Neoteric poets[227] nicely translated a line from Greek elegiac meter that mocks envy when he said, "Nothing is more just than envy: it constantly gnaws at an author and torments his spirit." And the blessed Cyprian[228] wrote a very excellent book about jealousy and envy.[229] The one who reads it will not hesitate to list "envy" among the "works of the flesh." Between the envious (*invidum*) and the envied (*invidiosum*) there is this difference, that the envious man envies one who is happier; but the envied man is one who suffers envy from another.

"Drunkenness" holds the fourteenth place among the "works of the flesh." For "drunkards will not obtain the kingdom of God."[230] Also the Lord says to his disciples, "Beware, lest perchance your hearts be weighed down with wine and drunkenness."[231] A man's senses are undermined by wine, the feet slip, the mind staggers, lust is fanned into flame. This is why the apostle exclaims, "And wine in which there is excess."[232] Each one has authority over his own opinion. I myself follow the apostle, that in wine there is "excess," in wine there is "drunkenness." Now that "drunkenness" and "excess" are listed among the "works of the flesh," no one can deny who is conquered by these very passions. And although some think that I deserve to be reproached for that book I wrote about preserving one's virginity, when I said that young people should flee from wine as if it were poison,[233] I do not

---

227. The Neoterics were Latin poets at Rome, such as Catullus and Propertius, who aimed at imitating Greek models, cultivating a studied elegance in vocabulary, word order, meter, and narrative form, and bringing Callimachean refinement to Latin poetry.

228. Cyprian was the bishop of Carthage (ca. 248–58) who wrote important treatises: *On the Lord's Prayer, On the Lapsed, On the Unity of the Church,* as well as *Epistles.* His biography, which is really a panegyric, was written by the deacon Pontius. He was beheaded in 258. See ANF 5.

229. See Treatise 10, ANF 5.491–96.

230. Cf. 1 Cor 6.10; Mt 24.49–50.

231. Lk 21.34.

232. Eph 5.18.

233. Cf. Ep. 22.8 to Eustochium.

regret this statement. For in that passage I was condemning the effect of wine, rather than God's creation, and I made use of outspokenness (*licentiam*) to an individual virgin, burning in the ardor of youth, to prevent her, on the occasion of drinking a little, from drinking too much and perishing. On the other hand I was aware both that wine is consecrated in the blood of Christ[234] and that Timothy was commanded to drink wine.[235] But "drunkenness" can happen both from wine and from other kinds of drinks that are processed in various ways. This is why it is even said of saints, "He will not drink wine and strong drink."[236] Strong drink is translated "drunkenness" and, lest anyone who does not drink wine thinks that something else has to be drunk, this pretext is excluded, since everything that is capable of causing inebriation is taken away equally with wine.

"Carousing" is the fifteenth and last of the "works of the flesh." "The people ate and drank and rose up to play."[237] "Excess is always linked to "drunkenness." A well-known orator, when he was describing the drunken man roused from slumber, said nicely: "The drunken man when roused could not sleep or stay awake."[238] By this statement he expressed that the man was so to speak neither dead nor alive.

It would have been a long task to enumerate all the "works of the flesh" and make a catalogue of vices. So Paul has wrapped them all up with the words "and things like these." I wish that we could avoid these vices as easily as we understand them! He says, "I tell you now, just as I told you before, that those who do such things will not obtain the kingdom of God." When had he previously "told them before"? He said, "Let not sin reign in your mortal body to obey its desires."[239] Sin has all these outward forms, in the distinguishing of which we have now been delayed, perhaps more than was necessary. Therefore, in the

234. Cf. Mt 26.27.
235. Cf. 1 Tm 5.23.
236. Lk 1.15.
237. Cf. Ex 32.6; 1 Cor 10.7.
238. Cicero, *Pro Caelio*, or *frg*. Quint, *Instituto oratoria* 4.2.124.
239. Rom 6.12.

soul in which sin reigns, the "kingdom of God" cannot reign. "For what fellowship is there between justice and iniquity? What communion is there between light and darkness? What agreement is there between Christ and Belial?"[240] And do we think that we will "obtain the kingdom of God" if we should be immune [merely] from "fornication, idolatry, and sorcery"? Behold "enmity, contention, anger, quarreling, dissension, drunkenness," and the other things, which we think are trivial, exclude us from the "kingdom of God." He does not report that someone is excluded from blessedness by one, or by several, since they all equally exclude.

In the Latin manuscripts "adultery, lewdness, and murder" are also recorded in this catalogue of vices. But one should know that no more than fifteen "works of the flesh" were named, and we have discussed them.

5.22–23.   *But the fruit of the Spirit is love, joy, peace, longsuffering, kindness, goodness, faithfulness, meekness, continence; against such things there is no law.* What else deserves to hold the first place among the "fruits of the Spirit" if not "love," without which the other virtues are not reckoned to be virtues and from which is born all that is good? For indeed both in the law and in the gospel, love holds primacy: "You will love the Lord your God with all your heart and with all your soul and with all your strength,"[241] and "you will love your neighbor as yourself."[242] Above we have briefly touched upon the extent of the good things with which "love" is packed. Now let it suffice to have said just a little. Love "does not seek what is its own"[243] but what pertains to the other; and even though someone by his own fault may be an enemy to the one who loves and strive to stir up his tranquility into a floodtide of hatred, nevertheless he is never disturbed, he never reckons God's creation worthy of hatred. For "love covers a multitude of sins."[244] That is

---

240. 2 Cor 6.14–15.
241. Dt 6.5; Mt 22.37.
242. Lv 19.18; Mt 22.39.
243. 1 Cor 13.5.
244. 1 Pt 4.8.

also what is said by the Savior: "A good tree cannot bear bad fruit, nor can a bad tree bear good fruit."[245] I believe he declared this not so much about men as about the "fruit" of the flesh and "of the spirit." For the Spirit can never produce the vices that are enumerated among the "works of the flesh"; nor can the flesh abound in these "fruits" that arise from the "Spirit." But it can come to pass that through the negligence of the possessor both that the Spirit who lives in man does not have his own fruits; and that, on the other hand, the flesh stops sinning, when its works have been put to death.[246] Yet they do not advance so far in that direction that both the neglected tree "of the Spirit" produces "works of the flesh" and that the cultivated tree "of the flesh" bears spiritual "fruit."

"Joy" is recorded in the second place among the spiritual "fruits." The Stoics too, who make rather subtle distinctions between words, think it is something different from gladness. For joy, they say, is "elation of the mind over things that are worthy of the one rejoicing";[247] whereas gladness is the "unbridled elation of mind that knows no moderation and is glad even in those things that are mingled with vice." Others put pleasure outside of the region of joy: not that pleasure that incites the body to lust, titillates the senses, flatters with sweet feeling; but another kind of pleasure, which goes by the same name (ὁμώνυμον). The latter is without moderation and without any of the elegance of gladness; it raises its own voice in laughter. But if this is true, and the distinction between these words is not misleading and deceptive, let us consider whether perhaps it may not be said on this account, "Do not rejoice with the impious, says the Lord."[248] But at the same time the following should be noted, that after love "joy" follows. For the one who loves anyone always rejoices in his happiness; and if he sees him led astray into some error and fallen on the slippery slope of sins, he will grieve deeply and strive to rescue him. Yet he will not be able to turn

---

245. Mt 7.18.
246. Cf. Col 3.5.
247. Cf. Cicero, *Tusculanae disputationes* 4.13.
248. Is 57.21 (Septuagint).

his joy into sadness, for he knows that no rational creature perishes forever with God.[249]

"Peace" is the third "fruit of the Spirit." Even Solomon, who came before as a type of Christ, took his name from it, and of the church the Psalmist sings, "Her place has been made in peace."[250] And in the midst of the eight benedictions in the gospel it is written, "Blessed are the peacemakers, for they will be called sons of God."[251] In the first Psalm of Ascents as well, it is sung, "I was a peacemaker among those who hated peace."[252] We should not suppose that peace is only to be sought in this, if we do not quarrel with another; rather the peace of Christ, that is, our inheritance, is "among" us if a tranquil mind is undisturbed by any passions.

After "peace" follows "longsuffering," or patience, since we can translate μακροθυμίαν both ways. The opposite of this is fainthearted-ness of which it is written, "The fainthearted is exceedingly foolish; but he who is patient and endures all things is a wise man."[253] And by ex-tension (*cum* ἐπιτάσει) the wise man is frequently called this, as for example in Proverbs it is written, "The longsuffering man abounds in wisdom."[254]

Likewise "kindness," or pleasantness—since among the Greeks χρηστότης expresses both—is a mild virtue, alluring, tranquil, and suited to partnership in all good things. It invites to familiarity with it-self, it is pleasant in conversation, even-keeled in character. After all, the Stoics define this virtue as follows: "Kindness is an affable virtue, ready of its own accord to do good."

"Goodness" is not much different from "kindness." For it too seems "ready to do good"; but it differs in this, that "goodness" can be

---

249. This passage again suggests that the early Jerome did not reproach Ori-gen's conjectures concerning the future restoration of all rational creatures. See note at 3.21–23 (p. 148, n. 140).

250. Ps 76.2.

251. Mt 5.9.

252. Ps 120.6–7.

253. Prv 14.29 (Septuagint).

254. Prv 14.29.

more serious, and it can do good, to be sure, and to offer what is asked, but with a brow that is wrinkled because of its grave character. And yet it is not charming in its associations and it does not invite everyone by its sweetness. The followers of Zeno[255] define this virtue too as follows: "goodness is a virtue that benefits, or a virtue from which benefits arise, or a virtue for its own sake; indeed, it is an affection which is the font of benefits."

Among the "fruits of the Spirit," "faith" holds the seventh and more sacred place. Elsewhere it is even recorded as one of three: "hope, faith, and love."[256] Nor is it remarkable that hope is not included in this list, since the object of hope is found in "faith." Thus does the apostle define it when writing to the Hebrews: "But faith is the substance of what is hoped for, the evidence of things that do not yet appear."[257] For indeed what we hope for is still to come and is not yet present in the "faith" we possess. We hope to grasp what we believe. It is also asked how "faith" is found in "love." The one who loves never considers himself injured, he never suspects anything else except that he loves and is loved. But when love is far removed, "faith" too leaves at the same time.

After "faith" is listed "meekness." This is the opposite of anger, quarreling, and dissension. It is never provoked to contradict. It truly sprouts good "fruit" from the good tree of the "Spirit." By this virtue Moses the servant of God merited receiving the testimony of Scripture which says, "Moses was meek beyond all the men over the earth."[258] "Over the earth," it says, for he could not be "over" those who saw God face to face.[259] For we are often compelled to do many things through the weakness of the flesh. Although many think that the following was prophesied of our Lord (which we too do not deny), the Holy Spirit sings of David too, as a type of the one to come, "Lord, re-

---

255. That is, the Stoics.
256. Cf. 1 Cor 13.13.
257. Heb 11.1.
258. Nm 12.3.
259. Cf. Gn 32.30.

member David and all his meekness."[260] Did not his "meekness" become clear in the manner of his opposition to Saul,[261] Absalom,[262] and especially Shimei?[263] One of these men wanted to kill him, another tried to deprive him of power by creating a revolution, and the third threw stones at him, tossed up dust, shouted, and said, "Begone, begone, you wicked man."[264]

"Continence" is recorded as the last of the "fruits of the Spirit." We should understand it not merely in respect to chastity, but also in respect to food and drink, to anger too, and the vexation of the mind, and to distracting lust. Now between modesty and "continence" there is this difference, that modesty exists in men who are perfect and of consummate virtue, of whom the Savior says, "Blessed are the meek, for they will inherit the earth";[265] and of himself, "Learn from me, for I am meek and humble and gentle of heart."[266] "Continence," on the other hand, is on the road to virtue, to be sure, but it has not yet reached the goal, since desires still arise in the thoughts of the one who is "containing" himself. They defile the seat of his mind, though they do not have the upper hand and do not lure into action the one thinking them. But not only is "continence" required in respect to desires and longings, but also in respect to the three remaining strong emotions, namely, grief, exuberance, and fear.

"Against such" fruits of the Spirit, "there is no law." For "the law is not laid down for the just man, but for the unjust and insubordinate, for the impious and the sinners."[267] The "law" says to me, "You shall not commit adultery, you shall not kill, you shall not speak false testimony, you shall not defraud, you shall not desire what belongs to

---

260. Ps 132.1.
261. Cf. 1 Sm 24.1–22.
262. Cf. 2 Sm 19.1–24.
263. Cf. 2 Sm 16.5–14.
264. 2 Sm 16.7.
265. Mt 5.4.
266. Mt 11.29. Notice Jerome's expansion of the original.
267. 1 Tm 1.9.

another, you shall not commit perjury, you shall not steal."[268] If I do not do all these things with "love," the "fruit of the Spirit," reigning in me, then the commands of the "law" are superfluous to me. After all, even the wise men of the world conjectured on the basis of philosophy that what the public laws force men to do by compulsion, love persuades this to be done by the will.

5.24.　*But those who are Christ's have crucified the flesh with vices and lusts.* Origen links this passage to what precedes and reads it as follows: "Against such there is no law, who have crucified the flesh of Christ with vices and lusts." Thus it does not express, as it does in the Latin, that he is saying that those "who are Christ's have crucified" *their own flesh* "with vices and lusts," but the "flesh" *of Christ,* which was crucified by those things "together with vices and lusts." And he asks how in those who have the fruits of the Spirit and against whom the law has ceased to be, the crucifixion of the Lord's "flesh" is recorded in praise, when to the Hebrews it is recorded in vituperation: "Crucifying again to themselves the Son of God and holding him up for public exposure."[269] (The Greek is better in that a single word, ἀνασταυροῦντες, stands for "crucifying again"; we can translate it as "re-crucifying.") Well then, the first thing to note is that it is one thing "to crucify," something else "to re-crucify." Secondly, it is not the same thing "to re-crucify the Son of God" and "to crucify the flesh of Christ with vices and lusts." For the "flesh of Christ" is not fundamentally and properly the Son of God. On the contrary Christ Jesus, who although as God the Word he was in the beginning with the Father,[270] became flesh[271] and emptied himself, taking the form of a slave,[272] in order to crucify the flesh and despoil the authorities and powers, triumphing over them on the cross.[273] And the apostle's statement was fulfilled: "For what he

---

268. Ex 20.13–17; Mk 10.19.
269. Heb 6.6.
270. Cf. Jn 1.1.
271. Cf. Jn 1.14.
272. Cf. Phil 2.7.
273. Cf. Col 2.15.

died, he died to sin once."[274] Therefore, if our bodies are members of Christ,[275] the consequence is that our flesh is the "flesh of Christ," which we "crucify" by putting to death through it "upon the earth" "fornication, uncleanness, passion, evil desire, and greed."[276] And it is now recorded of us in praise, "those who have crucified the flesh of Christ Jesus with the vices and lusts," and who always carry around the mortification of Jesus in our body,[277] so that also his life is manifested in our flesh.[278] Now it is a matter of no small effort to live in the present world in such a way that even now the life of Jesus is manifested in our flesh. For thus will our mortal bodies be made alive through the Spirit who dwells within us.[279]

Where the Latin translator recorded "vices," in Greek it reads παθήματα, that is, "passions." And because a "passion" can signify both pain and other necessities of the frail body, the apostle has carefully introduced "desires," so that he would not appear to be rejecting the *nature* of the body in spiritual men but its "vices." And so let this warning be heard, if we follow the common edition and read "but those who are Christ's have crucified the flesh with the vices and lusts," that we should not say that they have "crucified the flesh of Christ" but their own.

I almost forgot the second interpretation. For I had said earlier that everything that follows should be referred to the law and to circumcision.[280] And so, this is the meaning: Those in whom the fruit of the Spirit is found—love, joy, and so forth—have "crucified" the bodily understanding of Scripture, which is here called "the flesh of Christ," together with its passions and desires, which give rise to alleviation from the vices in little children and nursing babes.[281] He has "crucified that flesh of Christ" who fights not according to the "flesh" of history, but who follows the lead of the Spirit of allegory.

---

274. Rom 6.10.
275. Cf. 1 Cor 6.15.
276. Cf. Col 3.5.
277. Cf. 2 Cor 4.10.
278. Cf. 2 Cor 4.11.
279. Cf. Rom 8.11.
280. Cf. on 5.15.
281. 1 Cor 3.1–2.

5.25.   *If we live by the Spirit, let us also walk by the Spirit.* Let us use this testimony against those who do not want to understand the Scriptures spiritually. But who is the one who "lives by the Spirit" if not our hidden man, who also sometimes is accustomed "to live according to the flesh"? But when he "lives by the Spirit," he "walks by the Spirit." When he wants to "walk" in the flesh, though alive, he is dead. The perfect man in Christ always "lives in the Spirit," obeys the Spirit; he never "lives" in the flesh. On the other hand, the one who gives himself completely to the flesh and is associated with the passions never "lives in the Spirit." Among these there are those in between, whom we can call neither spiritual nor fleshly; but who vacillate between the virtues and the vices. They are sometimes drawn back to better things and are Spirit, sometimes they are made to stumble on the slippery slope of the flesh and they are flesh.

5.26.   *Let us not become desirous of vainglory, provoking one another, envying one another.* The Latin translator has expressed in the roundabout way of three words what is one word in Greek, κενόδοξοι. Countless books of the philosophers and two volumes of Cicero, which he wrote on glory, are an indication of what detailed definitions and significances glory has. But since we are not trying to discuss the etymologies of words but the meaning of Scripture, we will link this passage with what precedes in the following way: "If we live by the Spirit," we would comply with the Spirit, "serving one another" not through the law but through love. We should not be contentious about the interpretation of the Scriptures and say, "circumcision is better," "no, uncircumcision is better," "history should be rejected and allegory must be followed," "on the contrary allegory is vain and esoteric (*umbratica*)[282] and is not sustained by any rootedness in the truth." This is how it comes to pass that envy arises among "one another." He says, "For they want to exclude you in order that you should be zealous for them."[283] They do not want to teach the truth of the law so much as to conquer it.

---

282. Lit. too fond of shade; retired, private.
283. Gal 4.17.

But lest we completely pass over the word "glory" without touching upon it, let us leave to the philosophers their own nonsense and review a few things from the Scriptures. The term "glory" expresses the opinion of the crowd and the praise of men sought by favor, where it is said, "But everything they do is in order to be glorified by men";[284] and elsewhere, "How can you believe when you seek glory from one another?"[285] It is further used in a good sense in the same passage, "And do not seek glory from him who is alone."[286] From this we understand that the same word sometimes indicates a virtue, sometimes a vice. If I seek "glory" from men, it is a vice; if I seek it from God, it is a virtue. For he even exhorts us to true "glory" when he says, "But I will glorify those who glorify me."[287] In the divine Scriptures "glory" signifies something else when something very majestic and divine offers itself to human view. The Lord's "glory" was seen in the tabernacle,[288] and there was "glory" in the temple that was constructed by Solomon,[289] and in the face of Moses when he did not know that his face had been glorified.[290] I think that it was of this "glory" of his face that the apostle even says, "But we all with unveiled face, contemplating the glory of the Lord, are being transformed into the same image from glory into glory, just as from the Spirit of God."[291] And the Savior himself is called the "splendor of glory" and the "figure of God's substance."[292] And Stephen saw the "glory" of God and Jesus standing at his right hand.[293] But let us presume the freedom for ourselves to fashion names (since for new things, as they say, new names need to be fashioned). Therefore, since it is said here, "let us not become desirous of vain (or *empty*) glory," let us assert that they are "desirous of *full* glory" who desire

---

284. Mt 23.5.
285. Jn 5.44.
286. Jn 5.44.
287. 1 Sm 2.30.
288. Cf. Ex 40.32.
289. Cf. 1 Kgs 8.11.
290. Cf. Ex 34.35.
291. 2 Cor 3.18.
292. Cf. Heb 1.3.
293. Cf. Acts 7.55.

God's glory and the praise that is truly owed to virtue and that shows a vision of something rather divine. This is also why in the majority of passages our people have translated "glory" by *majesty*.

I have long since desired to burst out into words, but I am held back by the fear of speaking. Yet I will speak and I will not conceal my passion, a nearly common passion, not for wealth, not for power, not for beauty and charm of bodies (for these things are manifestly listed among the works of the flesh). Almsgiving is "vainglorious," if it is done for the sake of praise;[294] [so are] long prayers[295] and the paleness that follows from fasting.[296] These are not my words but the Savior's, who thunders against this in the gospel.[297] Even chastity itself among the married, widows, and virgins often seeks human acclaim. And what I have long since been afraid to say, but what must be said: martyrdom itself, if it is done in order for us to be regarded with admiration and praise by our brothers, is blood poured out in vain. Let the apostle speak, let the vessel of election[298] speak: "If I hand over my body in order to boast,[299] but have not love, it does not profit me at all (*glorier*)!"[300] He who had said, "I know a man in Christ who fourteen years ago—whether in the body, I do not know, or apart from the body, I do not know, God knows—was caught up to the third heaven";[301] and after a little bit, "He was caught up to Paradise and heard secret words, which it is not permitted to a man to speak";[302] that man, I say, who labored more than everyone,[303] to prevent the greatness of the revelations from puffing him up, was given a thorn in his flesh, an angel of Satan who buffeted him that he might not become puffed up.[304] And at

---

294. Cf. Mt 6.1.
295. Cf. Mt 6.5.
296. Cf. Mt 6.16–18.
297. Cf. Mt 6.1–6, 16–18.
298. Cf. Acts 9.15.
299. *Glorier* is cognate with *gloria* ("glory").
300. 1 Cor 13.3.
301. 2 Cor 12.2.
302. 2 Cor 12.4.
303. Cf. 1 Cor 15.10.
304. Cf. 2 Cor 12.7.

least three times he asked the Lord to remove it from him,[305] but he said to him, "My grace is sufficient for you; for my power is perfected in weakness."[306] What is so much the work of God as reading the Scriptures, preaching in the church, desiring to be a priest, ministering before the altar of the Lord? But even these things arise from the desire for praise, if someone does not guard his heart with all diligence. You should consider how the majority of people write their own books out of a contemptible glory (even Cicero says this) and for the sake of the glory of their own name prefix a title page.[307] We interpret the Scriptures, we often turn over the pen,[308] we write what is worth reading: and if this is done not for the sake of Christ but for remembrance in later generations and fame among the people, then the entire effort will be pointless and we will be as a sounding drum and a clashing cymbal.[309] You should consider that the majority of people argue about the Scriptures among themselves and turn discussions into wrestling matches. They challenge one another, and if they happen to be conquered, they become envious, for they are desirous of "vain glory."

I know that in the Latin copies, in this testimony that I recorded above, "if I hand over my body in order to boast," in place of "boast" they have "burn." But this error became firmly established in our copies owing to the similarity of a word. For in Greek one part of a letter distinguishes "burn" from "boast," that is, καυθήσομαι from καυχήσομαι. Moreover, even in the the Greek copies the readings are diverse.

6.1. *Brothers, even if a man is caught in some transgression, you who are spiritual, instruct such a one with a spirit of meekness; watching yourself, lest you too be tempted.* Paul knows that he is a worshiper of the God who does not will the death of the sinner but his repentance.[310]

---

305. Cf. 2 Cor 12.8.
306. 2 Cor 12.9.
307. Cf. Cicero, *Tusculanae disputationes* 1.34.
308. That is, to erase.
309. Cf. 1 Cor 13.1.
310. Cf. Ezek 18.23, 32; 33.11.

He knows that apart from the Trinity, every creature is able to sin, even though it may not sin. Thus he exhorts even "the one who is spiritual" to fear for himself, lest he should sin, to reach out his hand to the one who is falling. And he nicely calls the one "caught in a transgression" a "man," who is able to die. Thus he shows from the very term the frailness of the condition, that the one who, as a "man," has been deceived by error, and who has plunged himself into an abyss, is worthy of pardon. He cannot raise himself without help and assistance. But the term "man" is not added to "spiritual," but the command is given, as it were, to a god, that he should "instruct the man caught in a transgression," or (according to the Greek text, which is better), that he should "perfect" [him] with a spirit of gentleness. Now the one who is "perfected" does not lack all things, but some things. After all he has not gone astray into many sins, but he has been "caught in some" vice. The one who is "spiritual" should exhibit "a spirit of meekness" and gentleness in the correction of the sinner. He should not be stern, angry, or gloomy in his desire to correct the one who is astray. Instead he should challenge him, pledging salvation, promising remission, and offering the testimony of Christ. For he invites to his yoke, which is gentle and light, those who are weighed down with the heavy burden of the law and of sins. Let them learn that he is humble, meek, and gentle of heart, that they may find rest for their souls.[311]

We should use this testimony against heretics who fabricate myths about different natures and say that the spiritual [nature] is the good tree and never bears bad fruit.[312] Behold the apostle, whose authority they themselves follow, says that those "who are spiritual" are able to sin, if they become puffed up through the loftiness of their heart and fall (which even we admit). He also says that the earthly (*choicos*)[313] become spiritual, if they turn to better things. What is written to the Corinthians can be cited in opposition to us: "What do you want? Should I come to you with a rod or in love and in a spirit of meekness?"[314] For if

---

311. Cf. Mt 11.28–30.
312. Cf. Mt 7.17–19.
313. Cf. 1 Cor 15.47–49.
314. 1 Cor 4.21.

he says there that he is coming to sinners not "in a spirit of meekness" but "with a rod," how is it that here, to those who are caught in some sin, he displays not a rod but "a spirit of meekness"? But in the former passage he is speaking to those who did not perceive their error after committing sin. They were unwilling to be subjected to the elders and corrected by penance. But when the sinner understands his wound and entrusts himself to the physician to be cured, then a rod is not necessary but a spirit of gentleness.

Moreover, the following may perhaps be asked: If the reason one should "instruct" the sinner "in a spirit of gentleness" is because one needs to "watch himself, lest he himself be tempted,"[315] then should not the just person, who is certain of his own mind, who knows that he cannot fall himself, "instruct" the sinner "in a spirit" of gentleness? To this we say that even if he has conquered, since the just knows with what great effort he overcame, he should extend pardon to the sinner all the more. For even the Savior was tempted in all ways like us without sin, in order that he would be able to be compassionate and to suffer with our weaknesses, having learned by example how difficult is victory in the flesh. If someone remains a virgin until old age, he should pardon one who was once deceived by the burning passion of youth. For he knows how difficult it was for him to pass through that period of life. If someone who has been tortured for confessing the name sees that someone else has denied him under torture, let him show compassion toward the wounds of the one who denied. Let him marvel not so much that the other man was overcome as that he himself overcame. Pay attention too to the caution of the writer. For he did not say, "watching yourself lest you too" should fall, but, "lest you too should be tempted." For being overcome or overcoming is sometimes in our own power. But being tempted is in the power of the tempter. For if the Savior "was tempted,"[316] who can be secure that he will cross the sea of this life without temptation?

---

315. Gal 6.1.
316. Cf. Mt 4.1; Heb 4.15.

Those who think that Paul has spoken in accordance with his humility and not truly when he said, "And if I am unskilled in speech, yet not in knowledge," defend the coherence of this passage. For in terms of orderly sequence he should have said, "You who are spiritual instruct such ones in a spirit of gentleness," *watching yourselves lest you too be tempted.* He should not have introduced the singular number to what was in the plural.[317] Therefore, the Hebrew of Hebrews,[318] and the one who was very learned in his native language, was incapable of expressing deep meanings in a foreign language; nor did he greatly care about words, since he safely grasped the meaning.

These things pertain to the simple understanding. However that may be, in order that we may pursue the orderly sequence of the second exposition, this passage should be clarified from the end of the epistle to the Romans. For there, when in a similar fashion he was writing about foods and the observances of the Jews and those strong and perfect ones, who thought little of the precepts of the law according the letter, he was in fact speaking about those who were still from old habit being regarded as weak and infants. He saw that this quarrel was occurring between the spiritual and the fleshly. Thus he admonished the spiritual not to think little of the fleshly, and he says, "But receive the one who is weak in faith, not in disputes about thoughts. For one believes that he may eat all things; but the one who is weak eats vegetables. Let the one who eats not look down on the one who does not eat; and let not the one who does not eat judge the one who eats, for God has received him. Who are you to judge another's slave? He stands or falls to his own master. But he will stand, for God is able to establish him."[319] And when discussing many things in between about this theme, he added at the end, "Do not for the sake of food destroy the work of God";[320] and again, "But we who are stronger ought to put up

---

317. In the lemma (Gal 6.1) Paul addresses the spiritual in the plural in 6.1b, but switches to the singular in the third clause (6.1c).
318. Cf. Phil 3.5.
319. Rom 14.1–4.
320. Rom 14.20.

with the weaknesses of the weak and not please ourselves. Let each one of you please his neighbor leading to good edification."[321]

6.2.   *Carry the burdens of one another and so you will fulfill the law of Christ.* The psalmist also attests that sin is a "burden": "My iniquities have risen over my head, as a heavy burden they weigh down upon me."[322] And Zachariah sees iniquity in the outward form of a woman sitting upon a talent of lead.[323] The Savior bore this "burden" for us,[324] teaching by his own example what we ought to do. For he himself "carries" our iniquities and feels pain for us and invites those who are overwhelmed by the burden of sins and of the law to the light "burden" of virtue, saying: "My yoke is gentle and my burden is light."[325] Therefore, the one who does not lose hope for his brother's salvation but extends his hand to the one who begs, and as far is it lies within him weeps with him who weeps,[326] is weak with the weak,[327] and counts another's sins as his own, that is one who "fulfills the law of Christ" through love. What is the "law of Christ"? "This is my commandment that you love one another."[328] What is the "law" of the Son of God? "Love one another just as I have loved you."[329] How did the Son of God love us? "There is no greater love than this, that someone lay his own life down for his friends."[330] He who does not have mercy and is not clothed with the bowels of mercy and tears, though he may be "spiritual," he has not "fulfilled the law of Christ."

Moreover, let us link this passage with the preceding; for we are following a twofold mode of interpretation. If someone is weak in faith

---

321. Rom 15.1–2.
322. Ps 38.4.
323. Cf. Zec 5.7–8.
324. Cf. 1 Pt 2.24.
325. Mt 11.30.
326. Cf. Rom 12.15.
327. Cf. 1 Cor 9.22.
328. Jn 15.12.
329. Cf. Jn 13.34.
330. Jn 15.13.

and is still nourished on the milk of infancy,[331] and is unable to move too quickly from legal observance to the spiritual mysteries, you who are "stronger,"[332] "carry his burdens." Otherwise, through your knowledge the brother may perish for whom Christ died.[333] He too "carries" the necessity of the brother, who helps a poor man weighed down with the "burden" of need and who makes friends for himself from unjust mammon.[334] Christ addresses this one after the resurrection: "Come to me,[335] blessed of my Father, inherit the kingdom prepared for you from the foundation of the world. For I was hungry and you gave me to eat; I was thirsty and you gave me to drink."[336] Paul teaches Timothy as well in accordance with this meaning in another letter when he added, "Instruct the rich of this world not to be high minded (in place of *not to be haughty*), nor to place their hope in the uncertainty of riches, but in God, who gives all things abundantly for enjoyment; to live well; to be rich in good works, to be ready to give, to share, to lay up a treasure for themselves as a good foundation for the future, that they may lay hold of the true life."[337] The one who "lays hold of the true life," namely, him who says, "I am the life,"[338] has "fulfilled the law of Christ." This law has life as its aim.[339]

6.3.   *For if anyone thinks that he is something, when he is nothing, he deceives himself.* If someone does not want to "carry the burdens" of another and is merciless, contented with his own works and virtues alone, seeking not the things of others but what is his own, this one is merely a lover of self, not a lover of God as well;[340] "he deceives him-

---

331. Cf. 1 Cor 3.1–2.
332. Cf. Rom 15.1.
333. Cf. Rom 14.15; 1 Cor 8.11.
334. Cf. Lk 16.9.
335. Cf. Mt 11.28.
336. Mt 25.34–35.
337. 1 Tm 6.17–19.
338. Jn 14.6.
339. Cf. Rom 7.10.
340. 2 Tm 3.2, 4.

self." But this can be read in two distinct ways: either, "If someone thinks he is something when he is nothing"; or thus, "If someone thinks he is something," and after this we introduce, "since he is nothing he deceives himself." This separation resonates more with the Greek than with the Latin. Here is the meaning of the former way of dividing up the sentence: the one who "thinks that he is something" and is "nothing," deceives "himself." The second meaning is more profound and I approve of it more: "If anyone thinks that he is something," in that he thinks that "*he* is something" and judges himself, not on the basis of mercy toward his neighbor but on the basis of his own works and effort, contented merely with his own virtue, he becomes "nothing" on the basis of this very arrogance, and "he deceives himself." This is expressed better in the Greek, φρεναπατᾷ, that is, he "deceives his own mind," than in what the Latin translator recorded, "he seduces himself." Now he "deceives his own mind" who thinks that he is a wise man and, according to Isaiah, is "wise in himself" and "understanding in his own sight."[341]

The understanding of this passage is thus linked to circumcision and the law: He who is spiritual and has no compassion for his neighbor, despising the lowly because he himself is loftier, "deceives himself," not knowing that this is the law of the Spirit,[342] that we love one another.[343]

6.4.   *But let each one test his own work, and thus he will have glory only in himself and not in another.* Here is the meaning: You who reckon yourselves spiritual and you who are stronger in respect to another's weakness, you ought not to take consideration of the weakness of the one lying there, but of your own strength. For it is not the case that, if another is unable to make a perfect transition from Judaism to Christianity, therefore you are a perfect Christian; but if your own conscience does not sting you, you have "glory" in yourself "and not in the

---

341. Cf. Is 5.21.
342. Cf. Rom 8.2.
343. Cf. Rom 13.10; Jn 15.12.

other." The reason an athlete is strong is not because he has defeated the weak and has overcome the feeble limbs of his opponent, but if he is strong and glories in his own strength, not in the weakness of the other.

It can also be understood in another way. The one who has awareness of a good "work," and upon considering himself does not reprehend "his own work,"[344] ought not to glory about this before another and establish his own praise outwardly, and communicate this with everyone, and seek boasting from the favor of men. But let him "have glory in himself" and let him say, "But far be it from me to glory, except in the cross of our Lord Jesus Christ, through whom the world has been crucified to me and I to the world."[345] To the one who seeks glory from another, the world has not been crucified, nor is he himself nailed up with Christ.[346] For he has received what he was searching for from men, his own reward.[347]

6.5.   *For each one will carry his own burden.* This seems to contradict the words above where he says, "Carry the burdens of one another."[348] For if "each one will carry his own burden," he will not be able "to carry the burdens of one another." But one must see that he was there commanding us, as those who sin in this life, to support one another and be a help to one another in the present age. Here, on the other hand, he is speaking of the Lord's judgment of us, which is not based on the sin of another and by comparison with what is worse, but according to our work we are judged by him either as sinners or as saints. For each one receives back "in accordance with his own work."[349]

It may be that this brief maxim obscurely teaches us a new doctrine that keeps concealing itself: while we are in the present world we are able to be helped by one another, either by prayers or pieces of counsel;

---

344. Cf. 1 Jn 3.21.
345. Gal 6.14.
346. Cf. Gal 2.19.
347. Cf. Mt 6.2.
348. Gal 6.2.
349. Cf. Rom 2.6; 2 Cor 5.10.

but when we come before the tribunal of Christ, neither Job nor Daniel nor Noah can plead for anyone,[350] but "each one carries his own load."

6.6. *But let him who is instructed in the word share with him who instructs him in all good things.* Marcion interpreted this passage in such a way that he thought that the faithful and the catechumens ought to pray together and that the teacher ought to share in prayer with the disciples (at that point he became particularly puffed up with what comes next, "in all good things"), since assuredly, if the words had been about prayer, it ought not have been commanded to the one who "is instructed," but to him who "instructs," that is, not to the disciple but to the teacher.[351] On that basis as well, the other things that follow are not congruent with his explanation, "What a man sows, this also he will reap,"[352] and, "But let us not fail to do good: for by not failing we will reap in time."[353] Consequently, this is the meaning: above he had commanded to the spiritual that they should instruct those who had been caught in some transgression in a spirit of gentleness and should carry the burdens of one another, fulfilling the law of Christ. Now, on the other hand, he commands those who were still rather weak, who were both disciples and fleshly, that just as they reap spiritual things from their teachers, so they should supply fleshly things to their teachers.[354] For the teachers devote themselves completely to study and divine learning and are in need of the necessities of this life. Therefore, let what is written about the manna be done: "He [that gathered] much had nothing over, and he [that gathered] little had no lack."[355]

---

350. Cf. Ezek 14.14, 20.

351. Harnack, *Der kirchengeschichtliche Ertrag,* p. 149, comments on this passage: "This can only have been written by someone who knew Marcion precisely, as Origen did." Tertullian also reports that Marcion eliminated the customary rankings within the church.

352. Gal 6.8.

353. Gal 6.9.

354. Cf. Rom 15.27.

355. Ex 16.18; cf. 2 Cor 8.15.

Now in the present passage the "good things" he is speaking of are food and clothing and other things that men count among their "goods" by common usage and common custom. "For having food and clothing, we are content with these."[356] It is not surprising if Paul has signaled with the designation "good" the things that are necessary to the body, since our Savior too said to those who had not yet ascended to the summit of the virtues but were still proceeding in a rather lowly manner and were requesting that faith be added to them, "If then you, though you are evil, know how to give *good gifts* to your sons, how much more will the heavenly Father give good things to those who ask him!"[357] I think that even Job, when he was speaking to his wife, as to one of the foolish women, spoke from consideration of her who thought this way about physical riches, "If we have received *good things* from the hand of the Lord";[358] and again concerning trials and pressures and temptation, which may bring victory, "Why should we not endure evils?"[359] Since assuredly evils and goods are not recorded in respect to riches and afflictions, but in respect to virtues and vices (as the just man says in the Psalm, "Who is the man who wants life, who desires to see good days? Keep your tongue from evil and your lips from speaking deceit. Turn away from evil and do good").[360] Properly speaking, evil is what must be avoided, good is what we ought to do. That rich man in the gospel, who did not have "knowledge of good and evil,"[361] thought correctly that the abundance of his fields were "goods." He said, "Soul, you have *goods* laid up for many years; rest, eat, drink, be merry."[362] And another who was reclining in purple and was overflowing with luxuries hears from Abraham in the underworld, "You have received your *goods* in your life."[363]

---

356. 1 Tm 6.8.
357. Mt 7.11.
358. Job 2.10.
359. Job 2.10.
360. Ps 34.12–13.
361. Cf. Gn 2.9.
362. Lk 12.19.
363. Lk 16.25.

The following must also be considered, whether perhaps this too may not be possible to understand here: a commandment is given to the disciples that they should share with, docilely obey, and readily offer themselves as teachable to those who "instruct them in the word," but only in those things that are "goods," which are spiritual and not heretical or perverted by Judaic depravity.

6.7.   *Do not go astray, God is not mocked; for what a man sows, this also he will reap.* He foresees in the Spirit that those who are being taught and who ought to furnish sustenance for the necessities of life to their teachers might plead poverty and say, "My fields have been scorched by drought, hail has destroyed my vineyards, taxes have taken the revenue that might have been, I do not have the means to give what is commanded." Therefore, he has added, "Do not go astray, God is not mocked." He is saying: he knows your hearts, he is not unaware of your resources. However much a seemingly valid excuse can placate a man, it cannot deceive God. And at the same time he offers encouragement to exhibit what has been commanded, naming it seed, lest one should think of it as lost, what will be received when the capital has been multiplied. To the Corinthians too he has taught the method of giving and receiving by a similar example: "He who sows sparingly will also reap sparingly; and he who sows with blessing will also reap with blessing. Each one, as he has purposed in his heart, not from grief or from necessity; for God loves a cheerful giver."[364]

6.8.   *For he who sows in his own flesh, from the flesh he will also reap corruption; but he who sows in the Spirit, from the Spirit will reap eternal life.* All that we say, do, or think is sown in two fields, the "flesh" and the "Spirit." If what comes forth from our hand, mouth, and heart are goods, having been sown "in the Spirit," they will produce the fruits of "eternal life." If bad things are taken out of the field of the "flesh," they will produce a crop of "corruption" for us. Here is another interpretation: he who understands the law carnally also awaits carnal

---

364. 2 Cor 9.6–7.

promises and those that are corrupted in the present age. But he who is a spiritual hearer "sows in the Spirit," and "from the Spirit will reap everlasting life." At the same time the order of the words should be noted and linked with the preceding. He is called a "man" who "sows in the Spirit" who, when he begins to "reap everlasting life," perhaps ceases to be a "man."

Cassian (*Cassianus*),[365] who introduces putative flesh of Christ, thinks that every union between male to female is unclean.[366] Indeed the very fierce heresiarch of the Encratites[367] has used such an argument against us on the occasion of the present testimony: If "he who sows in the flesh, from the flesh will reap corruption," but he who is joined with a woman sows in the flesh, then even the one who enjoys his wife and "sows in" her "flesh" will "reap destruction from the flesh." We will respond to him, first, that Paul did not say "he who sows in *the* flesh," but "in *his own* flesh"; but no one has intercourse with himself and sows "in his *own* flesh." Second, as this observation that we have noted, "in his own flesh," let us concede more than enough to him. One must add that according to him those too who eat and drink and sleep

---

365. Migne reads "Tatianus." For Tatian see n. 367 below. According to Clement, *Stromateis* 3.13.91.1–92.2, Julius Cassian was the "founder of docetism" (which he certainly was not) and denied that sexual intercourse had God's approval. He is not known outside of Clement and statements from Jerome that depend on Clement. Smith and Wace, in DCB 1.412–13, suggest that Cassian's Docetism was closely linked with his Encratism, for it provided an answer to the orthodox challenge to his doctrine of continence: that if the birth of children were essential evil, then the Lord's own birth was evil, and his mother an object of blame. Cassian evidently met this objection by denying the reality of the Lord's body.

366. Harnack, *Der kirchengeschichtliche Ertrag*, p. 150, traces this passage with certainty to Jerome's source in Origen.

367. The Encratites were a heretical sect of the second century whose name derives from the Greek word for "self-controlled" (ἐγκρατής). Irenaeus, in *Adv Haer* 1.28.1 (ANF 1.353), says they rejected marriage and the eating of flesh, and that they denied Adam's salvation. He says that their originator was Tatian (110–72), disciple of Justin. Origen, in *CRm* 10.1, also says that the Encratites abstain from types of food and drink that they believed were opposed to chastity. Epiphanius (*Panarion* 67) has a more cynical view and says that the Encratites abstain from certain foods not for the sake of continence or piety, but from fear and for appearance's sake.

and do anything for the refreshment of their bodies "sow in the flesh" and from it "reap corruption." But if he takes refuge by saying that those who either drink or eat or sleep, yet they do it all with reason in the name of the Lord, they do not "sow in the flesh" but "in the Spirit," we will likewise respond to him that they too who, guided by reason, follow the first statement of God, "increase and multiply and fill the earth," do not "sow in the flesh" but "in the Spirit." And so, his syllogism is futile and doomed to fail. First he deceives the hearer by a sophism, but upon more careful inspection the problem is easily resolved. For we cannot say that Abraham, Isaac, Jacob, and the other holy men who were born from the promise, indeed that the very forerunner of the Lord,[368] since he was born in the flesh, sprouted from a stock of corruption.

The following should likewise be observed, that "he who sows in the flesh" is recorded with an addition: "in *his own* flesh." But with respect to, "he who sows in the Spirit," it is not said, "in *his own* spirit," but simply, "in the Spirit." For the one who "sows" good things "sows" not in *his own* "spirit" but in God's, from whom he will also "reap eternal life."

6.9. *But let us not fail to do good; for in due time we will reap if we do not relax.* He encourages them to strive for perseverance, those who unwittingly await the wage of good works in *this* life. For just as with seed, there is one time for sowing and another for harvesting, so also the work of sowing is in the *present* life (these works are now cast either "in the Spirit" or "in the flesh"); but the harvest pertains to the *future* judgment upon works. And in view of the quality or diversity of the sowing, we produce different measures: a hundredfold, sixtyfold, and thirtyfold fruit.[369] No one who "fails" can "reap" this crop, for "he who

---

368. John the Baptist.

369. Cf. Mt 13.8, 23. O'Connell, *The Eschatology of St. Jerome,* p. 9, cites this passage to prove that Jerome held the doctrine that the works for which we will be judged can be performed only during this life. "Once this life is finished, the possibility of performing them is finished too."

perseveres until the end will be saved."[370] He also says, "Be not faint."[371] But what is going on when sinners every day increase their evil works, yet we are worn out in the doing of good works?

6.10.   *Therefore, while we have time, let us work the good toward all, but especially toward the members of the household of faith.* The "time" of sowing, as we said, is the present time and the life that we pass. In this life it is allowed to us to sow what we want. When this life passes, the "time" for working is removed. This is why the Savior says, "Work while it is day; night will come, when no one can work any longer."[372] The word of God has risen for us, the true sun, and the "*beasts* have been gathered into their dens."[373] Let us go forth as *men* to our work and labor until evening, just as it is mystically sung in the Psalm: "You put in place the darkness and it became night. The beasts of the forest will pass through it, young lions roaring, to seize and seek food for themselves from God. The sun has risen and they were gathered and slept in their dens. Man goes forth to his task and to his work until evening."[374] Whether we are sick or healthy, lowly or powerful, rich or poor, unknown or honored, hungry or fed, let us do all things in the name of the Lord[375] with patience and equanimity, and what is written will be fulfilled in us: "But for those who love the Lord, all things work together for the good."[376] If I keep myself in check in respect to anger, lust, and injustice that desires vengeance; if for God's sake I keep quiet; if upon the occasion of each of these unsettling pricks and provocations of vices, I recall that God is looking down upon me, then these very things become to me an occasion for triumphs.

Let us not say when we give, "This man is my friend, that one I do not know." "This one should receive, that one should be overlooked."

---

370. Mt 10.22; 24.13.
371. Is 5.27.
372. Jn 9.4.
373. Ps 104.22.
374. Ps 104.20–23
375. Cf. Col 3.17.
376. Rom 8.28.

Let us imitate our Father who "makes his sun rise upon the good and the evil and who rains upon the just and the unjust."[377] The font of goodness is open to "all": slave and free, common man and king; rich and poor drink equally from him. When a lamp is kindled in a house it gives light equally to "all."[378] But if the halter upon generosity is loosened indiscriminately to everyone, how much more to the "members of the household of faith" and to Christians who have the same Father, who are registered under the name of the same teacher![379] It seems possible to me that this passage is rooted in what precedes. Thus he is using the name "members of the household of faith" to refer to the teachers whom he had previously commanded to be ministered to by the hearers, with respect to all that is regarded as "goods."[380]

The course of this life is brief. The very things that I speak, what I dictate, what is written, what I correct, what I reread, either increases or wastes some of my time. Titus the son of Vespasian, who in avenging the Lord's blood entered Rome as a victor when he overthrew Jerusalem, is said to have been a man of such great decency that when late on a certain night he was recalling at dinner that he had done nothing good that day, said, "Friends, today I have wasted a day."[381] Do we think that an hour is not lost to us, a day, moments, time, ages, when we speak an idle word, for which we will render an account on the judgment day?[382] But if he[383] both said and did this naturally, without the law, without the gospel, without the teaching of the Savior and the apostles, what ought we to do, in condemnation of whom both Juno[384]

---

377. Mt 5.45.

378. Cf. Mt 5.15.

379. Cf. Mt 23.8–9.

380. Cf. Gal 6.6.

381. Cf. Suetonius, *Titus* 8.

382. Cf. Mt 12.36.

383. Titus.

384. Juno (Greek Hera) was one of the chief deities of Rome and was widely worshiped as the Roman goddess of women.

has her widows (*univiras*),[385] Vesta[386] her virgins, and the other idols[387] their continent ones? Blessed John the evangelist, when he was staying in Ephesus until extreme old age, used to be carried to church with difficulty by the hands of the disciples. He was not able to put many words together with his voice and was accustomed to utter nothing but this during every gathering: "Little children, love one another."[388] Finally, the disciples and the brothers who were present became irritated because they constantly heard the same thing over and over, and they said, "Teacher, why do you always say this?" He answered with a statement worthy of John: "Because it is the Lord's command, and if it alone is done, it is enough." This has been said in view of the apostle's present command: "Let us work good toward all, but especially toward the members of the household of faith."

6.11. *See with what sort of letters I have written to you by my own hand.* Those who wanted the Galatians to be circumcised had spread it around that Paul acted one way and preached something else, destroying his words by his deeds. For he who proclaimed the abolition of the law was himself found under the law. Paul could not refute this opinion in person in the sight of all (for he was prevented by the chains[389] that he endured as a testimony [*martyrium*] to Christ). Therefore, he

---

385. Lit. "women of one husband." The word also occurs in Tertullian, *De exhortatione ad castitatis;* Jerome, *Adversus Jovinianum* 1.11. The women in question, devotees of Juno, apparently remained widows voluntarily.

386. Vesta was the Roman goddess of the hearth, whose cult was believed to have been introduced into Rome by Pompilius Numa. Though she bore the title "mother," she was thought of as a virgin. Her priestesses, the Vestal Virgins, had sacred status and were required to maintain strict sexual purity during their minimum of thirty years of service. Violations were punished by living entombment. Cf. Jerome, *Adversus Jovinianum* 11.

387. For example, the goddess Diana (Greek Artemis), the virgin goddess of hunting, whose devotees forsook marriage.

388. According to Harnack, *Der kirchengeschichtliche Ertrag,* pp. 150–51, this story must be traced to Origen.

389. Cf. Acts 21.33; 26.29; 28.20; Eph 6.20; 2 Tm 1.16.

represents himself through his letter. And to prevent any suspicion from arising that the letter was false, he himself has written it from this point right to the end, which shows that the preceding part was written by someone else.[390]

Now he demonstrates that letters were sent in his name by false teachers [in the letter] to the Thessalonians too, when he writes, "Now we ask you, brothers, through the coming of our Lord Jesus Christ and our gathering in him, not to be quickly moved from your frame of mind, nor to be frightened either by a spirit or through words or through a letter, as though sent from us, as if the day of the Lord is at hand. Let no one seduce you in any way."[391] And in order to rescue the entire letter that he sent from the suspicion of falsehood, he undersigns it at the end "with his own hand" and says, "My greeting by the hand of Paul, which is the sign in every epistle: thus I write. The grace of our Lord Jesus Christ be with you all."[392] In a similar manner he under-signed the letter that he dictated to the Colossians as well: "My greeting by the hand of Paul. Remember my chains."[393] And wherever he knew that false teachers were present, who were capable of sowing new doc-trines by means of the authority of an apostle, he undersigned the letter with his own hand. Finally, even when writing to the Corinthians, among whom there were schisms and heresies, with each one saying, "I am of Paul, and I am of Apollos, but I am of Cephas,"[394] he signed his epistle with such a notation: "My greeting by the hand of Paul. If any-one does not love the Lord Jesus Christ, let him be anathema. Mara-natha,"[395] and so on.

For this reason, then, because he wants to remove every opportu-nity from the false teachers, who turned the Galatians away from the truth of the gospel, he completed the end of the letter with a notation by his own hand, and says, "See with what sort of letters I have written

390. Cf. Rom 16.22.
391. 2 Thes 2.1–3.
392. 2 Thes 3.17–18.
393. Col 4.18.
394. 1 Cor 1.12.
395. 1 Cor 16.21–22.

to you." It is not that the letters themselves were large (for in Greek this is expressed by πηλίκοις), but that the marks of his own "hand" were known to them. Thus when they recognize the angles and contours of the letters, they would imagine that they had seen the very man who had written the letter. On this passage I marvel at the ridiculous thing spoken by a very learned man in our times. He says, "Paul was a Hebrew and did not know Greek letters, and because necessity demanded that he undersign the letter as it were 'with his own hand,' contrary to custom, and with difficulty, he pressed out the curved tracks of the letters with large angles, showing even in this the signs of his love for the Galatians, because he was trying for their sake what he was not even capable of doing."[396] Therefore, Paul wrote the epistle in large letters because the meaning in the letters was great and had been traced out by the Spirit of the living God, not by pen and ink. But with respect to what he has recorded, "with my hand," in the "hands" we should understand works. For this reason in the prophets as well it is frequently said, "The word of God that came into the *hand* of Jeremiah,"[397] or Haggai.[398] Thus we recognize that the word of God came in similar fashion "into the hand" of Paul too. Paul writes large letters not only at that time to the Galatians, but also today he writes them to everyone. Although they may be small angles with which his epistles are written, nevertheless the "letters" are great, since in the "letters" there is great meaning.

6.12.   *As many as want to please in the flesh, they compel you to be circumcised, only in order that they not suffer persecution for the cross of Christ.* He showed higher up from which passage he undersigned with his own hand; now he unfolds something that he wrote. Gaius [Julius]

---

396. Marius Victorinus speaks of Paul giving them a "sign of his love" by writing in his own hand. I have not been able to confirm that he says the rest of what Jerome quotes here.

397. Jer 37.2.

398. Hg 1.1.

Caesar,[399] Octavian Augustus,[400] and Tiberius,[401] the successor of Augustus, had promulgated laws that permitted the Jews, who had been dispersed throughout the whole sphere of the Roman Empire, to live by their own rites and observe their ancestral ceremonies.[402] Whoever had been circumcised, therefore, even if he believed in Christ, was reckoned as a Jew by the Gentiles. But anyone without circumcision, who proclaimed by his foreskin that was not a Jew, became liable to persecution, both from Jews and from Gentiles. So those who were subverting the Galatians, wishing to avoid these persecutions, were persuading the disciples to circumcise themselves for protection. This is what the apostle now calls "confidence in the flesh,"[403] namely, because they were proposing circumcision in persecution, both to Gentiles, whom they feared, and to the Jews, whom they wanted to please. For neither the Jews were able to persecute them nor could the Gentiles, whom they saw both circumcise converts and themselves keep the precepts of the law.

---

399. Gaius Julius Caesar (100–44 BC) was a Roman general and statesman and sole dictator in Rome after the defeat of his rival Pompey. An accomplished orator and prose stylist, his commentary on the conquest of Gaul and the civil war with Pompey are the best examples of unadorned narrative in Latin. Suetonius in his *Twelve Caesars* reports that the Jews especially mourned his death, since they detested his rival Pompey, who had desecrated the temple of Jerusalem.

400. Gaius Julius Caesar Octavianus Augustus was the first emperor of Rome (27 BC–AD 14). He was the great nephew and adopted son of Julius Caesar, and also his heir. With Mark Antony and Lepidus he was the victor in the civil war against his uncle's murderers, Brutus and Cassius. The title of Augustus was borne by all subsequent Roman emperors.

401. Tiberius Julius Caesar Germanicus was Roman emperor from 14–37. He was stepson of the Emperor Augustus.

402. Harnack, *Der kirchengeschichtliche Ertrag,* pp. 152–53, suggests that this factual material is unlike Jerome except when he is copying (from Origen). A standard study of the theme in question is E. M. Smallwood, *The Jews Under Roman Rule: From Pompey to Diocletian* (Leiden: Brill, 1976).

403. Cf. Phil 3.3–4.

6.13.   *For not even do those who are circumcised keep the law, but they want you to be circumcised in order to glory in your flesh.* Because of weakness, he says, the law of the flesh cannot be fulfilled.[404] This is why the Jews "keep" the precepts and teachings of men rather than the commandments of God,[405] while they do not *do* either the corporeal law (for that is impossible) or the spiritual [law], which they do not understand. Whence it comes about that all that they strive for, do, rely upon is in order to "glory" over the injury done to "your flesh," and to vaunt that Gentiles have been circumcised by their own instruction. But they do all this in order to please the Jews and to quell the ill-will over the embattled law.

6.14.   *But far be it from me to glory except in the cross of our Lord Jesus Christ, through whom the world has been crucified to me and I to the world.* He is able to "glory only in the cross of Christ" who takes it up and follows the Savior;[406] who has crucified his own flesh with its lusts and desires;[407] who has died to the world and does not contemplate the things that are seen, but what are unseen;[408] who sees that the world has been crucified and its form is passing.[409] Now the "world" that is "crucified" to the just man is that one of which the Savior says, "I have overcome the world,"[410] and, "Do not love the world,"[411] and, "You have not received the spirit of the world."[412] The "world has been crucified" to that man for whom the world is dead; and the consummation of the "world" comes to him and he is made worthy of the "new heaven and the new earth,"[413] and the new covenant.[414] He sings

---

404. Cf. Rom 8.3.
405. Cf. Mk 7.7–8.
406. Cf. Mt 16.24.
407. Cf. Gal 5.24.
408. Cf. 2 Cor 4.18.
409. Cf. 1 Cor 7.31.
410. Jn 16.33.
411. 1 Jn 2.15.
412. 1 Cor 2.12.
413. Cf. Rv 21.2.
414. Cf. Lk 22.20.

a "new song"[415] and receives a "new name written on a stone, which no one knows except the one who receives it."[416]

It is asked how Paul now says, "But far be it from me to glory except in the cross of our Lord Jesus Christ," when in a different passage he "glories" about other things, as for example when he says, "through your *glory* which I have in Christ Jesus";[417] and again, "I will gladly *glory* in my weaknesses, that the virtue of Christ may indwell me";[418] and in another passage, "But it would be better for me to die than for anyone to deprive my *glory*";[419] and the other things which are written in this way. But one should know that all this *glorying*, when it is related to the cross, *is* the glory of the cross, and anything worthy that is done in respect to the virtues is done for the sake of the Lord's passion.

6.15. *For neither circumcision nor uncircumsion is anything, but the new creation.* Just as a believer and an infidel, though they are one in nature, are divided in two according to the diversity of understanding, since the apostle says, "You must strip off the old man with his works and put on the new [man], who is renewed in knowledge according to the image of the Creator";[420] so also the world, though it is one according to its nature, according to its meaning it first becomes one thing, then another. To a sinner the world is old, to a saint it is new. For when the world is crucified to a saint, by no means is there "circumcision and uncircumcision" to him,[421] nor "Jew or Gentile," but a "new creation" in which the "body of our humiliation is transformed like the body of the glory of Christ."[422] "For old things have passed away, behold all things have become new."[423] And just as "there is one glory of

---

415. Rv 5.9.
416. Cf. Rv 2.17.
417. 1 Cor 15.31.
418. 2 Cor 12.9.
419. 1 Cor 9.15.
420. Col 3.9–10.
421. Cf. Col 3.11.
422. Cf. Phil 3.21.
423. 2 Cor 5.17.

the sun, another of the moon, another of the stars, for star differs from star in glory, so also the resurrection of the dead."[424] Daniel harmonizes with this when he says with the equivalent language, "Many of those who sleep will rise from the dust of the earth, some to eternal life and some to reproach and eternal confusion";[425] and, "Those with understanding will shine like the splendor of the firmament";[426] and of the just, "Many [will be] like the stars forever."[427] For it is not in respect to the sun and moon, the firmament and stars, that "circumcision or uncircumcision" avails anything; but it is in respect to the new condition without these parts of bodies that can be cut off. So then, even we who "love God,"[428] for whom have been prepared "what neither eye has seen nor ear heard nor has ascended into the heart of man,"[429] when we have been "transformed from the body of lowliness into the body of the glory of the Lord Jesus Christ,"[430] we will have that body that neither the Jew can cut nor a Gentile preserve in the state of uncircumcision. It is not that it is different in its nature, but diverse in its glory. "For it is necessary that this mortal put on immortality and this corruptible be clothed with incorruption."[431] This is like what the blessed evangelist John perceived when he said, "Dearly beloved, now we are sons of God, and it is not yet manifest what we will be. We know that if it becomes manifest, we will be like him, because we will see him just as he is."[432] Since, therefore, that "body of the glory of Jesus Christ"[433] is not yet manifest, which after the resurrection both had the prints of the nails[434] and entered through closed doors,[435] we

---

424. 1 Cor 15.41–42.
425. Dn 12.2.
426. Dn 12.3.
427. Dn 12.3.
428. Cf. Rom 8.28.
429. Cf. 1 Cor 2.9.
430. Cf. Phil 3.21.
431. 1 Cor 15.53.
432. 1 Jn 3.2.
433. Cf. Phil 3.21.
434. Cf. Lk 24.40; Jn 20.25, 27.
435. Cf. Jn 20.26.

who have already now risen together with Christ in baptism,[436] having been renewed in the new man,[437] should serve neither "circumcision nor uncircumcision." But we should believe that even now we are what we will be.

6.16.   *And whoever follows this rule, peace and mercy on them and on the Israel of God.* All things are directed toward the norm, and whether they are crooked or straight, when the "rule" is laid down, they are exposed. So also the doctrine of God is, so to speak, like a norm for our words, which judges between just and unjust things. The one who "follows" it will have in himself the "peace, which surpasses all understanding";[438] and after "peace," "mercy," which is a particular characteristic of the "Israel of God."

In fact he has said "Israel of God" to distinguish it from that Israel that ceased to be God's. For they "claim to be Jews and are not," but they are lying, since they are from the "synagogue of Satan."[439] You should not be surprised if there is a carnal Israel in imitation of spiritual Israel, who have neither "peace" nor "mercy." (It is written of them to the Corinthians: "Consider Israel according to the flesh.")[440] For in imitation of God and of the Lord as well, there are "many gods and many lords, whether in heaven or on earth."[441] But with a single expression, when he was concluding the epistle in terms of the thesis of the argument, he has nicely spoken of the "Israel of God," namely, so that everything that was said above may be shown to have been argued not without reason, but with reason.

6.17.   *Henceforth let no one be troublesome to me.* It is not as if he has failed in his teaching, but that a farmer has this "labor,"[442] if the plants

---

436. Cf. Rom 6.4; Col 2.12.
437. Cf. Col 3.9–10.
438. Cf. Phil 4.7.
439. Cf. Rv 2.9.
440. 1 Cor 10.18.
441. Cf. 1 Cor 8.5.
442. The Greek has κόπους, which can mean "toil, trouble, suffering."

he has planted dry up; and a shepherd has this anxiety, if the animals that he had gathered in are scattered and ravaged. This is why it reads better in the Greek: "Henceforth let no one give me *labor*," namely, lest once again I should have the need to *labor* among you. He gives "labor" to a teacher who lives and thinks differently from what the teacher did and taught.

He can even forestall contention with them, if anyone wants to contradict him from that point forward. He grasped this when writing to the Corinthians about the veiling of the female's head and the non-veiling of the male's.[443] After many things he says, "But if anyone seems to be contentious, we do not have such a custom, nor does the church of God."[444] That is to say, we have said what seemed honest and just to us; but if anyone who does not want to comply with the truth looks for something to say in response and upon which he may insist, let him know, on the contrary, that the one who is ready to contend, rather than to be taught, is not worthy of a response.

6.17.   *For I bear the stigmata of our Lord Jesus Christ on my body.* The one who is circumcised in the flesh after the coming of Christ does not "bear the stigmata of the Lord Jesus." On the contrary he glories in his own confusion. But the one who was "flogged beyond measure, frequently in prison, was beaten three times with rods, was once stoned," and who suffered all the other things that are written in his catalogue of glorying,[445] this is the one who "carries the stigmata of the Lord Jesus on his body." Perhaps also the one who "buffets his body and subjects it to servitude, lest after preaching to others he may be found to be rejected,"[446] "bears the stigmata of the Lord Jesus on his own body." Also the apostles rejoiced that they were worthy to suffer mistreatment for the name of Jesus.[447]

---

443. Cf. 1 Cor 11.4–5.
444. 1 Cor 11.16.
445. Cf. 2 Cor 11.23–29.
446. 1 Cor 9.27.
447. Cf. Acts 5.41.

6.18. *May the grace of our Lord Jesus Christ [be] with your spirit, brothers. Amen.* "May" not dissension, not servitude to the law, not quarreling, not wrangling, but "the grace of our Lord Jesus Christ be with your spirit." He does not say with the *flesh* or with the *soul,* either because you who have become spiritual have ceased being flesh and soul or because the things that are lesser are embraced in the principal part.[448] For the soul and the flesh are subjected to the "spirit," of which even Ecclesiastes speaks: "The spirit will return to him who gave it."[449] And Paul says in another passage, "The Spirit himself bears witness with our spirit."[450]

But this "grace of the Lord Jesus" is not with everyone, but with those who merit being called "brothers" by the apostle, faithful "brothers" and true "brothers." This is what the Hebrew word "amen" signifies. For the seventy translators translated "amen" by "let it be done." Aquila, Symmachus, and Theodotion translated it "faithfully," or "truly." And just as in the Old Testament, God confirms his words by a certain custom of swearing, when he says, "I live, says the Lord,"[451] and he also swears by holy men, "Your soul lives";[452] so also our Savior in the Gospel shows by the word "amen" that the things he is saying are true. But that "amen" signifies the agreement of the hearer and is a seal of truth. The first letter to the Corinthians teaches us this as well, where Paul says, "But if you speak a blessing in the spirit, how will the one who occupies the place of the uninstructed speak the "Amen" over your blessing, since he does not even know what you are saying?"[453] From this he shows that the uninstructed cannot reply that what is said is true, unless he understands what is being taught.

---

448. Compare Origen's similar use of Stoic categories in human anthropology in *CRm* 5.6.3; 9.23.2.

449. Eccl 12.7.

450. Rom 8.16.

451. Nm 14.28.

452. Jdth 12.4.

453. 1 Cor 14.16.

Commentary on

Titus

ONE BOOK OF THE COMMENTARY ON THE

EPISTLE TO TITUS BY SOPHRONIUS

EUSEBIUS JEROME, PRIEST OF STRIDON

Preface

Although those who have nullified their first faith[1] are not worthy of
the faith—I am speaking of Marcion,[2] Basilides,[3] and all the heretics,
who tear the Old Testament to pieces—nevertheless, we should endure
them to some extent, at least if they keep their hands on the New and
do not dare to do violence to the evangelists or apostles of Christ, "the
Son of the good God" (as they boast). But now, since they have both
demolished his Gospels and made the epistles of the apostles to be not
of Christ's apostles but have made them their own, I marvel at how
they dare to lay claim to the name of Christians for themselves. For to

---

1. Cf. 1 Tm 5.12.
2. See p. 56, n. 47 above.
3. See p. 70, n. 135 above.

say nothing of the other epistles, from which they erased anything they had seen that was opposed to their own doctrine, they have believed that some of them deserved to be rejected in their entirety, namely, those to Timothy, to the Hebrews, and to Titus, which even now we are endeavoring to expound. And indeed if they were to offer reasons why they do not think that they are the apostle's, we would attempt to answer something in response, and perhaps give satisfaction to the reader. But let them now declare with heretical authority and say, "This epistle is Paul's; that one is not." By this authority let them understand that they are refuted on behalf of the truth by which they are not ashamed to feign false things.

But Tatian,[4] patriarch of the Ebionites,[5] who also himself repudiated some of Paul's letters, believed that this one, especially the one to Titus, had to be declared to be the apostle's. He cares little for the claim of Marcion and of the others who agree with him in this respect. Well then, O Paula and Eustochium, the apostle is writing from Nicopolis, which is located on the coastline at Actium; now indeed it is the greatest part of your possession.[6] And he writes to his disciple and son in Christ, Titus, whom he had left in Crete to instruct the churches. And he commanded him to come to Nicopolis himself, when one of the two, Artemas or Tychicus, had landed at Crete.[7] For it was just that the one who had said, "my anxiety for all the churches,"[8] and who, having set out from Jerusalem, had established the gospel of Christ all the way to Illyricum,[9] would not allow the Cretans to be abandoned due to the absence of himself and Titus. The seeds of idolatry first sprouted from

---

4. Tatian is mentioned by Irenaeus, *Adv Haer* 3.36–37, as a hearer of Justin Martyr, who became a heretic who denied Adam's salvation and declared all marriage to be fornication. Harnack, *Der kirchengeschichtliche Ertrag*, p. 166, remarks that this mention of Tatian confirms that Jerome's preface is based on Origen.

5. See p. 55, n. 42 above.

6. Paula and Eustochium came from this region.

7. Cf. Ti 3.12.

8. 2 Cor 11.28.

9. Cf. Rom 15.19.

the Cretans; but he would send to them Artemas or Tychicus in place of himself and Titus, whose teaching and solace would be greatly cherished.

The book begins here.

1.1. *Paul, a slave of God, but an apostle of Jesus Christ.* In the Epistle to the Romans he began this way: "Paul a slave of Jesus Christ, called apostle."[10] In this one, however, he calls himself "a slave of God, but an apostle of Jesus Christ." For if the Father and the Son are one,[11] and the one who believes in the Son will believe also in the Father, then the apostle Paul's slavery too should be referred equally to the Father or to the Son. But this slavery is not that of which the apostle himself says, "For you have not received a spirit of slavery again unto fear, but you have received the Spirit of adoption[12] in whom we cry: Abba, Father."[13]

Truly it is a noble slavery of which even David says to God, "I am your slave, the son of your maidservant."[14] And blessed Mary says to the angel: "Behold the maidservant of the Lord; be it done to me according to your word."[15] Even Moses had this slavery, of whom the Lord says to Jesus,[16] son of Nun, "Moses my servant is dead."[17] And in another passage, "Moses the servant of the Lord died in the land of Moab by the word of the Lord."[18] For far be it from us to believe that Moses and Mary had the spirit of slavery in fear[19] and not in the love of God.

---

10. Rom 1.1.

11. Cf. Jn 10.30.

12. A textual variant adds "of sons."

13. Rom 8.15.

14. Ps 116.16.

15. Lk 1.38.

16. Heb. Joshua. I preserve the Latin form to keep the link to Jesus (Christ) before the reader's eyes.

17. Jos 1.2.

18. Dt 34.5.

19. Cf. Rom 8.15.

It is no wonder that men, no matter how holy, are nevertheless called slaves in a noble sense, seeing that the Father says to the Son through Isaiah the prophet, "For you it is a great thing that you are called my boy."[20] In Greek this says: μέγα σοί ἐστι τοῦ κληθῆναί σε παῖδά μου. Now since in Greek "boy," that is, παῖς, can mean both servant and son, we have looked in the Hebrew and have found that it was not written, "my son," but "my slave," that is, *abdi*. This is why the prophet Obadiah, which translates as "slave of the Lord," was named from servitude to God.

It may trouble someone that the Lord and Savior, who is creator of the universe, is called God's slave. He will not be troubled if he listens to the same one who speaks to the apostles, "Whoever wants to be greatest among you, let him be slave of all,"[21] and, "The Son of Man came not to be served, but to serve."[22] Lest he should seem to teach this in words only, he showed it by example. "For when he had taken a towel, he girded himself, filled a basin with water, and washed the disciples' feet."[23] And so, it is not impious to believe that he who had assumed the form of a slave[24] had done those things that belong to slaves, in order that it would be said that he served the Father's will, since he himself served his own slaves. But this slavery is that of love, through which we are commanded to serve one another mutually.[25] And even the apostle himself, though he was free from all, made himself a slave of all.[26] And in another passage he says, "Your slave for the sake of Christ."[27] He is a slave of God who is not a slave of sin. The apostle, then, who was not a slave of sin, is rightly called slave of God the Father and of Christ.

---

20. Is 49.6.
21. Mt 20.26–27; cf. Mk 9.35.
22. Mk 10.45.
23. Cf. Jn 13.4–5.
24. Cf. Phil 2.7.
25. Cf. Jn 13.14, 34.
26. Cf. 1 Cor 9.19.
27. Cf. 2 Cor 4.5.

It seems to me that what he says further, "but an apostle of Jesus Christ," is as if he had said, "commander of the praetorian guard of Augustus Caesar, master of the army of Emperor Tiberius." For just as the judges of this world appear more noble in relation to the rulers whom they serve, and they are assigned titles from the office to which they are elevated, so also the apostle, by laying claim for himself among the Christians to the great dignity, he has first designated himself with the title of "apostle of Christ," that he might strike awe into his readers by the very authority of the name, indicating that all who believe in Christ must be in submission to him. And besides, what we have recorded a little bit earlier as written to the Romans, "slave of Jesus Christ,"[28] is no different from his having said slave of wisdom, slave of justice, slave of sanctification, slave of redemption. "For Christ became for us from God the Father, wisdom, justice, sanctification, and redemption."[29]

1.2–4.   *According to the faith of God's chosen ones and the knowledge of the truth, which is in accordance with piety in the hope of eternal life, which God, who does not lie, promised before the eternal ages. But he manifested his word in his own time in the preaching, which was entrusted to me according to the command of our God and Savior. To [my] dearly beloved son Titus in accordance with [our] common faith. Grace and peace from God the Father and Christ Jesus our Savior.*

The one who had said, not by way of humility, as many think, but truly, "And if I am unskilled in speech, but not in knowledge,"[30] the "Hebrew of Hebrews, according to the law a Pharisee,"[31] does not unfold profound meanings in the Greek language. Moreover, he scarcely expresses in words what he is thinking. Therefore let us discuss each of these details, as they are written, in accordance with the sequence of thought and the composition of the realities, rather than of the words.

---

28. Rom 1.1.
29. 1 Cor 1.30; cf. *CRm* 1.1.3.
30. 2 Cor 11.6.
31. Phil 3.5.

He says, "according to the faith of God's chosen ones." This refers to what is higher up, what he began with: "Paul a slave of God, but an apostle of Jesus Christ according to the faith of God's chosen ones";[32] that is to say, [faith] of those who have not only been called, but have been chosen.[33] In view of the variety of their works, thoughts, and words, there is a great diversity even among the chosen ones themselves. The one who is chosen by God does not immediately possess "faith in accordance with election," or have the "knowledge of the truth in accordance with the faith." And this is why the Savior said to the Jews who had believed in him, "If you abide in my word, you will know the truth, and the truth will set you free."[34] And the evangelist testifies that he said these things to those who indeed believed, but who did not know the truth, which they were able to attain, if they would have abided in his words. And having become free, they would have ceased being slaves.

It is asked, why does he add to what he says, "according to the faith of God's chosen ones and the knowledge of the truth," the words, "which is in accordance with piety." Is there a truth recorded that is not "in piety"? And is "knowledge of the truth" now introduced to distinguish it from that which is "in accordance with piety"? Plainly there is truth that does not have piety: if someone knows the art of grammar, or dialectics, so that he possess the means of speaking correctly and judges with discernment between what is true and false. Geometry too and arithmetic and music have truth the knowledge of their subject matter; but that knowledge does not belong to piety.

The knowledge of piety is to know the law, to understand the prophets, to believe the gospel, not to ignore the apostles. And, on the other hand, there are many who have true knowledge of piety, but they do not automatically also possess the truth of other arts and of those that we mentioned above. This truth, therefore, the knowledge of which is "in accordance with piety" is recorded as "in the hope of eter-

---

32. Ti 1.1.

33. Cf. Mt 22.14; *CRm* 1.2.1.

34. Jn 8.31–32.

nal life," which immediately bestows the reward of immortality to him who knows himself. Apart from piety, however, the knowledge of the truth delights for the moment, but it does not possess an eternity of rewards, [an eternity] "which God, who does not lie, promised before the eternal ages and manifested it in his own time in Christ Jesus."

Now to whom did he "promise beforehand," and afterward acted to make it "manifest," if not to his own wisdom, which was always with the Father,[35] when he "was glad in the perfected world and rejoiced over the sons of men"?[36] And he promised that whosoever would believe in that [wisdom] would possess eternal life.[37] Before he laid the foundations of the world, before he diffused the seas, established the mountains, suspended the sky, made the land solid by driving it into a mass,[38] God, in whom there is no lying, promised these things. It is not that he is capable of lying and is unwilling to bring forth false words, but that he who is the Father of truth has no lie in him,[39] according to this: "But let God be true, but every man a liar."[40] So this is why he is called the "God who does not lie" and when he promises certain things in the prophets with an oath, this is in order that *we* may become more certain, that *we* may hope all the more that the things which were spoken will happen, and by believing this with our whole mind, *we* will be prepared for the attainment of the things that are coming.

It does not seem off topic to glance briefly at the question: Why is it said with the voice of the apostle that God alone is true, and every man a liar.[41] And unless I am mistaken, just as he *alone* is said to have immortality,[42] though he made both angels and many rational creatures to which he gave immortality, so also he *alone* is called true. It is not that the others are not immortal and lovers of truth, but that he

---

35. Cf. Prv 8.27.
36. Prv 8.30–31.
37. Cf. Jn 3.16.
38. Cf. Prv 8.27–29.
39. Cf. Jn 8.44.
40. Rom 3.4.
41. Cf. Rom 3.4.
42. Cf. 1 Tm 6.16.

alone is by nature both immortal and true. The others, however, attain to immortality and truth as a gift from him. And it is one thing to *be* true, to have something by means of oneself; it is something else to be under the authority of one who gives what you possess.

But I do not think the following point should be silently passed over: How did the "God who does not lie" promise eternal life "before the eternal ages"? According to the history of Genesis the world was created by him.[43] Through the alternation of nights and days, and also of months and years, time was created. In this cycle and circuit of the world, time passes and comes, and it will either come or it has been. This is why some philosophers do not think that time is present, but either past or future. For everything that we say, do, or think, is awaited, either while it is happening, passes by, or if it has not yet happened.[44] Before the time of this world, then, one should believe that there was a certain eternity of the ages in which the Father was always with the Son and the Holy Spirit.

And thus I would say that God's time alone is an entire *eternity;* or rather, time is incalculable, since he himself is infinite, who being prior to times transcends all time.[45] But a thousand years of our world are not yet fulfilled, and what great prior eternities, how much time, what great beginnings of ages must one think have existed in which angels, thrones, dominions, and other powers served God![46] And they existed at God's command, apart from the alternations and measure of time! And so, before all this time, which neither words dare to utter, nor mind to comprehend, nor hidden thought to reach, God the Father of

---

43. Cf. Gn 1.1.

44. My colleague, Jay Martin, informs me that this passage approximates a Stoic philosophy of time, which brings Heraclitus, Parmenides, and Plato into synthesis. Zeno, the founder of Stoicism, held both that the present is but mere mediation between being and nonbeing (past and future) and that all events are causally determined, which would render the future a very robust reality as well as the changeless past.

45. Cf. Jerome, Ep. 18 to Damasus.

46. Cf. Col 1.16.

his own wisdom promised that his own Word, both his own very wisdom itself and the life of those who would believe, would come into the world.

Pay careful attention to the text and sequence of the reading: for the eternal life that "God who does not lie promised before the eternal ages" is nothing else but the Word of God. For it says, He "manifested his word in his own time." Therefore the eternal life that he had promised is itself his own Word, which was in the beginning with the Father.[47] "And the Word was God,"[48] "and the Word became flesh and dwelled among us."[49] But that the Word of God, that is, Christ himself, is life, is testified in another passage, which says, "I am the life."[50] But the life is not fleeting; it is not circumscribed by any time. On the contrary it is perpetual and eternal. It was manifested in the final age through the proclamation that was entrusted to Paul, doctor of the Gentiles, and teacher,[51] in order to be proclaimed in the world and become known to men, "in accordance with the command of God [our] Savior," who wanted to save us[52] by fulfilling what he had promised.

Now the apostle writes to Titus, "most dearly beloved son," which is expressed in Greek as γνησίῳ τέκνῳ. This cannot be rendered into Latin speech, for γνήσιος expresses more the idea that someone is called faithful and is one's own and, so to speak, is legitimate or genuine. There is no comparison to another. From this we understand that there were very great differences among Paul's sons. He considered some to be γνησίους, that is, very genuine and united with himself and offspring of a true marriage and of free [woman].[53] But others were, so to speak, from a maidservant and from Hagar, who cannot receive an inheritance with Isaac, the son of the free woman. For the words and wisdom and teaching by which Titus was instructing the churches of

---

47. Cf. Jn 1.1.
48. Jn 1.1.
49. Jn 1.14.
50. Jn 14.6.
51. Cf. 1 Tm 2.7.
52. Cf. 1 Tm 2.4.
53. Cf. Gal 4.21–26.

Christ made him into the apostle's own son, and separated him from all association with others.

After this let us consider what follows: "according to the common faith." When he speaks of "common faith," does he mean common to all who believed in Christ or "faith common" only to himself and Titus? Now indeed what seems better to me is that the faith of the apostle Paul and of Titus was common, rather than that of all the faithful in whom faith too could not have been common, but diverse, because of the variety of minds.

But finally, [notice that] the prefatory part of the epistle and the greeting found in the apostle's preface to Titus is completed with the following sort of conclusion: "Grace and peace from God the Father and from Christ Jesus our Savior." It is either to be understood that both grace and peace are both from God the Father and from Christ Jesus, and both can be given by either one; or that grace is attributed to the Father, peace to the Son. One should not move on from here without hesitation, since the apostle prayed for certain people that grace and peace would be multiplied.[54] But now to Titus peace and grace are recorded without multiplication. Noah, a just man,[55] who alone was preserved from the shipwreck of the world,[56] is not said to have found in the sight of God many graces, but one grace.[57] And Moses said to the Lord, "If I have found grace before you."[58] And if anywhere else grace is recorded in the name of the saints, "seek and you will find"[59] that they did not find *graces,* but *grace.* That merchant from the Gospel, who had many pearls, in the end he found one precious one. Of many pearls this is the only one he buys.[60] For it belongs to the perfect to buy one pearl and one treasure, by means of all their pearls and by trading

54. Cf. 1 Pt 1.2; 2 Pt 1.2.
55. Cf. Gn 6.9.
56. Cf. 1 Pt 3.21.
57. Cf. Gn 6.8; *CRm* 4.5.4–5.
58. Ex 33.13.
59. Mt 7.7.
60. Cf. Mt 13.45–46.

all their other goods.[61] But it belongs to beginners and to those who are still en route not yet to have only one, but many.

1.5a. *For the sake of this matter I left you in Crete, that you might correct the things that were wanting.* It belongs to apostolic dignity to lay the foundation of the church, which no one can lay down except the architect.[62] "But there is no foundation other than Christ Jesus."[63] The ones who are lesser craftsmen can build the temple upon the foundation. And so Paul is like a wise architect,[64] and he strives with all effort not to boast in things done previously, but where Christ had not yet been proclaimed.[65] After he had softened the hard hearts of the Cretans for faith in Christ, and had subdued them by both words and signs,[66] and had taught them to believe not in their native Jove, but in God the Father and in Christ, he left his disciple Titus in Crete in order to strengthen the rudimentary lessons of the nascent church and to correct anything that seemed wanting. He himself traveled on to other nations in order once again to lay down among them the foundation of Christ.

Now his words, "that you correct what is wanting," show that they had not yet come to a complete knowledge of the truth; and although they were corrected by an apostle, nevertheless they still need correction. Now everything that is corrected is imperfect. For in the Greek a preposition is attached, so that it is written ἐπιδιορθώσῃ. This does not express the same thing as διορθώσῃ, that is, "correct," but it means, so to speak, "super-correct." Thus he means, let the things that have been corrected by me and have not yet been treated again[67] to the full line of truth, be corrected by you and let them receive an equal standard.

---

61. Cf. Mt 13.44–46.
62. Cf. 1 Cor 3.10.
63. 1 Cor 3.11.
64. Cf. 1 Cor 3.10.
65. Cf. 2 Cor 10.16.
66. Cf. Acts 14.3; 15.12; Rom 15.19; 2 Cor 12.12.
67. A textual variant reads "retouched."

1.5b.   *That you should appoint priests in every city, just as I arranged for you.* Let the bishops who have the authority to appoint priests in the individual cities hear by what kind of law the ranking of ecclesiastical appointments should be maintained. Let them not think that these are the apostle's words, but Christ's, who says to his disciples, "He who rejects you, rejects me; but he who rejects me, rejects him who sent me."[68] So also, "he who hears you hears me; but he who hears me hears him who sent me." From this it is clear that those who wish to confer ecclesiastical status on someone not by merit but as a favor, having despised the apostle's law, act contrary to Christ, who in what follows has described through his apostle what sort of priest ought to be appointed in the church. Moses, God's friend, to whom God spoke face to face,[69] surely was able to appoint his own sons to be the successors of his rule, and to leave behind his own dignity to posterity. Instead, he selected Jesus,[70] an outsider from a different tribe.[71] This was so that we would know that rule among the people should not be conferred by blood ties but by manner of living. And at the present time we perceive that very many make appointments as a favor. Thus they do not look for those who can help the church the most, they do not set up pillars in the church, but those whom either they themselves like, or by whose flattery they have been won over, or a man whom one of the elders has requested. I better keep quiet about worse situations, those who have obtained their rank in the clergy by means of [financial] gifts.

Let us pay careful attention to the words of the apostle who says, "that you should appoint priests in every city, just as I arranged for you." He discusses what sort of priest ought to be ordained in what follows when he says, "If anyone is without fault, a husband of one wife,"[72] and so on. Later he added, "For a bishop must be without fault, as a

---

68. Lk 10.16.

69. Cf. Ex 33.11; Dt 5.4; 34.10.

70. Heb. Joshua.

71. Cf. Dt 31.3. According to Nm 13.8, 16; 1 Chr 7.27, Joshua is a descendant of Ephraim. Moses was of Levi (cf. Ex 2.1–10; 6.16–20; 1 Chr 6.3).

72. Ti 1.6.

steward of God."[73] It is therefore the very same priest, who is a bishop, and before there existed men who are slanderers by instinct, [before] factions in the religion, and [before] it was said to the people, "I am of Paul, I am of Apollos, but I am of Cephas,"[74] the churches were governed by a common council of the priests. But after each one began to think that those whom he had baptized were his own and not Christ's,[75] it was decreed for the whole world that one of the priests should be elected to preside over the others, to whom the entire care of the church should pertain, and the seeds of schism would be removed.[76]

If someone thinks that this is our opinion, but not that of the Scriptures—that bishop and priest are one, and that one is the title of age, the other of his duty—let him reread the apostle's words to the Philippians when he says, "Paul and Timothy, slaves of Jesus Christ, to all the saints in Christ Jesus who are in Philippi, with the bishops and deacons, grace to you and peace,"[77] and so on. Philippi is a single city in Macedonia, and at least in one city several were not able to be bishops, as they are now thought.[78] But because at that time they called the same men bishops whom they also called priests, therefore he has spoken indifferently of bishops as if of priests.

This may still seem doubtful to someone unless it is proven by another testimony. In the Acts of the Apostles it is written that when the apostle came to Miletus, he sent to Ephesus and summoned the priests of that church to whom later he said among other things, "Watch yourselves, and the whole flock in which the Holy Spirit appointed you bishops to feed the church of God, which he acquired through his own

---

73. Ti 1.7.
74. 1 Cor 1.12.
75. Cf. 1 Cor 1.13.
76. Likewise in Ep. 146 to Evangelus, Jerome equates priests and bishops and argues that the move to elevate one priest over the rest was made to remedy schism and to prevent each individual from rending the church of Christ by drawing it to himself. In Ep. 52.7 to Nepotian he defends the rights of priests.
77. Phil 1.1–2.
78. A textual variant reads: "as the bishops are now thought."

blood."[79] And observe here very carefully how, by summoning the priests of the single city of Ephesus, later he has spoken of the same men as bishops.

If anyone wants to receive that epistle which is written in Paul's name to the Hebrews,[80] even there care for the church is shared equally by many. For indeed he writes to the people, "Obey your leaders, and be in subjection; for they are the ones who watch over your souls, as those who will give a reckoning. Let them not do this with sighing; for indeed this is advantageous to you."[81] And Peter, who received his name from the firmness of his faith,[82] speaks in his own epistle and says, "As a fellow priest, then, I plead with the priests among you, and as a witness of Christ's sufferings, I who am a companion also of his glory that is to be revealed in the future, tend the Lord's flock that is among you, not as though by compulsion but voluntarily."[83]

These things [have been said] in order to show that to the men of old the same men who were the priests were also the bishops; but gradually, as the seed beds of dissensions were eradicated, all solicitude[84] was conferred on one man. Therefore, just as the priests know that by the custom of the church they are subject to the one who was previously appointed over them, so the bishops know that they, more by custom than by the truth of the Lord's arrangement, are greater than the priests. And they ought to rule the Church commonly, in imitation of Moses who, when he had under his authority to preside alone over the people of Israel, he chose the seventy by whom he could judge the people.[85] Therefore let us see what sort of priest, or bishop, ought to be ordained.

---

79. Acts 20.28.

80. Notice the hesitation on Jerome's part about the attribution of Hebrews to Paul. His comment here is probably based on Origen, whom he is following throughout his exposition.

81. Heb 13.17.

82. Cf. Mt 16.18.

83. 1 Pt 5.1–2.

84. Cf. 1 Cor 11.28.

85. Cf. Nm 11.16–17.

1.6.   *If someone is without fault, a husband of one wife, having faithful children,*[86] *not accused of excess or insubordinate. For a bishop must be without fault, as a steward of God, not brash, not prone to anger, not given to wine, not a striker, not one who seeks after disgraceful gain.* First of all, then, he should be without fault. I think that in another word to Timothy this is termed "irreproachable."[87] It is not that he is to be without any fault merely at that time when he is to be ordained and washes away past blemishes by a new manner of life; but from that time when he was reborn in Christ, he should not be plagued by any consciousness of sin. For how can the one in charge of a church "remove evil from its midst,"[88] who falls into the same sin? Or by what license can he correct the one who sins, when he tacitly responds to himself that he has perpetrated the very same things that he is correcting?

And so "he who desires the episcopacy desires a noble task."[89] "Task," he says, not honor, not glory. "But he ought to have a good testimony with those who are outside, so that he does not fall into reproach, and into the snare of the devil."[90] Now as for his words "husband of one wife," we should understand them as follows: It is not that we are to think that every monogamous man is better than the one who has been married twice; but that he is able to exhort unto monogamy and continence, who offers the example of himself in his teaching. For let there be some young man who has lost his spouse, and overcome by the necessity of the flesh has taken a second wife, whom he also immediately loses. Then he lives continently. But let there be another man who was married to an older woman and made use of his wife, as the majority think happiness consists, and he never ceased from the work of the flesh. Which of the two seems better to you, chaster, more continent? Surely it is the one who was unhappy (*infelix*)[91] even in the second

---

86. Lit. "sons."
87. Cf. 1 Tm 3.2.
88. Cf. 1 Cor 5.13.
89. 1 Tm 3.1.
90. 1 Tm 3.8.
91. Other mss. read *felix,* happy.

marriage and afterward lived chastely and piously, and not the one who was not separated from his wife's embrace in old age. Therefore let him not congratulate himself, whoever is chosen as if monogamous, that he is better than every twice-married man, since in him happiness is chosen more than will.

Certain ones think the following about this passage. It was a Judaic custom, they say, to have two or more wives, because even in the old law we read this about Abraham and Jacob.[92] And they want this to be a command now, lest the one who is to be chosen bishop equally should have two wives at the same time. Many, more superstitiously than truly, think that likewise those ones are not to be chosen for the priesthood who, when they were pagans and had one wife, who was lost, after the baptism of Christ, married another. Though assuredly, if this is to be observed, those ones ought to be excluded from the episcopate who, while practicing wandering lust among prostitutes previously, having been reborn, took one wife. And it would be much more detestable that he has fornicated with many than to be found twice-married, since in one there is the unhappiness of marriage, in the other there is a lasciviousness that is prone to committing sin.

Montanus[93] and those who are adherents of the schism of Novatus[94] presume for themselves the name of the "purified." They think that second marriages are to be kept from communion of the church, though the apostle, when giving this instruction about bishops and priests, assuredly relaxed [it] in respect to the rest. It is not because he

---

92. Cf. Gn 25.1; 29–30.

93. Montanus, a native of Ardabau, a village in Phrygia, in the late second century (155–60) originated a schism that took its name from him (Montanism) and spread far and wide. It even won Tertullian for an adherent in 207. He claimed to be a prophet and a mouthpiece of the Holy Spirit. Prisca and Maximilla were two of his female disciples who outdid him in prophesying. Both had been previously married and left their husbands.

94. Novatian, founder of the sect of the Novatians, denied the possibility of a second repentance after an act of apostasy. Harnack, *Der kirchengeschichtliche Ertrag*, p. 166, thinks that Jerome added Novatus to an original discussion based on Origen that mentioned only Montanus.

is encouraging them to second marriages, but that he makes a concession to the necessity of the flesh. Tertullian too wrote a heretical book about monogamy, which no one who reads the apostle will fail to know is contrary to the apostle.[95] And indeed it is under our control that a bishop or priest be without fault and have one wife. Otherwise, what follows, "having faithful children, not given to the accusation of excess, and not insubordinate," is outside of our will.

For let it be so that parents have instructed their children well and have constantly educated them from early childhood in the Lord's commands. If at a later time they devote themselves to excess and are overcome by vices and let go of the restraints to lust, will the fault redound to the parents? Will the sins of the child defile the father's sanctity? If anyone educated his children well, I think that Isaac was among them. Assuredly he should be believed to have instructed his son Esau well. But Esau, a fornicator and a profane man, sold the rights of the firstborn for one meal.[96] Samuel was also such, so that he called upon the Lord and the Lord heard him, and he obtained winter's rain at the time of the harvest.[97] He had sons who turned aside after greed, and they accepted [financial] gifts and exhibited themselves as such unjust judges that the people could not bear it and demanded a king over them in imitation of the other nations.[98] Well then, if there were an election of priests, both Isaac, on account of Esau, and Samuel, on account of his sons, would have been deemed unworthy of the priesthood. And though the sins of the parents are not imputed to the children, since that pronouncement is no longer in force, "The parents ate sour grapes, and the children's teeth are set on edge,"[99] will the children's vices prejudge the parents?

---

95. According to Quasten, *Patrology*, v. 2, p. 305 Tertullian's work *De Monogamia* (217 AD) makes clear that he had joined forces with the Montanists. He claimed to represent the golden mean between the repudiation of marriage by the Gnostics and Catholic licentiousness in permitting repeated marriages. He judges second marriages illicit and the next thing to adultery.

96. Cf. Gn 25.33; Heb 12.16.

97. 1 Sm 12.18.

98. Cf. 1 Sm 8.1–5.

99. Ezek 18.2.

And so, first of all it should be said that the name of priesthood is so holy that even the things that are placed outside of us are required of us. This is not in order that we not become bishops on account of our vices, but because we need to be hindered from taking this step on account of the incontinence of [our] children. For by what freedom can we correct the children of others and teach what is right, when the one who has been corrected could immediately hurl at us, "First teach your own children"? Or with what effrontery do I correct an outside fornicator, when my own conscience responds to me, "Disinherit then the fornicating child; cast out your children who are enslaved to the vices"? But when a bad child lives together with you in the same house, do you dare to remove the speck from the other's eye, not seeing the beam in your own?[100] Consequently a just man is not defiled by the vices of his children, but the apostle restricts the freedom of the ruler of the church, that he may become such a kind who is not afraid that outsiders reproach him for the vices of his children.

Next the following must be added because of those who grow puffed up from the episcopate and think that they have obtained not a stewardship of Christ but power to command. For they are not at once superior to all those who have not been ordained bishops. From the fact that they themselves have been chosen, let them consider themselves more approved; but let them understand that some have been removed from the priesthood because their children's vices hindered them. But if the sins of the children prohibit a just man from the episcopacy, how much more should each one who considers himself and who knows that the "powerful suffer powerful torments"[101] withdraw himself from what is not so much an honor as a burden. Let him not campaign to occupy the place of others who are more worthy.

Finally the following should be said, that in the Scriptures by "sons," λογισμοὺς, that is, thoughts are understood; but daughters are understood as πράξεις, that is, deeds. And he ought to be instructed now to become a bishop who has both his thoughts and deeds under

---

100. Cf. Mt 7.3–5.

101. Wis 6.6. Notice this citation from the "Deuterocanonical" work.

his own control, and who truly believes in Christ and is not defiled by any blemish of surreptitious vices.

1.7.   *For a bishop should be without fault, as a steward of God. [He must not be brash or subject to anger or given to wine; he should not be a striker or seek disgraceful gain.]* "Among stewards, then, it is sought that one be found faithful."[102] Let him not eat and drink with drunkards and strike his male and female servants.[103] Instead, let him await the uncertain advent of God and give food to the fellow servants at the proper time.[104] Now the sole distinction between a household steward and the family is that a fellow slave is appointed over his fellow slaves.

And so, let the bishop and priest know that the people are not slaves, but they are fellow slaves with him. The other things that follow are recorded on our behalf. Let the bishop not be "brash," that is, not "puffed up" and one who pleases himself, but like a good household steward, let him seek what is beneficial to the majority. "Not subject to anger." He who is always angry is "subject to anger." He is provoked by the light breeze of a response and of a sin, as if by the wind through the leaves. And in fact there is nothing more disgraceful than an enraged teacher, who, though he ought to be gentle and [act] according to what is written, "But a servant of the Lord ought not be quarrelsome, but humble toward all, a teacher, patient, instructing in gentleness those who contradict."[105] That one, on the other hand, clamors and shouts with a twisted expression, quivering lips, wrinkled brow, unbridled insults, a countenance that alternates between pale and bright red. He does not so much lead back toward the good those who are astray, as plunge them headfirst into evil by his savageness. This is what Solomon also says, "Anger destroys even wise men,"[106] and, "A man's anger does not work the justice of God."[107] But neither is he "subject to anger"

---

102. 1 Cor 4.2.
103. Cf. Mt 24.49.
104. Cf. Mt 24.45.
105. 2 Tm 2.24–25.
106. Pr 15.1.
107. Jas 1.20.

who now and then becomes angry, but he is said to be "subject to anger" who frequently is overcome by this passion.

He also forbids that a bishop be "given to wine." He writes to Timothy about this: "not given to much wine."[108] Now what sort of thing is it to see a bishop "given to wine," so that while his senses are overrun he raises a laugh contrary to proper decorum and dignity. His lips let loose with uncontrollable laughter; or, if he suddenly remembers something sad, in the midst of his cups he breaks down in sobs and tears. It would take too long to go into detail and describe the madness that drunkenness gives rise to. You should see how some men turn their cups into missiles and hurl goblets at the face of their own dinner guests. Another rushes forth with clothes that have been torn by wounds inflicted by others; some shout, others fall asleep. The one who drinks the most is reckoned to be strongest. It is an occasion for an accusation when one who has sworn loyalty to the king has not gotten drunk frequently enough. They vomit in order to drink; they drink in order to vomit. The belly's digestion and the throat are occupied with a single duty. Let it suffice for now to have said this, which accords with the apostle: "In wine there is excess."[109]

And wherever there is overabundance and drunkenness, there lust is in control. Look at the belly and the genitals, the arrangement of the members [has] in view the nature of the vices.[110] I will never regard a drunken man as chaste. Even if he is lulled to sleep by the wine, nevertheless he could have sinned through the wine. But are we surprised that the apostle condemned wine drinking in bishops or priests, when

---

108. 1 Tm 3.8.

109. Eph 5.18.

110. Cf. the parallel in Tertullian, *On Fasting* 1: "Lust without voracity would certainly be considered a monstrous phenomenon; since these two are so united and concrete, that, had there been any possibility of disjoining them, the pudenda would not have been affixed to the belly itself rather than elsewhere. Look at the body: the region (of these members) is one and the same. In short, the order of the vices is proportionate to the arrangement of the members. First, the belly; and then immediately the materials of all other species of lasciviousness are laid subordinately to daintiness: through love of eating, love of impurity finds passage" (ANF 4.102).

in the old law too it is commanded that priests, when they enter the temple to minister to God, not drink wine at all?[111] Moreover the Nazarene is not defiled as long as he takes care of his sacred hair, does not look upon anything dead, abstains both from wine, dried grapes, weaker drinks that usually come from grape-skins, and from all strong drinks, which distort the mind from complete soundness.[112] Let each one say what he wants to; I speak my conscience. I know that abstinence, when interrupted, has harmed me, and when renewed has brought benefit.

Now after wine drinking he commands this: "he should not be a striker." This, of course, edifies the hearer when understood literally, that he should not readily stretch forth his hand to strike; he should not burst out in a rage to punch someone else in the mouth. But it is better to say that one is "not a striker" who is gentle and patient so that he knows what should be said at the moment, what should be held in silence; not to "strike" the conscience of the weak with unhelpful words. For the apostle, when forming the ruler of a church, forbids him to be a boxer and a pancratiast[113] (which is reproached even among the common people and in pagans if it happens), but as I have said [pay heed to] this: let not the abusive and garrulous man ruin one whom he was able to correct with modesty and mildness.

He who will be a bishop ought to be estranged too from being a seeker after "disgraceful gain." For there are many who teach what is not fitting for the sake of "disgraceful gain," who subvert entire households and think that piety is profit. But according to Solomon "a modest acceptance is better with justice than much produce with iniquity."[114] And one should rather choose a good name with poverty than an evil name with riches.[115] A bishop who desires to be an imitator of the apostle, "having food and clothing," ought to be content with these alone.[116]

---

111. Cf. Lv 10.9.
112. Cf. Nm 6.1–4.
113. An athlete who contested in the skills of boxing and wrestling.
114. Prv 16.8.
115. Cf. Prv 22.1.
116. Cf. 1 Tm 6.8.

Those who serve at the altar live from the altar.[117] They do not live, he says, who become rich. This is why copper is shaken out of our belts, we wear only one tunic;[118] we do not think about tomorrow.[119] The appetite for "disgraceful gain" indicates that one is thinking more about the present. Up to this point the apostle's words have instructed what the bishop or priest should not have; now, on the other hand, he explains what he should have.

1.8–9.   *But hospitable, a lover of good things, chaste, just, holy, continent, abstinent, holding fast to that which accords with doctrine, faithful in speech, so that he is able to offer consolation in sound doctrine and to refute those who contradict.* Before everything "hospitality" (*hospitalitas*) is officially announced in the future bishop. For if everyone desires to hear the following from the Gospel, "I was a stranger (*hospes*) and you received me,"[120] how much more should a bishop, whose home ought to be a common lodge for all! For a layman will fulfill[121] the duty of hospitality by receiving one or two or a few [strangers]. A bishop is inhumane if he does not receive everyone.

But I am apprehensive that, just as the Queen of the South who came from the ends of the earth to hear the wisdom of Solomon will judge the men of her own time;[122] and just as the men of Nineveh who did penance at the preaching of Jonah will condemn those who scorned listening to the one who was greater than Jonah, the Savior;[123] so in the same way very many among the people will judge the bishops who dissociate themselves from their ecclesiastical rank and practice things that do not befit bishops. I think that John is writing to Gaius about them: "Beloved, you do faithfully whatever you achieve among the brothers, and [you do] this for strangers who gave testimony to your

117. Cf. 1 Cor 9.13.
118. Cf. Mt 10.9–10; Mk 6.8–9; Lk 9.3.
119. Cf. Mt 6.34.
120. Mt 25.35.
121. A textual variant reads, "has fulfilled."
122. Cf. Mt 12.42.
123. Cf. Mt 12.41.

love before the Church, whom you do well if you send them ahead worthily of God; for they went out on behalf of his name, taking nothing from the Gentiles."[124] And with the Holy Spirit truly speaking in him what is to come upon the churches,[125] even then he rebukes, saying, "I wrote likewise to the church, but he who desires to exercise primacy among them, Diotrephes, does not receive us. Therefore when I come I will admonish his works that he is doing, detracting from us by means of evil words. And it is not enough that he does not receive the brothers himself, but he even hinders those who want to, and he expels [them] from the church."[126]

Truly, now it is to discern what has been said first, that in very many cities the bishops or priests, if they see that the laity are "hospitable, lovers of good things," they envy them, they complain, they excommunicate, they expel them from the church. [They act] as if it is not permitted to do what the bishop is not doing. The very fact that the laity are such is a condemnation of the priests. And so they resent them, and regard them as if they were burdens on their necks, in order to lead them away from good works, to unsettle them by various forms of persecution.

But let the bishop be "chaste," which the Greeks call σώφρονα, and the Latin translator, fooled by the ambiguity of the word, translated "prudent" instead of "chaste." But if laymen are commanded to abstain from intercourse with their wives for the sake of prayer,[127] what is one to think of a bishop, who will daily offer intact victims for his own sins and the people's? We should reread the books of Kingdoms and we will find that the priest Abimelech was unwilling to give any of the bread of proposition to David and his men before he had first asked whether the men were "clean from woman," assuredly referring not to someone else's spouse but to their own.[128] And until he had heard that they had been free from the conjugal act since yesterday and the day

124. 3 Jn 5–7.
125. Cf. Rv 1.1.
126. 3 Jn 9–11.
127. Cf. 1 Cor 7.5.
128. 1 Sm 21.4.

before, he did not allow them the bread that he had at first denied. How great is the difference between the bread of proposition and the body of Christ? It is the difference between shadow and bodies, between image and truth, between copies of things to come and the realities themselves which were prefigured through the copies.[129]

And so, just as gentleness, patience, sobriety, moderation, abstaining from profit, hospitality, too, and kindness, ought to be in a bishop in particular, and they ought to be eminent among all the laity, so also there should be in him a unique chastity and, so to speak, a priestly purity, so that he not only keeps himself from the unclean act but even from the glance of his eye and from straying in his thoughts. Let his mind be free to confect the body of Christ. The bishop should be just and holy as well, so that he is preeminent in justice among the people among whom he labors, rendering to each man what he deserves, showing no partiality in judgment. The difference between the justice of a layman and of a bishop is this, that a layman can appear just to a few people, but a bishop [can] practice justice among as many people as are subject to him.

Now "holy," which in Greek is expressed by ὅσιος, signifies more the idea of sanctity itself combined with religiousness. It is referred to God. For the one whom we call *holy,* the Greeks call ἅγιον. But what they call ὅσιον we can call pious toward God.

Let the bishop also be "abstinent," not only, as some think, from lust and from the embrace of a woman, but from all disturbances of the mind. Let him not be incited to wrath; let not sadness cause him to be dejected; let not fear scare him away; let him not be carried away by excessive gladness. Now abstinence is listed by the apostle among the fruits of the Spirit.[130] And if it is demanded of everyone, how much more of the bishop, who ought to bear the vices of sinners with patience and gentleness: "console the faint-hearted, endure the weak,"[131] "render to no one evil for evil,"[132] but "overcome evil by good."[133]

---

129. Cf. Heb 10.1.
130. Cf. Gal 5.22.
131. 1 Thes 5.14.
132. Rom 12.17.
133. Rom 12.21.

Finally let the one who is in accordance with doctrine hold fast to "faithful speech," that just as the word of God is faithful, and worthy of all acceptance, so also he should show himself to be such that everything that he says is reckoned to be worthy of the faith and his words should be worthy of the rule of truth.

Let him also be "able to console" those who are stirred up by the storms of this world, and to destroy weak precepts by means of "sound doctrine." Now "sound doctrine" is spoken of in distinction from feeble and weak doctrine. Let him be such too that he refutes "those who contradict," heretics or Jews, and the wise of this age.[134] Now the things that he recorded higher up in respect to the virtues of the bishop pertain to life; but what he says now, "So that he may be able to console in sound doctrine and refute those who contradict," should be referred to knowledge. For if merely the life of the bishop is holy, the one living thus can bring benefit to himself. If he is further educated both in doctrine and speech, he can instruct himself and others; and not only instruct and teach his own people, but also strike back against his adversaries, who, unless they are refuted and overcome, can easily destroy simple hearts.

This passage opposes those who, in their personal devotion to laziness, idleness, and sleep, think that it is a sin to read the Scriptures; and who despise as "garrulous and unprofitable" those who meditate on the law of the Lord day and night. They do not notice that the apostle, after his catalogue of the bishop's way of life, has likewise given instruction about his doctrine as well.

1.10–11.   *For there are also many who are insubordinate, vain talkers, and deceivers of minds, especially those who are from the circumcision, upon whom it is fitting to impose silence, who overturn entire homes, teaching what is not fitting, for the sake of disgraceful profit.* He who will be a ruler of the church should have eloquence combined with integrity of life, lest the deeds without words be mute, and the words be ashamed because of the deeds that are lacking. This is especially the

---

134. Cf. 1 Cor 1.20.

case since they are not few but "many" who are "not subordinate but
brash," who do not care that the Psalmist says, "Is not my soul subject
to God?"[135] who destroy by their worthless persuasion the good seed of
minds[136] that has by nature the knowledge of God.[137] (For it seems to
me that Paul thought this, since he says φρεναπάται, not as the Latin
translator rendered it literally, "deceivers," but "deceivers of minds.")

And indeed, without the authority of the Scriptures, their garru-
lousness would not be believable, if these men did not seem to cor-
roborate their perverse doctrine as well by divine testimonies. They are
Jews of the circumcision who at that time endeavored to destroy the
nascent church of Christ and to introduce the precepts of the law. Paul
develops this quite fully both [in the Epistles] to the Romans and to the
Galatians. And a few months ago we dictated three books in explanation of the Epistle to the Galatians. A teacher of the church to whom
the souls of the people have been entrusted should overcome such men
by means of reasoning from the Scriptures. By the weight of testimonies he should impose silence on those who overturn not one or two
homes, but all homes, masters together with their families. These men
teach about the differences between foods, about the already long ago
abolished Sabbath, about the injury of circumcision. Would that they
did this from the zeal of faith; then it could be partly forgiven, since the
apostle says, "I confess, they have zeal for God, but not according to
knowledge."[138] But because their belly is god,[139] for the sake of disgraceful profit they want to make their own disciples,[140] so that as teachers
they may be taken care of by their adherents.

But we can interpret what has been said in another way: "for the
sake of disgraceful profit." Let us consider that the apostle has used a
common saying whereby all the heretics, when they teach perverse

---

135. Ps 62.1.

136. A textual variant reads, "the seed of good minds."

137. Cf. Rom 1.19–21.

138. Rom 10.2.

139. Cf. Phil 3.19.

140. Cf. Mt 23.15.

things, customarily assert themselves as profiteers of men; though to destroy the souls of the deceived is not profit, but perdition. On the other hand, he who corrects his erring brother in accordance with the gospel, if he is converted, he has gained him.[141] For what greater profit (*lucrum*) can there be, or what is more precious, than if someone gains a human soul? Every teacher of the church, therefore, who persuades by the right method to faith in Christ is an honest profiteer (*lucrator*). And every heretic who deceives men by certain tricks and is deceived, "speaks what is not fitting for the sake of disgraceful profit."

1.12–14. *One of themselves, a prophet of their own said, "Cretans are always liars, evil beasts, lazy bellies." This testimony is true. Therefore, rebuke them sharply, that they may be sound in the faith, not attending to Judaic fables, and to the commands of men who turn themselves away from the truth.* In terms of the text itself and as far as it pertains to the content of the passage, what he says, "One of themselves, a prophet of their own said," seems to refer to those of whom he said above, "especially those who are of the circumcision, whom it is necessary to restrain, who overturn entire homes, teaching what is not fitting for the sake of disgraceful profit."[142] Thus it follows: "one of themselves, a prophet of their own said." But since this brief hexameter verse is not found in any of the prophets who prophesied in Judea, to me it seems that there are two ways this should be read. Thus when what he says, "one of themselves, a prophet of their own said," is joined with what precedes, "For the sake of this matter, I left you in Crete, so that you would correct the things that were lacking,"[143] it follows, "one of themselves, a prophet of their own said," that is, one of the Cretans.

But because there are many things in between, and this seems absurd, and perhaps no one would receive it, therefore one should apply it in another manner with the preceding things that are nearer to it, so that we read, "For there are also many who are insubordinate, vain

---

141. Cf. Mt 18.15.
142. Ti 1.10–11.
143. Ti 1.5.

talkers, and deceivers of minds, but especially those who are of the circumcision."[144] "It is necessary to restrain many who are insubordinate, vain talkers, and deceivers of minds, along with those who are of the circumcision, who overturn entire homes, teaching what is not fitting for the sake of disgraceful profit."[145] "One of themselves, a prophet of their own said." Thus his words, "a prophet of their own," refers not particularly to the Jews, and to those especially "who are of the circumcision," but to the "many who are disobedient and vain talkers and deceivers of minds."[146] Especially because they were in Crete, they must be believed to have been Cretans.

Now this brief verse is said to be found among the oracular sayings of the Cretan poet Epimenides.[147] In the present circumstances he has either mockingly called him a prophet, namely, because such Christians deserve to have prophets like this, just as there were also prophets of Baal[148] and prophets of confusion and others of stumbling blocks, and whatever other corrupt prophets Scripture mentions; or he has truly called him one, because he had written about oracles and responses that both predict the future itself and tell well ahead of time the things that are coming. After all, the book itself is marked on the title page "Oracles." Because it seemed to promise something divine, for this reason I think the apostle looked into it to see what the divination of the pagans promised. And on the occasion of writing to Titus, who was in Crete, he used (*abusum*)[149] this little verse in order to crush the false teachers of the Cretans by means of an author from their own island.

Now it is noticeable that Paul does this not only in this passage but also in others. For in the Acts of the Apostles, when he was assembled

---

144. Ti 1.10.
145. Ti 1.11.
146. Ti 1.10.
147. See p. 187, n. 390 above. Harnack, *Der kirchengeschichtliche Ertrag*, p. 168 says that anyone familiar with the parallel passages in Origen cannot doubt that Jerome has added a few sentences of his own to Origen's discussions.
148. Cf. 1 Kgs 18.19–40; 2 Kgs 10.19.
149. *Abusum* can also mean "abused."

with the people and was involved in discussion on the Areopagus, which is the Senate Building of the Athenians, among other things he says, "Just as one of your own poets said: 'For we are indeed his offspring.'"[150] This half-line is read in the *Phaenomena* of Aratus,[151] which Cicero translated into the Latin language,[152] as well as Germanicus Caesar[153] and recently Avienus[154] and many whom it would take too long to enumerate. [He also does this in his letter] to the Corinthians, who were themselves polished by Attic eloquence. And because of the proximity of locations, they are seasoned with a taste of the Athenians. There he took an iambic line from a comedy of Menander: "Bad company ruins good morals."[155]

It is not surprising if on occasion he makes use (*abutatur*) of lines from pagan poets, since he even changes some things from the inscription of an altar and says to the Athenians, "For while passing through and observing your objects of worship, I even found an altar in which it was inscribed: 'To an unknown God.' And so, what you worship in ignorance, this I proclaim to you."[156] Now the inscription of the altar

---

150. Acts 17.28.

151. Aratus of Soli was an outstanding poet and scholar of the third century BC, famous at Rome above all for his astronomical poem, the *Phaenomena*. This work had a large number of Latin translators, as Jerome mentions, and it influenced the whole tradition of didactic poetry, in particular Virgil's *Georgics*, Ovid, and Manilius.

152. Cicero's hexameter translation of Aratus's *Phaenomena* is considered his most successful poetic work. Considerable portions are extant. Cf. G. Conti, *Latin Literature: A History* (Baltimore: The Johns Hopkins University Press, 1994), p. 200.

153. Germanicus (15 BC–19 AD) was adoptive son of the emperor Tiberius and his designated successor, who left behind a thousand hexameters that are a version of Aratus's *Phaenomena* and *Prognostica*.

154. Rufius Festus Avienus, a friend of Symmachus, was associated with Claudian (370–404). He published a translation of Aratus's *Phaenomena*.

155. 1 Cor 15.33. Menander (341–290 BC), the most distinguished author of Greek New Comedy, was imitated by the Romans Plautus and Terence, thus indirectly exerting a great influence on European literature.

156. Acts 17.23.

was not precisely as Paul claimed: "to an unknown God," but "to the gods of Asia and of Europe and of Africa, to the unknown and foreign gods." But because Paul did not require several unknown gods but only one unknown God, he used the word in the singular, in order to teach that that God is his own, whom the Athenians had designated on the inscription of the altar; and that by knowing him in the right way, they ought to worship him whom they were venerating in ignorance and whom they were unable not to know.[157] Now Paul did this seldom and as the occasion of the passage demanded, rather than from ostentation, in the manner of bees, which are accustomed to store up honey from different flowers and to fit together the little storerooms of their honeycombs.

There are those who think that this verse has been taken from the poet Callimachus of Cyrene[158] and to some extent they are not wrong. For in fact he himself, while repeatedly writing in praise of Jove against the Cretans, who boasted that they displayed a tomb, says, "Cretans are always liars, who by their sacrilegious mind have fabricated even his tomb." But, as we said above, the apostle took the entire verse from the poet Epimenides. And his Callimachus made use of an introduction in his poem. Or, without plagiarism of someone else's work, he rendered into meter a common proverb in which the Cretans were called liars.

Some think that the apostle should be rebuked because he imprudently slipped, and while accusing false teachers he approved of that little line, that the reason the Cretans are said to be liars is because they inanely built Jupiter's tomb. For if, they say, the reason Epimenides, or Callimachus, prove that the Cretans are liars and evil beasts and idle bellies is because they do not perceive divine things; and they imagine

---

157. Jerome's teacher, Didymus of Alexandria, *Commentary on 2 Cor 10.5,* also thought Paul changed "gods" to "God" in his reference here. F. F. Bruce, *The Acts of the Apostles: The Greek Text with Introduction and Commentary* (Grand Rapids: Eerdmans, 1986), p. 336, says in response to this that "there is no reason why there should not have been an altar dedicated exactly as Paul describes."

158. Callimachus (305–240 BC) was a distinguished scholar who settled in Alexandria and whose *Aetia* (*Origins*) was imitated by Catullus.

that Jove, who reigns in heaven, is buried on their island; and that which they said is proven to be true by the apostle's judgment; then it follows that Jupiter is not dead but alive. Unskillfully, therefore, Paul, the destroyer of idolatry, while he pleads against perverse teachers, has asserted the gods whom he was fighting against.

One should briefly respond to them as follows. Just as in what he says, "Bad company corrupts good morals," and in this, "For we are his offspring," he has not all at once approved of the entire comedy of Menander and book of Aratus; but he has made use of the occasion of a brief line; so also in the present passage. By one little verse he has not affirmed the whole work of Callimachus or Epimenides, one of whom sings Jove's praises, the other who writes often of oracles; but he merely rebuked the mendacious Cretans for a vice that is characteristic of their nation. He silences them by means of an author from their own country, not on account of that opinion by which they are convicted by the poets, but on account of their inborn readiness to lie.

But those who think that someone who uses a part of a book is obligated to follow the entire book seem to me to be receiving among the Scriptures of the church the apocrypha Enoch from which the apostle Jude has cited a testimony in his epistle,[159] and the many other things that the apostle Paul has spoken about recondite matters. For by this argument we could say the following: among the Athenians he said that they worshiped the unknown God whom they pointed out to him on the altar. Paul ought to follow the other things as well that were written on that altar, and he should do the things that the Athenians were doing. For he had partly agreed with the Athenians in the worship of the unknown God. Far be it from me to drag his argument and scholarship from elegance into calumny in this way.

There is no one who is so much a murderer, so much a parricide, so much a poisoner, that he does not do something good once in a while. Well then, if I see and approve of the one good thing in such men, am I immediately burdened by the necessity to approve the other evils things that they do? If an enemy who is against us is scolded and

---

159. Jude 14–15.

cries out, does he not speak some truth amidst the words of enmity and wrangling, which are not faulted absolutely, even by us against whom he is speaking? And so, both Callimachus and Epimenides have not therefore spoken truly, that Jove is a god and the remaining things that are contained in their poems, just because the Cretans are liars; but they have spoken truth only in that matter, since they have expressed a congenital vice of mendacity in the Cretans, who because they are liars have not immediately not spoken truth as well once in a while. For Jupiter would not therefore be a god, if the Cretans spoke truth; but even with them being silent, he who was dead would not have the name of god.

Finally, that we might know that the apostle did not speak fortuitously and as it pleased him in passing (as they think), but in a considered fashion and circumspectly, and has spoken in a way so that every aspect protects him against the Cretans, he says, "This testimony is true"; not "this entire poem" from which the "testimony" was taken, not the entire work, but merely "this testimony," this brief line in which they are called liars. And assuredly he who agrees with merely one part of a poem should be believed to have rejected the rest. Now the sense in which the Cretans are branded as liars, and the Galatians as foolish, or Israel as stiff-necked, or each individual province by their own unique vice, we have explained in [our commentary] on Paul's epistle to the Galatians.[160] And since there is nothing more which we can bring forth here, we are content with that.

Therefore, he says, "Rebuke them severely," for they are "liars and evil beasts and idle bellies,"[161] who persuade false things, who in the manner of beasts thirst for the blood of the deceived. And they do not "work quietly eating their own food."[162] "Their god is their belly and their glory is in their shame."[163] Moreover, "rebuke [them] that they may be sound in the faith." He speaks of this "soundness of faith" also in what follows: "[Bid] the older men to be sober, honest, chaste, sound

160. See the preface of book two in the *Commentary on Galatians*.
161. Ti 1.12.
162. 2 Thes 3.12.
163. Phil 3.19.

in faith, and in charity and in patience."[164] The soundness of doctrine is also named in a way that is similar to that of faith. He says, "There will be a time when they will not be content with sound doctrine."[165] There are also words of soundness of which he speaks to Timothy in the first epistle: "If someone teaches otherwise, and is not content with sound words of our Lord Jesus Christ and which are in accordance with the piety of doctrine."[166] And in the second [epistle]: "Having an example of sound words, which you heard from me."[167] Those who have this soundness of faith and doctrine and words will not "attend to Jewish myths and the commands of men who turn themselves away from truth."

Let us "be content" with the Jews for a little while, and let us patiently listen to the nonsense of those who are called wise among them; and then we will understand what are the "Jewish myths" without the authority of Scripture, without any claim on reason, of those who fabricate certain fabulous things,[168] of whom Isaiah prophesied, saying, "This people honors me with their lips, but their heart is far from me. But without reason do they worship me, teaching the doctrines and commands of men."[169] The Savior approves this testimony in the Gospel and accuses them of having preferred the commands of men to the law of God. "For God says, 'Honor father and mother'; but they have handed down that whoever says to his father and mother, 'Any gift there is from me will be useful to you,' and he has not honored his father and mother."[170]

---

164. Ti 2.2.
165. 2 Tm 4.3.
166. 1 Tm 6.3.
167. 1 Tm 1.13.
168. In *Contra Celsum* 4.17, Origen speaks of the impossibilities found in the Old Testament law. "We find an animal called the goat-stag, which cannot possibly exist, but which, as being in the number of clean beasts, Moses commands to be eaten; and a griffin, which no one ever remembers or heard of as yielding to human power, but which the legislator forbids to be used for food." Jerome may have this sort of thing in mind among the "fabulous things."
169. Is 29.13.
170. Mt 15.3–5.

If, after the coming of Christ, someone is "mutilated," and not circumcised,[171] he serves "Judaic myths" and the commands of men who turn away the truth. "For it is not the one manifest who is a Jew, but the one in secret; and circumcision is of the heart in the Spirit, not the letter."[172] If someone does not keep the Passover "with the unleavened bread of sincerity and truth,"[173] so that he removes from his soul all the "old leaven of malice and wickedness,"[174] that person attends to "myths," follows shadows, and neglects the truth. If someone does not rise up with Christ to seek not the things above,[175] but the things below, and says, "Do not touch, do not taste, do not handle, which things are unto corruption with their very use in accordance with the precepts and doctrines of men,"[176] that person follows a justice that is not good, and "precepts that are not good."[177] But where there is truth and the spiritual law, there there are good justifications and the best precepts; the one who does such things will live in them.[178]

1.15.   *To the pure all things are pure, but to the defiled and unbelieving nothing is pure; but both their mind and conscience is polluted.* He had said above, "For there are many who are insubordinate, vain talkers, and deceivers, especially those who are of the circumcision."[179] And of those who had been deceived by them, he added in what follows, "Rebuke them sharply, that they may be sound in the faith, not giving heed to Judaic myths and to the commands of men who turn away the truth."[180] And just as he treats in great detail to the Galatians and to the Romans, they thought that there was a distinction between foods, since some seemed pure, some impure, therefore he adds now, "To the

---

171. Cf. Phil 3.2–3; Gal 5.12.
172. Rom 2.28.
173. 1 Cor 5.8.
174. 1 Cor 5.8.
175. Cf. Col 3.1.
176. Cf. Col 2.21–22.
177. Cf. Ezek 20.10–11, 25.
178. Cf. Lv 18.5.
179. Ti 1.10.
180. Ti 1.14.

pure all things are pure," namely, to those who believe in Christ and know that every created thing is good and nothing is to be rejected that is received with thanksgiving.[181] "But to the defiled and unbelieving nothing is pure," because "their mind and conscience are polluted." Therefore even what is pure by nature becomes impure to them. It is not that something becomes either pure or impure, but in view of the nature of those eating, it becomes pure to the pure and impure to the defiled.

In any case, even the bread of benediction and the Lord's cup does not help any unbelievers and defiled, since the one who eats of that bread and drinks of the cup unworthily eats and drinks judgment upon himself.[182] At the coming of Christ all things have been cleansed.[183] What he cleansed, we cannot make common.[184] But one should take heed that in treating these matters we do not give opportunity to that heresy which, according to the Apocalypse[185] and according to the apostle himself too when writing to the Corinthians,[186] thinks that one should eat from things sacrificed to idols, since "to the pure all things are pure."

For the apostle did not at this time propose to discuss those things that are sacrificed to demons.[187] Instead, his discussion is directed against the Jews who think that certain things are pure, others impure, in accordance with the discipline of the abolished law. He says, "For we cannot be sharers in the table of the Lord and the table of demons; nor can we simultaneously drink the Lord's cup and the cup of demons."[188] And so, to eat either pure or impure things lies in us. For if we are pure, to us the created thing is pure. But if on the other hand we are impure and unbelieving, everything becomes common to us, either through

---

181. Cf. 1 Tm 4.4.
182. Cf. 1 Cor 11.29.
183. Cf. Mk 7.19.
184. Cf. Mk 7.18.
185. Cf. Rv 2.20.
186. Cf. 1 Cor 10.14–22.
187. Cf. 1 Cor 10.20.
188. 1 Cor 10.21.

the heresy inhabiting our hearts or through the consciousness of transgressions. Further, if our conscience does not rebuke us, we will have the confidence of piety before the Lord.[189] "We will pray in the Spirit, we will also pray with the mind."[190] And we will be far removed from those of whom it is now written, "Both their mind and conscience is polluted."

1.16.   *They confess to know God, but by their deeds they deny him; they are detestable, disobedient, and rejected for any good work.* Those whose "mind and conscience" are polluted "confess to know God, but they deny [him] by their deeds" according to what is said in Isaiah, "This people honors me with their lips, but their heart is far from me."[191] Therefore, just as someone with the lips honors and in the heart withdraws far away, so someone confessing God in words denies him in deeds. But the one denying God by his works, since his confession is feigned, is rightly "detestable" and profane; and being in no way convinced of the truth, he is called "disobedient and unbelieving." This is how it comes to pass that he is "rejected for every good work," namely, because even the things that he did, perhaps good things, when his natural goodness had the upper hand, are not good things when they are rejected by the perversity of mind.

Some think that God is denied only in the case of someone who is arrested by the Gentiles during a persecution and denies that he is a Christian. But behold the apostle asserts that God is denied by all deeds that are perverse. Christ is wisdom, justice, truth, sanctity, fortitude.[192] Wisdom will be denied by foolishness, justice by injustice, truth by falsehood, sanctity by baseness, fortitude by weakness of heart. And as often as we are overcome by vices and sins, just that often do we deny God. And on the other hand, as often as we do anything good, we confess God.

---

189. Cf. 1 Cor 4.4; 1 Jn 3.21.
190. 1 Cor 14.15.
191. Is 29.13.
192. Cf. 1 Cor 1.24, 30; Jn 14.6.

Let it not be thought that on the day of judgment only those will be denied by the Son of God who have denied Christ in respect to martyrdom.[193] On the contrary, by all works, words, and thoughts, Christ denies when he is denied. He confesses when he is confessed. I think that it was concerning this "confession" that he instructed the disciples, saying, "You will be my witnesses in Jerusalem and in all Judea and Samaria, and to the ends of the earth."[194] Thus in all good works and words, the mind devoted to itself "confesses" Christ. There is even a certain praiseworthy form of denying of which the apostle himself speaks: "Thus denying impiety and worldly desires, let us live chastely, justly, and piously in the present world, awaiting the blessed hope and coming of our Savior and God."[195] He who denies this denial and wants to follow the Savior, who says, "Whoever wants to come after me, let him deny himself,"[196] having stripped off the old man with his works, and having put on the new,[197] will follow his God.

But we need to contemplate how someone denies himself. A chaste man denies the fornicator that he once was; a wise man denies the imprudent man, the just man the unjust, the strong the weak. And that I may speak with universal application concerning everything, however often we deny ourselves, just so often do we tread upon former vices, cease to be what we were, and begin to be what we were not formerly.

2.1. *But you, speak what befits sound doctrine.* It is one thing to speak sound doctrine, something else to teach what agrees with sound doctrine. For the former consists merely in simple instruction, the latter takes place when together with what you teach [there is] also improvement of life. "For he who breaks one of the least of these commandments and teaches men thus shall be called least in the kingdom of heaven."[198] The Savior commands his disciples not only to labor at meditating on the Scriptures, to reflect upon the things that are written,

---

193. Cf. Mt 10.32.
194. Acts 1.8.
195. Ti 2.12–13.
196. Lk 9.23.
197. Cf. Col 3.9–10.
198. Mt 5.19.

and to store them up in the treasury of their memory; but first they are to do what has been commanded. "But whosoever does and teaches, he will be called great in the kingdom of heaven."[199] For unless our justice surpasses the justice of the Scribes and Pharisees, we cannot enter the kingdom of heaven.[200] They are those who, although they sit upon Moses' seat, they say and do not do, and they bind burdens that cannot be carried, which they place on men's necks, and they themselves are unwilling to touch with the least finger.[201] This then the apostle now teaches Titus his son in Christ and his own disciple that he should speak what agrees with sound doctrine. For at that time when the teacher's doctrine is equally in agreement with his life, there is soundness of doctrine.

2.2.   *[Tell] the older men to be sober, honest, chaste, sound in faith, and in love and in patience.* Previously he instructed Titus in a general way in what he ought to speak to everyone, in that he says, "But you, speak what befits sound doctrine."[202] Now, he explains what befits each age by specific cases. First [he deals with] the things that befit the older men, then what befits older women, third what things are suitable for the young, both males and females. Although in the instruction of the older women he has laid down commands concerning young women, it is not so much that he himself was teaching the young women as explaining what they should be taught by the older ones. The final precepts he has befittingly laid down concern slaves and specific ages and conditions, so that his words are a rule of life and character.

So then, older men are to be "sober" or vigilant, since νηφάλιοι among the Greeks expresses both. They are to be "honest," so that the dignity of their character may adorn the dignity of their age; "chaste," lest they should practice the excess that belongs to another period of life, lest they whose blood is already cold in respect to lust should be a ruinous example to the young men. They should be "sound in faith," of

<hr>

199. Mt 5.19.
200. Mt 5.20.
201. Cf. Mt 23.2–4.
202. Ti 2.1.

which "soundness of faith" we have spoken above. They are to be "sound," however, not only "in faith" but also "in love" and "in patience," so that when they have the first soundness of faith, they may hear from the Savior, "Your faith has made you whole."[203] And elsewhere, "I have not found such great faith in Israel."[204]

And on account of the same "soundness of faith" they may become sons of Abraham, of whom it is written, "Abraham believed God and it was reckoned to him for justice."[205] And Habakkuk mentions this soundness of faith when he says, "But the just lives from my faith."[206] Reread the apostle Paul's letter to the Hebrews (or whosoever you think it is, since it is now received among the ecclesiastical [writings]), and list off that entire catalogue of faith in which it is written, "By faith Abel offered to God a greater sacrifice than Cain";[207] and, "Enoch was translated so that he would not see death";[208] and Noah, believing God concerning those things which he could not yet see, built the ark;[209] and Abraham went forth into a land which he did not know.[210] And lest it seem that Scripture gives no example of faith to women, in the same letter it is written that Sarah received the power to conceive seed at a time of life when this was already out of place, since she considered him faithful who had made the promise.[211] Isaac's faith is praised there,[212] and Jacob's,[213] Joseph's,[214] Moses' too,[215] and Rahab's,[216] and that of the rest whom the one who reads that letter can know better.

---

203. Mk 10.52.
204. Mt 8.10.
205. Gn 15.6.
206. Hab 2.4.
207. Heb 11.4.
208. Heb 11.5.
209. Heb 11.7.
210. Heb 11.8.
211. Heb 11.11.
212. Cf. Heb 11.20.
213. Cf. Heb 11.21.
214. Cf. Heb 11.22.
215. Cf. Heb 11.23–28.
216. Cf. Heb 11.31.

Well then, just as there is "soundness in faith," so there is also the same soundness "in love." But who possesses the soundness of love if not he who loves God first with his entire soul and with his whole heart and with all his strength?[217] Then, upon hearing Christ's command respecting the neighbor, "You shall love your neighbor as yourself,"[218] he divides his love, since in these two commandments the entire law and prophets depend.[219] The one who has soundness of love "is not jealous, he is not puffed up, he does not do wrong or act dishonorably, he is not incited to wrath, he does not think evil, he does not rejoice over injustice, but he rejoices together in the truth; he endures all things, believes all things, hopes all things, expects all things."[220] And because love never falls away, the one who is in soundness of love also himself never falls. For indeed, "neither tribulation, nor anguish, nor hunger, nor persecution, nor nakedness, nor danger, nor sword will be able to separate him" from the soundness of love, which he has in Christ Jesus.[221] Why should I speak about the sword and other lesser things that are not able to divide him who possesses the soundness of love, when neither death nor life nor angels nor principalities nor things present nor things coming nor strength nor height nor depth nor any other created thing can separate him who has the soundness of love in Christ Jesus?[222]

If we have understood the soundness of love, let us take an example from the Scriptures of those who are in the weakness of love. The Savior says concerning the last times, "For when iniquity is multiplied, the love of many will grow cold."[223] Now love is hot among those who are fervent in spirit; but it is cold and icy and chilly in those

---

217. Cf. Mt 22.37; Dt 6.5.
218. Mt 22.39.
219. Cf. Mt 22.40.
220. Cf. 1 Cor 13.4–7.
221. Cf. Rom 8.35.
222. Cf. Rom 10.38–39.
223. Mt 24.12.

who have endured the very severe winds of the North. "For from the North evils will flare up against all the inhabitants of the earth."[224] And it was from this coldness of love that Ammon grew cold in respect to his sister Tamar.[225] Therefore, one should be afraid lest perhaps even we should one day be overcome by the weakness of love. For sometimes it comes to pass that at first our love toward a virgin or toward some woman is holy; and when the mind softens in affection, gradually out of weakness the soundness of love fades and begins to grow weak, and it carries off the one in love to final death.

This is also why the apostle cautiously and prudently instructs Timothy that he should exhort young women in "all chastity."[226] Now "all chastity" is in flesh, spirit, and soul.[227] Let not the eye stumble; let us not be ensnared by the beauty of a woman's face; let it not entice us to hear flattering words; let not our previously hardened mind begin to wither at single words. Let them beware, then, as we have said, both young men and old, both young women and old, and let them guard their hearts with all diligence, lest through the soundness of love, the illness of love may sneak in and through holy love it may become unholy love that drags them down to Gehenna.[228]

Let the one who is *sound in faith*, who is sound *in love*, be sound *in patience* too. And *patience*, which is especially tested in temptations, because it is of no benefit to have possessed what we listed above unless all the wealth and merchandise with which the ship is loaded down is preserved through the storm, and with the winds blowing here and there, the things that have been well distributed should be delivered without a shipwreck.[229] "For he who perseveres to the end will be saved."[230]

---

224. Jer 1.14.
225. Cf. 2 Sm 13.15.
226. Cf. 1 Tm 5.2.
227. Cf. 1 Thes 5.23.
228. Cf. Mt 5.27–30.
229. Cf. 1 Tm 1.19.
230. Mt 24.13.

2.3–5.   Likewise [bid] the older women to be of holy disposition, not slanderers, not enslaved to much wine, teaching well, so that they may instruct the young women in chastity, to love their husbands, to love their children, to be pure and chaste, keeping house diligently, kind, submissive to their husbands, so that the word of God is not blasphemed. Even if the apostle Peter commands that husbands should honor their wives as the weaker vessel,[231] one should not think, however, that the wife, who may have the weaker bodily vessel is at once also weaker in soul. This is why it is now commanded to them that in them too the apostle's words are fulfilled: "Power is perfected in weakness."[232] And it is said that they should have everything that the older men have been commanded to know commonly, namely, in that passage where he says, "*Likewise* [bid] the older women," that is, just as the older men, "in everything to be sober, honest, chaste, sound in faith, love, and patience."[233] And they should have this unique thing in view of their sex, to be "of holy disposition," or as it reads better in Greek, ἐν καταστήματι ἱεροπρεπεῖς, so that their very gait and movements, countenance, speech, silence, should present a certain dignity of holy elegance.

And because this kind of young women is accustomed to be garrulous, in accordance with this he says, "Besides that, they learn to be idlers, going about from house to house, but not only idlers but also loquacious meddlers, speaking what is not fitting."[234] Therefore, he does not want them to be slanderers, that is, accusers. They should not be the type to detract from some in order to please others. Or, at least, because they themselves have already passed beyond adolescence, they would discuss with the ages of the younger women and would say, "She is adorned thus, she wears her hair thus, she proceeds thus, she loves him, she is loved by him." Even if these things are true, she should not so much accuse others as correct herself secretly by the love of Christ,

---

231. 1 Pt 3.7.
232. 2 Cor 12.9.
233. Ti 2.2.
234. 1 Tm 5.13.

and let her not prefer to teach in order to avoid doing, to accuse her in public of what she herself has done.

These periods of life are accustomed to devote themselves to wine for the sake of lust, because they have grown cold from bodily excess[235] (although there are very many who are not ashamed of their own flesh and, being timid young virgins, they are composed as they come before the flock of playboys). And when in the midst of their cups they seem wise and eloquent in their own eyes, they assume as it were an austerity of manners, speaking what seems good to themselves, and not remembering what they were. And therefore let the older woman be forbidden to drink wine excessively, since that which leads to lust in young men leads to drunkenness in the old. Or how can an older woman teach younger women chastity seeing that, if the young woman imitates the drunkenness of the older woman, she cannot be chaste?

It is significant, however, that he has expressed, "Not enslaved to much wine." For enslavement is a kind of extreme condition. The senses of a man occupied with wine are not his own but the wine's. Since therefore he has first taught what sort the older women ought to be, and after these things what things they have in common with the older men, he has likewise explained their own unique characteristics, that they should be filled with an honest and holy disposition and with all decorum; they should not be accusers or detractors of others, they should not have their senses occupied with wine. Now, consequently, he permits them to have the bridles of doctrine, so that when they become such, they may have the freedom to teach, namely, to teach what are good things. For although in another passage he said, "But I do not permit women to teach,"[236] it should be understood thus, that lofty teaching should be for their husbands.

However that may be, let them teach the younger women, as if they were their own daughters, first of all, "chastity," since the adversary fights against this all the more in the one blooming with youth;

---

235. A textual variant reads, "they have chilled bodily excess."
236. 1 Tm 2.12.

and all his power against women is in the navel of the belly.[237] Then, they are to love their husbands and esteem their children. What is the teaching to love husbands? When it is constituted not in the eloquence of the one teaching but in the heart of the one who loves. He wants them to love their husbands "chastely"; he wants there to be chaste esteem between a husband and wife, so that with shame and modesty, and, as it were, by the necessity of sex, she should render what is owed to the husband rather than that she herself demands it from him.[238] And let her believe that they are doing the works [that lead to the birth] of children before the eyes of God and of the angels, so that she will not be ashamed even of the secret bedroom, and of the darkness of night, and of her own enclosed room, since she reflects on the fact that everything lies open to the eyes of God.

Now they love their children in this way, if they educate them in the instruction of God. But to be unwilling to cause them grief by teaching what is good, and to give them license to sin, this is not to love the children but to hate them. Let the younger women be instructed too to keep house carefully. And since it could come to pass that care for the house will be thrown off by austerity, and through this command of the apostle, the mother would become more severe toward the young slaves, therefore he has linked the word "kind" so that she believes she rules the husband's house well when she has commanded the young slaves with "kindness," not terror. And besides, "submissive to their husbands," lest perhaps they do not remember the riches and nobility of God's pronouncement that has been wafted in, through which they have been subjected to their husbands. For he says to the woman, "Your turning (*conversio*)[239] [will be] toward your husband; and he will rule over you."[240]

One should take consideration of the prudence of holy Scripture in this. For the Lord did not speak this to the man and say, "You will

---

237. Cf. Job 40.16.
238. Cf. 1 Cor 7.3.
239. Cf. ἀποστρόφη in Gn 3.17 (Septuagint).
240. Cf. Gn 3.16.

rule your wife"; but to the woman herself, that he would leave to her a reward for obedience while she is under his authority, if she wills to obey God's commands, serve the man, and be subject to the husband. Thus in a manner she would be free of servitude and full of love, therefore she serves her husband while she fears offending him. For indeed "the man was not created for the woman, but the woman for the sake of the man."[241] And since the man is the head of the woman, but Christ is the head of the man,[242] any wife who is not subject to her husband, that is, to her head, is guilty of the same sin of which the husband is guilty too, if he is not subject to Christ his head.

Now the word of the Lord is "blasphemed," either while God's initial pronouncement is despised[243] and regarded as nothing; or when the gospel of Christ is defamed while, contrary to the law and faith of nature, she who is Christian and subjected by God's law, desires to command the husband, when even pagan women serve their husbands by the common law of nature.

2.6–7. *Likewise exhort the younger men to be chaste in all things, offering yourself as an example of good works, in doctrine, in integrity, in chastity, in sound and irreproachable speech, so that the one who is an adversary may show reverent fear, having nothing evil to say about us.* Just as in respect to what he had commanded above, saying, "Likewise [bid] the older women to be of holy disposition,"[244] we had mentioned that the comparison of the older women was to be related to the older men, so now in respect to what he has added, "Urge the younger men likewise to be chaste," we think that the comparison of younger men should be applied to the older women and through the older women to the older men. Thus they should have the sobriety of the older men, and they should be honest and chaste and sound in faith, love, and patience.[245] Now in respect to the sanctity of the disposition of the older

241. 1 Cor 11.9.
242. Cf. 1 Cor 11.3.
243. Cf. Gn 3.16.
244. Ti 2.3.
245. Cf. Ti 2.2.

women, they are not to be accusers, enslaved to much wine, but they should teach well, and so on.[246] But he has recorded uniquely of the younger men that they are to be chaste "in all things," namely, both in mind and in body, both in deeds and in thoughts, so that there is no suspicion of baseness in the young man. And although certain of the Latins think that this should be read thus, "Urge the young men likewise to be chaste," and after this they add, "offering yourself as a model of good works in all things"; nevertheless we should know that "in all things" is to be referred to what comes above it, that is, "urge them to be chaste in all things."

One should also know that continence is necessary not only in respect to deeds of the flesh and desires of the mind but in all affairs. Let us not seek honors we do not deserve. Let us not be set on fire by greed; let us not be overcome by any passion. He says, "offering yourself as a model of good works." It is not profitable for someone to be trained in teaching, and to have sharpened his tongue for orating unless he teaches more by example than by words. After all, one who is unchaste, even if he is eloquent, if he exhorts his audience to chastity, his speech is infirm and he has no authority to exhort. And on the other hand, though someone may be a rustic and slow of speech, if he is chaste, he can incite men by his example to imitate his life.

Now as for what he says, "in incorruption," it should be understood as follows: "incorruption" expresses virginity proper. After all, even in public those who are virgins are called the incorrupt; and those who have ceased being virgins are named the corrupt. And we say, she who was once a virgin is corrupt. This is why I think that even Titus, before he was involved with the deeds of the flesh believed in the gospel and received baptism; and he remained a virgin, and now is advised by the apostle to offer himself as a model in respect to incorruption. Now we do not see this incorruption in Timothy. For when he said to him, "Let no one despise your youth, but be a model for the believers in speech, in way of life, in love, faith, and chastity,"[247] he was silent about "incorruption" and recorded only "chastity."

---

246. Cf. Ti 2.3.
247. 1 Tm 4.12.

Now chastity can be understood also of celibacy without virginity. Unless perhaps we take chastity in respect to the mind, but incorruption in respect to the body, in accordance with what is written elsewhere as a definition of a virgin: "so that she may be holy in body and spirit."[248] And he himself now added in what follows: "in doctrine, in incorruption, in chastity." We could interpret even chastity as incorruption likewise in respect to the integrity of doctrine, except that what uniquely follows, "in sound and irreproachable speech," contains its own command for the instruction of doctrine. Now as for his words, "in irreproachable speech," it is not that anyone is of such great eloquence and prudence that no one reproaches him (for even the apostles and evangelists are reproached by heretics and pagans), but that he should neither say nor do anything worthy of being reproached, even though there are adversaries prepared to reproach.

And since there are "many who are insubordinate, vain talkers, and deceivers of minds,"[249] who "hate him who reproved in the gate and abhorred holy speech,"[250] therefore we should offer ourselves as an example "in all things," in doctrine, in integrity, in chastity, in sound and irreproachable speech, so that the adversaries of life and those who are terrified by the soundness of our doctrine may not dare to accuse, that is, to fabricate anything factually true as an accusation. And indeed until today we see that there are some in the church of such great dignity and continence (although he is a rare bird) that they are even attested by their adversaries,[251] and it is said, "That is a great man and one of holy life and with proven character, were he not a heretic." For no one is of such limitless impudence that he could accuse sunbeams of being dark and could cover over a bright light with the darkness of night. This is why the apostle takes precautions against these very things and says, "that I might remove the occasion from whose who want an occasion."[252]

---

248. 1 Cor 7.34.
249. Ti 1.10.
250. Amos 5.10.
251. I believe he means "heretical adversaries."
252. 2 Cor 11.12.

Now it is possible to interpret "the one who is opposed" as the devil, because he is the accuser of our brethren, as John the evangelist asserts.[253] Since he has nothing evil to raise as an objection against us, he is ashamed and the incriminator will not be able to incriminate. Now "devil" expresses "incriminator" in the Latin language.

2.9–10.   *Slaves should be submissive to their masters in all things, so that they may be pleasing, not contradictory, not stealing; but displaying all good faith, so that they may adorn the doctrine of our Savior and God in all things.* Since our Lord and Savior, who in the gospel says, "Come to me, you who labor and are heavy laden and I will give you rest,"[254] thinks that no condition, age, or sex is unsuitable for blessedness, therefore the apostle now lays down commands even for slaves, namely, as for a part of the church and for members of the body of Christ. And just as higher up he showed Titus what he needed to teach older men, older women, younger women, and younger men, so now he lays down precepts that are suitable for slaves.

First of all, that "they should be submissive to their masters in all things." Now in these "all things" that are not contrary to God, the slave should be subjected to the master, when and if the master commands things that are not opposed to Holy Scripture. But if he commands things that are contrary, let him obey the master more in spirit than in body. Pay careful attention to how he issues commands that are congruent with the persons. "Slaves," he says, "should be submissive to their masters in all things." While carrying on a discussion about children in another passage, he says, "Children, obey your parents."[255] For it is befitting that children "obey" their parents, but slaves are to be "subjected" to the master who gives orders.

It is not that we should think that this contradicts what he says in another letter, "Wives should be subjected to your husbands,"[256]

253. Cf. Rv 12.10.
254. Mt 11.28.
255. Eph 6.1; cf. Col 3.20.
256. Eph 5.22; Col 3.18.

whereas in this one he asserted that wives are subjected to their husbands, as if he has used the same word both in respect to slaves and in respect to wives. For in what way is the husband the lord of the wife? He says, "He will rule over you."[257] Also the Savior was subjected to his parents,[258] but when he was still twelve years old and was no different from a slave, he was Lord of all.[259] For he had not yet reached the perfect age of manhood, which could receive the inheritance. Moreover, elsewhere it is written of him, "For when all things have been subjected to him, then the Son himself will be subjected to him who subjected all things to himself, that God may be all in all."[260] Now all things will be subjected to him when he says, "The Lord [says] to my Lord, sit at my right hand until I put your enemies as a footstool for your feet."[261] The Lord is subjected in the subjected slaves. And just as he is said to be a curse for us,[262] though he is not a curse but a true blessing, so for us he is recorded either as subjected or not subjected, if we become either subjected or not subjected to God.

Some read this passage as follows: "Slaves should be subjected to their masters," and after they have punctuated up to this point, they add, "Let them please [them] in all things"; though the order of the reading is different in Greek, that is, "Let slaves be subjected to their masters in all things"; so that it follows: εὐαρέστους εἶναι. This does not fully please us, nevertheless we can translate it to some extent as: "so that they may please themselves," namely, lest God's pronouncement upon their condition should seem unjust to them. But just as a poor man can be saved in accordance with his own measure; and a woman is not excluded from the kingdom of God for the weakness of her sex, and every condition can receive beatitude in accordance with its own rank; so also slaves may be pleased with themselves that they are slaves. They should not think that, because they are subjected to

---

257. Gn 3.16.
258. Cf. Lk 2.51.
259. Cf. Gal 4.1.
260. Cf. 1 Cor 15.28.
261. Cf. Ps 110.1.
262. Cf. Gal 3.13.

men, on that account they cannot serve God. On the contrary in that respect, if they become subjected in all things to their masters and please themselves in their own condition, they can please the will of God all the more. And let them pursue what the apostle commanded next, that they not be "contradicters" or "thieves." To contradict masters is the very great vice of slaves. When the masters command anything, they mutter to themselves. And so, he warns Titus to remove this sort of passion from those who are Christian slaves by means of sound teaching. For if the slave regards it as necessary to fulfill the things the master commands, why should he not do this with good will? Why should he instead offend the master and yet do what is commanded, especially since God too was offended at the water of contradiction?[263] And in another passage he speaks to the people about murmuring: "Let their murmuring cease and they will not die."[264]

After correcting "contradicting" and the other vice of slaves, Christ's doctrine says, "Do not be thieves." Now a thief should be judged not only in great things but in lesser matters. For it is not what is taken away by theft that is attended to, but the mind of the thief. Just as in fornication and adultery, fornication or adultery would not on that account be different, if a promiscuous girl or an adulterous woman is pretty or rich, unshapely or poor. On the contrary no matter how she is, the fornication or adultery is one. The same applies to theft. However much a slave has taken, the crime of theft is incurred. This is why in the law of Moses thieves are compelled to pay back, sometimes sevenfold, sometimes fourfold.[265] And sometimes they are killed,[266] sometimes the thief himself is sold for his theft.[267] I remember recently explaining these things to you (*vobis*)[268] on Leviticus. Now if this is forbidden in the slave, how much more in the free man, lest either a judge

---

263. Cf. Nm 20.24.

264. Nm 17.10.

265. Cf. Ex 21.37; 2 Sm 12.6.

266. Cf. Dt 24.7.

267. Cf. Ex 22.3.

268. The Latin *vobis* is plural. This must be addressed to Paula and Eustochium.

snatches what belongs to others, or a soldier who is scarcely contented with his wages plunders what belongs to others?

A very dignified man made a nice response when the integrity of a certain judge was being praised to him. The one who was doing the praising said about him, "He is no thief." The man replied, "He would have made an excellent slave, if he were not a runaway. The mere suspicion of theft ought to be foreign to all free persons." Therefore let slaves be subject to their masters in everything; let them be pleasing to their condition; let them not endure their servitude with bitterness; let them not contradict their masters; let them not steal.

And after these things let them "display good faith in all things, so that they may adorn the doctrine of our Savior and God in all things." For if with their fleshly masters they become faithful in the least thing, greater things will begin to be entrusted to them with God.[269] Now he "adorns the doctrine" of the Lord who does the things that are suitable to his condition. And on the other hand, he confounds it who is not subjected in all things, to whom his condition is displeasing, who as a contradicter and deceiver displays good faith in no respect. For how can he be faithful with God's property who was not able to exhibit faithfulness to a fleshly master?

2.12–14.   *For the grace of God [our] Savior has dawned upon all men, teaching us to renounce impiety and worldly desires, to live chastely, justly, and piously in this world, awaiting the blessed hope and coming of glory of the great God and of our Savior Jesus Christ, who gave himself for us, to redeem us from all iniquity and to purify for himself an exceptional people, zealous for good works.* After the catalogue of doctrine for Titus, what he ought to teach older men, older women, younger women, and younger men, and lastly slaves, he now has rightly added, "For the grace of God [our] Savior has dawned upon all men." For there is no difference between free and slave, Greek and barbarian, circumcised and uncircumcised, woman and man, but we are all one in Christ.[270] We are all invited to the kingdom of God. We are all to be

---

269. Cf. Lk 16.10–12.
270. Cf. Gal 3.27–28.

reconciled[271] to our Father after stumbling,[272] not through our merits but through the grace of the Savior. This is either because Christ himself is the grace, living and subsisting from God the Father, or because this is the grace of Christ, God and Savior. And we are saved not by our merit according to what is said in another passage, "You will save them for nothing."[273] This grace, then, "has dawned on all men to teach us to renounce impiety and worldly desires, to live chastely and justly and piously in this world."

Now I am confident that what it means to "renounce impiety and worldly desires" can be understood from what we have explained above: "They confess to know God, but they deny him by their deeds."[274] Through opposites, opposites are explained.[275] Therefore "desires" are "worldly" that are suggested by the ruler of this world.[276] And since they are "of the world," they pass away with the clouds of this world.[277] But when we live in Christ "chastely" and "justly," that is, sinning neither in body nor in mind, we should also live "piously" in this world. This piety "awaits a blessed hope and the coming of glory of the great God and of our Savior Jesus Christ." For just as impiety dreads the advent of the great God, so piety awaits him, confident concerning its works and faith.

Where is the serpent Arius?[278] Where is the snake Eunomius?[279] The "great God" is called "Jesus Christ the Savior," not the firstborn of

---

271. A textual variant reads, "have been reconciled."
272. Cf. Rom 11.32.
273. Ps 56.7.
274. Cf. Ti 1.16.
275. Cf. *CRm* 3.1.7.
276. Cf. Jn 16.11.
277. Cf. 1 Jn 2.16–17.
278. Arius (260–336) was a priest from Alexandria whose doctrine was condemned at the Council of Nicaea in 325. He taught that Christ is a creature in the proper sense of that word, and as such does not share in the divine nature. Arius believed that the Father created the Son in time, and, therefore, the Son has not always existed. The notorious Arian affirmation was, "There was a time when he (the Son) was not (did not exist)."
279. Eunomius of Cyzicus (bishop, 360–364) was the greatest exponent of radical Arianism in Jerome's day. His apologies for "Arianism" were refuted in detail by Basil and Gregory of Nyssa.

every creature,[280] not the Word of God[281] and wisdom,[282] but Jesus and Christ, which are designations of the humanity he assumed. But we do not call the one, Jesus Christ, the other, the Word, as a new heresy falsely states. But we name the very same one, both before the ages and after the ages, both before the world and after Mary, or rather from Mary, the "great God our Savior Jesus Christ," who gave himself for us to redeem us from all iniquity[283] by his precious blood[284] and to purify for himself a περιούσιον people (for this what the Greek has) and that he might make them "zealous for good works."

Though I have often pondered what the word περιούσιον means and have questioned the wise men of this world in the hope that they may have read it somewhere, I was never able to discover anyone who could explain to me what it meant.[285] For this reason I was forced to consult the Old Testament (*Instrumentum*) from which I thought the apostle had taken what he had said. For since he was a Hebrew and "according to the law a Pharisee,"[286] assuredly recorded in his epistle what he knew he had read in the Old Testament (*Testamento*). And so, in Deuteronomy I have found, "For you are a people holy to the your Lord, and the Lord your God is pleased with you; so that you are to be to him a περιούσιον people from all the peoples who are on the face of the earth,"[287] and in the one-hundred-thirty-fourth Psalm, where we have, "Sing to his name, for it is sweet; for the Lord chose Jacob for

---

280. Cf. Col 1.15.
281. Cf. Jn 1.1,14.
282. Cf. 1 Cor 1.30.
283. Cf. Gal 1.4.
284. Cf. 1 Pt 1.19.
285. Such allegedly autobiographical statements in Jerome are most often translated directly from his *Vorlage,* the Greek Origen. G. Bardy, "Jérôme et ses maîtres hébreux," *Revue Bénédictine* 46 (1934), pp. 145–64, has shown that Jerome took from Origen all of what he claimed to know firsthand from the Jews. This seems also to apply to his consultations of the Old Testament, since the readings Jerome cites are from the Septuagint.
286. Cf. Phil 3.5.
287. Dt 7.6.

himself, Israel for his possession."[288] In place of what we have as "for his possession," in Greek it is recorded as εἰς περιουσιασμὸν. In fact Aquila[289] and the fifth edition[290] expressed this as εἰς περιούσιον. But the Septuagint and Theodotion[291] in rendering it περιουσιασμὸν made an alteration of a syllable, not of the sense. Symmachus,[292] therefore, for what stands in Greek as περιούσιον, in Hebrew as *sogolla*, expressed it as ἐξαίρετον, that is, exceptional or excellent. In another book using Latin speech this word is translated "peculiar."

Therefore, Christ Jesus our "great God and Savior" rightly redeemed us by his blood to make the Christian people "peculiar." They would be able to be "peculiar" if they show themselves as "zealous for good works." This is also why what is written according to the Latin

---

288. Ps 135.3–4. For "possession," the Septuagint has περιουσιασμόν.

289. Aquila was a second-century Jew who published a slavishly literal Greek translation of the Hebrew Old Testament that was intended to replace the Septuagint, which was in use by the Christians. He was a native of Sinope in Pontus and lived under Emperor Hadrian. Jerome and Origen admitted the fidelity of his translation to the Hebrew. Aquila's text occupied the third column of Origen's *Hexapla*.

290. The "fifth edition" evidently refers to additional Greek translations of the Old Testament (beyond those of Aquila, Symmachus, Theodotion, and the Septuagint) that Origen added to the text of the Psalms in his *Hexapla*. Rufinus of Aquileia, in his Latin translation of Eusebius's *Historia Ecclesiastica,* also reports that Origen added a fifth, sixth, and seventh version in the Psalms, and he arranged all of them in columns in such a way that each could be compared either with the others or with the Hebrew. See J. Oulton, "Rufinus's Translation of the Church History of Eusebius," *Journal of Theological Studies* 30 (1929), pp. 150–74; "Hexapla," in *DCB* 3.

291. Theodotion was the author of a Greek version of the Old Testament composed during the reign of Commodus (180–192). Irenaeus says he was a proselyte at Ephesus (*Adv Haer* 3.21.2). Jerome calls him an Ebionite (*Vir Ill* 54). Epiphanius calls him a disciple of Marcion (*On Weights and Measures* 17). Theodotion's translation is essentially a revision of the Septuagint, harmonized with the Hebrew text. His version occupied the sixth column of Origen's *Hexapla*.

292. Symmachus was the late second-century translator of the Greek version of the Hebrew Old Testament. Eusebius and Jerome considered him an Ebionite, but Epiphanius called him a Samaritan who went over to Judaism (*On Weights and Measures* 16). Symmachus's translation formed the fourth column of Origen's *Hexapla*.

translators in the gospel as "give us today our daily bread"[293] reads better in Greek as "our ἐπιούσιον bread," that is, excellent, exceptional, peculiar, namely, him who when coming down from heaven says, "I am the bread who came down from heaven."[294] For far be from us who are forbidden to think about tomorrow[295] to be commanded in the Lord's prayer to ask for that bread that after a little while must be digested and expelled into the drain.[296] There is not much difference between ἐπιούσιον and περιούσιον; for only the preposition is changed, not the word. Some think that in the Lord's prayer the bread was called ἐπιούσιον because it is beyond all ὀυσιας, that is, beyond all substances. But if this is accepted, it does not differ much from that meaning that we have explained. For whatever is exceptional and excellent is outside everything and beyond everything.[297]

2.15.   *Speak and exhort these things, and rebuke with all authority.* He has recorded three things: "speak, exhort, rebuke." Now his word, "speak," apparently refers to doctrine. But what he added, "exhort," that is, παρακάλει, signifies in Greek something different than in Latin; for παράκλησις expresses more the idea of "consolation" than "exhortation." This word is used above about the younger men, "Likewise *console* the young men to be chaste in all things."[298] We have commented on this just as it reads in Latin, as if "exhort" were written. Therefore, he *consoles* the hearer who says: "We plead on Christ's behalf, be reconciled to God,"[299] and who humbles and subjects himself, in order to "gain" the one he is consoling.[300]

However, the third term, "rebuke," seems to me to be the opposite of consolation. Thus whoever despises the consolation becomes worthy

293. Mt 6.11.
294. Jn 6.51.
295. Cf. Mt 6.34.
296. Cf. Mt 15.17; Mk 7.19.
297. For a similar discussion, see Jerome's *Commentary on Matthew* 6.11.
298. Ti 2.6.
299. 2 Cor 5.20.
300. Cf. 1 Cor 9.19.

of a rebuke and deserves to hear, "You have forgotten the *consolation* which speaks to you as sons."[301] To Timothy too we read of another "consolation" and another "rebuke" when the apostle says, "Be ready in season and out of season, convict, rebuke, console."[302] And indeed there the rebuke is employed first, and afterward the severity is tempered by consolation. But here he wants to console the disciples first, and if they do not make progress by means of the consolation, then he wants them to be corrected, and corrected "with all authority." For this is how I understand what is said: "Rebuke *with all authority*," that the added phrase refers particularly to the rebuke; it does not apply generally to the two previous terms. For it is not right to say: console "with all authority," and speak "with all authority," but only, "rebuke with all authority."

2.15. *Let no one look down on you.* Someone may think that the same thing is now being written to Titus that was said to Timothy: "Let no one look down on your youth."[303] But we think, in accordance with the difference of the Greek words, that περιφρονείτω, which is written here, means one thing, and καταφρονείτω, which is said to Timothy, means something else, and that the prepositions περὶ- or κατὰ- make the sense different. Now that it is not by chance and as it pleases him that the apostle Paul uses not only terms and words but even diverse prepositions, in view of the variety of causes, can be clarified from what he says, "For the woman is *from* the man, but the man is *through* the woman."[304] And elsewhere, "For *from* him and *through* him and *in* him are all things."[305] And moreover, there is the following, "Paul an apostle not *from* men, nor *through* a man."[306] And so, we think that καταφρόνησιν pertains to contempt proper, as when someone

---

301. Heb 12.5.
302. 2 Tm 4.2.
303. 1 Tm 4.12.
304. 1 Cor 11.12.
305. Rom 11.36.
306. Gal 1.1.

stretched out between the torture rack and the plates[307] shows contempt for the pain and fears neither the threats of the judge nor the loud buzz of approval from the people standing around. On the contrary, for the sake of confession of martyrdom, he shows contempt for and despises all punishments.

Now on the other hand, there is also a bad kind of contempt, of which Habakkuk testifies with the Holy Spirit speaking in him, "Look, you despisers, and see marvelous things and vanish."[308] In accordance with what we said was written to Timothy too, "Let no one show contempt for your youth,"[309] that is to say: I do not want you to show yourself to be such a person who could deservedly be shown contempt by anyone. Now περιφρόνησις expresses this. Nevertheless, as the Stoics claim, who make subtle distinctions between words, one who is confident in himself that he is better than someone else, "despises" the one whom he regards as inferior; and the "super-," that is, wiser, man, thinks that the lowlier man is worthy of contempt.

One of the Greeks is mocked for being puffed up like this by the vanity of pride, and for despising heaven itself and the sun, as having said, Ἀεροβατῶ καὶ περιφρονῶ τὸν ἥλιον, which we can say in Latin as, "I tread on air and I know that I am greater than the sun."[310] Therefore, περιφρόνησις, which is not written to Titus, has this sense: Let none of those who are in the churches, by your negligent behavior, live in such a way that he thinks that he is better. For what sort of edification of a disciple will there be if he understands himself to be superior to his teacher? This is why not only bishops, priests, and deacons especially ought to take care to preside over all their people, to excel in their manner of life and speech, but also the lesser ranks, exorcists, lectors, sacristans, and absolutely everyone who serve the household of God. For it severely undermines the church of Christ that the laity are better than the clerics.

---

307. That is, plates that are heated by fire and used to torture slaves or the accused.

308. Hab 1.5.

309. 1 Tm 4.12.

310. Stepsiades says this in Aristophanes' *Clouds* 1503.

*3.1–2.   Remind them to be subject to rulers and authorities, to be obe-
dient, to be ready for every good work, to blaspheme no one, not to be
contentious, modest, showing all gentleness toward all men.* Something
like this is also written to the Romans: "Let everyone be subject to the
higher authorities. For there is no authority except from God."[311] Indeed, I think that this command, both this one here and that one there,
was published because the doctrine of Judas the Galilean was still in
force at that time and he had very many adherents. Mention is made of
this in the Acts of the Apostles, when the Scripture reports, "For before these days Theudas arose claiming to be someone great, and about
three thousand men joined themselves to him."[312] And, "after this in
the days of the census Judas the Galilean rose up."[313] Among other
things he was probably making this known on the basis of the law, that
no one was to be called Lord except God alone; and that those who
registered the tithes at the temple were not to pay tribute to Caesar.

This heresy had increased to such an extent that it even threw a
large portion of the Pharisees and the people into confusion, so that
this question was even referred to our Lord: "Is it permissible to give
tribute to Caesar or not?"[314] The Lord responded to them prudently
and cautiously, when he says, "Render to Caesar the things that are
Caesar's, and to God the things that are God's."[315] The apostle Paul
agrees with this response and teaches that believers ought to be subject
to the rulers and authorities. For Ἀρχαὶ that is read in the Greek expresses rulerships rather than rulers, and it signifies the authority itself,
not those men who are in authority.

But because he had said, "Remind them to be subject to principalities and authorities," an occasion for denying [him] could have
been given to those who dread torture. In accordance with the apostle's
statement, they could have claimed that they were subject to the prin-

---

311. Rom 13.1.
312. Acts 5.36. The modern text has "four hundred."
313. Acts 5.37.
314. Mt 22.17.
315. Mt 22.21.

cipalities and authorities and did what they had commanded. For this reason he added, "Be obedient in every good work." If what the emperor or ruler orders is good, follow the will of him who orders. But if it is evil and has in mind things contrary to God, respond to him what is from the Acts of the Apostles: "It is necessary to obey God rather than men."[316] We should understand this both of slaves with their masters and of wives with their husbands and of children with their parents, that they should only be subject to those masters, husbands, and parents in things that would not go contrary to God's commands.

But what follows, "Be ready," should be read in two senses, either that one should supply in thought, "Be ready for every good work," or, at least, it should be linked with what comes above, which says, "Be obedient in every good work," and be terminated at that point, as if it is its own separate and unique command, "Be ready." This accords with what is written in Leviticus: "The goat that is sent bearing the curses of the people is handed over to the hands of a *ready* man."[317] If anyone therefore is "ready" to hold the ἀποπομπαῖον,[318] and to lead it out into the desert, and there disperses it and as far as lies in him banishes the fate of the curse, when he obeys, he will also be "ready for every good work." Now, "Be ready" can also be understood in another way. Everything whatsoever that can come to pass prefigures[319] itself in the mind, and when all these things happen, they endure nothing as if it were a new thing, but all things have been prepared in advance for them.

"Blaspheme no one" also is not to be taken literally. For he does not say to "blaspheme" no human being, but absolutely no one: no angel, no other creature of God. For everything that has been made by God are very good things. "When Michael the archangel was disputing with the devil about the body of Moses, he did not dare to bring

---

316. Acts 5.29.

317. Lv 16.21.

318. This neologism is used in the Septuagint of Lv 16.8 and means "the one who carries away." The Masoretic text has "Azazel."

319. A textual variant reads, "fixes."

a judgment of blasphemy, but he said, 'May God command you.'"[320] If, therefore, Michael did not dare to bring a judgment of blasphemy against the devil, and against one who was most certainly worthy of cursing, how much more should we be free from all cursing? The devil deserved the curse, but blasphemy should not proceed from the mouth of an archangel.

Reread the old books and see what tribes are established on Mount[321] Gerizim in order to bless the people, and which ones are on the other mountain in order to curse.[322] Reuben, who defiled the couch of his father,[323] and Zebulon, the last son of Leah,[324] and the children of the maidservants, are placed on mount Ebal in order to curse those who are worthy of cursing.[325] It would take too long to enumerate at this time how Jacob, who had called his sons to the blessing, saying "that I may bless you,"[326] afterward, as if he is sharing in the blessing, says, "accursed is their anger for it is brash."[327] And the Lord himself would say in Genesis, "Cursed is the land in your works."[328]

Let it suffice for now to have said only this, that it is not right for disciples of Christ to "blaspheme"; and it is added, "nor to be contentious." For if we are sons of peace and want peace to rest upon us[329] and are approaching the heavenly Jerusalem,[330] which was named from peace, let us have peace with those who hate peace. As far as in us lies, let us be at peace with all men,[331] not only with the modest but also with the quarrelsome. For there is no virtue in bearing with those who are

---

320. Jude 9.
321. Reading *monte* for Migne's *mente.*
322. Cf. Dt 11.29; 27.12; Jos 8.33.
323. Cf. Gn 35.22; 49.4.
324. Cf. Gn 30.20.
325. Cf. Dt 27.13.
326. Cf. Gn 49.1.
327. Gn 49.7.
328. Gn 3.17.
329. Cf. Lk 10.6.
330. Cf. Heb 12.22.
331. Cf. Rom 14.19.

meek; let us leave room for wrath,[332] showing all gentleness to all men. It is not that from a desire for vain glory we should show ourselves to be gentle with all men, but while we bear all men and do not pay back injury in turn for an injury, let these very works become better known to all. Someone can feign gentleness among certain people and fabricate goodness on account of boasting and the opinion of the crowd and popular favor. But when his gentleness is not true, genuine, and real, I do not know whether he can convince everyone that he is gentle.

3.3–7.   *For we ourselves were once foolish, disobedient, led astray, slaves to various passions and pleasures, passing our days in malice and envy, hated, hating one another. But when the goodness and humanity of God our Savior dawned, he saved us, not because of works of justice that we did; but in accordance with his own mercy, by the washing of regeneration and renewal of the Holy Spirit, whom he poured out upon us richly through Jesus Christ our Savior, so that having been justified by his grace, we might become heirs according to the hope of eternal life.* Someone may ask how Paul was "foolish, unbelieving, led astray," and "enslaved to various desires and pleasures" in malice and "envy, hated, and hating," before the "goodness" and clemency of our "Savior by the washing" of the second "rebirth saved" him, "not because of works of justice that he had done, but from his own mercy," when the "Holy Spirit" was abundantly and "generously poured out" upon the apostles and believers "through Jesus Christ," so that, having obtained the inheritance of grace, they took possession of the "hope of life" forever. And certainly we read that according to the "justice that is in the law," he was "without fault, circumcised on the eighth day, a Hebrew of Hebrews, according to the law a Pharisee, from the tribe of Benjamin."[333] He was educated at the feet of Gamaliel and instructed from infancy in the sacred literature.[334]

---

332. Cf. Rom 12.19.
333. Cf. Phil 3.5.
334. Cf. Acts 22.3.

The following response is given to this. The Jews who before the Savior's advent and his suffering and resurrection lived in the law, although they did not have full justice, nevertheless had some measure of justice, just as both Simeon[335] and Anna the prophetess[336] were found serving in the temple of God. But after the people shouted out together, "Crucify him, crucify him; we have no king but Caesar";[337] and, "His blood is upon us and upon our children";[338] and, "the kingdom of God" was "taken away from them and given to a nation bearing its fruit";[339] from that time he who has not believed in Christ has become "foolish, led astray, unbelieving" and "enslaved to various pleasures."

Or does Paul not seem to us to have been "foolish" when he had "zeal for God but not according to knowledge"?[340] And when he "persecuted the church"[341] and kept watch over the clothing of those who stoned Stephen?[342] When he was goaded on and burned with such great hatred of the Savior that he received letters from the priests to go to Damascus to lock up those who had believed in Christ?[343] Or could he have had any virtues without the virtue of Christ Jesus?[344] Or could he have extinguished the burning flame of "pleasure" when he was not God's temple? But what greater malice and ill will can there be than to take letters against those who are not present and to lay waste to the disciples of Christ everywhere? To be unwilling to be saved himself, and to envy others who could have been saved? To hate the Christians and, as a consequence, to earn everyone's hatred? And what greater error and senseless disobedience is there than, after the day has expired and the shadows have passed, to want to preserve the law that has been

---

335. Cf. Lk 2.25–35.
336. Cf. Lk 2.36–38.
337. Jn 19.15; cf. Mt 27.23.
338. Mt 27.25.
339. Cf. Mt 21.43.
340. Cf. Rom 10.2.
341. Cf. 1 Cor 15.9.
342. Cf. Acts 7.58.
343. Cf. Acts 9.2.
344. Cf. 1 Cor 1.24.

abolished and to say, "Do not handle, do not touch, do not taste,"[345] and when solid food for adults has appeared, to long to drink the milk of infancy?[346]

Let us pay more careful attention,[347] and we will find in the present section the clearest manifestation of the Trinity. For the "kindness and clemency of God our Savior," none other than of God the Father, "by the washing of regeneration and renewal of the Holy Spirit that he poured out upon us abundantly through Jesus Christ our Savior," has "justified" us unto "eternal life." The salvation of believers is the mystery of the Trinity. Some understand this passage as follows: they think the statement is not about Paul and the apostles, but about others under the persona of the apostles. Thus, just as he spoke about dissention and schism under his own persona and Apollos's and Cephas's, which he proved to be in existence among the Corinthians, so likewise in the present text, by naming himself and the apostles, he is pointing to all who had believed in Christ, what sort they were before the regeneration of the life-giving washing. But at the same time his humility is also to be admired, because he who despised all humility (*humilitatem*)[348] and justice of the law as worthless offscourings,[349] rightly relates that he was enslaved to all vices when he was without Christ.

3.8.   *Faithful are the words, and concerning these things I want to affirm you, that those who believe in God may have concern to excel in good works. These are good and useful to men.* His statement, "Faithful are the words," should be linked to what is above, in which he had said first, "so that having been justified by his grace, we may become heirs according to the hope of eternal life."[350] For the "words" concerning the inheritance of God and concerning the hope of eternal life are

---

345. Col 2.21.
346. Cf. 1 Cor 3.2; Heb 5.12–13.
347. Cf. Heb 2.1.
348. Var. *utilitatem*, "advantage."
349. Cf. Phil 3.7–8.
350. Ti 3.7.

worthy of credence. This is why it is proper to believe "concerning these things," no doubt, and, that the rest may believe, to "strengthen" the one who is not himself afraid; but not only this, but one must also strengthen this one together with these others who want to believe. This is why he says, "And I want to strengthen you concerning these things."

Now it is necessary for those who believe that these things are true to have concern for good works, through which the inheritance of God and the hope of eternal life is being prepared. And it is beautiful how he made faith greater by saying, not "who believe in men," but "who believe in God." For it is necessary that they have concern for good works, which, when fulfilled and carried out with all zeal, are good and useful to those who believe.

3.9.   *But stay away from foolish questions and genealogies and contentious issues and quarrels that come from the law, for they are useless and vain.* Because questions are many and diverse, Solomon spoke about those who were seeking God and says, "But those who seek him rightly have found peace."[351] Therefore, those who do not seek God rightly cannot find peace. There are very many examples of those who do not seek God rightly. The Jews seek God wrongly, hoping that they can find him without Christ. The heretics sound out with a vain clamor of words seeking one whom they are not able to find. The philosophers too and the pagans hold various opinions about God and have sought God. But because they have not sought rightly, the "questions" of those who thought that God could be comprehended by human thought were "foolish." Therefore, Paul calls us to back away from these "questions."

However that may be, he exhorts and invites wise [questions] instead, and things that are supported by the authority of the Scriptures. He was not ignorant of the Savior's commands in which he says, "Seek and you will find; knock and it will be opened to you; ask and it will be given to you. For everyone who seeks finds, and he who asks will re-

---

351. Prv 16.5 (16.8 in the Septuagint).

ceive, and the one who knocks, it will be opened to him."[352] Only may our body not be subject to sins, and wisdom will enter into us.[353] May our senses be trained, may our mind daily feed on the divine reading, and our questions will not be "foolish questions."

Now as for what he says, "Stay away from genealogies and contentious issues and quarrels, which come from the law," this is directed particularly against the Jews, who boast in it and who think that they know the law, if they grasp the names of individual things. Since these things are foreign and we do not know their etymologies, for the most part we make them known with corruptions. And if by chance we err in accent, in the lengthening and shortening of a syllable, or if we lengthen short syllables or shorten long ones, they customarily deride our lack of skill, especially in aspiration and in producing certain letters with a rasping of the throat.

Now this happens because the seventy translators through whom the divine law was translated into Greek expressed particularly the letters *heth* and *ayin* and others of this sort with other letters added (since they were unable to translate into the Greek language with a double aspiration). For instance for *Rahel* they said *Rachel;* for *Jeriho, Jericho;* for *Hebron, Chebron;* and for *Seor, Segor.* But in other words this attempt failed them. For we and the Greeks have only one letter *s,* but they have three—*samech, sade,* and *sin*—which have different sounds. *Isaac* and *Sion* are written with *sade; Israel* with *sin,* and yet it does not sound as it is written but as it is not written. *Seon,* king of the Amorites, is pronounced and written with the letter *samech.* If therefore these peculiar ἰδιώματα of names and language, namely foreign characteristics, are not expressed by us as they are expressed by the Hebrews, they usually raise a loud laugh and swear that they simply do not know what we are saying.

This is also why we have been careful to correct all the books of the old law that the learned man Adamantius[354] had arranged in the

---

352. Mt 7.7–8.
353. Cf. Wis 1.4.
354. This is another name for Origen of Alexandria. Cf. *HE* 6.14.10; Jerome, Ep. 43.

Hexapla, having transcribed them from the library of Caesarea, by means of these authentic copies in which the very Hebrew words were written out in their own characters and expressed in the next column in Greek letters. Aquila likewise and Symmachus, the seventy too, and Theodotion occupy their own column. But some books, especially those that were composed in verse among the Hebrews, have three other added editions, which they call the fifth, sixth, and seventh translation, editions that have followed the authority of the translators without their names.[355] That immortal genius[356] gave us these things by his own effort, so that we should not greatly fear the haughtiness of the Jews who rejoice with their loose lips, contorted tongue, gurgling saliva, and shaved jaw.[357]

And there is another occasion for arrogance by them. Just as we who are Latins easily commit to memory Latin names and things that originate in our language, so from earliest infancy they have imbibed in their deepest thoughts terms that are indigenous to their speech (and from the beginning with Adam until the end in Zerubbabel, they

---

355. This applies to the Psalms.

356. Jerome calls Origen an "immortal genius" in *Vir Ill* 54.8.

357. Origen does not mock the Jews in this way, but in his letter to Julius Africanus (ANF 4) on the authenticity of Daniel 13, he does say that he undertook the project of the *Hexapla* with the Jews in mind. He writes, "Nor do I say this because I shun the labor of investigating the Jewish Scriptures, and comparing them with ours, and noticing their various readings. This, if it be not arrogant to say it, I have already to a great extent done to the best of my ability, laboring hard to get at the meaning in all the editions and various readings; while I paid particular attention to the interpretation of the Seventy, lest I might to be found to accredit any forgery to the Churches that are under heaven, and give an occasion to those who seek such a starting-point for gratifying their desire to slander the common brethren, and to bring some accusation against those who shine forth in our community. And I make it my endeavor not to be ignorant of their various readings, lest in my controversies with the Jews I should quote to them what is not found in their copies, and that I may make some use of what is found there, even although it should not be in our Scriptures. For if we are so prepared for them in our discussions, they will not, as is their manner, scornfully laugh at Gentile believers for their ignorance of the true reading as they have them."

run through the generations of everyone so swiftly and accurately that you would think they are referring to their own name).

As for us who have either learned other literature, or at least who have believed in Christ late, or even if we have been delivered to the church as infants, let us follow the meaning of the Scripture rather than the words. If perchance we do not know it in this way, they consider themselves to be more learned in the references to names, in the calculation of years, and in the listing of grandsons, great-great-grandsons, grandfathers, great-grandfathers, great-great-great-grandfathers. I myself heard one of the Hebrews who pretended that he believed in Christ in Rome raise a question about the "genealogies" of our Lord Jesus Christ, which are written in Matthew and Luke, namely, that from Solomon to Joseph they do not agree with one another either in number or in the equivalence of the names. This man perverted the hearts of the simple as if he were announcing certain kinds of solutions, as it seemed to himself, from sanctuaries and by oracle, though he should have sought the justice, mercy, and love of God.[358] And after this, if perchance the occasion would have arisen, he should have discussed names and numbers. Perhaps we have said enough about the superciliousness of the Hebrews and more than was necessary. But the occasion was given to us from the discussion of "genealogies and contentious issues and quarrels that come from the law."

The dialecticians of whom Aristotle is the chief are accustomed to lay out nets of arguments and to conclude the rambling freedom of their rhetoric in the thorny thickets of syllogisms. Therefore, those who waste all their days and nights in it, as they either ask questions, give responses, state a proposition, accept, assume, confirm, and conclude, call certain ones "contentious" who, as it pleases, dispute not from reason but from a taste for quarrelling. If therefore they do this, those whose unique skill is "contention," what should the Christian do but flee from "contention" entirely? "Quarrels over the law" too should be completely repudiated and left to the folly of the Jews. For they are "useless and vain." They have merely the appearance of knowledge, but they do not benefit either those who speak or those who listen.

---

358. Cf. Mt 23.23.

For how does it help me to know how many years Methuselah lived,[359] at which year of his life Solomon obtained a wife, lest perchance Rehoboam should be believed to have been born when he was in his eleventh year? And there are many other things of this sort that either are difficult to discover, on account of the variations between the books and the errors that are embedded in them (while gradually incorrect readings are recorded based upon incorrect readings), or even if we discover the answers by great effort and study, we recognize that there will be no benefit. Frequently it occurs that we have "quarrels over the law," not on account of the desire for truth, but for the sake of boasting. Among those who listen, we want to be counted as learned; or at the least we pursue "disgraceful profit" from this sort of gossip. For what use are foaming lips and chatter like that of barking dogs when a simple and restrained answer either could satisfy you if it is true or, if false, be corrected by you gently and peacably?

3.10–11.   *Avoid a heretical man after one rebuke, knowing that his sort is ruined and is a transgressor, who is self-condemned.* The term "heresy" is recorded in the epistle to the Corinthians: "For it is necessary that there be heresies among you, that those who are approved may become manifest."[360] And to the Galatians it is listed among the works of the flesh: "Now the works of the flesh are manifest, what they are: fornication, uncleanness, excess, idolatry, sorcery, enmities, contentions, strife, wrath, quarrels, dissentions, "heresies," envy, drunkenness, carousing, and other similar things, which I declare to you in advance, just as I said before, that those who do these things will not possess the kingdom of God."[361] In these things, one must carefully observe that just as the other vices that are enumerated among the works of the flesh exclude us from the kingdom of God, so also "heresies"

---

359. The answer is 969; cf. Gn 5.27.

360. 1 Cor 11.19. On this passage, the excerpts from Origen's *Commentary on Titus* that are preserved in Pamphilus's *Apology for Origen* 33 show significant agreement with Jerome's exposition.

361. Gal 5.19–21.

take away the kingdom of God from us. And it does not matter *how*, only *that* someone is excluded from the kingdom.

Now what may be rather surprising is what seems to require a re-reading from the Acts of the Apostles, that our faith in Christ and in the Church's instruction already then was called a "heresy" by perverse men. The Jews say to the apostle Paul, "For we have received no letter from you about Judea,[362] nor have any of the brothers come and declared to us, nor has anyone spoken of you in respect to evil. But we seek to hear from you what you think, for this "heresy" is known to us, since everywhere it is spoken against."[363] And although in Miletus the term "heresy" is not mentioned by Paul, nevertheless its works are identified, when he says to the priests of the church, "I know that after my departure fierce wolves will come among you, not sparing the flock; and men from your very midst will arise speaking perverse things, to lead away disciples behind them."[364] These things would have been said in passing, when even elsewhere heresy was named. Now it appears that the term itself needs to be very fully displayed.

Heresy is the Greek word for choice, namely, because each one chooses for himself what seems better to him. The philosophers, too, the Stoics, Peripatetics, Academics, and Epicureans, are called heresies of this one or that one. It is superfluous to go into detail and to list Marcion, Valentinus, Apelles, Ebion, Montanus, and Manichaeus, together with their doctrines, since it is very easy for each one to find out for which errors these individuals are regarded. Would that Arius and Eunomius and the author of a new heresy were not so well known. Perhaps they would not have deceived so many! Therefore, "avoid a heretical man after one rebuke," or as is expressed better in the Greek, νουθεσίαν. Now νουθεσία signifies more admonition and teaching without a rebuke. In the Latin copies (which, however, father Athanasius also approved) it is read, "After a first and second rebuke," namely, because it may not be sufficient merely to correct him once, or to

---

362. A variant reads, "about you from Judea."
363. Acts 28.21–22.
364. Acts 20.29–30.

admonish one who is corrupted by some error, but even a second teaching would have to be administered to him, so that by the mouth of two and three witnesses every word may be established.[365]

But he gives the reasons why after the first and second rebuke he is to be avoided, when he says, "Because his sort are ruined and he sins, since he is self-condemned." For one who has been rebuked once and twice, when his error has been heard, does not want to be corrected; he thinks the one who corrects him is in error. And instead he prepares himself to fight and wrangle over words. He wants to win over the one by whom he is being taught. For this reason, however, he is said to be "self-condemned." For the fornicator, adulterer, murderer, and the other vices are expelled from the church by the priests.[366] But heretics pass judgment on themselves, by withdrawing from the church by their own choice. This withdrawal seems to be the condemnation of private conscience. I think that the difference between heresy and schism is that heresy contains perverse doctrine, schism separates from the church on account of episcopal dissension. To be sure this can be understood this way to some extent in the beginning. However that may be, no schism fails to concoct some heresy for itself, so that it may appear to have withdrawn from the church rightly.

3.12.   *When I send Artemas to you, or Tychicus, hasten to come to me in Nicopolis, for I have decided to spend the winter there.* We read in the beginning of this epistle, "For this reason I left you in Crete, that you may correct the things that were lacking and appoint priests throughout the cities, just as I directed you."[367] Thus, because the Cretans had recently believed, when Paul withdrew and passed on to other churches, they were not to be left as orphans[368] but were to have an apostolic man, who could correct the things that seemed to be missing. Since, therefore, after the foundation of other churches, Titus was necessary, who was to build upon the edifice,[369] he writes to him, that when he

---

365. Cf. Mt 18.16.
366. Cf. 1 Cor 5.11–13; 6.9–10.
367. Ti 1.5.
368. Cf. Jn 14.18.
369. Cf. 1 Cor 3.10.

had sent Artemas or Tychicus, evidently one of the two who had been with him, this man would fill his place. He himself was to go to Nicopolis and there, he testifies, he will spend the winter.

From this we may prove Paul's paternal affection for the Cretans. He considers Titus to be necessary to the ministry of the gospel; yet he does not want him to come to himself unless his successor, either Artemas or Tychicus, arrives in his place. Nicopolis itself was named after Augustus's victory, who had defeated Antony and Cleopatra there.

3.13. *Diligently send ahead Zenas, the teacher of law, and Apollos, so that nothing is lacking them.* This is the Apollos of whom he writes to the Corinthians, "Each of you says: I am of Paul, I am of Apollos, and I am of Cephas."[370] He was an Alexandrian man from the Jews, very eloquent and perfect in the law,[371] bishop of the Corinthians. One must conclude that on account of the dissensions that were in Corinth, he crossed over to the nearby island of Crete with Zenas, the teacher of law. When Paul's epistles had quelled the dissensions that had arisen in Corinth, he again returned to Corinth.

We cannot tell from another passage of Scripture who "Zenas the teacher of law" may have been, save only this: that he, being an apostolic man, had that task which Apollos was exercising, to build up the churches of Christ. And so Paul commanded Titus that since they were about to sail from Crete to Greece, he should not cause them to lack provisions, but have the things that are necessary as travel provisions.

3.14. *But let our own [people] learn to excel in good works in cases of urgent needs, so that they are not unfruitful.* Above he had said, "Diligently send ahead Zenas the teacher of law and Apollos, so that nothing may be lacking to them."[372] Well then, a secret reply could have arisen, that not so much Titus as any reader of the letter had said this. And for this reason any reader of the letter should be generous to Titus, as to those who do not have travel provisions. Paul answers this

---

370. 1 Cor 1.12.
371. Cf. Acts 18.24.
372. Ti 3.13.

question, and as if nothing should be opposed to him, he shatters this possible interpretation by saying, "Let our own people learn to excel in good works in cases of urgent needs, so that they are not unfruitful." He calls those who had believed in Christ "our own people"; those who, because they belonged to Christ, rightly deserved to be named Paul's and Titus's. You have authority among the disciples, he says; teach them not to be unfruitful, but to minister to the evangelists and apostolic men, who serve good works, and to minister not in just any causes, but in "cases of urgent needs." "For having food and clothing, with these we should be content."[373] And those who serve at the altar, let them live from the altar;[374] and those who have become sharers of our spiritual things ought to share their fleshly things with us.[375]

And lest perchance they should lightly show contempt either for the epistle of Paul or for the command of Titus, he calls "unfruitful" anyone who will not minister to the evangelists. And Solomon says in the Proverbs, "fruit for a man [is] alms."[376] And Paul himself calls love the first fruit of the Spirit.[377] Now love is proven especially in sharing and in service. He says, "so that they are not unfruitful." "For every tree that does not produce good fruit will be cut down and thrown into the fire."[378] Now I say this, he who sows sparingly will also reap sparingly.[379] To be unwilling to give to apostolic men and to Christ's evangelists in respect to "urgent needs" is to condemn oneself for sterility.

3.15.   *All who are with me greet you.* Either he has made use of his usual custom, in order to say that Titus is greeted by all those who were with him; or possibly, it is unique to Titus, because he was the kind of man who earned the love of all those who were with Paul. But it is Titus's great distinction to be greeted by everyone through Paul.

---

373. 1 Tm 6.8.
374. Cf. 1 Cor 9.13.
375. Cf. Rom 15.27.
376. Cf. Prv 3.9.
377. Cf. Gal 5.22.
378. Mt 3.10.
379. Cf. 2 Cor 9.6.

3.15. *Greet those who love us in the faith.* If everyone who loves, were loving "in the faith," and there were not others who loved without faith, Paul would never have added faith to love, saying, "Greet those who love us in the faith." For even mothers love their children, so that they are ready even to meet death for them, but they do not love "in the faith." And wives love their husbands with whom they very frequently die together, but that love is not of the "faith." Only the love of the saints loves "in the faith." To the extent that even if that one who is loved is an infidel, nevertheless a saint loves him "in the faith" in accordance with the following: "Let all your things be done in faith."[380] And elsewhere: "Love your enemies."[381] A saint loves his own enemies, and therefore he loves "in the faith," since he believes in him who promised that he will pay back a reward for the fulfillment of this command.

3.15. *The grace of our Lord [be] with all of you.* One should know that in the Greek copies it is written as follows: "Grace [be] with all of you"; thus neither "Lord" nor "our" features in the authentic books.

And so, he pleads for grace commonly for saints and believers, for Titus and the others who were with him. And just as Isaac the patriarch blessed his son Jacob,[382] and Jacob himself blessed the twelve patriarchs,[383] the apostles too, upon entering a house, said, "Peace be upon this house."[384] And if the house was worthy, their peace rested over it; but if it showed itself unworthy, it returned to those who had invoked it. So also now at the end of his epistle, the apostle invokes grace upon the believers, which with prayer was effective.[385] And it was under the believers' control if the one who was blessed wanted to offer himself to be of the sort as one giving the blessing.

---

380. Cf. 1 Cor 16.14.
381. Lk 6.35.
382. Cf. Gn 27.
383. Cf. Gn 49.
384. Mt 10.12.
385. Cf. Jas 5.16.

Commentary on

Philemon

COMMENTARY ON THE EPISTLE TO

PHILEMON. ONE BOOK BY S. EUSEBIUS

JEROME, PRIEST OF STRIDON

Preface

Those who are unwilling to receive among the epistles of Paul this one written to Philemon say that the apostle did not speak at all times or all things with Christ speaking in him.[1] For human weakness was not able to bear the Holy Spirit without interruption, and the needs of his frail

---

1. Harnack, *Der kirchengeschichtliche Ertrag,* pp. 141–42, conjectures that Jerome's discussion here is based upon (at least) two sources: Origen's *Commentary on Philemon,* where the canonicity of Philemon is accepted, and a commentary based upon Origen's, in which Philemon is rejected. While Origen had himself conceded that the apostle had not always spoken in the condition of divine inspiration, he nevertheless defended the authenticity of Philemon based upon its universal reception in the Church as an authentic letter of Paul. He had also defended the letter against the charges of containing mundane details. However, a commentary based on Origen, to which Jerome also had gained access, challenged the authenticity of Philemon using arguments that were based upon Origen's concession about Paul not always speaking under direct inspiration.

body were not always satisfied by the presence of the Lord, so as to arrange for his breakfast, taking in food, being hungry, being satisfied, digesting things ingested, and filling in what had been emptied out, to say nothing about other things. They reflect upon these things carefully and strictly, so that they assert that there was a time when Paul would not have dared to say, "Now I no longer live, but Christ lives in me";[2] and this, "Or do you seek proof of him who speaks in me, Christ?"[3] What sort of "proof of Christ" is it, they say, to hear, "When you come, bring the cloak that I left with Carpus in Troas";[4] and what he writes to the Galatians, "Would that those who are troubling you would be mutilated";[5] and in this very epistle, "But at the same time, prepare a lodging for me"[6]?

Now [they say that] this happened not only to the apostles but similarly to the prophets as well, which is why quite often it is reported to be written, "The word of the Lord came to Ezekiel,"[7] or to any other of the prophets. For after the prophecy was fulfilled, the man returned from being a prophet and became himself again, a common man. And with the exception of our Lord Jesus Christ, [they say that] the Holy Spirit remained in no one. And John the Baptist had received this sign, that upon whom he saw the Holy Spirit descending and remaining in him, he would recognize that he was the one.[8] From this he shows that the Holy Spirit descends on many, but uniquely the sign of the Savior is this, that He remains in him.

With these and other things of this sort, they maintain either that the epistle that is written to Philemon is not Paul's; or, if it is likewise Paul's, that it contains nothing capable of edifying us; and that it was rejected by very many of the ancients, since it is written merely out of the duty to commend someone, not for teaching.

---

2. Gal 2.20.
3. 2 Cor 13.3.
4. 2 Tm 4.13.
5. Gal 5.12.
6. Phlm 22.
7. Ezek 22.1.
8. Cf. Jn 1.33.

But on the other hand, those who defend it as possessing genuine authority say that it would never have been received in the whole world by all the churches unless it were believed to be the apostle Paul's;[9] and by this principle they should not even receive the second letter to Timothy and the letter to the Galatians, concerning that even they themselves have published examples of human weakness: "When you come bring with you the cloak that I left with Carpus in Troas,"[10] and, "Would that those who trouble you would be mutilated."[11] [They say further] that very many things are found even in the letter to the Romans and in those to the other churches, and especially in those to the Corinthians, that have been dictated quite remissly and almost in everyday speech. Among these things are the apostle's words, "But to the rest, I say, not the Lord."[12] Since those very letters contain things like this, either they should not be considered to be Paul's epistles, or if they are received as such, the one to Philemon should also be received by following the precedent that things that are similar ought to be received. [And they say that] they are plainly very far astray if they think that it is a sin to buy food,[13] prepare a lodging,[14] procure clothing,[15] if they assert that the Holy Spirit is banished if for a little we serve bodily needs. The apostle says, "Do not grieve the Holy Spirit in whom you were sealed for the day of redemption."[16] The prophet records what works grieve the Holy Spirit. After compiling a list of many vices and sins in order, at the end he adds, "By all these things you grieved me."[17] In any case would it be a sin to offer a cup of cold water,[18] to wash feet,[19] to

---

9. According to Harnack, *Der kirchengeschichtliche Ertrag*, p. 142, Origen is Jerome's referent here.

10. 2 Tm 4.13.

11. Gal 5.12.

12. 1 Cor 7.12.

13. Cf. Ti 3.13–14.

14. Cf. Phlm 22.

15. Cf. 2 Tm 4.13.

16. Eph 4.30.

17. Ezek 16.43.

18. Cf. Mt 10.42; 25.35.

19. Jn 13.14; 1 Tm 5.10.

sacrifice a calf,[20] to prepare breakfast,[21] when we know that some are adopted as sons of God on the basis of these things?[22]

It is not the time to respond to all these things, since we have not included everything that they are accustomed to propose. But if they do not think that the small things belong to those to whom belong also the great things, they ought to introduce to me, in accordance with Valentinus,[23] Marcion,[24] and Apelles,[25] one Creator of the ant, worms, gnats, and locusts, another of the heaven, earth, sea, and angels.[26] Or does it belong rather to the same power to affirm that the talent which you exercised in greater matters, you likewise exercised in lesser matters?

And since we have mentioned Marcion, let them be led by their authority Marcion, that the epistle to Philemon at least is Paul's. Though he either did not receive Paul's other epistles,[27] or he altered and blotted out certain things in them,[28] he did not dare to lay his hands on this one alone, since brevity defended that letter of his.[29] But it seems to me, when they convict this epistle of simplicity, they betray their own ignorance, failing to understand what power and wisdom lies hidden underneath each of the words. With the help of your prayers, and by the

---

20. Cf. Lk 15.23.

21. Cf. Jn 21.12.

22. Cf. Mt 5.45.

23. See p. 60, n. 76 above.

24. See p. 56, n. 47 above.

25. See p. 66, n. 111 above.

26. Harnack, *Der kirchengeschichtliche Ertrag*, p. 143, traces Jerome's formulation here both to Origen and to Tertullian, *Adversus Marcionem* 1.17. He adds, however, (p. 143, n. 1) that Marcion had not distinguished the Creator of locusts from the Creator of the heaven and earth.

27. Evidently Marcion did not receive 1 Tm, 2 Tm, and Ti. Cf. Tertullian, *Adversus Marcionem* 5.21.

28. Cf. *CRm* 10.43.2 where it is reported that Marcion interpolated and removed material from Paul's texts in Romans.

29. Jerome is following Tertullian here; cf. *Adversus Marcionem* 5.21 (ANF 4.473): "To this epistle alone did its brevity avail to protect it against the falsifying hands of Marcion."

supply of the Holy Spirit himself to us, we will endeavor to explain these things in their own passages. But if brevity is held in contempt, Obadiah, Nahum, Zephaniah, and the other of the twelve prophets should be held in contempt. In those books the things that are recorded are so wonderful and so dignified that one does not know whether you should admire the brevity of the words in them or the greatness of the thoughts. But if those who repudiate the letter to Philemon understood this, they never would have looked down upon its brevity, which in place of the entangled burdens of the law is written with evangelical decorum, while the "Lord makes his words abbreviated and consummated upon the earth."[30] But now the apostle's own words need to be set down, which begin as follows.

Here begins the book.

1–3. *Paul a prisoner of Christ Jesus and Timothy our brother, to Philemon, our beloved fellow-worker, and to Apphia our sister and Archippus our fellow soldier, and to the church which is in your house: Grace to you and peace from God our Father and the Lord Jesus Christ.* You decided that I dictate on Paul's epistles in a preposterous and perverse order. For when you repeatedly asked me to do this, O Paula and Eustochium, I obstinately refused to do it, and you compelled me at least to comment on the brief letter as for example in the number of its verses and thus the one that seemed to you to be the last one too in meaning and order. And so, I will attempt the subject of the beginning at the end. What someone else seeks immediately in the introduction to the apostle, namely, why did he receive the name of Paul from Saul? When did this happen, and who gave him his surname? I am compelled to do this now. Before today I have not even dared to make a grunt, as they say,[31] about him.

But one should not think, as is read by the more simple among the Latins, that he was previously called Saulus, and not Saul. For he was

---

30. Cf. Is 10.23; Rom 9.28.

31. According to Varro, "to make a μῦ" refers to saying the least thing. Cf. Jerome, Ep. 12 to Antony; Erasmus, *Adages,* I, viii 3.

from the tribe of Benjamin[32] in which this name was deemed quite fa-
miliar, since indeed that Saul, the king of Judea and persecutor of
David, was from the tribe of Benjamin. But it is not surprising that we
say Saulus, since Hebrew names are declined in imitation of Greek and
Latin case endings, as for example one says in our language and speech
Josephus for Joseph, Jacobus for Jacob, so too Saulus for Saul.

It is asked, therefore, why, or at whose command, he either lost his
old name or took up the new one.[33] That Abraham was named from
Abram was accomplished by God's command;[34] that Sarah's name
came from Sarai was equally God's command.[35] And to come to the
New Testament (*Instrumentum*), that Simon received the name Peter,[36]
and the sons of Zebedee were called *Bane reem,* that is, sons of thunder, was commanded by the voice of our Lord Jesus Christ.[37]

But no Scripture records why Paul was named from Saul. And so I
will be bold, but perhaps truly confirm my conjectures from the Acts of
the Apostles. There we read that the Holy Spirit said in Antioch, "Separate for me Barnabas and Saul for the work to which I have taken them.
Then they fasted and prayed, laid hands on them, and sent them off."[38]
When they had gone down to Seleucia of Syria, they sailed for Salamis
of Cyprus and reached it, which is now called Constantia. And they
had with them for ministry John[39] (on account of whom afterward a
quarrel was stirred up among the builders of the church).[40]

---

32. Cf. Phil 3.5; Rom 11.1.

33. The explanation of the origin of Paul's name seems to be taken from Origen, who discusses this in his *CRm,* Preface 9, in a passage that may have been inserted there from its original location in Origen's *Commentary on Philemon.* Cf.
Harnack, *Der kirchengeschichtliche Ertrag,* p. 143. Rufinus admits that he has added
this discussion from elsewhere (*CRm,* Preface of Origen 11). Interestingly, Origen
himself was not convinced of this explanation, which he reported as being from his
predecessors.

34. Cf. Gn 17.5.

35. Cf. Gn 17.15.

36. Cf. Mk 3.16.

37. Cf. Mk 3.17.

38. Cf. Acts 13.2–3.

39. Cf. Acts 13.5.

40. Cf. Acts 15.36–41.

And having traveled through the whole island, they came as far as Paphos and found a certain magician and false-prophet named Bar-Jesus with the proconsul Sergius Paulus, a prudent man.[41] He summoned Barnabas and Saul and desired to hear the word of God from them.[42] And so, when the magician put up resistance to this and turned Sergius away from the right faith,[43] "Saul," the Scripture says, "who was also Paul, filled with the Holy Spirit, looked at him and said, 'You son of the devil, enemy of all justice, full of all deceit and all lying, do you not leave off undermining the straight paths of the Lord? And now, behold, the hand of the Lord is upon you, and you will be blind, not seeing the sun for a time.' And immediately mist and darkness fell upon him, and he went about seeking someone to give him a hand. Then the proconsul believed, when he saw what had occurred, for he was astonished at the teaching of the Lord. And when Paul and those who were with him set sail from Paphos, they came to Perga in Pamphylia."[44]

Pay careful attention, because here he first received the name of Paul. For as Scipio[45] assumed the name of Africanus for himself when Africa was subjugated, and Metellus[46] brought back to his family the insignia of Creticus when the island of Crete was subjugated, and the Roman emperors even now are named after subjected nations, Adiabenicus,[47] Parthicus,[48] Sarmaticus,[49] so also Saulus, who was sent to

---

41. Cf. Acts 13.7.

42. Cf. Acts 13.7.

43. Cf. Acts 13.8.

44. Acts 13.9–13.

45. Scipio Africanus (236–183 BC), Roman general who as consul planned the successful invasion of Africa and defeated Hannibal at the battle of Zama, thus ending the Second Punic War.

46. Q. Metellus, Roman general, who subjugated Crete.

47. The title derives from Adiabena, Ἀδιαβηνή, a region in the northern part of ancient Assyria.

48. In other words, victor over the Parthians.

49. That is, victor over the Sarmatians.

preach to the nations, brought back from the initial spoils of the church, the proconsul Sergius Paulus, the trophy of his victory, and he raised a standard so that he was called Paulus from Saulus.[50]

But if a translation of his name is sought, Paul in Hebrew expresses "wonderful." In fact, it is wonderful that after being Saul—which is translated "asked for," because he had been asked by the devil to harass the church—from being a persecutor became a vessel of election.[51] Perhaps I have discussed more than was fitting here, but it was necessary.

Now in no epistle does he use the surname that follows, "prisoner of Jesus Christ," although within the corpus of his letters, namely to the Ephesians, Philippians, and Colossians, he testifies that he is in chains for the confession.[52] But to me it seems to be a matter of greater pride that he calls himself a "prisoner" of Jesus Christ than apostle. For the apostles boasted that they were worthy to suffer mistreatment for the name of Jesus Christ.[53] But the authority of chains was necessary. Being about to ask for Onesimus, such a person was obliged to ask who could procure what he was requesting. Happy no doubt is he who boasts not in wisdom, not in riches, not in eloquence and secular power, but in the sufferings of Christ.[54] With such words he also concludes the epistle to the Galatians, saying, "Finally, let no one trouble me; for I carry on my body the stigmata of the Lord Jesus Christ."[55]

Now not everyone who is imprisoned is a "prisoner of Christ," but whoever is imprisoned for the name of Christ and for his confession, that one truly is called a "prisoner of Jesus Christ," so that that blood alone when shed makes a martyr, blood that is poured out for the name of Christ. Therefore, while chained up in prison in Rome, he writes to

---

50. Origen concludes his discussion of this conjectural explanation for Paul's name change: "Not even we think that this explanation is to be discarded entirely. However, because no such custom is detected in the Holy Scriptures, let us rather seek a solution in those things which are our patterns"; *CRm*, Preface 9–10.

51. Cf. Acts 9.15.

52. Cf. Eph 3.1; 6.20; Phil 1.7,14; Col 4.3.

53. Cf. Acts 5.41.

54. Cf. Col 1.24; 2 Cor 11.30; Gal 6.14.

55. Gal 6.17.

Philemon at that time, it seems to me, when the epistles to Philippians, Colossians, and Ephesians were dictated. The reason I think this is first of all because he writes to the Philippians with Timothy alone, which he also does in this epistle.[56] Second, because he says that his chains have become manifest for the sake of Christ among the whole praetorian.[57] Now he indicates at the end of that epistle where the praetorian is: "All the saints greet you, but especially those who are of Caesar's house."[58] When sent to prison by Caesar, he became better known to his family and made the house of the persecutor into a church of Christ. Moreover, he says, "But some proclaim Christ from contention, not sincerely, thinking that they stir up affliction by my chains."[59] Further, the introduction of the letter to the Colossians is similar: "Paul an apostle of Jesus Christ through the will of God, and Timothy [our] brother."[60] And in what follows he says, "Whose minister I, Paul, have become, who now rejoice in the sufferings for you; and I fill up what is lacking of the sufferings of Christ in my flesh for the sake of his body, which is the church."[61] And in the conclusion: "I Paul write this greeting with my own hand. Remember my chains."[62] [I have cited] this that we may know that these letters too were dictated from prison while in chains.

Now the letter to the Colossians contains the following unique characteristic, that the same Onesimus, who is now being commended to Philemon, was likewise the bearer of the same words. After all, he says, "Tychicus will make known to you about all my affairs; he is a beloved brother and faithful minister and fellow servant in the Lord whom I have sent to you for this very purpose, that he may find out about your affairs and may console your hearts, together with Onesimus, the faithful and beloved brother, who is one of yourselves."[63]

---

56. Cf. Phil 1.1; Phlm 1.1.
57. Cf. Phil 1.13.
58. Phil 4.22.
59. Phil 1.17.
60. Col 1.1.
61. Col 1.23–24.
62. Col 4.18.
63. Col 4.7–8.

Now if Philemon, to whom this epistle is written, is Onesimus's master, or rather, has begun to be his brother in the Lord,[64] and if it is reported in the letter to the Colossians that Onesimus is one of them, reason and order itself leads us to deduce that Philemon too is a Colossian; and at the same time when Onesimus carried a general letter to the whole church, he took along a private letter of recommendation of himself to his master.

There is another indication of this in that in this same letter Archippus is also named, to whom here it is written [that he is] with Philemon. He says, "Tell Archippus, 'See that you fulfill the ministry that you have received in the Lord.'"[65] What is the ministry that Archippus received from the Lord? We read in the letter to Philemon: "And to Archippus our fellow soldier, and to the church that is in your house."[66] Therefore, I think that he was either the bishop of the Colossian church, whom he reminds to preside zealously and diligently, as a preacher of the gospel; or, if he is not that, to me the following suffices [to say] for the present: that Philemon, Archippus, and Onesimus himself who carried the letters were Colossians, and four letters (as we said earlier) were written at the same time.

But the reason [I think] Ephesians [was written at this time] is this: he says there as well that he was imprisoned for the sake of Christ,[67] and the same things that he had commanded to the Colossians,[68] he orders at the end of this letter too, that wives be subjected to their husbands, and husbands should love their wives, that children obey their parents, that parents not provoke their children to anger, that slaves obey their fleshly masters, that masters leave aside their threats and offer things that are just to the slaves.[69] Finally, he ends his epistle with this conclusion: "What I am doing Tychicus will make known to you,

---

64. Phlm 16.
65. Col 4.17.
66. Phlm 2.
67. Cf. Eph 3.1.
68. Cf. Col 3.18–22.
69. Cf. Eph 5.22, 28; 6.1–5.

the beloved brother and faithful minister in the Lord, whom I sent to you for this purpose, that you may find out about my affairs, and he may console your hearts."[70] Now Tychicus is the one who is sent with Onesimus to the Colossians, and he had Onesimus as a companion at that time when Onesimus carried the letter to Philemon.

"And Timothy [our] brother." In other letters Sosthenes,[71] Silvanus,[72] and sometimes Timothy, are adopted.[73] In four letters Timothy alone [is mentioned], either because they were dictated at the same time as the rest, or because Timothy was present. Now I think this was done for two reasons, so that the epistle that was not written by one man would have greater authority, and because there was no jealousy among the apostles. Suppose for instance that while Paul was dictating something, the Spirit suggested something to another. Without any regret Paul would have added it to the letter what he was dictating. This is accordant with what he himself commanded the Corinthians, that if when one person is prophesying, something is revealed to someone else, the one who was prophesying first should be silent.[74] Thus he too was himself fulfilling his own command in deed, and on account of the few things that he had added at the other's suggestion, he signed the epistle as his own as well as of the other.

He says, "to the beloved Philemon." The Greek does not have ἠγαπημένῳ, which means "beloved," but ἀγαπητῷ, that is, "lovable." Now the difference between "beloved" and "lovable" is that even one who does not deserve love can be called "beloved." But only he who is loved deservedly is "lovable." After all, we are commanded to love even our enemies,[75] who are "beloved," not "lovable." For we love them not because they deserve to be loved, but because it is commanded that they are not be held in hatred. Also, the words that form the heading

---

70. Col 4.7–8.
71. Cf. 1 Cor 1.1.
72. Cf. 1 Thes 1.1; 2 Thes 1.1.
73. Cf. 2 Cor 1.1; Col 1.1.
74. Cf. 1 Cor 14.30.
75. Cf. Mt 5.44.

and title of the forty-fourth Psalm, "for the beloved," are expressed better in Greek as "for the lovable." This passage is very manifestly understood to refer to Christ. For although the Jews think that Solomon was called Jedidiah,[76] that is, "loved of God"[77]—which name was conferred upon him by God on account of his wisdom[78]—yet who can be called "loved of God" more than he of whom the Father says in the Gospel, "This is my beloved Son in whom I am well pleased. Listen to him."[79]

After all, even in Isaiah it is written as follows: "I will sing a song to my beloved of my lovable vineyard. The vineyard has become my beloved's."[80] And the circumcision, thinking that this must be understood concerning the Judaic people, dashed against the rock of offense and the stone of stumbling.[81] They did not consider that the vine which was transferred from Egypt[82] is the house of Israel and that Christ is here called either lovable or beloved, provided that he himself deserves to be loved by the saints and the saints love him, by offering love to him rather than by demanding any rewards of love. Therefore Paul and Timothy write "to the beloved coworker Philemon," who is called "beloved" because he is involved in the same work of Christ.

Also "to Apphia the sister," one who does not have anything false in herself[83] and of feigned sisterhood; and "to Archippus the fellow soldier," whom I think had emerged with Paul and Timothy as victor in the combat against the adversaries on behalf of the name of Christ. And the reason he is now called "fellow soldier" is because he prevailed in the same struggle and war.

It is also written "to the church which is in his house." But this is ambiguous, whether it is "to the church which is in *Archippus's* house" or "to the *one* which is in *Philemon's* house." But it seems to me that it

---

76. Cf. 2 Sm 12.25.
77. Cf. 2 Sm 12.24.
78. Cf. 1 Kgs 3.9–10.
79. Lk 9.36.
80. Is 5.1.
81. Cf. Is 28.16; Rom 9.32–33.
82. Cf. Ezek 17.8.
83. Cf. Jn 1.47.

does not refer to the person of Archippus but to that of Philemon, to whom the epistle itself is reckoned. For although Paul and Timothy are both writing to Philemon, Apphia, Archippus, and the church, yet in what follows it is attested that Paul is writing only to Philemon. One man converses with one man. "I always thank my God when I remember *you*."[84] Now you will be able to find this manner of writing in several of his epistles, that when several are recorded in the preface and [the letter is addressed] to several, afterward, throughout the whole body of the epistle, one disputant is introduced. This is what the apostle says when writing to the Galatians, that in the faith of Christ it makes no difference whether someone is a Gentile or Jew, man or woman, slave or free.[85] Likewise this becomes clear in this passage. For between the two apostolic men, between the coworker of Paul and his fellow soldier, the name of Apphia is inserted in between, so that such a woman,[86] who is propped up by an attendant on both sides,[87] does not seem to be ranked by her sex, but by her merit.

Now as for what he says, "Grace to you and peace from God our Father and the Lord Jesus Christ," this is still being written by two men to several, and in nearly all the epistles the introduction is the same. Thus grace and peace are invoked upon them from God the Father and from Christ the Lord. From this it is shown that the nature of the Son and the Father is one, since the Son can bestow what the Father can, and it is said that what the Father can bestow is what the Son can.[88] Now it is grace by which we are saved with no merit or work.[89] Peace is that by which we are reconciled to God through Christ, as for example in this passage: "We beseech you on Christ's behalf, be reconciled to God."[90] Then follows:

---

84. Phlm 4. The pronoun *tui* is singular, which is Jerome's point.
85. Cf. Gal 3.28.
86. Reading the variant, *talis*.
87. Cf. Ex 17.12.
88. The ongoing validity of Jerome's Christological argument here has essentially been confirmed in the recent study by G. Fee, *Pauline Christology: An Exegetical-Theological Study* (Peabody, Mass.: Hendrickson, 2007), pp. 52–55.
89. Cf. Eph 2.8–9.
90. 2 Cor 5.20.

4–6.   *I thank my God always when I remember you in my prayers, because I hear of your love and of the faith that you have in the Lord Jesus and in all his saints, that the sharing of your faith may become evident in the knowledge of every good that is in us in Christ.* He says these things now to Philemon and the others, not as Paul and Timothy, but as Paul alone to Philemon alone, saying, "I give thanks when I remember you[91] in my prayers." In fact the statement is ambiguous, whether he thanks his God always, or remembers him in his prayers always. And both can be understood. For he who commands others to give thanks to God in all things[92] can be confined by no difficulties that would result in his not always returning thanks to God. But if Paul were always praying for the saints and for each of those who are better (but Philemon is also a saint, who has such great faith and love in himself that he was known not only by hearsay about him but also by deed), then it is credible that Paul always prayed for Philemon, namely, that the faith and love that he had in Christ and in all his saints would be preserved by the mercy of Christ by means of the "sharing of his faith" and the working of his "knowledge in every good thing." And indeed the interpretation of the "love that he had in Christ Jesus and in all his saints" is not difficult. It is that love with which we are commanded, after God, to love our neighbors.[93]

Now the following question is asked: how can someone have the same faith in Christ Jesus and in his saints? For ἀπὸ κοινοῦ [by commonality][94] he repeats the "love that you have for the Lord Jesus" and for all his saints, and the "faith that you have in the Lord Jesus and in all his saints." To explain this passage, let us take an example from Exodus: "The people believed God and his servant Moses."[95] One and the same belief is related in Moses and in God, so that the people who believed in the Lord are said equally to have believed in the servant. But this applies not only to Moses but to all his saints, so that whoever

---

91. The pronoun is singular.
92. Cf. Eph 5.20; 1 Thes 5.18.
93. Cf. Mt 22.37–38.
94. Cf. Jerome, *Commentary on Matthew* 5.22.
95. Ex 14.31.

has believed in God is not able to receive faith in him in any other manner than if he believes also in his saints. For love and faith in God are not perfect, when they are weakened by ill will and unbelief in his servants.

Now what I am saying is the following: Someone believes in the Creator God.[96] He is not able to believe unless he first believes that the things that are written about his saints are true: that Adam was formed by God;[97] that Eve was fashioned from his rib and side;[98] that Enoch was translated;[99] that Noah alone was saved from the shipwrecked world;[100] that Abraham, when first commanded to depart from his land and kinsmen,[101] left to his descendants circumcision, which he had received as a sign of future offspring;[102] that Isaac should be offered as a victim, and in his place a ram was sacrificed;[103] and having been crowned with thorny briars, he sketched out the passion of the Lord; that Moses and Aaron afflicted Egypt with ten plagues;[104] that at the prayers of Jesus[105] son of Nun, the sun stood over Gibeon and the moon over the valley of Aijalon.[106]

It would take too long to run through all the deeds of the Judges, the whole story of Samson, to trace the mystery of the true sun (for this is what his name means). I will come to the books of Kingdoms when at the time of the harvest, as Samuel prayed, rains [fell] from heaven and the rivers suddenly overflowed;[107] and David was anointed king;[108] and Nathan and Gad prophesied;[109] when Elijah was taken away in a

---

96. Cf. Gn 1.1. See Pamphilus, *Apology for Origen* 125, FOTC 120, pp. 96–98.
97. Cf. Gn 2.7; Wis 10.1.
98. Cf. Gn 2.21–22.
99. Cf. Gn 5.24.
100. Cf. Gn 6–8.
101. Cf. Gn 12.1.
102. Cf. Gn 17.
103. Cf. Gn 22.
104. Cf. Ex 7–11.
105. Heb. Joshua.
106. Cf. Jos 10.12–14.
107. 1 Sm 12.17–18.
108. Cf. 2 Sm 5.3.
109. Cf. 2 Sm 7; 24.11–14.

fiery chariot;[110] and Elisha, having died, raised the dead by the Spirit that had been doubled.[111] Unless someone believes all these things, and the other things that are written about the saints, he will not be able to believe in the God of the saints, nor be led to faith in the Old Testament, unless he approves whatsoever history narrates about the patriarchs and prophets and other distinguished men. Thus does he go from the faith of the law to the faith of the Gospel,[112] and the justice of God is revealed in him from faith to faith,[113] just as it is written: "But the just lives from faith."[114]

In another passage it is commanded, "Be holy, for I am holy, the Lord your God."[115] The same holiness is owed to the slaves and the Lord, for the one who sanctifies and those sanctified are all from one.[116] Let us not think that the proclamation about Philemon is trivial, if he has the same faith in the saints as also in God. He who believes that God is holy assuredly is not in error. But if someone believes that a man is holy who is not holy, and joins him to the fellowship of God, he outrages Christ, of whose body we all are members.

It says, "He who calls the just unjust, and the unjust just, both [are] abominable before God."[117] Likewise, he who says that the holy is not holy, and again who claims that the unholy is holy, is abominable before God. According to the apostle, all of us believers are made the body of Christ.[118] As for the one who goes astray in the body of Christ and slips, claiming either that his member is holy when it is not, or that it is not holy when it is holy, see with what sort of crime he becomes guilty. Isaiah says, "Woe [to those] who call sweet bitter and bitter

---

110. 2 Kgs 2.11.
111. Cf. 2 Kgs 9.9; 13.21.
112. Cf. *CRm* 1.15.
113. Cf. Rom 1.17.
114. Hab 2.4; cf. Rom 1.17.
115. Lv 19.2.
116. Cf. Heb 2.11.
117. Cf. Prv 17.15.
118. Cf. 1 Cor 12.13, 27; Eph 5.30.

sweet, putting darkness for light and light for darkness."[119] Moral purity is sweet, I think; the opposite of moral purity is bitter. Likewise light can be understood as moral purity, darkness as the opposite of moral purity.

Which of us, as a shrewd money changer, do you think will test the coins and not be in error in the discrimination of the saints? Whoever has an equal love for God and his saints, and faith; he should have no disparity in the sharing of his faith. Thus, just as he believes and loves, so he will complete his love and faith by his works. This is why he says, "Let it become evident in knowledge of every good"—or, as it reads better in Greek, "efficacious," for ἐνηργής can be properly translated "efficacious" or "operative"[120]—so that we do not merely "believe" that faith can suffice for us, and the love for God and for his saints; but let us complete what we believe by works. Now it can happen that someone has faith and consummates it by works, but it is a plain and bare faith; it does not have the recognition or knowledge of him in accordance with the following words of the apostle: "I confess they have a zeal for God, but not according to knowledge."[121] Today too there are very many simple people who do works of justice and do not have knowledge of those things which they themselves are achieving. This is why he added, "so that the sharing of your faith may become operative in the knowledge of every good thing."

With what great strides and advances does the apostolic word strive toward deeper things! Someone has love and faith in God and in his saints; but perhaps he may not share it impartially with everyone. Perhaps he shares it with everyone, but he does not fulfill it in works. Someone may fulfill his will even in works, but he is not able to have

---

119. Is 5.20.

120. Jerome is referring to the word rendered "evident" in the Latin. J. B. Lightfoot, *Saint Paul's Epistles to Colossians and to Philemon: A Revised Text with Introductions, Notes, and Dissertations,* 7th ed. (London: Macmillan, 1884), p. 335, notes that the Latin translators must have read ἐναργής rather than ἐνεργής, since they render the word *evidens* or *manifesta*. Cf. Origen, *Contra Celsum* 1.25; 2.52; 4.89.

121. Rom 10.2.

perfect acquaintance with his own actions. There may be such a one too who has both works and knowledge, but does not have it "of every good thing"; for in carrying out many things justly, gently, and zealously, he is ill matched to some extent to his own virtues. Or is Philemon not like this? For he has a sharing in operative faith and love "in the knowledge of every good thing." When this sharing is directed toward the apostles, we should not think that it is perfect merely on that account, if it is directed toward them; but that it is entire in this, because he is Christ's. Thus any good that is both praised in Philemon and taken from the example of the apostles is a good precisely because it is derived from the font of Christ.

7.   *For we have great joy and consolation in your love, [my] brother, because the hearts of the saints have been refreshed through you.* He is emphasizing and showing more fully why he said, "I thank my God always when I remember you in my prayers."[122] For indeed it was fitting to give thanks for the love of Philemon, who had refreshed the interior affection of the heart and the deep recesses of the souls of the saints by his receiving [them]. And this is a characteristic of an apostle, that when he wants to point to the full love of mind he always speaks of the "heart." This is why when he is "rejoicing with those who rejoice"[123] and believes that he was refreshed with those who had been refreshed, he has no transitory and light "joy," which can happen by chance, but a "great" and surpassing kind, like the love that was in Philemon. The consolation that descended upon Philemon's love increased this joy. His love had been filled by the Father of mercies and the God of all consolation.[124]

8–9.   *Accordingly, having much confidence in Christ to command you to do what is profitable on account of love, I prefer to appeal, since you are such a person, as Paul, an old man, but now also a prisoner of Jesus*

122. Phlm 4.
123. Cf. Rom 12.15.
124. Cf. 2 Cor 1.3.

Christ. He first spoke many things in praise of Philemon, since the matter for which Philemon will be asked is such that it is useful both to the one discharging it and to the one who is asking. Paul could have commanded rather than "appealed." And this came from that confidence that he who had done such great works for the sake of Christ assuredly was not able to be unlike himself in other things. But he wants to "ask" rather than command, setting forth the great authority of one who is "asking." By this authority the apostle "pleads," both as "an old man" and as "a prisoner of Jesus Christ." But the whole of what he asks for is this: Onesimus, Philemon's slave, had capped off his secret flight by stealing some of the household possessions. Traveling to Italy to prevent his being able to be easily apprehended from the neighboring vicinity, he had squandered his master's money through luxurious living.

Lest anyone think that we have invented this explanation rashly and as it pleases us, let him learn from what follows. For Paul would never have said, "If he has harmed you at all or owes you anything, charge it to me. I Paul have written with my hand, I will repay."[125] He would not have become guarantor of the wealth that had been taken unless what had been taken had been squandered. This man, therefore, when Paul was imprisoned in Rome for the sake of confessing Christ, believed in Christ, and having been baptized by him, he washed away the stains of his former life by a worthy repentance, so much so that the apostle himself became a witness of his conversion, the apostle who had once rebuked Peter who was not going on the right foot in the truth of the gospel.[126]

As far as it pertains to the sin, therefore, and to the crime that had wounded the man, he does not deserve pardon; but as far as pertains to the apostle's testimony, he who knows that he has been fully converted is pressed by a great burden, because from being a runaway slave and plunderer he is asked to become the apostle's ministry partner. Now what other ministry did the apostle have but the gospel of Christ Jesus?

---

125. Phlm 18.
126. Cf. Gal 2.14.

He was to be pardoned no longer as if by a master, but as if by a fellow slave and a fellow evangelist. For he was likewise a slave and minister of Christ.

10–13.   I appeal to you concerning my son, Onesimus, whom I have begotten in my chains, who formerly was useless to you; but now he is useful to you and to me, whom I have sent back to you. But you, receive him, that is, my heart, whom I would have wanted to keep with me, in order that he might minister to me on your behalf in the chains of the gospel. Wanting to procure what he is asking for, he claims that he is "pleading," no longer on behalf of Philemon's slave, but for his own son, that "son" whom he "begot in the chains of the gospel." The chains refer to the things that Paul endured for the gospel of Christ. Though previously he was merely useless to his master (for a thieving and runaway slave has harmed no one else but his own master), now, on the other hand, in compensation for his usefulness, whereby he is useful to the master himself and to Paul, and to others through Paul, he deserves love rather than the ill will he had previously merited. This is why he says, "who formerly was useless to you." "To you" alone, he says, not to others; "but now he is useful both to you and to me."

He was useful to his master because he could serve Paul on behalf of his master; but he was useful to Paul because, when he was detained in prison and in chains, he could minister to him in the gospel. But at the same time one must stand in awe of the apostle's greatness of soul and of his mind that is on fire for Christ. He is being held in prison, he is bound by chains, he is in physical squalor, separated from dear ones, plunged into prison darkness; and he does not feel the harm, he is not tortured by grief. He knows nothing else but to think of the gospel of Christ. He knew that the slave, the runaway, the onetime plunderer was converted to faith in Christ. It is a matter of great effort for a man like that to persevere in what he began. Therefore, he emphasizes that he is his son, the son of his chains, and minister of the gospel established in chains. And he repeats that this Philemon, who was merely prudently and diplomatically praised in the prefatory remarks, should not dare to say no. Otherwise he would seem unworthy of the words of praise.

Now let us consider what he says, "But you, receive him, that is, my heart (*viscera*)." This refers to what I said a little earlier, that *viscera* signifies the internal affection of the heart and the full will of the soul, since the entirety of whatever is in us is received from the one who is asked.[127] Now elsewhere all children are the heart of their parents.[128]

14.   *But I did not want to do anything without consulting you in order that your good might not be by compulsion* (ex necessitate) *as it were, but of your own free will* (voluntarium). The present passage is able to solve a question asked by many and very frequently discussed: why did God, when he made man, not create him good and upright? For if God is good of his own free will and not by compulsion, when he made man he ought to have made him according to his own image and likeness, that is, that he himself be good "of his own free will" and not "by compulsion." Now those who claim that he ought to have been made this way, as incapable of receiving evil, say this: he who is good of necessity is obliged to become such and it is not by free will (*voluntate*). But if he who perfected the good not by free will but by necessity had been made that way, he would not be like God, who is good because he wills it, not because he is forced. From this it is plain that they are demanding among themselves the opposite situation. For from the fact that they say man ought to have been made like God, they are demanding that he should have been made with free choice, just as God himself is. But in view of the fact that they add that he ought to have been made in such a way that he was incapable of receiving evil, when they introduce to him compulsion to the good, they think that man was not made like God.

And so, even the apostle Paul was able to detain Onesimus with himself for ministry without the free consent (*voluntate*) of Philemon. But if he had done this without the free consent of Philemon, it would have been a "good" to be sure, but not a "freely willed" (*voluntarium*) [one]. But what was not "freely willed" was exposed in another respect

---

127. Cf. Mt 7.7.
128. *Unde?* Cf. Sir 30.7; Wis 10.5.

as not being "good." For nothing can be called "good" except what is voluntary (*ultroneum*).[129] The reason the apostle's prudence needs to be considered is because he sends back a runaway slave to the master in order to benefit his own master; one who was not able to benefit, if he was held back from his absent master. The question posed higher up, therefore, is resolved as follows: God could have made man good without free will (*voluntate*). Moreover, if he had done this, "good" would not have been "freely willed" but "of necessity." But what is good by necessity is not good, and is exposed as evil in another respect. Therefore, by leaving us to personal choice, he made [us] rather in his own image and likeness.[130] But to be like God is good absolutely.

15–16.   *For perhaps this is why he departed for an hour, that you might have him back eternally, no longer as a slave but more than a slave, as a beloved brother, especially to me, but how much more to you, both in the flesh and in the Lord.* Sometimes an evil becomes the occasion of good things, and God turns the depraved plans of men to uprightness. What I mean will become clearer by an example. Joseph's own brothers were incited by the goads of jealousy to sell him to the Ishmaelites for twenty pieces of gold.[131] This was the commencement of all good things both for his father, his brothers, and for all of Egypt.[132] After all, he himself afterward says to his brothers, "You gave consideration concerning me in terms of evils, but God gave consideration concerning me in respect to good things."[133]

---

129. Or "of one's own accord."

130. The argument resembles that of Tertullian, *Adversus Marcionem* 2.5–8; 4.41, that the endowment with freedom of will is the meaning of man's being made in the image of God. It also corresponds to a major emphasis in Origen's theology.

131. Cf. Gn 37.11, 25–28. "Gold" is the Septuagint reading of Gn 37.28. In *Commentary on Matthew* 26.15, Jerome rejects this reading and says that "Joseph was sold not for twenty gold pieces, as many think, in accordance with the Septuagint, but, according to the Hebrew truth, for twenty silver pieces."

132. Cf. Gn 45.4–8; 50.20.

133. Gn 50.20.

Commentary on Philemon 373

We can understand something similar in respect to Onesimus, that his initial evils became the occasion of a good. For if he had not fled his master, he never would have come to Rome where Paul was locked up in prison. If he had not seen Paul in chains, he would not have received faith in Christ. If he had not had faith in Christ, he never would have become Paul's son and have been sent for the work of the gospel. Therefore, gradually and by his own stages, by a conversion of the thought, the reason Onesimus became a minister of the gospel is because he fled from his master.

He nicely adds "perhaps" to tone down his thought. For the judgments of God are hidden, and it is excessively bold to pronounce what is doubtful as something certain. He says "perhaps this is why he departed" cautiously, hesitantly, with trepidation, and not with a standpoint that is completely fixed, lest, if he had not set down "perhaps," all slaves would need to run away in order to become apostolic men.

Now as for what he has added, "for an hour," we ought to understand "hour" for time. For in comparison with eternity, all time is brief. "That you might have him back eternally." There is no eternal master of one's own slave; for his authority and the condition of both is limited by death. But Onesimus, who by faith in Christ became eternal to eternal Philemon (since he himself had believed in Christ), having received the Spirit of freedom,[134] he began to be no longer a slave, but a brother from being a slave, a beloved brother, an eternal brother, to the eternal apostle himself and to his Lord, to whom, just as previously the condition of the flesh was uniting Onesimus, so afterward the [the condition] of the spirit unites them.[135]

And indeed, at that time when he was subjected to him in the flesh, he had not been united with him in the Lord; but now he is united with him both in the flesh and in the Lord. From which we understand that a slave who believes in Christ is bound by law to his master in two respects: he is joined to him "for a time" by the necessity of the flesh, and he is united "eternally" by the Spirit.

---

134. Cf. 2 Cor 3.17.
135. Cf. 1 Cor 6.17.

17.   *So if you consider me a partner, receive him as you would receive me.* Philemon desired to regard Paul as a "partner," and in Christ; he assuredly wanted to make the kind of progress that he would become like Paul and would share with him in his chains. Therefore let us consider how much Onesimus is being praised here, how much progress he is said to have made, since he is to be received just as the apostle; and thus his master ought to long for his companionship just as if it were Paul's. Briefly what he is saying is this: If you want to regard me as a partner, regard Onesimus this way too, whom I hold to be a partner and my son and my heart. If you do not receive him and are unwilling to regard like this, you yourself understand that you cannot have me.

18.   *But if he has wronged you at all, or owes you anything, charge that to me.* He is an imitator of his Lord and has Christ speaking in him. To the best of his ability, he is obligated to do what Christ does. For if he carried our infirmities[136] and felt pain from our welt,[137] justly does the apostle lay himself down for Onesimus and stand surety for what that man owed. But, as we said above, this is the whole point, that what was taken by theft and wasted by excess could not be discharged; for Philemon was paying out at a great price, so long as in place of the runaway slave and the lost money, he would receive a beloved brother, and an eternal brother, and by means of him he should make the apostle a debtor to himself.

19.   *I, Paul, have written this with my own hand. I will repay it—to say nothing of your owing me even your own self.* What he is saying is this: What Onesimus seized by theft, I promise that I will repay it. Of this promise this epistle and this hand is personal witness, which I have dictated not in my customary manner, but I have written it myself with my own hand. Therefore, believe me when I make promises on Onesimus's behalf. But I say this as though speaking to an outsider. However

---

136. Cf. Is 53.4.
137. Cf. Is 53.5.

that may be, if I return to my rights, in view of the words of Christ, whom I preached to you, and in view of your becoming a Christian, you owe your own self to me. But if you are mine, all that is yours is mine; if, however, all that is yours is mine, Onesimus, too, who is yours is mine. Therefore, I could have used him as my own, but I leave it to your free will (*voluntate*), so that you may have a reward for forgiving.

20.   *So, brother, I would enjoy you in the Lord. Refresh my heart in Christ.* The Latin wording does not exhibit the unique character of the Greek. For what he says, ναὶ, ἀδελφέ, is a kind of adverb of one who is flattering. But we translators are expressing something or other in a rather watered down and diluted way by, "So, brother"; this is rather different from what is written. For just as that Hebrew word *anna,* for which the seventy translators frequently rendered ὦ δή, in our language means the affection of one pleading. This is why Symmachus sometimes translated *anna* as δέομαι, that is, "I entreat." Thus we [Latins] too suffer the same violence in respect to the Greek language that the Greeks endure in respect to the Hebrew.

But his words, "I would enjoy you in the Lord," is understood much differently than is thought. The apostle does not "enjoy" [anyone] but one who has within himself many harmonious virtues and all that is said to be Christ's for a variety of reasons, namely, wisdom, justice, continence, gentleness, moderation, chastity.[138] He pleads for these virtues for Philemon, so that when he abounds with them, Paul himself may be filled with deep enjoyment of him. And lest you think that it is called enjoyment whereby we ourselves often are delighted by people's presence among ourselves, he has added, "in the Lord." Thus from the fact that the name of the Lord has been subjoined, it should be understood that there is also another kind of enjoyment in which someone fully enjoys [something] apart from the Lord.

"Refresh my heart in Christ." Just as he himself wants to "enjoy" Philemon "in the Lord," so he wants his own heart, Onesimus, whom

---

138. Cf. *CRm* 1.1.3.

even above he identified by means of the same term,[139] to be "refreshed" through Philemon. The words are ambiguous, whether Onesimus is Paul's heart in Christ, or Paul's heart, Onesimus, is to be refreshed through Philemon in Christ. If you want to understand the former, Paul's heart in Christ will rightly be called Onesimus, whom he begot in Christ in his chains.[140] If [you prefer] the latter, Onesimus is to be refreshed in Christ by Philemon while he is instructed in Christ by his words.

21.   *Confident from your obedience, I have written to you, knowing that you will do even more than I say.* One who presumes the request he is about to make judges in advance, as it were, by that very presumption, so as not to allow him to deny the request. Further, if the one who is requesting more than he has asked for knows that what has been requested will be [granted], therefore he is asking for less, so that the request may be of one's free will (*voluntariam*) and may receive a greater wage as its payment. If, however, Philemon does this at the command of a man, how much more will he do it for the sake of the love of God? This is also why he is deservedly praised by the apostle's voice, because he attends first to his commands in his deeds and is able to say, "May the free-will offerings (*voluntaria*) of my mouth please you, O Lord."[141] By doing more than has been commanded, he would surpass those who have done merely what has been commanded and are ordered to say, "We are useless servants, because we did what we were obligated to do."[142] Virginity too is crowned with a greater reward for this reason, because it does not have a command of the Lord, and it directs itself beyond what has been commanded.

22.   *But at the same time, prepare a lodge (*hospitium*)[143] for me.* I do not think the apostle was so wealthy and filled with such great furnish-

---

139. Cf. Phlm 12.

140. Cf. Phlm 9.

141. Ps 119.108.

142. Lk 17.10.

143. Jerome seems to understand this term not of a guest room within a house, but of an inn or a separate house for lodging.

ings that he pleaded for the preparation of a "lodge" and was not content with one small room. He thought that the small space of his own body was a very roomy house. Rather it is the case that, while Philemon awaits his future arrival, he may do more than what was asked. But if anyone thinks that this has been commanded not diplomatically (*dispensatorie*)[144] but truly, that he should have "prepared a lodge" for himself, a lodge ought to be prepared for the "apostle," rather than for "Paul." Being about to come to a new city to preach the Crucified and to reveal doctrines unheard of before, he knew that very many would flock to him. There would be need first of all for a house in that well-known location of the city to which one could easily come to meet. In the second place, it needed to be free from all inappropriateness, to be spacious so that it would have room for a great number of hearers. It was not to be in a location near the theaters, so that it would not be abhorrent because of its shameful locale. Finally, it was to be situated on the ground floor rather than on the upper floor. This is also the reason I think that he remained in Rome for two years in a rented house.[145] The dwelling was not small, I imagine, to which crowds of Jews daily gathered.[146]

22.   *For I am hoping to be granted to you through your prayers.* God when asked grants a son to a father, and a brother is often saved by the prayer of a brother. But an apostle is granted by the prayers of the whole church on account of the benefit that comes to those who will hear him. And this gift is said to be not so much in him who is separated from martyrdom, prepared for martyrdom, as in those to whom the apostle is sent. But because Paul was in prison frequently, and was set free from his chains, he himself says in another passage, "frequently in prison"[147] from which he was released, sometimes by the Lord's

---

144. Harnack, *Der kirchengeschichtliche Ertrag,* p. 144, thinks that Origen's discussion and use of οἰκονομικῶς underlies this passage.
145. Cf. Acts 28.23, 30.
146. Cf. Acts 28.23.
147. 2 Cor 11.23.

help,[148] frequently by the persecutors themselves,[149] who found nothing worthy of death in him.[150] For the decrees of the Senate had not yet proceeded against the name of Christian; not yet had Nero's sword consecrated Christian blood.[151] But having been cast into prison because of the novelty of the preaching, whether by the envious Jews[152] or by those who saw their own idols destroyed,[153] when the people were incited to fury, they were released again when the fury of the attack was set aside. And the Acts of the Apostles testifies that it is as we say, where even Felix says to Agrippa that Paul could have been released if he had not appealed to Caesar;[154] and that he found no case except for certain questions about their own religion and about a certain Jesus whom Paul was proclaimed was alive.[155] From this we notice that they could have been released by other judges in a similar way, as the Lord acted to disseminate the new proclamation in the whole world.

23–24.   *Epaphras, my fellow prisoner in Christ Jesus, sends greetings to you, [and so do] Mark, Aristarchus, Demas, and Luke, my fellow workers.* What we were saying at the beginning,[156] that the epistle to the Colossians was written at the same time as the one to Philemon was written and [was carried] by the same letter carrier, even the names of those who are added as greeters shows. For in the former letter it is signed as follows: "Aristarchus my fellow prisoner greets you, and Mark the cousin of Barnabas, and Epaphras, who is one of you, a servant of Christ";[157] and a little further down, "Luke the beloved physician and Demas greet you; and say to Archippus, 'See that you fulfill

---

148. Cf. Acts 16.25–27.
149. Cf. Acts 16.36–39.
150. Cf. Acts 26.31.
151. Cf. Tacitus, *Annals* 15.44; Origen, *Homilies on Joshua* 9.10.
152. Cf. Acts 5.17–17; 13.45; 17.5.
153. Cf. Acts 19.23–41.
154. Festus says this to Agrippa more or less in Acts 25.21; Agrippa says this to Festus in Acts 26.32.
155. Cf. Acts 25.19.
156. Cf. 1–3.
157. Cf. Col 4.10, 12.

the ministry that you have received in the Lord'";[158] and, "Remember my chains."[159] Now if someone thinks that they were not written at the same time because there are a few names recorded in Colossians that are not reported here, let him know that not all these men are either friends or acquaintances with everyone, and that a private letter written to one man is one thing,[160] a public letter written to the whole church is something else.[161]

"Epaphras my fellow prisoner in Christ Jesus greets you," he says. We have received the following story about this Epaphras, Paul's fellow prisoner.[162] They say that the apostle Paul's parents were from the region of Giscala in Judea; and that when the whole province was laid waste by the hands of the Romans, and the Jews were dispersed into the world, they were moved to the city of Tarsus in Cilicia.[163] As a young man he followed the condition of his parents. And thus what he testifies about himself can be confirmed: "Are they Hebrews? So am I. Are they Israelites? So am I. Are they Abraham's seed? So am I."[164] And again elsewhere he says, "Hebrew of Hebrews,"[165] and the other things that indicate that he was a Jew more than a man of Tarsus. But if this is so, we can conjecture that Epaphras too was arrested at that time when Paul was taken, and that having been found with his own parents in Colossae, a city of Asia, he later received the word about Christ. This is why it is written to the Colossians, as we said above, "Epaphras, who is one of you, a slave of Christ, greets you, being always earnest over you in his prayers."[166]

---

158. Cf. Col 4.14.17.

159. Col 4.18.

160. That is, Philemon.

161. In other words, Colossians.

162. According to Harnack, *Der kirchengeschichtliche Ertrag*, p. 145, Jerome's source is Origen, but Origen's source is unknown. Harnack adds that no objection can be raised against this information.

163. This evidently refers to the conquest of Judea by Pompei in the mid-second century BC.

164. Cf. 2 Cor 11.22.

165. Phil 3.5.

166. Col 4.12.

If this is so, Aristarchus too, who is called his fellow captive in the same letter, will be brought to the same understanding, unless perchance he is pointing to something hidden and mysterious in the word captivity, as some think, that having been equally made captive and conquered, they were brought to this vale of tears.[167] But if neither is received, from the added words "in Christ Jesus," we can surmise that he sustained for the sake of Christ the same chains in Rome that Paul did. And as a prisoner of Christ, he could thus also be called his captive. Or at least it may be understood in this way, that he himself is "outstanding among the apostles," like Andronicus and Julia[168] of whom it is written to the Romans, "Greet Andronicus and Julia, kinsmen and my fellow captives who are outstanding among the apostles, who were in Christ Jesus before me."[169] These things have been said concerning Epaphras.

However that may be, [he speaks of] "fellow workers of the gospel and of his chains." When he wrote the epistle to Philemon, he records Mark, whom I think is the author of the Gospel, and Aristarchus, of whom we have made mention above, and Demas, of whom he complains in another passage: "Demas has left me, being devoted to the present world, and has gone to Thessalonica."[170] And he records "Luke the physician,"[171] who, by leaving behind a Gospel and the Acts of the Apostles for the churches, converted from being a physician of bodies into a physician of souls, just as the apostles became being fishers of men from being fishers of fish.[172] Of Luke he says in another passage,

---

167. Cf. Ps 84.6. The "some" must refer to Origen, and the interpretation would involve the idea that preexistent souls are "imprisoned" in bodies through their birth into human life. Rufinus, *Apologia adversus Hieronymum* 1.40 in his invective against Jerome refers to this text as one in which the early Jerome transmits Origen's controversial views without reproach.

168. This is an early textual variant for *Junias*.

169. Rom 16.7.

170. 2 Tm 4.10.

171. Cf. Col 4.14.

172. Cf. Mt 4.19; Lk 5.10.

"With him [Titus] I have sent the brother whose praise is in the gospel throughout all the churches."[173] However often Luke's book is read in the churches, just that often does his medicine not run out.

25.   *The grace of the Lord Jesus Christ be with your spirit.* Just as the people of Israel are numbered from the better part of man, the head, when the Scripture says, "according to their heads,"[174] so in the whole man, indeed, and in every part of the saints, there is the grace of the Lord Jesus Christ. But from the greater and better part, that is, from the spirit, it is spoken of the whole man by συνεκδοχήν. "The grace of the Lord Jesus Christ be with your spirit." Now when grace comes into the spirit, it makes the whole man spiritual, so that the flesh serves the spirit and the soul is not overcome by the flesh, and, having been rendered at the same time into a spiritual substance, they cleave to the Lord because he who cleaves to the Lord is one spirit.[175]

Now according to the Hebrews "Paul" translates as "admirable,"[176] "Timothy" as "generous," "Philemon" as "wonderfully given," or "mouth of bread," from "mouth," not "bone." "Apphia" means "continent," or "freedom." "Archippus" means "length of work." "Onesimus" means "responding," "Epaphras," "fruitful," and "seeing" or "increasing." "Mark" means "lofty by the commandment," "Aristarchus" means "mountain of more abundant work," "Demas" means "silent," "Luke" "he himself rising together."

If you want to understand these names according to their translation, it is not difficult for "admirable" [Paul] and "generous" [Timothy] to write particularly to him to whom all vices have been pardoned and his "mouth" is open to the heavenly bread [Philemon]. Then he writes to "continent" and "free" [Apphia] and to "length of work" [Archippus], because he never ceases from holy labor. But he writes on behalf

---

173. 2 Cor 8.18.

174. Nm 1.2. See Origen, *Homilies on Number,* trans. Thomas P. Scheck (Downers Grove: Intervarsity, 2009).

175. Cf. 1 Cor 6.17.

176. See on v. 1.

of him who "responds" [Onesimus] by his own testimony, and certainly the one to whom the epistle is dedicated is greeted especially by "increasing abundance" [Epaphras]. And he is greeted by the one who has become more "lofty" through the "commands" [Mark] and by that one who has "increased" through greater works into a "mountain" [Aristarchus]; by him too who has placed a guard on his mouth and a fortified gate on his lips, who perhaps was "silent" [Demas] for this reason, because he had abandoned the apostle for a little while.[177] And finally he is greeted by him who "himself rising together" [Luke] through himself grows daily and makes progress, while the world is filled with his gospel, and as often as it grows, so often does the hearing and the reading of it edify.

---

177. Cf. 2 Tm 4.10.

Select Bibliography

Primary Texts and Translations

St. Jerome (by editor/translator)

Bucchi, Federica. *Commentarii in Epistulas Pauli Apostoli ad Titum et ad Philemon.* S. Hieronymi Presbyteri Opera, Pars I Opera Exegetica 8. CCSL 77C. Turnhout: Brepols, 2003.

Fremantle, W. H. *St. Jerome: Letters and Select Works.* NPNF2 6. Grand Rapids, Mich.: Eerdmans, 1893.

———. *St. Jerome: Apology to Rufinus.* NPNF2 3. Grand Rapids, Mich.: Eerdmans, 1892.

Halton, T. *St. Jerome: On Illustrious Men.* FOTC 100. Washington, D.C.: Catholic University of America Press, 1999.

Raspanti, Giacomo. *Commentarii in Epistulam Pauli Apostoli ad Galatas.* S. Hieronymi Presbyteri Opera, Pars I Opera Exegetica 6. CCSL 77A. Turnhout: Brepols, 2006.

Richardson, E. C. *St. Jerome: Lives of Illustrious Men.* NPNF2 3. Grand Rapids, Mich.: Eerdmans, 1892.

Scheck, Thomas P. *St. Jerome: Commentary on Matthew.* FOTC 117. Washington, D.C.: Catholic University of America Press, 2008.

Origen (by editor/translator)

Balthasar, H. Urs von. *Origen: Spirit and Fire; A Thematic Anthology of His Writings.* Trans. R. J. Daly. Washington, D.C.: Catholic University of America Press, 1984.

Barkley, G. W. *Homilies on Leviticus, 1–16.* FOTC 83. Washington, D.C.: Catholic University of America Press, 1990.

Bruce. B. *Homilies on Joshua*. FOTC 105. Washington, D.C.: Catholic University of America Press, 2002.

Chadwick, H., and J. E. L. Oulton, eds. *Alexandrian Christianity: Selected Translations of Clement and Origen*. Library of Christian Classics 2. Philadelphia: Westminster, 1954.

Dively Lauro, E. A. *Homilies on Judges*. FOTC 119. Washington, D.C.: Catholic University of America Press, 2009.

Heine, R. *The Commentaries of Origen and Jerome on St Paul's Epistle to the Ephesians*. Oxford: Oxford University Press, 2002.

———. *Homilies on Genesis and Exodus*. FOTC 71. Washington, D.C.: Catholic University of America Press, 1981.

Heintz, M. *Homilies on Psalms 36–38*. FOTC. Washington, D.C.: Catholic University of America Press, forthcoming..

Lawson, R. P. Origen: *The Song of Songs, Commentary and Homilies*. Ancient Chrstian Writers 26. Westminster, Md.: Newman, 1957.

Lienhard, J. *Homilies on Luke, Fragments on Luke*. FOTC 94. Washington, D.C.: Catholic University of America Press, 1996.

Scheck, T. P. *Commentary on the Epistle to the Romans*. 2 vols. FOTC 103, 104. Washington, D.C.: Catholic University of America Press, 2001–2.

———. *Homilies on Ezekiel*. Ancient Christian Writers 62. Mahwah, N.J.: Paulist Press, 2009.

———. *Homilies on Numbers*. Ancient Christian Texts. Downers Grove: Intervarsity, 2009.

———. *Pamphilus' Apology for Origen*. FOTC 120. Washington, D.C.: Catholic University of America Press, 2010.

Smith, J. C. *Homilies on Jeremiah, Homily on 1 Kings 28*. FOTC 97. Washington, D.C.: Catholic University of America Press, 1998.

Secondary Works

Adkin, N. "Ambrose and Jerome: The Opening Shot," *Mnemosyne* 46 (1993), pp. 364–66.

———. "Jerome on Ambrose: The Preface to the Translation of Origen's *Homilies on Luke*." *Revue Benedictine* 107 (1997), pp. 5–14.

Bammel, C. P. "Augustine, Origen and the Exegesis of St. Paul." *Augustinianum* 32 (1992), pp. 341–68.

———. "Justification by Faith in Augustine and Origen." *Journal of Ecclesiastical History* 47 (1996), pp. 223–35.

———. "Origen's Pauline Prefaces." In *Origeniana Sexta: Origène et la Bible/ Origen and the Bible*, ed. G. Dorival and A. Le Boulluec, pp. 495–513. Leuven: Leuven University Press, 1995.

———. "Patristic Exegesis of Romans 5:7." *Jounal of Theological Studies* 47 (1996), pp. 532–42.

Bardy, G. "Jérôme et ses maîtres hébreux." *Revue Bénédictine* 46 (1934), pp. 145–64.

Cain, A. *The Letters of Jerome: Asceticism, Biblical Exegesis, and the Construction of Christian Authority in Late Antiquity.* Oxford: Oxford University Press, 2009.

———. "*Vox Clamantis in Deserto*: Rhetoric, Reproach, and the Forging of Ascetic Authority in Jerome's Letters from the Syrian Desert." *Journal of Theological Studies* 57.2 (2006), pp. 500–25.

Cain, A., and J. Lössl, eds. *Jerome of Stridon: His Life, Writings, and Legacy.* Aldershot, 2009.

Carriker, A. "Augustine's Frankness in His Dispute with Jerome over the Interpretation of Galatians 2:11–14." In *Nova Doctrina Vetusque: Essays in Honor of F. W. Schlatter,* D. Kries and C. Tkacz, pp. 121–38. New York: P. Lang, 1999.

Clark, E. *The Origenist Controversy: The Cultural Construction of an Early Christian Debate.* Princeton: Princeton University Press, 1992.

Cole-Turner, R. "Anti-heretical Issues and the Debate over Galatians 2:11–14 in the Letters of St. Augustine and St. Jerome," *Augustinian Studies* 11 (1980), pp. 155–66.

Cooper, S. *Marius Victorinus' Commentary on Galatians.* Introduction, translation, and notes by Stephen Andrew Cooper. Oxford: Oxford University Press, 2005.

Erasmus, Desiderius. *Hyperaspistes I and II.* C. In *Controversies: Hyperaspistes 1 and 2,* ed. C. Trinkhaus, trans. Clarence H. Miller. CWE 76, 77. Toronto: University of Toronto Press, 1999, 2000.

Eusebius. *The History of the Church from Christ to Constantine.* Trans. G. A. Williamson. Revised and edited by Andrew Louth. Penguin Books, 1965, 1989.

Grech, P.. "Justification by Faith in Origen's Commentary on Romans." *Augustinianum* 36 (1996), pp. 337–59.

Grützmacher, G. *Hieronymus: Eine Biographische Studie zur alten Kirchengeschichte.* 3 vols. *Band 2: Sein Leben und seine Schriften von 385 bis 400.* Berlin: Scientia Verlag, 1901–8, repr. 1969.

Hale Williams, Megan. *The Monk and the Book: Jerome and the Making of Christian Scholarship.* Chicago: University of Chicago Press, 2006.

Hammond, C. P. "The Last Ten Years of Rufinus' Life and the Date of His Move South from Aquileia." *Journal of Theological Studies* 28 (1977), pp. 372–429.

Hammond Bammel, C. P. "Die Hexapla des Origenes: Die *Hebraica veritas* im Streit der Meinungen." *Augustinianum* 28 (1988), pp. 125–49.

————. "Philocalia IX, Jerome, Epistle 121, and Origen's Exposition of Romans VII." *Journal of Theological Studies* 32 (1981), pp. 50– 81.

Harnack, A. *Der kirchengeschichtliche Ertrag der exegetischen Arbeiten des Origenes.* Leipzig: Hinrichs, 1919.

Hengel, M., and A. M. Schwemer, eds. *Die Septuaginta zwischen Judentum und Christentum.* Tübingen: J. C. B. Mohr, 1994.

Kelly, J. N. D. *Jerome: His Life, Writings, and Controversies.* New York: Harper & Row, 1975.

Levy, I. C. "*Fides qua per caritatem operatur:* Love as the Hermeneutical Key in Medieval Galatians Commentaries." *Cistercian Studies Quarterly* 43.1 (2008), pp. 41–61.

Lightfoot, J. B. *The Epistle of St. Paul to the Galatians.* Grand Rapids, Mich.: Zondervan, 1968; repr. of 1865 ed..

Longenecker, R. *Galatians.* Word Biblical Commentary 41. Dallas: Word Books, 1990.

Lubac, Henri de. *History and Spirit: The Understanding of Scripture according to Origen.* Trans. A. Nash. San Francisco: Ignatius, 2007. Orig. pub. as *Histoire et esprit: L'Intelligence de l'Ecriture d'après Origène.* Paris: Editions Montaigne, 1950.

————*Medieval Exegesis,* vol. 1, *The Four Senses of Scripture.* Trans. M. Sebanc. Grand Rapids, Mich.: Eerdmans, 1998. Orig. pub. as *Exégèse médiéval,* vol. 1, *Les quatre sens de l'écriture,* Paris: Aubier, 1959.

————. *Medieval Exegesis,* vol. 2, *The Four Senses of Scripture.* Trans. E. M. Macierowski. Grand Rapids, Mich.: Eerdmans, 2000. Orig. pub. as *Exégèse médiéval,* vol. 2, *Les quatre sens de l'écriture,* Paris: Aubier, 1959.

McGuckin, J., ed. *The Westminster Handbook to Origen.* Louisville: Westminster John Knox Press, 2004.

Metzger, Bruce M. *A Textual Commentary on the Greek New Testament.* Stuttgart: United Bible Societies, 1971; corr. ed., 1975.

Montague, G. T. *First and Second Timothy, Titus.* Catholic Commentary on Sacred Scripture. Grand Rapids, Mich.: Baker, 2008.

Murphy, F. X. *Rufinus of Aquileia (345–411): His Life and Works.* Washington, D.C.: Catholic University of America Press, 1945.

————. "Saint Jerome." *New Catholic Encyclopedia,* 2d ed, 7.756–59. Washington, D.C.: Catholic University of America Press, 2003.

Murphy, F. X., ed. *A Monument to Saint Jerome.* New York: Sheed & Ward, 1952.

Oberhelman, S. "Jerome's Earliest Attack on Ambrose: On Ephesians, Prologue (ML 26: 469D-70A)," *Transactions and Proceedings of the American Philological Association* 121 (1991), pp. 377–401.

O'Connell, John P. *The Eschatology of Saint Jerome.* Dissertationes ad Lauream 16. Mundelein, Ill.: Pontificia Facultas Theologica Seminarii Sanctae Mariae ad Lacum, 1948.

Plumer, E. *Augustine's Commentary on Galatians. Introduction, Text, Translation, and Notes*. Oxford: Oxford University Press, 2003.

Schatkin, M. "The Influence of Origen upon St. Jerome's Commentary on Galatians." *Vigiliae Christianae* 24 (1970), pp. 49–58.

Scheck, T. *Origen and the History of Justification: The Legacy of Origen's Commentary on Romans*. Notre Dame, Ind.: University of Notre Dame Press, 2008.

Simonetti, M., ed. *Matthew 1–13*. ACC. New Testament 1a. Downers Grove: Intervarsity Press, 2001–2.

———. *Matthew 14–28*. ACC. New Testament 1b. Downers Grove: Intervarsity Press, 2001–2.

Souter, A. *The Earliest Latin Commentaries on the Epistles of St. Paul*. Oxford: Clarendon Press, 1927; repr. 1999.

Steinmann, J. *Saint Jerome and his Times*. Notre Dame, Ind.: University of Notre Dame Press, 1959.

Verfaillie, C. *La doctrine de la justification dans Origène d'après son commentaire de l'Épître aux Romains*. Thèse de la Faculté de théologie catholique de l'Université de Strasbourg. Strasbourg, 1926.

Wenham, D. *Paul and Jesus: The True Story*. Grand Rapids, Mich.: Eerdmans, 2002.

———. *Paul: Follower of Jesus or Founder of Christianity?* Grand Rapids, Mich.: Eerdmans, 1995.

White, C., ed. *The Correspondence (394–419) between Jerome and Augustine of Hippo*. Lewiston: Edwin Mellen Press, 1990.

Wiles, M. F. *The Divine Apostle: The Interpretation of St. Paul's Epistles in the Early Church*. London: Cambridge University Press, 1967.

Index of Scriptural Passages

Jerome's commentaries are referenced by the lemma (chapter/verse) or Preface (Pref) of Galatians (Gal), Titus (Ti), and Philemon (Phlm).

Old Testament

Genesis

1.1: Ti 1.2–4; Phlm 4–6

2.7: Phlm 4–6

2.9: Gal 3.13b–14; 6.6

2.21–22: Phlm 4–6

2.24: Gal 5.19–21

3.1–7: Gal 3.13b–14

3.14: Gal 3.13b–14

3.15: Gal 5.19–21

3.16: Gal 4.19; Ti 2.3–5; 2.9–10

3.17: Gal 3.13b–14; Ti 2.3–5; 3.2

4.8: Gal 4.17–18

4.10: Gal 3.8–9

4.11: Gal 3.13b–14

4.26: Gal 3.8–9

5.24: Gal 1.6–7; Phlm 4–6

5.27: Ti 3.9

6–8: Phlm 4–6

6.3: Gal 1.16b; 5.19–21

6.8: Ti 1.4

6.9: Ti 1.4

9.21: Gal 5.13a

9.25: Gal 3.13b–14

12.1: Phlm 4–6

12.1–8: Gal 3.6

12.3: Gal 3.7; 3.8–9

12.7: Gal 3.15–18

14.18–19: Gal 5.2

15.3: Gal 4.6

15.5–6: Gal 3.8–9

15.6: Gal 5.6; Ti 2.2

15.16: Gal 3.15–18

16.4: Gal 4.22–23

16.6: Gal 4.22–23

16.9: Gal 4.22–23

16.10: Gal 4.22–23

16.12: Gal 4.22–23

17: Phlm 4–6

17.5: Phlm 1–3

17.10: Gal 5.2; 5.3

Genesis (*cont.*)
17.15: Phlm 1–3
17.15–21: Gal 3.6
17.18–21: Gal 4.22–23
17.19: Gal 4.22–23
17.21: Gal 4.22–23
18.18: Gal 3.7
18.9–14: Gal 3.6
21.2: Gal 4.22–23
21.4: Gal 5.3
21.9: Gal 4.29–31
21.10: Gal 4.29–31
21.12: Gal 3.6; 4.29–31
22: Phlm 4–6
22.1–14: Gal 3.6
22.18: Gal 3.15–18
25.1: Gal 5.13a; Ti 1.6
25.29–30: Ti 1.6
25.33: Ti 1.6
27.27: Ti 3.15
28.9: Gal 1.4–5
29.20: Gal 1.4–5
30.13: Gal 4.6
30.20: Ti 3.2
32.30: Gal 5.22–23
35.22: Ti 3.2
37.11: Gal 4.17–18;
    Phlm 15–16
37.25–28: Phlm 15–16
38.14–18: Gal 5.13a
38.27–30: Gal 3.15–18
43.34: Gal 5.13a
45.4–8: Phlm 15–16
47.9: Gal 1.4–5
49: Ti 3.15
49.1: Ti 3.2
49.4: Ti 3.2
49.7: Gal 3.13b–14; Ti 3.2
50.20: Phlm 15–16

Exodus
2.1–10: Ti 1.5
3.6: Gal 3.19–20
3.10: Gal 1.1
4.13: Gal 1.1
4.24–26: Gal 5.6
6.12: Gal 5.6
6.16–20: Ti 1.5
7–11: Phlm 4–6
12.2–6: Gal 1.18b
12.3–6: Gal 4.10–11
12.15: Gal 4.10–11
12.18–20: Gal 4.10–11
14.15: Gal 4.6
14.31: Phlm 4–6
15.10: Gal 5.1
15.20: Gal Pref1; 5.19–21
15.22–25: Gal 3.13b–14
15.24: Gal 3.19–20
16.2: Gal 3.19–20
16.18: Gal 6.6
17.3: Gal 3.19–20
17.12: Phlm 1–3
19.5: Gal 5.8
20.13–16: Gal 5.13b–14
20.13–17: Gal 5.22–23
21.5–6: Gal 1.4–5
21.37: Ti 2.9–10
22.3: Ti 2.9–10
23.14–17: Gal 5.3
23.15: Gal Pref3
23.17: Gal 3.24–26; 4.10–11
23.22: Gal 5.19–21
29.38–42: Gal 5.3
29.39–41: Gal 5.3
32: Gal 3.19–20
32.4: Gal 3.19–20
32.9: Gal 3.1a
33.11: Gal 4.8–9; Ti 1.5

New Testament

General Index

The Translator's Introduction (int) is referenced by page number. Jerome's three Prefaces (Pref) to his Galatians commentary are referenced by book number; Jerome's commentaries are referenced by the lemma (chapter/verse) of Galatians (Gal), Titus (Ti), and Philemon (Phlm).

Reese, A., int 41
Rhoda, Gal Pref2
Rhone, Gal Pref2
Ridderbos, H., int 33
Rufinus, int 7, 8, 11, 14; Gal Pref1;
    Ti 2.12–14; Phlm 1–3; 23–24

Saguntum, Gal Pref2
Sallust, Gal 5.16
Sarmaticus, Phlm 1–3
Scheck, T., int 37, 44
Scipio Africanus, Phlm 1–3
Second Vatican Council, int 2
Seneca, int 4
Septuagint (LXX), int 7, 10–11;
    Gal 1.4–5
Sibyl, Gal Pref2
Simonetti, M., Gal 4.17–18; 5.9
Smallwood, E., Gal 6.12
Socrates (church historian),
    Gal 4.19
Stoics, Gal 1.15–16a; 4.24; 5.22–23;
    Ti 1.2–4; 3.10–11
Strepsiades, Ti 2.15
Stridon, int 3; Ti Pref; Phlm Pref
Stromateis(Origen), int 9; Gal Pref1;
    Gal 1.11–12; 2.15; Gal Pref2;
    Gal 5.13a; 5.19–21; 6.8
Suetonius, int 1; Gal Pref3; 6.10;
    6.12
Symmachians, int 21
Symmachus, int 7; Gal 3.10;
    3.13b–14; Ti 2.12–14; 3.9
synecdoche, Phlm 25
synergism, int 27

Tacitus, Gal Pref3; Phlm 22
Tartessos, Gal Pref2

Tascodrugitae, Gal Pref2
Tatian, Gal 6.8; Ti Pref
Terence, Gal 4.15–16; 4.24;
    Ti 1.12
Tertullian, Gal Pref1; Gal 1.1; 1.4–5;
    1.8–9; 2.11–13; Gal Pref2;
    Gal 3.15–18; 4.12b–14; 5.13;
    6.6; 6.10; Ti 1.6; 1.7;
    Phlm Pref; Phlm 14
Thebes, Gal Pref2
Thebistis, Gal Pref2
Theodore, Gal Pref1
Theodotion, int 7; Gal 3.10;
    3.13b–14; Ti 2.12–14; 3.9
Thomas Aquinas, St., Gal 3.13a
Tiberius, Gal 6.12
Titus, emperor, Gal 6.10
Trent, Council of, int 11, 40
Treveri, Gal Pref2
Trier, int 4
Trinity/Trinitarian, Gal 1.11–12; 4.6;
    6.1; Ti 3.3–7
tropology, Gal 4.17–18

Valentinus, Gal 1.4–5; 1.15–16a;
    Ti 3.10–11; Phlm Pref
VanLandingham, C., int 29
Varro, Marcus Terentius, Gal Pref2;
    Phlm 1–3
Vespasian, emperor, Gal Pref3;
    Gal 6.10
Vesta, Gal 6.10
Victorinus, Marius, int 15–17,
    21–23; Gal Pref1; Gal 1.1; 1.16b;
    2.21; 4.6; 6.11
Villegas, V., int 3
Virgil, Gal 1.4–5; 1.15–16a; 3.1a;
    Gal Pref2; Gal Pref3; Ti 1.12

Thomas P. Sheck

is assistant professor of classics and theology at Ave Maria
University. He is the author of *Origen and the History of Justification:
The Legacy of Origen's Commentary on Romans*
(University of Notre Dame Press, 2008).